Aimee
Love & Pray 4 ua...
child of God.
Matt. 43 - 45 from chap. 5
Aileen Chow 9/30/18

JAHAR

THE LONE BOSTON BOMBER #2

THE STORY ABOUT DZHOKHAR TSARNAEV
FROM HIS CAPTURE TO HIS TRIAL

Aileen Lee

Jahar The Lone Boston Bomber #2

Aileen Lee
Book Interior and Cover designed by Aileen Lee
ABC Publishers, 2016
Printed by CreateSpace

Revised Edition, 2018

© 2018 AILEEN LEE

This is a copyright free book. This is a work of a documentary research about a true event. The work is based on Twitter or tweets from the reporters who reported the news during the trial. The author has made every effort to ensure the accuracy of the information in this book is correct. Although the author uses her thoughts to write the narration of the story, she gives the reporters credit and the book could not have been written or accomplished without their observations. The author uses quotes, comments, excerpts and references from the media and from court documents accessed from the public domain.

ISBN-13: 978-1539735229

This book is dedicated to those who uttered a word of prayer or forgiveness to love thy enemies. We got to know Dzhokhar A. Tsarnaev since his arrest in 2013 and his trial from January - May 2015. I hope this book will continue our faithful commitment to follow much of the news and remember Jahar, the lost sheep. He shall never be forgotten in our hearts. We will continue to pray for his salvation and think of him from time to time.

He was captured for bombing the Boston Marathon. When he woke up at the hospital people called him a monster. His family was in disbelief. Did he have remorse?

How could he murder the innocents?

"This was an extraordinary case."

– Judge George O'Toole

```
UNITED STATES OF AMERICA,
Plaintiff,
v.
DZHOKHAR A. TSARNAEV also
known as Jahar Tsarni,
Defendant.
```

PRAISE FOR THE BOOK

"What touched me is that you don't specify or focus on his guilt. Instead, your purpose for this book is focusing on praying for him and that is tremendous and is what we all should do." – *Jackie*

"This documentary presented a different perspective to readers. It does not go with the flow and that is good." – *Anonymous*

"Masterfully researched and brilliantly organized with the amazing ability to create a moving picture in our minds, Aileen Lee gives readers a compassionate, thorough and much-needed perspective of the story behind Dzhokhar Tsarnaev and the Boston Marathon bombing. We owe it to ourselves and to others to not simply adopt what the media feeds us. As a Christian, it is important to seek the truth and to remember and heed Matthew 7:1 which states, *"Do not judge lest ye be judged."* Aileen Lee does a stupendous job of pulling everything together. Her book is absolutely superb. – *G.S.*

"KUDOS for your well-written book! I love how you included all the web/video links in the book, so I don't need to do a google search. You've provided all the information I need to know, and you presented it systematically (and of course you've touched on details)." – *Dewi*

"I knew about Aileen's book two years ago and always looked forward to reading it since then. When I read it for the first time I was moved to tears. I am astounded by the story when the bomber was captured in the boat, and it made me think deeply about the tragedy that happened to him."
–Yang

"A compelling and easy read. Thoroughly informative and well-researched narrative on the Boston Bomber Dzhokhar Tsarnaev and his subsequent trial. I would highly recommend the book for those interested in the events surrounding the Boston Marathon bombing." – *Alice*

"I read the book. It brought back so many memories of Jahar and his trial. Of course, his story is heartbreaking, but still I could not stop reading. Thank you also for all the interactive links that bring further layers to the story. Everyone who cares about this case should know about this."
– Anonymous

"This book puts aside philosophical questions about malicious deeds in mankind. Every reader will think about morals and doubts through this book. This catastrophic event made us think deeper about where our consciousness is heading. We should never forget this catastrophic event!!"*– Anton W. Yun*

Table of Contents

FOREWORD

WHEN HIS NAME AND picture was finally released my exact thought in the moment was, "You have to be kidding me." It took me a while to believe it at first that someone so young could do something so cruel. I remember when a few different theories on *Tumblr* came out, within hours of the bombings; I immediately gained an interest in the case. I expected to see someone much older, than the 19-year-old college kid that came across my television screen. I vaguely followed the manhunt on Twitter. I don't have much of a memory the night of the shootout and when Dzhokhar was captured. But I had hoped that he would survive. When he was finally captured, I let out a sigh of relief. Even after everything that had happened during that week, I had faith in him that he was innocent. It took time for me to realize that he wasn't. I had so many questions.

I started following the case through *Tumblr.* Just like everyone else, I wanted to understand it more and piece together evidence. I became involved in discussions by asking bloggers questions unanimously. As I got more into the case, I learned more about him. The more I learned, the harder it became for me to associate him with what he committed. I started to care about him and have sympathy for him. I related with Dzhokhar in more ways than one. I shared his struggles and experiences with school. Excelling in high school but struggling through college, receiving poor grades, and not having as great of a family support system that I wish I had, etc. I couldn't help but find myself praying for him. I prayed for him every night for several months. Although I'm a nonbeliever, I'm not sure where I'll be at religiously six months from now or a year from now, but I still can't help but want to pray for him. So, I'm not sure what that says about me religiously.

When it became official that a trial was happening, I knew that I had to go. I attended May 5–7. I was able to get a seat inside Courtroom 9 on May 6. My heart was beating fast and I had a hundred thoughts racing through my head. It was the combination of nerves and anxiety, of not knowing what to expect. I walked in and my seat was the second to last bench on the right-hand side. By luck I was able to get an aisle seat. Having an aisle was the best shot at getting a good look at him, since the television monitor blocked most of the view. When I sat down, about a minute later Dzhokhar came out of the door on the right-hand side. He walked in with a "swagger." He didn't look up towards anyone when he made his way in, but I was able to get a good enough look at him. His appearance was almost like the CCTV footage from the Wai Kru gym, a few days before the bombing. When he was seated, it was hard to tell just how much weight he had lost. But when he stood with his back facing towards you, it was easy to tell just how much. I don't remember what shirt he was wearing, but his pants and suit jacket were a little too loose for him. His hair was a little unkempt, and not as curly in person. From my seat I had a pretty good look at his face, when he would come in and out of the courtroom as well as when he turned his head to the side. I couldn't see much of his facial injuries. But from what I could tell, his left side was visibly different than his right side.

It was surreal being in the same room as him. He had such a big presence to me and to others that I met that day. It was hard to not notice him in the room, even when he was slouched down in his chair. Some of the testimony from that day included Elmirza Khozhugov who is Ailina's ex–husband, (Ailina is one of Dzhokhar's sisters.) Deputy U.S. Marshal Kevin Michael Roche who witnessed Dzhokhar giving the middle finger on the day of his arraignment and a psychiatrist testifying about Anzor's mental health. I couldn't help but take moments to stare Dzhokhar down and observe him.

He would slouch down in his seat but not too often and sometimes had his head resting against his hand. To me he never appeared disinterested in listening to the testimonies. But I could be biased. One memory that I'll always hold close is from May 7. I was able to meet someone from *Christians 4 Jahar,* who I now consider a good friend. We sat together in the overflow room. Inside you're able to see Dzhokhar's face from the front on the TV monitors. Even though the picture wasn't as clear and a little grainy before testimony started I was able to see Dzhokhar's spirit perk up. I saw him smile and laugh with his lawyers, Miriam and Judy.

Eight days after I came back from Boston, the jury came back with a recommendation of death. I had the TV station on CNN as each count was read. I felt a sigh of relief and a strange sense of comfort, but I also felt anger. It's hard for me to describe why I felt the way I did. Throughout the trial my opinion on Dzhokhar was always changing. A big turning point for me was when we learned how he bought milk at Whole Foods minutes after he and Tamerlan detonated their bombs. As a strong death penalty supporter, his case always had me wavering back and forth between wanting natural life and wanting a death sentence. I still struggle today with what I feel is the appropriate sentence for him. His case has taught me so much over the last few years, and I've met so many great people who've also taught me things that I didn't know before. I continue to have hope not only for Dzhokhar but for his victims as well.

> 🔲 Follow
>
> **I'm praying for the man who is a bombing suspect.**
>
> 7:32 PM - 19 April 2013

During Tsarnaev's capture, someone is praying for him.

I'm not much of an avid reader, but when I found out a book about Dzhokhar was written I knew I wanted to read it. Even more so that it was written by someone who follows the case as closely as myself. I originally found Aileen's book through *Christians 4 Jahar*. I read the initial description, and I knew I wanted to reach out to her. I saw her book as a way to refresh my memory and to potentially learn something new. I haven't been able to stop reading. There's more than a handful of information regarding Dzhokhar and the case itself. You're sure to learn and take plenty away from the book. I know I'll be able to reference and hopefully share with family and close friends in the future. I have so much more to read of Aileen's book, but I think you'll be as impressed as I am. I highly recommend!

Christian C.

August 22, 2016

MY THOUGHTS ABOUT DZHOKHAR

Christians shared their thoughts about Dzhokhar

DZHOKHAR WAS A CHEERFUL boy. He was popular and had many friends surrounding him during high school. He got praises and love from friends and teachers. But, he planted hatred. He considered the war in Middle East as injustice. Radical thoughts in mind, and encountered setback in college life, led him to the wrong road of terrorism. It's a sad story of a lost sheep.

As a Christian, I have a great compassion for Dzhokhar's soul. I was wondering what he would be like if he had been born in a much more caring family. What he would be like if there was a wise elder who could have enlightened him when he was confused and frustrated in school, in life, and religion. The story of his life could be totally different.

At this time, Dzhokhar needs urgent and consistent prayers following God's will more than ever. Pray that he can repent and receive salvation because our God is merciful, and He is the Lord of sinners. Our sin is great, but His love is greater. Mercy triumphs over judgment. - (*James 2:13*). However, I also feel we Christians should repent first – remove the accusation spirit of Pharisees; love people who have hurt us with the love of God; and restore the relationships with each other. May the Holy Spirit abide in the residency in people's hearts. May the tender and loving spirit of Jesus touch the hearts of Dzhokhar and other Muslim brothers and sisters.

– Carol C.

WHEN I SAW THE bombings on the news, I was in a country on the other side of the world. At that time, I could not understand why I felt a desperate need to pray for this dying young man that I never knew – although I knew the Bible taught me to *"love your enemies and pray for those who persecute you"* (*Matthew 5:44*). I tried to find the answer or find someone who also shared the same "calling" as I did. I did find some Christians who shared the same experience with me on the internet. They know the knowledge of truth and have faith in Jesus, and that made me feel at ease and peaceful. It also made me realize that the Lord we trust is the one who is reluctant to give up on any person. *"Not wanting anyone to perish, but everyone to come to repentance"* (*2 Peter 3:9*). So, He moved some brothers and sisters to pray for Dzhokhar since then.

When I was reading the documentary book by Aileen, some descriptions of Dzhokhar made me think of my own brother, neighbors, classmates, friends and myself. My family background and surroundings are different from Dzhokhar's, but I am not any different from him. Dzhokhar is just like everyone who owns flesh, feeling, and soul. I think that is the way we should treat each other: acknowledge that everyone has their past, present and future, everyone has their times of laughs and cries, love and hatred, as well as the times of being kind and evil, strong and weak. More importantly we must realize that we are all loved and sought by the same Father. He wholeheartedly commits to pursue and save all human beings, whether they are ordinary people, good ones or wicked ones in people's eyes.

I appreciate God that we live in such day and age. It teaches and urges us to live and love like Jesus: no pride, no condemnation, pray continually, give thanks in all circumstances, and love your neighbor and enemy.

As Christians, we don't forget to pray and love Dzhokhar as we learn more about him, his victims and his trial. I hope this documentary can touch the hearts of many people, so they can pray for Dzhokhar's salvation and this generation which thirsts for healing.

May God break our heart for what breaks His; may He reveal himself more and more to Christians and churches today.

At last, I hope Jesus lives among everyone who reads this documentary and dispenses His heavenly mercy, compassion and love in people's hearts. I pray that all of us can be the demonstration of *"We love because God first loved us" (1 John 4:19)*. No matter how far a person seems to be away from salvation, the God of love always chases to bring the beloved child home.

- E

"He never seemed out of the ordinary…
He was just one of us."
Dzhokhar Tsarnaev, a student. (Picture is from *Tumblr*.)

PREFACE

WHEN I SAW JAHAR'S face on the front page inside a newspaper vending stand, my first reaction was that I felt pity for him. The large font size bold headline above the article read, "CAUGHT!" I had a weird feeling in my heart. I was concerned for him. As I left the newsstand near a restaurant where I ate that day I began contemplating, "Why did this young man…?" I could not complete my thought. I felt troubled. Jahar was caught, dying, bloody and injured when he was found inside a boat on April 19, 2013. I was curious about him and I wanted to find out why he bombed the Boston Marathon with his older brother, Tamerlan. I knew not everyone would care to know because he's a murderer and his murders were senseless. My preoccupation was to write what is in my heart. I didn't think I would write a book about him. This may not be the healthiest thing to do. However, I wanted to write about Jahar so that we can learn about terrorism. Hopefully, you can understand him and pray for him. Some people will not pray for him. You only saw his face in the news and thought: *"Oh, that murderer is a monster," "He is evil on earth," "This POS (piece of shit) doesn't deserve to breathe," "I have no sympathy for him," "This asshole should burn in hell," "Enough, and please let him die,"* or *"I wished they killed him on that boat."* Those are the words I would say if I didn't care. I ask, who cares about him right now?

But, I did care about Jahar and I hoped one day he would realize how he terrorized and hurt hundreds of people at the Boston Marathon. I'm not the only one who cared about him. There were many people. Christians all around the world united together to pray for Jahar. We cared about him for some reason and had made it their calling and commitment to care for his physical, emotional and spiritual well–being. We prayed for his salvation. We sent him books to read. We thought of him every day since his capture. As *Christians 4 Jahar*, we took what the Bible said – we remembered Jahar's sufferings as if we were chained with him.

There were many Muslims and nonbelievers who had a tremendous love or empathy for him also; they prayed for him and supported him in the same way. I don't know what drew many people to pray for him because this murderer did not deserve any mercy or support. We were disgusted by his crimes. He was like all the others that kill for no reason. But, we *(Christians 4 Jahar)* couldn't let him go to hell.

Jahar was a cool kid; however, circumstances within his family circle sucked him deep into their obsession. Jahar had dark secrets. He hid it from others. Jahar's full Russian birth name is Dzhokhar Anzorovich Tsarnaev and he was the convicted Boston Bomber who was caught hiding and bleeding in a boat behind a house in Watertown, MA. He was accused of terrorism, placing two pressure cooker bombs with his older brother, Tamerlan, at the Boston Marathon, an international long distance running event held every year in Boston. The bombs went off and killed three people and injured hundreds. Jahar would pay with his life for what he had done. What the brothers had done was beyond forgiveness. I was at home when I first heard the news about the bombings. I thought it was horrible and swore in my heart that those who did the bombings were "evil." It all brought me back to 9/11 and that horrible day.

I was inspired to write his story (before the trial) so you can pray for him. To document an American tragedy and a loss of innocence about a young man who had a promising future. I felt sad and sorry for the victims killed and those who became handicapped in the Boston Marathon bombings. I followed their stories closely. Many wanted to know why Jahar was the culprit of the crime.

When I saw Jahar on the news I thought he had a smug face when he zipped around the corner without his backpack. He looked very foreign to me and I was certain he was not born in the States.

A couple days later, after the younger brother was captured, a wise lady reminded people to pray for everyone in Boston. She included in her statement to pray for this 19-year-old suspect because he is a child of God, after all. I became moved by this woman's request to pray for this young man accused of hurting so many people.

I felt guilty for not loving my enemy. I should not judge him because the Bible teaches us not to judge others, as we are all sinners. I felt that Jahar was sad and in despair. I was pretty concerned about him during the whole manhunt. After he was caught, God gave me a heart to love my enemy and to pray for him. I said earlier, there were many Christians who loved him also and prayed for him every day! Jahar must know how everyone hates him. I asked myself how I can show love to this person. Jahar is a devout Muslim. His religion is Islam. He clings to his faith and praises his God, Allah; it draws him comfort. He is strong in his faith like his brother. As Christians we can show Christ's love for him, to love him, and to pray for him.

I, like many others, prayed for him to know the gospel, to be exposed to God's amazing grace, and to know the love and forgiveness of Christ. I respect Jahar's faith. I loved how he expressed his faith to Allah. Nevertheless, I prayed for him because everyone needs prayer. We must pray for the condemned. We must pray for those who try to kill us. We must love our enemies. It's so easy to hate someone like him. It is so easy to lock him up and throw away the key because he killed people.

Instead, let's go beyond the surface of things and look for the answers why this happened to him. This is a story about a family with two brothers: one a father and the other a college student. No one who knew them would imagine in their minds that they could be responsible for the bombings. Many of his survivors were trying to understand how a young kid can be involved in a horrible crime.

In this book, you will read about his radicalization. After the bombings I watched how Dzhokhar Tsarnaev was brought down to a non–human being. He was called anything from monster to a piece of shit. However, there were people who cared for him no matter if they thought he was guilty or called a terrorist. I believe some people cared about him because we kept praying for him in hope that one day he would come to repentance.

I remember that day when I saw his face in the paper while I was eating at a restaurant. Similarly, the restaurant had a TV on the wall and the news came on. The top news was the Boston Bomber's capture. The news repeatedly showed the infrared footage of the suspect hiding in the boat, and flash grenades were administered to get him out of the boat. I was sitting on the edge of my seat and my eyes were fixed on the screen. I couldn't imagine what he was feeling or going through when the SWAT team apprehended him.

When I saw the photos of Jahar coming out of the boat, I could not make him out in the picture at first. These photos were taken by ex-Massachusetts Police Sgt. Sean Murphy and were released from *Time magazine*. The pictures were too dark to see; however, I slowly began to see it was Jahar with one leg dangling, and he was slumped forward on the side of the boat with a bloody arm and hand. He had his head buried in his arm. He was defeated and injured. I was shocked when I saw the photo. It was difficult to comprehend why he did it. He could kill any one of us.

Dzhokhar slumped on the side of the boat.
Photo taken by ex-Mass. Police Sgt. Sean Murphy. April 19, 2013.
Photo credit to Associated Press.
(View more photos at
http://www.bostonmagazine.com/news/blog/2013/07/18/tsarnaev/

People said he should have been shot dead, but, by mercy the SWAT Team did not take him out. We desperately needed answers. We need to realize for some reason that his life was spared that night. Some had thought that it was because God loves him enough and shielded him that night in the boat. Maybe he could have a chance to hear the gospel.

I researched his story and complied together many news documents, videos, photos, tweets, quotes, comments and excerpts of opening/closing statements from the trial so that we all can learn and remember this tragic event.

Many would like Mr. Tsarnaev to disappear. This book was written for some of us who do care for Dzhokhar Tsarnaev can remember him as we pray for him. As a boy he was well liked, but now he is hated by many. Many people will be angry at me for writing about him. All I want to say is he needs our love and prayers.

This book is his story about his capture and the trial. I did not experience this event personally. I did not interview anyone. Nor could I talk to Jahar or his lawyers. No one could contact Jahar. A large section of this story is mostly tweets collected from news reporters tweeting at the trial. It begins in the chapter, "Jahar Appears." I had to use reporters' tweets during the trial to explain what transpired and what was said. The tweets would be *"quote like this with the reporter's last name,"* – Cullen. Or I would write a sentence and end it crediting the last name of the reporter who "reported" it or "observed" it.

The account where Jahar is in prison are fictionalized, but some of them are derived from people who knew the family. The messages he wrote to his parents are true. There will also be pictures of Jahar gathered from various *Tumblr* sites. A kindle eBook is also available, and it has numerous hyperlinks in the book to open or download many pictures, videos and documents online.

I started writing *Jahar The Lone Boston Bomber* book in November of 2014. I completed the book in January 30, 2016. In the beginning, I only gave the book to some of my friends who wanted to know more about the case. I wanted them to know who Dzhokhar was than what they had heard on the news.

I certainly hoped this book would be something more than just a court case documentary. As a Christian who prays for Dzhokhar to know Jesus, I hoped my Christian friends could also pray for him if they wanted to. However, at that time, I didn't want to have my book published. I wasn't ready for that.

Is this book only for Christians? Yes and no. Anyone can read this book if they are interested in this case. I've had some non-Christian friends read my book with interest. I've also had a Muslim believer who was interested in reading this book.

In July 7, 2016, I decided to post a blog online at *Christians 4 Jahar*, asking if anyone would like to have my book. I met a sister-in-Christ online, who encouraged me to publish this book, hoping that my book will reach a worldwide audience and would touch the hearts of many. I gave some thoughts about publishing and how this book could reach many people because at the moment my book was only given to my friends and a few Christians through *Christians 4 Jahar*. I finally decided to publish this book in mid-July. I was glad to meet other Christians who wanted to help me publish the book.

I admit the book is a long story, because it was a 3–5 months trial from jury selection to sentencing. It may take you awhile to get to the last chapter in this book, but the ending, it is all worth it as Judge George O'Toole had emphasized at the end of the Boston bombing trial, "This was an extraordinary case." No cameras were allowed in the courtroom to film the proceedings in this anticipated high-profile case.

Since this book was originally written for Christians and was later distributed at the *Christians for Jahar* site, this book was written for a purpose, and it's not to satisfy your curiosity or interest. This is not an investigative book about the Tsarnaevs and the bombings. There are plenty of other books about the investigated side of the case that may have straight forward answers, but you won't find any answers in this book. Other writers and journalists have already achieved this, but, I am more interested in conveying the compassion some people had for Jahar, and the testimony from Christians responding to the outcome and giving him hope.

I like to thank those who took time from their busy schedule to read my book and write a review for the "Praise for the Book" section. I also like to thank Carol and E for writing their thoughts about Jahar and giving us some scriptures, thereupon we can be reminded of God's words.

I am grateful that this book opens with a foreword written by Christian whom I met at *Christians 4 Jahar*. She loved the idea of my book and was willing to share her thoughts about Jahar, her experience at the trial and for introducing my book. I thank her for writing this. Her personal thoughts and her observations at the Tsarnaev's trial brought enrichment to this book.

The book cover is designed like an old journal book, so you will keep this book forever to remember the victims, survivors of the bombings and Jahar as well. You will read about some of the victims and survivors in this book and know more about their stories. We pray for their healing and recovery and we sincerely ask God to give them strength.

I hope people who still have ill-feelings for Jahar will be touched by his story and will be able to forgive him and pray for him. At last, I hope you will find the many stories contained in this book interesting, ranging from profound to heartfelt. For those who couldn't follow the news at that time, let me take you from the beginning of this case.

Aileen Lee
September 26, 2016

Caught!

"I told the people of Boston that they can rest easily, that the two people who were committing these vicious attacks are either dead or arrested, and I still believe that. From what I know right now, these two acted together and alone," he said. "I think we have to be ever vigilant, and we're learning as we go along, but as far as this little cell this little group – I think we got our guys."
– Watertown Police Chief Edward Deveau.[1]

BOOM! IT SOUNDED LIKE a loud firecracker.

A witness, who stood outside the Forum Restaurant, shook and felt a violent jolt. She heard the booming noise and cried, "Oh my god, what the hell was that?" The loud explosion near the finish line set off a wave of panic as people were watching the Boston Marathon runners finish the last mile of the race. "Something blew up!" yelled a spectator near the restaurant. White smoke enveloped the street. Suddenly, another explosion at the restaurant revealed the location of the second bomb near the tree as it burst into a ball of fire. People were thrown into the air. More screams and cries were heard by the victims. Terrified people fled from the smoke resulting in chaos. The blast tore away human body parts. Pieces of shrapnel lodged inside people's bodies. A celebrated event abruptly turned into frightening screams. Blood and falling debris were everywhere.

The twin explosions killed three innocent bystanders; it blew the limbs from seventeen people who lost part of their once whole bodies and injured two hundred sixty people. It was Monday, April 15, 2013, Patriots Day. The finish line of the Boston Marathon had become a major crime scene. Everything changed.

At the scene, several bomb technicians were collecting trace residues from bomb fragments scattered on the sidewalk. Ball bearings, nails and pieces of shrapnel littered the street. Some distance away investigators found a metal lid cover from a pressure cooker left behind. Chaos was everywhere.

After the explosions, investigators began viewing security footage. On Boylston Street, a security camera at the Lord & Taylor Department store caught images of two suspicious men walking. Suspect #1 was wearing a dark-colored baseball cap, sunglasses and a dark coat. The other man, called "Suspect #2" was wearing a white baseball cap backwards and had on a black jacket. Both men were carrying backpacks. Investigators could not view Suspect #1 clearly; he carried a gray-black backpack on his shoulder and was walking towards the finish line. Yet, the person they were most interested in was Suspect #2 and they called him "White Hat." Investigators reviewed the tape again to get a closer look at what he was doing. At about 2:49 p.m., White Hat placed his gray-white backpack on the ground in front of the Forum Restaurant near the sidewalk barricade. He lifted his phone to his ear and spoke.

When he finished speaking the first explosion detonated near the finish line. The ground shook and a blast of fire and smoke wafted the air and down the street. It shocked the spectators and the runners. Everyone turned their gaze to the finish line. Only White Hat remained unfazed by the event. Investigators thought his demeanor was chilling and suspicious. He calmly streamed out from the busy moving crowd without his backpack.

Ten seconds later, another deadly loud explosion blew up right where White Hat had placed his backpack. Investigators believed the pressure cooker bombs were concealed inside the backpacks and they wanted to capture the suspects and bring them to justice.

Four days later, on April 18, the world learned about the two men responsible for the crime when their faces were aired on national news as suspects of the bombings. The perpetrators were identified as brothers from Dagestan, Russia.

White Hat became known as Dzhokhar Tsarnaev. He was a nineteen-year-old college sophomore student at the University of Massachusetts at Dartmouth. He and his brother, Tamerlan, were both accused of placing two bombs near the finish line at the 2013 Boston Marathon. Tamerlan was an unemployed father who stayed at home with his two-year-old daughter.

Since investigators caught Dzhokhar on camera, he was also seen in photographs taken by people who were at the marathon. One of the photographs was a picture of him quickly turning around the corner of Hereford Street without his backpack. He was wearing a white hat that had a number "3" on the side. After he walked away from sight he sent a text message on his cell phone to his close friend, Baudy Mazaev.

Dzhokhar was a lean tall boy with curly brown hair. He had a thin face, a petite goatee on his chin and a pointy nose. Seemingly calm, he began typing... He was worried Baudy might have attended the marathon; he didn't want him to be hurt in the explosions. Upon hearing his friend described the mayhem of the bombings "Two bombs went off, people losing limbs."

Dzhokhar texted *"I automatically thought of yu [sic] man Boston and what not."* He added *"Alrighty man stay safe my man, keep in touch."*[2] He distanced himself, making light of the blasts. Before the bombings, he tweeted these messages hinting that something ominous was coming,

"Evil triumphs when good men do nothing." (March 20, 2013)
"If you have the knowledge and the inspiration all that's left is to take action."
"Most of you are conditioned by the media." (April 7, 2013)

On the day of the bombings, an hour later, he tweeted a couple of disturbing messages:[3]

"Ain't no love in the heart of the city, stay safe people." (April 15, 2013)

"There are people that know the truth but stay silent & there are people that speak the truth, but we don't hear them cuz they're the minority." (April 15, 2013)

On Tuesday, April 16, the day after the bombings, Dzhokhar went to Somerville in Middlesex County in Boston to retrieve his white Mercedes parked at a car repair shop. The car had no taillights and it was missing a bumper. Dzhokhar appeared nervous when he met Gilberto Junior, a mechanic, who was supposed to fix his car. He told him the damaged car apparently belonged to his girlfriend. He said nervously to him, "I need the car right now," and bit his fingernails. Junior told him it wasn't fixed yet.

Dzhokhar was agitated, "I don't care. I don't care. I need the car right now." Junior observed how shaky he was and thought he was on drugs. Dzhokhar almost lost his cool. Junior released the car and Dzhokhar drove off.[4]

Dzhokhar, a highly impressionable college student at nineteen was hiding the fact that he had completely helped his brother bomb the marathon. Later that day, Dzhokhar felt at ease and resumed his student life at UMass–Dartmouth. He talked to one of his sophomore friends on Tuesday. The friend said, "Hey Jahar, the marathon got bombed. Can you believe that?"

Dzhokhar replied, "It's crazy it's happening now. This is so easy to do. These tragedies happen all the time in Afghanistan and Iraq." His very last tweet was on Tuesday night: *"I am a stress free guy."*[5]

On Wednesday, April 17, Dzhokhar smoked inside the student lounge at Pine Dale with Dias Kadyrbayev, his UMass–Dartmouth college buddy from Kazakhstan. They talked briefly, and Dias observed Dzhokhar had cut his unruly dark curly hair shorter.

Dzhokhar went to work out at the Tripp Athletic Center gym with another friend, Azamat Tazhayakov, a student at UMass–Dartmouth who is also from Kazakhstan. The two boys loved to hang out, play video games, and smoke pot together.

At the gym he met other friends who were working out. Dzhokhar was sitting on a weight bench, listening to music on his iPod. His friends were shocked about the bombings and talked with him about it briefly. Dzhokhar, seemed exhausted, but exclaimed in disbelief saying, "Yeah, man, tragedies can happen anywhere in the world. It's too bad." He showed no signs of having any involvement in the crime to his friends. Dzhokhar grew tired and slept in his dorm room at UMass–Dartmouth.

On Wednesday night he was chillin' at a party with his pals from the intramural soccer team. Dzhokhar used to smoke marijuana at the parties but quit smoking before the bombings took place. During the party; he had a laid-back demeanor like he was living a regular college life; being 'Jahar.'

"Jahar" is his American nickname. Jahar got his name when Coach Peter Payack and others in his high school wrestling team had trouble pronouncing his foreign sounding name "Dzhokhar."

Tamerlan, the older twenty-six-year-old brother, who wore the black hat and concealed his identity wearing sunglasses when he bombed the marathon stayed home at their Cambridge apartment to care for his daughter, Zahara. He kissed Zahara goodnight and put her to bed. The next day, Tamerlan thought of his mother, Zubeidat Tsarnaeva, who lived in Dagestan, Russia. He called his mother and said tenderly, "I love you, Mama. I love you." Tamerlan missed his mother. He spoke, "Mama, I missed you."[6]

"Peep," the family fur ball cat meowed at Tamerlan for attention. *(Peep is the name of Dzhokhar's cat found on his Twitter account. This scene is purely imaginative from the writer.)* Tamerlan scooped up the cat in his arm and stroked him while he and his mother both shared small talk about the family pet, Peep.[6a]

On Thursday, April 18, Dzhokhar offered to take a friend, Andrew Gasby home to Waltham, but never did.

However, that afternoon Dzhokhar drove Azamat home where he attended a class at UMass–Dartmouth. He dropped him off at his New Bedford apartment.

After this time Dzhokhar became startled and left for Cambridge…home.

Meanwhile, the FBI made a daring and urgent move at 5 p.m., ET. They released pictures of the two male suspects and were on the manhunt to capture the bombers linked to the bombings. The brothers realized their identities were blown and they tried to make their escape out of the city. It was unplanned. They did not think they would get caught this soon.

Tamerlan was home. He made a quick call to Uncle Alvi Tsarni, his estranged uncle.

Uncle Alvi thought how odd it was to receive a call from his long, lost nephew. Tamerlan spoke a bit about himself, "I married an American and she is now Islamic." He later apologized to his uncle for their estranged relationship, "I want to have an uncle and I love you," he said with sadness in his voice.

There was a pause on the other end of the line. Uncle Alvi relented, "I love you, too, Tamerlan. Now, can we just be a family?"

"Yes" said Tamerlan. "Can I have Uncle Ruslan's number? I just want to make peace with him."

Uncle Alvi gave Tamerlan the number, yet he never called Uncle Ruslan.

Dias turned on the TV and noticed that one of the suspects bore a striking resemblance to his friend, Jahar. He texted Dzhokhar saying he looked like one of the bombing suspects the FBI were interested in capturing. Dzhokhar returned a text message:

"LOL, you better not text me. Come to my room and take whatever you want." 7

Dias told his friends, Azamat and Robel Phillipos, to meet him at the UMass–Dartmouth campus and head to Dzhokhar's dorm room. Dias texted Azamat at around 9 p.m. and alerted him to the breaking news of Dzhokhar being implicated in the Boston Marathon bombings. When all three friends got to the dorm room, Dzhokhar's roommate, Andrew Dwinells let them into the room and told them Dzhokhar had left a few hours earlier.

Before they went in to get things, Dias showed Andrew a text message from Dzhokhar. It said, *"I'm about to leave if you need something in my room take it."* When Azamat saw the message, he believed he would never see Dzhokhar alive again.

In Dzhokhar's dorm room, while they watched a movie they saw Dzhokhar's blue backpack by the side of the bed. Inside the pack they spotted fireworks that had been ripped opened and emptied of black powder. Robel who sat on Dzhokhar's bed counted seven tubular fireworks in the backpack. Dias took the backpack and Dzhokhar's laptop back to their New Bedford apartment.

After the breaking news the city was on high alert for the two suspects. The police believed they were armed and dangerous, and probably had more bombs to detonate. The brothers were fearless and were on the move. A night shift Massachusetts Institute of Technology police officer Sean Collier was shot dead in his patrol car on the school's Cambridge campus at 11 p.m. The authorities linked the killing to the Tsarnaevs.[8]

In Cambridge, Tamerlan hijacked a black Mercedes SUV at gunpoint and took the driver hostage. His name is Meng, an Asian man. While Meng drove, Tamerlan stared at him with a gun pointed directly at his face and said, "Do you know about the Boston Marathon explosions?"[9]

Meng was terrified of him. He said, "Yes, I know."

Tamerlan said proudly, "Well, I did it."

They pulled to a curb in Watertown and another car drove up and stopped. Dzhokhar stepped out of his green Honda sedan. In Meng's black SUV, Tamerlan told Meng to sit on the passenger side. Dzhokhar placed a couple packages into the SUV's trunk. He joined them sitting in the back seat of the SUV, Tamerlan now taking the wheel. They took Meng's ATM card and retrieved his money at an ATM machine.

Meng overheard one of the brothers tell the other to go to Manhattan, New York. However, the SUV was almost out of gas, so they stopped at a gas station in Cambridge. While Dzhokhar went inside the gas station store, Meng was planning to escape. When the opportunity arose, Meng ran across the street to another gas station convenience store. He arrived at the store, screaming "Call 911!"

Twelve-thirty at night, law enforcement officers were notified and initiated a search for the stolen black Mercedes SUV. Since the Mercedes was low on gas, the brothers had intended to abandon the Mercedes and unload the packages back into the Honda in their attempt at escape. Officers tracked and located the Mercedes using GPS in Watertown. The brothers drove down Dexter Avenue and then Laurel Street in Watertown. Dzhokhar drove his Honda sedan and Tamerlan drove the stolen black SUV. They encountered a police patrol car driving up behind Tamerlan and they stopped. Tamerlan stepped out of the SUV, uncovered his gun and then fired at the officer. The officer dodged the bullet and he was shaken by the incident. Neighbors heard the shots inside their homes.[10]

The city of Boston was attacked by terrorists again. Soon, other officers arrived and exchanged gunfire with Tamerlan. Meanwhile, Dzhokhar tossed pipe bomb explosives at the police. A pipe bomb detonated, and it awakened the neighbors. Gunfire continued. Boom! A second bomb was hurled at the police and it exploded.

Tamerlan's gun jammed when he confronted the police while they fired at him. He tossed the gun away and boldly walked towards the police. Officers tackled him while Tamerlan struggled to get up.

Suddenly, a screeching sound from the SUV came right in their path where the police were attempting to cuff Tamerlan. Dzhokhar in a panicked state zoomed right by the police. Tamerlan was clipped by the rear wheel of the vehicle and was dragged under the wheel. Dzhokhar escaped the police firing and sped out of sight down Laurel Street.[11]

During the melee, Officer Dic Donohue was shot and injured by friendly fire and was taken to the hospital. Tamerlan was gashed up and all bloody. He moaned and gasped in pain, after being run over by his brother. The officers arrested him and took him to the hospital for multiple bullet wounds. Tamerlan spat at the EMT's who took him to the hospital. His last words were, "Rot in hell" to an officer before he died.

The police identified Tamerlan at the morgue. On his body they found a trigger for an explosive device; they searched his name in the Intelligence database and discovered he had been interviewed by the FBI before. But, they found no evidence of terrorism. The police pulled up information about Tamerlan's family and Dzhokhar's DMV photo I.D. popped on screen... The police learned that Dzhokhar became a U.S. citizen on September 11, 2012 and his face exactly matched the suspect known as "White Hat." *This* is the suspect.[12]

Dzhokhar fled from the pursuing police. He had abandoned the SUV and smashed the evidence: the cellphone, GPS and ATM card. He hid them between concrete blocks. He was shot in the hand and leg and was bleeding as he fled on foot. Frantically, he looked from house to house down the street, bleeding and searching for a place to rest and hide. It was after midnight and all residents were asleep. He could no longer run or leave a trail of blood behind him. He hoped to find a place to crawl into and survive the night.

Down the corner block his eyes glanced to an unlit house on Franklin Street. Behind the house, he spotted a white 20-foot boat.

Dzhokhar limped to the vessel quietly, and felt around the boat, searching for a way inside. Immediately, he saw two pads holding down a tarp on the edge of the boat. He removed them carefully and the tarp spread apart, revealing a dark opening space to lie down in. The boat was his crypt and haven. He crawled in exhausted and hurt. Scared, he was hungry and shaking as he groped inside the boat to find a comfortable place to lie down. As his blood spilled onto the boat, he pressed his right hand on his wounds and gasped in agony. His eyes blinked and were getting heavy in exhaustion. As he fell asleep he thought about his brother's arrest. He hoped the police would not come looking for him.

Late that night, at the New Bedford Apartments, Dias puts Dzhokhar's backpack that he took from his dorm room into a black plastic trash bag and tossed it outside into a dumpster.

THE UNARMED TERRORIST

The following morning was windy. It was Friday, April 19. Five days after the bombings that killed three innocent spectators and injured hundreds of others at the marathon, Governor Deval Patrick, Boston's Mayor Thomas Menino, Chief Edward Deveau of the Boston police department, and U.S. Massachusetts Attorney Carmen Ortiz, decided to put the city on lockdown until they could capture the fugitive. Boston became paralyzed. It became a ghost town, settling into a dead silence that the nation had never seen before. The whole nation was on edge.

Surrounding communities were closed and authorities told people to stay off the streets. A manhunt was underway to hunt down the terrorist and to capture him alive. Outside media swarmed into the city to report the whole manhunt. Police rode in with tanks.

A massive force of law enforcement officers was on stand-by. The FBI and the SWAT Team arrived in heavy militarized equipment, all searching for Dzhokhar Tsarnaev. Police went house-to-house searching for him. They believed he was wounded during the shootout and thought he might hide in a residential home. Dzhokhar Tsarnaev was now a "Wanted Man." His face was plastered on billboards. A Wanted poster was dispersed through the media, warning anyone who saw Dzhokhar to call the FBI. They assumed he was armed and may be carrying bombs with him.

Dzhokhar awoke in the boat. His wound was deep, and he suffered pain in his leg. Ignoring the pain, he wrote busily with a pencil in his right hand he had found in the boat. He began etching jihadi messages on the inside hull and beam of the boat. It was a chilling confession…

He wrote that the bombings were in retribution for the U.S. wars against Muslims and the bombings were *"collateral damage…" when you attack one Muslim, you attack all Muslims."* He wrote how he did not *"mourn his brother, that he was a martyr in paradise…"* Dzhokhar quickly wrote these words on the boat hull, *"…and I will join him there."*

Later that afternoon, Azamat watched the garbage truck pick up the dumpster and drove away taking Dzhokhar's backpack to the garbage land fill.

Dzhokhar's relatives spoke to the media. Especially Uncle Ruslan Tsarni, an uncle living in Maryland who was interviewed by reporters. He did not want to blame groups, saying, "He (Dzhokhar) put a shame on our family…He put shame on the entire Chechen ethnicity because now everyone blames Chechens…When a Muslim or a person of color does something, someone always has to defend the whole community."

Ruslan became emotional and was deeply torn by the tragic deaths, delivering his condolences to the victims, "Those who were injured – this boy, this Chinese girl, the young 29-year-old girl – I've been following this from day one." He paused and pleaded for Dzhokhar on live television, "Dzhokhar, if you are alive, turn yourself in and ask for forgiveness from the victims, from the injured and from those who are left..."[13]

However, Dzhokhar never heard those pleading words from his uncle whom he had not seen in years. He was bleeding to death. He fell in and out of consciousness. Feeling dizzy and weak, he became unconscious.

Meanwhile, the authorities checked the database and discovered that he attended UMass-Dartmouth. The SWAT team advanced to the Pine Dale dorm and combed through the dorm rooms searching for Dzhokhar. They did not find him hiding there. Tired, their hopes wavered. It was critically important to them that they find him.

By evening the lockdown was lifted. The boat owner, David Henneberry, noticed how two pads had fallen out of the shrink-wrap. He went to check on his boat. When he pulled the straps, he wondered why it was loose. He lifted the loose tarp and peered inside. He saw blood smeared on the boat deck!

Inside his boat, Henneberry discovered the body of a man curled up, lying near the steering console, appearing to be severely injured. He gasped and was shocked to find the suspect the authorities were looking for. He feared the man had weapons, possibly more bombs. Later, he saw a trail of blood leading into the boat, and he quickly alerted authorities.

Immediately, cops rushed to the Henneberry's property. An officer yelled at the owner to move away. Mr. Henneberry told the authorities, "He's in the boat." Law enforcement moved in quickly but cautiously. They surrounded the boat; they did not know how badly injured Dzhokhar was.[14]

Dzhokhar's eyes jerked opened when he heard the rumbling noises and police sirens outside. A helicopter whirled above him. He wanted to check outside. He reached for a fishing gaff and lifted the white boat cover to get a peek. Officers outside saw movement inside the boat yet didn't know what weapons he had on him and they thought he had a rifle. They prepared to fire. Mr. Henneberry quickly warned them he had 45 gallons of gas in the boat.

Suddenly, shots rang out. Multiple shots fired all around the boat, hundreds of rounds. A bullet hit Dzhokhar in the left side of his neck and went out under the left ear. He flinched back and gasped in pain. Blood splattered and oozed out of his neck; he went down in a fetal position, crawling and throbbing in pain. He was stunned and scared; bullets were flying all around him. The boat's hull was riddled with bullets. Bullets struck him in the legs. Dzhokhar yelled amid the sounds of shots being firing at him, "I'm, I'm coming out! I'm coming out!"

David Henneberry, the boat owner stood next to the officers and was horrified to see his boat, the "Slip Away II," destroyed. The shooting halted. Dzhokhar's confession note on the boat's hull was punctured by bullet holes.

Dzhokhar was losing both blood and body heat. A helicopter probed the perimeter around the boat. The infrared camera inside the helicopter watched for Dzhokhar's movement. There were no movements. They noted his body was losing body heat. Dzhokhar was shot in the neck and was bleeding profusely from his mouth. He laid still.

The FBI wanted to negotiate with him to surrender. They used a flash bang grenade to force him out of the boat. A flash grenade was shot into the boat. Bang! Dzhokhar's body did not flinch. Another one hit him directly below his feet. This time, Dzhokhar's body jerked and flopped around, prompting FBI to report that there was movement in the boat.

Dzhokhar was frightened by the grenade. His ears began ringing and he could not hear. The impact broke his arm when the second flash bang exploded near him.

It was realized later that the assault was recorded. The world saw what was happening in real time, how the police were operating. It was shocking to see that one flash grenade nearly killed the suspect. A decision was made to cut the live feed.

When the flash bangs failed, a robotic device was sent to rattle the boat. The arm of the robot ripped off the boat cover. Dzhokhar was visible. He was too weak to move. He had lost a lot of blood from his injuries in the first gun battle. The robot probed him, and it checked for explosives. An officer shouted into a megaphone to talk to him, but Dzhokhar did not respond.

Meanwhile the SWAT teams, FBI special agents and the police kept watch over the boat. "This is a real battle," said a police officer. "We believe this man to be a terrorist. We believe this to be a man who's come here to kill people," he exclaimed.

An FBI agent negotiator with the FBI's Crisis Negotiating Unit thought Dzhokhar would not surrender himself. He shouted back to him in the boat, "Give it up, give it up! We know you are bleeding. We know you are tired." By evening, Dzhokhar would not move or come out of the boat.

The FBI agent remembered watching CNN that afternoon; the reporters interviewed Dzhokhar's former wrestling coach from high school, Peter Payack. Payack was more than a coach; he had loved Dzhokhar as his own son. Payack had sent a "direct appeal" for Dzhokhar to surrender that afternoon.

The agent remembered the coach's appeal to Dzhokhar. He used his message to negotiate with Dzhokhar. He brought up people who thought of him, especially his family. "Dzhokhar," he shouted. "It is getting late. Your family is thinking about you now. Your father spoke and wants you to give up. He wants you to come to justice alive. He is worried."[15]

Inside the boat, Dzhokhar heard the agent speak about his family. Dzhokhar was supposed to visit his father in Dagestan during the summer holidays. He lay still, listening.

"And Mr. Payack, your former wrestling coach thinks of you also."

Dzhokhar became emotional when the agent said Mr. Payack's name because he remembered his former coach as a dear friend and mentor. Coach Payack was also fond of him too. Dzhokhar remembered he was named captain of the wrestling team; his fellow wrestlers respected him as a leader. They were all like family to him when he was a high school student attending Cambridge Rindge and Latin. "Mr. Payack sends you this direct appeal. He wants you to hear this message. He said, 'Jahar, this is Coach Payack.'"[16]

Dzhokhar listened, lying in his blood.

The agent continued, "Jahar, there has been enough death, destruction. Please turn yourself in."

It was intense, and the police waited for him to surrender. Dzhokhar must have thought he was going to die a martyr; however, the cherished relationship he had with his wrestling coach gave him a reason to surrender... There was someone who loved him and wanted him to live instead of dying and becoming a martyr.

Coach Payack wanted Dzhokhar to live. Hopefully, one day he could talk to Dzhokhar, the man that he once knew, and not the mass murderer he had become.

"Coach Payack is on his way to be here and he wants you to turn yourself in," the agent called out again to Dzhokhar.

Coach Peter Payack and Jahar

Dzhokhar was in agony and needed help. He was ready to give himself up and face the authorities. He rolled onto his side. The metallic pieces of the flash grenade scarred his left eye and he was nearly blind and deaf from the blast. His bloody hand shook in pain; he was hurting and needed immediate help. He gathered all his might and strength to scream. As his voice quavered, he screamed in pain, "It hurts! Help! HELLLLP!"[17]

The SWAT team heard him. The FBI negotiator ordered him to get up and go to the side of the boat. But, Dzhokhar was screaming, "It hurts! It hurts!" Dzhokhar lifted himself up slowly and tried to stand.

The FBI negotiator told him, "You got to get out; you've got to do it on your own. Just keep your hands visible."

Dzhokhar put his hands to his side. He was bleeding and shaking. He slowly climbed out of the boat, one leg up over the boat. As he wobbled, the SWAT team watched. They feared he was reaching for a gun as Dzhokhar's hand went behind the boat.

His ears were ringing. He lost his balance. Grenade concussion sound waves pierced his eardrums. Disoriented, nearly unconscious, delirious and defeated he swooned. He bent over dangling on the edge.

He could not stand or move off the edge of the boat. The police yelled at him repeatedly to put his hands up and to lift his shirt up. Dzhokhar's response was very slow. He held up his shirt and raised his right hand. The SWAT team cautiously crept up to him aiming a laser gun sight dot on his forehead. An officer yelled, "Show me your hand!"

Dzhokhar extended his left bloody hand to them. As they came closer, the officers snatched Dzhokhar off the boat and knocked him onto the ground. He landed hard on his back and he yelped. The SWAT quickly pounced on top of him; searching to see if he had a detonator in his hands or on his extremities. Dzhokhar kept screaming in pain as the officers inspected him.

He was wounded, dying and yelling for help. An officer yanked Dzhokhar's sweatshirt up. He saw no bombs attached. No guns either. Dzhokhar did not move or fidget when the handcuffs were placed around his wrists. ATF Medical workers tended to his bleeding wounds.

As Dzhokhar was carried out on a stretcher, a group of fuming officers moved in and began spitting on his face. Dzhokhar was shocked and traumatized, not understanding the meaning of all this. One angry officer watched the terror suspect go by. He muttered, "We got you, motherfucker."[18] Once Dzhokhar was placed in the ambulance, the EMTs immediately attended to his wounds. After he was captured, the Boston police tweeted:

CAPTURED! THE HUNT IS OVER. THE SEARCH IS DONE! THE TERROR IS OVER! AND JUSTICE HAS WON! SUSPECT IS IN CUSTODY! [19]

Everyone ran out into the streets elated, shouting cheers wildly into the night. People stood by the roadsides began clapping and cheering for the officers driving by in their vehicles, and for all those involved in the manhunt! Dzhokhar nearly died in the ambulance ride to the hospital due to blood loss. He needed immediate medical attention.

REMEMBERING THE VICTIMS

The senseless murders of the Boston Marathon bombings killed three innocent spectators on April 15, 2013: the victims were an eight-year-old boy, and, two women, one from Boston, and another from China. Furthermore, the brothers were responsible for the murder of a MIT police officer on April 18, 2013. Their beautiful faces and smiles will never fade away. They should not be forgotten. May God be with them. I wrote a short description about them and dedicated a scripture verse to each of them to be remembered by. There are also memorial landmarks honoring the victims that you can visit.

MARTIN RICHARD IS "PEACE."

Martin Richard. There is a photo of him smiling and holding up a sign. He wrote on the sign "No more hurting people... Peace." He is remembered for these words. Martin Richard's Statue can be seen at Bridgewater State, MA.

To Martin: *"Turn from evil and do good; seek peace and pursue it."* (Psalms 34:14)

OFFICER SEAN COLLIER IS "CHERISH."

Sean Collier loved life. He was a passionate man who put everything he had into what he loved. Sean Collier's Memorial can be seen at MIT, Cambridge, MA.

To Sean: *"The one who gets wisdom loves life; the one who cherishes understanding will soon prosper."* (Proverbs 19:8)

LINGZI LU IS "JOY."

Lingzi Lu brought joy into people's lives. She had a very sweet smile.

To Lingzi: *"Be happy, young man, while you are young, and let your heart give you joy in the days of your youth. Follow the ways of your heart and see whatever your eyes see, but know that for all these things God will bring you to judgment."* *(Ecclesiastes 11:9)* This is Lingzi's biography: *Boston Remembering a Chinese Girl.*

KRYSTLE CAMPBELL IS A "HEART OF GOLD."

Krystle Campbell's mom said, "Krystle was a loveable person, a hard worker and a popular manager." Krystle Campbell's Peace Garden is in Medford, Boston, MA.

To Krystle: *"Now that you have purified yourselves by obeying the truth so that you have sincere love for your brothers, love one another deeply, from the heart."* (1 Peter 1: 22)

The Lone Surviving Suspect

"Boston–area residents were coming together in prayer and reflection Sunday after a tumultuous week as the lone surviving suspect in the Boston Marathon bombing lay hospitalized under heavy guard apparently in no shape for interrogation."
— Bridget Murphy and Katie Zezim of Associated Press, April 21, 2013

DZHOKHAR WAS RUSHED TO Beth Israel Deaconess Medical Center. He lay on the stretcher and moaned in pain.[20] At the hospital, nurses were still treating victims from the bombings. Nine nurses were selected to care for Dzhokhar. When the nurses learned they would be caring for the terrorist, they all agreed to their assignment. One of those nurses recalled a conversation earlier with her husband, she wasn't sure if she could nurse a terrorist. But, her husband insisted she treat him. "We have to do it, so we can get answers," he told her.

When Dzhokhar was admitted into the red zone trauma room, he was bloody and dying. He groaned in pain. He was scared being alone, knowing no one. The doctors and nurses began treating him immediately. A nurse named Marie took care of Dzhokhar. She stared at the bleeding suspect. Marie thought about the victims who had died. She would not be upset if Dzhokhar received the death penalty. She was ambivalent as she moved him to get a CT scan and then to the OR room.

In the OR, two thoracic surgeons and specialized surgeons were prepared to operate and stabilize this young man. All the nurses who treated him referred to him as the "boy." A nurse who worked in the trauma room saw the wounded Dzhokhar and thought he didn't look like a terrorist anymore. Another unidentified nurse said, "You see a hurt 19–year–old and you can't help but feel sorry for him."

This is a leaked photo of Dzhokhar at the hospital after surgery.

After the surgery, Dzhokhar was moved to the sixth floor where it was secured by Law enforcement, FBI representatives and police officers assigned to protect Dzhokhar. Two FBI investigators assigned to the investigation stood in the hallway and were very eager to interrogate Dzhokhar. They could not speak with him because he had been intubated. As Dzhokhar slept, Nurse Michele stood by him. She could only think what people thought of him. She said, "The world hates him right now. The emotions are like one big salad, all tossed around." The nurses caring for Dzhokhar were conflicted.[21]

The following day, Dzhokhar was still alive in a designated hospital room. He was intubated and on a breathing ventilator due to a tear from a gunshot wound. He slowly awoke in the unfamiliar surroundings, feeling dizzy and hungry. Due to the pooling of blood in and around his left eye, where there were sutures, his sight was restricted. He was non-verbal due to his jaw being wired together. His hearing was now impaired in his left ear. Gunshot wounds in his legs would require a painful recovery. In addition to this, his left arm was broken, and the left hand was bandaged making it difficult to adjust himself in the bed. His right hand was secured to the bed with a handcuff! Dzhokhar felt overwhelmed. He became emotional.

A nurse came in to check on Dzhokhar. *(There is an unverified story about a nurse who allegedly witnessed that Dzhokhar was crying at the hospital. But no one knew what he was crying about. This source is found in the article "Jahar's World" in Rolling Stone.[22])* She was startled to see him awake and she checked the ventilator. She glanced at Dzhokhar without emotion.

Dzhokhar glanced at her, using his good right eye. He began crying from his injuries and possibly the loss of freedom in his future. The nurse ignored him, left the room and told the two FBI agents at the door that he was awake.

The FBI agents entered to see Dzhokhar; they were careful not to tell him his brother Tamerlan was dead. Dzhokhar was weak, and he wanted to sleep. The multitude pain medication made him light-headed, sleepy and unfocused. The agents uncuffed his right arm so he could write on a pad with a pencil.

The agents began questioning him. They wanted to be sure there were no more bombs and they also asked about his involvement in the bombings.

"Are there more bombs?"

Dzhokhar wrote: "No."

"Did you and your brother act alone? Or did you have any help from anyone, foreign or domestic?"

"No, no help. We acted alone," Dzhokhar tried to write with his good hand.

"What is the cause or motive for this attack?"

Dzhokhar wrote: *"We were motivated by religious fervor and anger over U.S. involvement in the Iraq and Afghanistan wars."*[23]

As Dzhokhar was being interrogated, he wrote that the attack was launched without preparation and they did not test fire the pressure-cooker bombs before allegedly placing them near the crowd of spectators at the marathon finish line, where it killed three people and injured over 260 people.

Dzhokhar communicated to them through writing. Sometimes, he became extremely sleepy, and he fell asleep. He stopped writing and it appeared to trail off the edge of the page. He wrote: *"I'm hurt," "I'm exhausted,"* and *"Can we do this later?"* He was sleep deprived and the pain killers made him sick. He wrote on another note and passed it to them: *"I need to throw up. Leave me alone."* Dzhokhar asked the agents where his brother was and if he was still alive. The agents lied to him and told him he was still alive.

He wrote: *"Is my brother alive I know you said he is, are you lying Is he alive?"* Again, he persisted to see Tamerlan. He was disoriented and wrote: *"Is he alive, show me the news!"* *"What's today? Where is he?"* Lastly, he was awfully tired and distraught throughout the interrogation he wrote: *"Can I sleep?"* *"Can you not handcuff my right arm?"* *"Where is my bro [sic] Are you sure [sic]"* [24a] [24b]

Dzhokhar admitted his part in the plot and told them his brother was the actual mastermind of the bombings. He and his brother watched sermons of Anwar al–Awlaki online. They had planned a suicide attack on July 4th but finished the bombs early, therefore the marathon became the alternative target.

While the agents questioned Dzhokhar's motive, it occurred then that he desperately needed a lawyer. He became afraid of the interrogation; he felt he was cornered by the agents asking him several questions. He did not know if Tamerlan was alive or not. The agents deliberately avoided telling him where his brother was. Intensely nervous, there was much weighing on him that he began to realize he had lost his freedom and his future and would never see his friends and family again. As the agents continued questioning him, he wrote and circled *"lawyer"* ten times on a piece of paper! He was questioned for sixteen hours before he was advised of his Miranda rights.[25]

After the agents left him, he cried for two days straight.[26]

One day, a nurse came to move him. Dzhokhar moaned when she touched him. She blurted out, "I am really sorry, hon." She couldn't help calling him *"hon"* that she made a pact with the other nurse if they spoke with terms of endearment to him. Nine nurses spent time caring for the boy and they were emotionally ambivalent to admit they had empathy for him.

After a week in the hospital, Dzhokhar's condition improved, but he was still unable to appear at his court hearing. The court appointed judge for the Hearing was U.S. Judge Marianne Bowler. She went to the hospital for a brief visit to conduct the court hearing.

Dzhokhar answered her questions. He uttered the word *"no"* when asked if he could not afford a lawyer. He nodded that he understood his rights. Then Judge Bowler read his constitutional rights. She told him he would face the death penalty for the bombings. Suddenly, Dzhokhar was quiet. He stopped talking when he was asked to answer some more questions.[27]

At the end of the week at the hospital, the U.S. Marshals transferred Dzhokhar to Devens Medical Center prison facility forty miles outside of Boston. His life was now in their control. They wheeled him out of the loading dock at the back of the hospital in the middle of the night into a large transport vehicle out of Boston.

Meanwhile, America wondered about the surviving brother. Why did he do it? Did he have remorse? The photo I.D. circulated by the media, revealed his youthful features; however, some people perceived the soulless eyes of a monster. He was dehumanized and was called the Devil. He had placed the bomb behind that little boy. Uncle Ruslan, looked forward to meeting his nephew in prison. He wanted to tell Dzhokhar that there was still time for evil and hate to leave his body, and that he was still loved. Ruslan believed his family was not so different from many others. "We all think we know each other, but in fact we don't," he said. [28a 28b]

After Dzhokhar was captured, prayers started pouring in to pray for both the Boston Bomber suspect and for the victims of the bombings. The prayers never stopped. The memories of the bombings, the horror of the tragedy remained in the hearts of all who lived it.

Our God is a God of mercy And just. As brothers & sisters of Christ, we must pray for the captured suspect, for he is still a child of God.

Pray for the captured suspect, that if he is guilty he repents and confesses his sins.

THE TSARNAEV FAMILY

Dzhokhar Anzorovich *"Jahar"* Tsarnaev (joh–HAHR' tsahr NEYE'ehv) was born on July 22, 1993, in Kyrgyzstan. He is half–Chechen (North Caucasus) and half–Avar (North Caucasus mountaineers).

Dzhokhar, also known as "Jahar," is the youngest of four children in his family. He was born to a devout Muslim mother, Zubeidat Tsarnaeva (an Avar). His father, Anzor Tsarnaev (a Chechen), once worked as a car mechanic and was a former boxer.

Jahar immigrated with his family to the States from Russia in 2002 seeking asylum after claiming they were persecuted in Russia for being ethnic Chechens. His mother, Zubeidat, called him "dwog" which means "heart." Jahar was her sweet dark, curly-haired boy and close to his mother's heart. Long ago, she called him "Jo-Jo" for short. The name Dzhokhar means "Jewel."[29] His mother claims, "Dzhokhar was pleased and proud of his name. He has always been a happy boy."

Jahar's parents, who live in Dagestan, were shocked and saddened by Tamerlan's death and Jahar's arrest. Tears slid down Anzor's face when he heard that Jahar had been caught alive. He wanted to send his son this message. "Tell police everything. Everything. Just be honest," said Anzor. A couple days earlier, he said, "I spoke to my sons by phone earlier this week after the bombings." His sons reassured him, "'Everything is good, Daddy. Everything is very good.'" Now that Anzor learned the truth about his sons, he denied that his sons had any involvement in the terrorist attack. "They never could have done this. Never, ever, ever!" said Anzor. He believed that they had been framed.[30]

At a press conference in Dagestan, Russia, Zubeidat and Anzor were reconciled after a divorce. Zubeidat was visibly upset about the bombings. The tragedy of the bombings drew their relationship closer together. She wore a black hijab and cried, saying she preferred not to live in America, "Why did I even go there? Why did I go there? I thought America would protect us, our kids, it's going to be safe, but it happened." Zubeidat cried and was distraught as she spoke with her hands in the air. She said hopelessly, "America took my kids away from me." Anzor sat passively beside her, not speaking to the press.[31]

A heartbroken mother, who mourned the loss of her eldest, Tamerlan, talked to the press about the close brotherly relationship between Tamerlan and Dzhokhar. She said they loved each other. Tamerlan was the favorite in the family. He was mature, big and strong. Tamerlan would go up to little Jahar and hug him. He would hold Jahar up in the air, carrying him on his shoulders because he was his big brother. He adored and kissed him. Jahar idolized Tamerlan. Tamerlan would likewise kissed his two sisters, Bella and Ailina.

Bella, the second oldest child withdrew from high school and married in Kazakhstan. Her marriage failed after she had a baby. She returned to the United States, moving to Cambridge, Massachusetts. Bella had a previous run in with the law and was arrested on marijuana charges.

Ailina, the third child of this family had an arranged marriage at age sixteen. It lasted one year and produced one child. Like Bella, she had broken the law. Ailina had a relationship with another man and they had a child together. She fought a custody battle for the child. Later, in August 27, 2014, Ailina was charged for allegedly making a bomb threat to her boyfriend's ex-girlfriend with the intention of keeping her away from him. She pleaded not guilty and is no longer in police custody. She is now focused on raising her children.[32] Both sisters have been through the legal system.

In 2002, Jahar was eight-years-old when he immigrated to the United States with his parents. Once they arrived, the family applied for asylum.[33a] [33b] In Kazakhstan, an uncle cared for Tamerlan, Bella and Ailina. In 2003, when Tamerlan was sixteen, he and his sisters arrived in the States and were reunited with their parents.

They settled in Cambridge in Boston. The family lived in a narrow, cramped top-floor apartment at 410 Norfolk. Jahar and Tamerlan shared a bedroom. Because the kitchen table was small for the family, Jahar and Tamerlan would routinely sit on the couch in the living room and eat their meals while they watched television. The two boys as companions engaged themselves playing video games while their parents ate and talked in the kitchen.

Both siblings had different roles while growing up. Tamerlan stood 6-foot 3 and was called "a big friendly giant." He was always the leader and his siblings obeyed and listened to him. All the children followed the big brother's example. The family's big dream for Tamerlan was for him to become an Olympic boxer. Anzor helped coach Tamerlan with his boxing. The family regularly attended his practices and matches. Jahar was remembered as a little kid who had big ears and a sweet smile. He liked tagging alongside his brother like a puppy to the boxing gym. He hung out and watched his brother fight and practice; Tamerlan would teach him boxing. But, Jahar would pick up wrestling as his sport.[34]

In America, the Tsarnaevs tried to fit into their new society while observing their customs. The hardworking, immigrant family struggled financially and was on welfare. They received public assistance for five years and in 2002 received food stamps benefits. They lived in a crowded apartment; no one from Jahar's school came to visit the Tsarnaev's home.

Anzor developed chronic arthritis and headaches, making it difficult for him to support his family. He had an unpredictable temperament caused by the abuse he suffered in Kyrgyzstan. Anzor was tortured in a Russian camp during the Russian/Chechen war.

Zubeidat opened a local salon in her home and gave beauty treatments to her customers. She also became a devout Muslim.

Tamerlan dropped out of Bunker Hill Community College because he said he had no friends. He became depressed and wasn't adjusting easily to American culture. He became schizophrenic. He was hearing voices in his head. Once Tamerlan came home late smelling like smoke and alcohol. He had been partying. Zubeidat disapproved of her son's lifestyle and encouraged him to seek Islam to search for his identity. Together, mother and son began studying the Qur'an which influenced Tamerlan to become a devout Muslim.

Jahar lived and went to school in Makhachkala, Dagestan from 1999 to 2001. Makhachkala is the capital city of the Republic of Dagestan. His former teachers described him as a normal child.[35] When he came to America, Jahar was thankful to live in Cambridge. He embraced the freedom of living in America. He loved Boston, his high school – Cambridge Rindge and Latin. He furthermore expressed love for American music from artists like Michael Jackson, Billy Joel, Eminem, Jay Z and Kanye West. He loved to eat American food such as pizza, cheeseburgers, peanut butter fluff and Nutella. Jahar ate other kinds of foods as well. A Chinese journalist accidentally found a local Chinese restaurant Jahar frequented during his high school. The journalist learned Jahar would often go there alone to order lunch specials, ordering fried rice, fried chicken and fried noodles.[36]

In high school, Jahar excelled in his studies and earned a $2,500 college scholarship. He enjoyed wrestling and was captain of the team for two years. He also worked at the Harvard University's pool as a lifeguard. He posted this message on Twitter about how much he enjoyed working as a lifeguard: *"I didn't become a lifeguard to just chill and get paid, I do it for the people, saving lives brings me joy."*

Jahar
@J_tsar

i didn't become a lifeguard to just chill and get paid, i do it for the people, saving lives brings me joy #lifeguardoftheyear

1:13pm - 29 May 12

Jahar went to UMass–Dartmouth because he couldn't afford to go to a better private college. He paid some of his college tuition by himself (parents provided little). Jahar's college dorm was provided by the State. He was a straight "A" student.

His parents still supported him, sometimes sending him money for food. In his sophomore year, he told his close friends he was failing courses at UMass–Dartmouth because it was harder than he thought. He switched majors from engineering to biology. But, he was unhappy there and began hating life. He did not have many friends in college. During class, he was quiet and kept to himself. Jahar's closest friends from high school were gone so he hung out with Dias Kadyrbayev and Azamat Tazhayakov because they spoke Russian. He began selling marijuana, making money out of the cash. He owned a gun for protection, and smooth talked his way around police officers.[37]

The Tsarnaev family was in chaos. In 2011, the family finally broke apart. Jahar's parents filed for divorced. They were married for twenty–five years. There was no chance of reconciling their differences because Zubeidat embraced Islam tradition. Anzor decided to return home to Dagestan to treat his mental illness.

Later, Zubeidat also moved back to Russia to set up her own business.[38] Suddenly, Tamerlan became the father-figure to Jahar. However, their lifestyle was observed by Rinat Harel, a long-time neighbor who knew the Tsarnaevs. He said the brothers were like two obnoxious boys. They would hold loud parties in the courtyard and drink into the night. With their parents' divorce and absence, the kids were left to do whatever they wanted. Jahar partied at many gatherings and became addicted to both cocaine and marijuana.

JAHAR WAS A WAS LOVELY KID, BUT WHAT HAPPENED?

Jahar was never a religious person until he learned Islamic religion through his mother and brother. At the time Jahar immersed himself in American culture, he was well-respected and liked by his teachers. They questioned how he could have developed this hatred and yet act notably cordial.

"He was grateful to be in America. He was so grateful to be at the school. He was so grateful to be accepted. He was pleasant, careful, jovial – there was nothing remotely like this at all. He was a lovely, lovely kid, an outstanding athlete and never a troublemaker," said former wrestling coach, Larry Anderson.[39]

The business owners like the local Chinese restaurant in Cambridge, said Jahar came into their restaurant as a regular customer and they had positive thoughts regarding him. They thought he was an adorable and polite teenager. He seemed like a better kid than the other high school students. The owners were shocked and in disbelief when they learned that Jahar was one of the bombers of the Boston marathon.[40]

Coach Peter Payack who demanded Jahar to surrender that night in the boat said, "When he lived in Cambridge, at one point in his life, he was "beloved." He wanted to go to UMass–Amherst to become an engineer. But, he did not get in; instead he attended UMass–Dartmouth." Coach Payack said Jahar was a nice kid, not a hot head, but someone who would always help people. He thought Jahar would become a dentist or a nurse. He was a life guard in the past. He had as well volunteered in "Best Buddies," a program helping the disabled.

Anzor believed in his son's compassion. He spoke to the press from Russia. He had learned that his eldest son, Tamerlan, had been killed when the police were in a hot pursuit hunting for both sons. "My son is a true angel. Dzhokhar is a second–year medical student in the U.S. He is such an intelligent boy. We expected him to come home for the holidays here," said his father to the press.

Jahar's high school classmates were all shocked to learn that their close friend whom they had trusted and liked was involved in terrorism.

"It's scary. It's completely scary," said Sonia Ribeiro, a classmate of Tsarnaev. "Who would have thought that somebody you know, someone that you're friends with, can be capable of doing something like this? So, it's scary because it's home," Ribeiro said. "I really liked this kid. He was nice. He was cool. I don't know. I'm just in shock."[41]

All his friends said the same things. They were shocked and searched for answers; they thought Jahar was a typical American kid, they never expected he would hurt someone.[42] This is what they had to say:

"Never thought I would see something like this for sure. I still can't consider him guilty. If you knew him, he was a nice guy; there was no reason to not like him at all. He was nice, calm. He was nice. He wouldn't even make a joke because it seemed like he wouldn't even want to bring any harm towards anybody."

"I started crying. That wasn't the Jahar I knew. The Jahar I knew wasn't trying to throw sticks and dynamites. He was respected so much. The Jahar that I knew, he wasn't extreme in any way. He said I'm a Muslim, but I'm not really a Muslim. He talked like that."

Jahar was comical and liked to be the class clown, cracking jokes; however, he gave the teachers a hard time. He had a bright smile and an infectious laugh. He was well-liked by many of his classmates and friends called him Shaggy from *Scooby-Doo*. He had a lot of friends whom he could share his life with. They said the following: He was goofy (spreading cheese strings on a couch, and a friend hairstyling his curly hair and putting it in pigtails.) He was a risk taker (driving a car backwards down a one–way street.) He liked music (he wore ear buds in his ear, coming into class listening to hip-hop music). He would arrive late to class and take a short nap on his desk for 15 minutes.

Friends remembered him smoking outside of his car, just chillin' out. Jahar was one of the chilliest kids. He was cute. Girls had crushes on him. Close friends remember conversations with Jahar one time as he drank a shot of vodka, debating to himself whether to or not to talk to a cute girl at a party. Friends thought of him as shy, gentle, compassionate and sweet. A month before the bombings, he gathered many of his friends, including his best friend, Junes, and they played and set off fireworks near Charles River.[43]

His tweets were amusing like a typical college kid: [44]

Back to terrible food, hot pockets and school bs. Dam I'm just tryina be at that stage in life where I'm coming home to my wife from work.

2 essays down, one to go baby.

I hate these college desks, way too small to sleep on.

Some of his tweets were meaningful about his views on life:

No matter where life takes me you'll still find me with a smile.

Gratitude is the attitude of the blessed. A smile isn't just mouth movement; one can distinguish between fake & real smiles by the shimmer of happiness in the persons eyes.

All Dzhokhar's Photos are from various "Jahar" *Tumblr* sites.

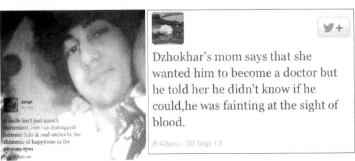

Dzhokhar's mom says that she wanted him to become a doctor but he told her he didn't know if he could,he was fainting at the sight of blood.

8:43am - 30 Sep 13

However, it is sad that Jahar failed to live up to his dreams and to pursue a profession helping people. Instead, Jahar was completely consumed in Jihad. He lost focus in studying. It is unfathomable to his friends that he was capable of being this cold-blooded mass murderer. How could this have happened? What changed him? Coach Payack felt a contributing factor may be Jahar leaving his little nest or home (school family) in Cambridge where he had close friends and relationships. There was no discrimination regarding whether someone was a Muslim, Jewish or Catholic. "When he left Cambridge to attend UMass–Dartmouth it wasn't his family. Anything could be cold than where he came from," explained Coach Payack.

"In Cambridge we coddled him. We not only coddled him, but the whole wrestling team. We bonded. We're all like one family." Coach Payack recalled how Jahar visited him six months before the bombings to practice wrestling with the high school team. It was hard for Coach Payack to believe that Jahar was the accused bomber. When he learned that the suspect, who killed and maimed people, was one of his own he felt like he was shot in the heart. The coach could never forget the little boy, Martin Richard, who was killed in the bombings. It upset him to think that the Jahar he knew and loved as his own son would allegedly do such a heinous murder.

"What was he thinking?" He said, "He betrayed us, he betrayed his friends, his school, his coach, his community and America who harbored him and gave him his citizenship. Not only did he hurt a lot of people, but he also hurt himself." The once mentor who loved Jahar believed he was groomed in a cult to kill people alongside his older brother, Tamerlan. "He took away millions of people's lives," he said.[45]

A WOUNDED BOY

Jahar lay in bed in a medical prison doctor's office. He was drowsy. He had a bandage over both of his eyes. He tried to move his injured left hand. It would not move. There were five bullet wounds in his hand. Jahar was deaf in his left ear. He could not move his neck sideways. A bullet had punctured and had torn through his left cheek, traveling from the left inside of his mouth and exiting out the left lower face. His throat injury left him incapable of eating. He had a couple of gash knife wounds (from shrapnel explosion) extending from the top of his neck down to his collarbone. His jaw was – *"fragmented,"* but was not infected. His skull base was fractured. He had wounds on his left arm and shoulder. His legs also took in five bullet shots: three bullets in his right leg, and two in his left. He was unable to walk. Altogether, there were sixteen deep wounds in his body as described by a family friend.[46]

(Jahar stayed at Devens Medical Center, a prison facility outside of Boston. This scene is from the testimony by one of Tsarnaev's U.S. Marshals who guarded him. Supporters of Tsarnaev's family shared updates about Jahar to people who cared about his injuries. The messages Jahar wrote to his parents are true.)

A deputy U.S. Marshal stood near him, observing his shot–up swollen face. As Jahar lay in the doctor's office, he must have thought about his mother and father. Moreover, he wondered where Tamerlan was, but no one would tell him where his brother was. He was unaware that Tamerlan had died in the Watertown shootout with police.

Nobody wanted to claim Tamerlan's body, not even his wife, Katherine Russel, a health aid. She claimed to officials that she did not have any prior knowledge regarding the bombing plot. She was a Christian, converted to Islam after she met and married Tamerlan in 2009. She quickly retreated to her home and family in Rhode Island with her daughter, Zahara.

Tamerlan's dead body was treated like a disease. No cemeteries wanted him buried in Boston. Therefore, Uncle Ruslan went to the morgue and took Tamerlan's corpse. He gave him a proper funeral and buried his nephew's body in an unmarked grave site in Virginia.[47]

Jahar thought about Tamerlan. Long ago, his brother would say to him, "Pray to Allah in times of difficulty." Jahar was too lethargic to pray. His left eye was shut, due to his injuries. He sensed someone coming into the room to check up on him. The door opened, and his doctor came in to check on his wounds. The doctor worked on rebandaging his wounds.

Weeks passed and Jahar's wounds slowly healed. His swollen cheek was healing. His throat was getting better. Due to his injuries, he had a hard time speaking. However, when he could finally speak, he asked for the Qur'an. While the doctor removed the bandage and patch covering his left eye, *"it was sadder than usual,"* wrote a close friend to the Tsarnaev's. The corner of the eye was bent down, (a result of nerve damage) which made him look like the actor Stallone in the movie *Rocky*. His vision remained normal. His left ear did not hear very well. He had a broken arm. His hand was slow to move when he flexed it. It was still healing from the bullet wounds. His fingers were moving better. Jahar *"was in his usual calm and balanced"* state. He could eat. He ate a bit of chicken and rice. He got around using a wheelchair. Slowly, he resumed walking again, and he did walk out for the first time in months... He saw a patch of sky from his cell.

A typical Special Housing Unit prison cell outside is a limited area, surrounded by high concrete gray walls and floor. Jahar left his 10 x 10 cell to visit the area outside. It was depressing. Jahar suffered solitary confinement. It motivated him to draw closer to God. He prayed to Allah and when he was well he wrote to his parents.

"Mamuyla," Jahar wrote to his mother, Zubeidat. *"My mommy and daddy, my lovelies, hello. Don't worry about me.... I start walking. They gave me Qur'an and I read it. It is easy to get through these times with the Qur'an. Everything is in God's hand. I'm very proud of you and our family. I love you."*

The prison allowed him to call home once. Jahar called his mother in Russia for the first time. In a phone call filled with tears, Zubeidat was worried, "I want to feel the life of my child," she said. Zubeidat recalled how she cried and cried for him over the phone. Jahar said calmly, "I am absolutely fine. My wounds are healing. Everything is in God's hands. Be patient. Everything will be fine."

A mother's heart aches for her son and she was understandably upset. Her son had been traumatized by the officers that apprehended him. The anger and level of disgust directed at him from the officials was hard for Jahar to forget. "Mentally he is normal, but the child is shocked. It was really hard to hear him and for him to hear me. The conversation was very quiet," she said in the report. "It was my child. I know he is locked up like a dog, like an animal." Zubeidat told *The Associated Press*, from a recent conversation with her son, "He didn't hold back his emotions either, as if he were screaming to the whole world: What is this? What's happening?" She felt her son was very confused, "I could just feel that he was being driven crazy by the unfairness that happened to us, that they killed our innocent Tamerlan." [48]

When Jahar started to walk again, he walked with a limp. By the end of May, Jahar had recovered and could move about and speak freely enough. He called his mother to proclaim his and his brother's total innocence. In their conversation, his mother asked him if he was in pain.

Jahar answered, "No, of course not. I'm already eating and have been for a long time. They are giving me chicken and rice, everything's fine."

Zubeidat cried over the phone, "You are my life. You need to be strong."

Jahar replied, "Everything is good. Please don't say anything." She reassured him with her love. "We love you. Muslims and non–Muslim all love you." Anzor spoke with his son, "We will meet again in heaven. We will be together."

Sadly, Zubeidat and Anzor were barred from entering the United States. Zubeidat had an outstanding warrant charge for shoplifting at Lord & Taylor. If she returned to the States, the authorities would arrest her for allegedly stealing $1,600 of clothes. She also faced a grand larceny charge for leaving the States because she avoided going to court.[49]

Zubeidat was in despair. She would never ever see her son again. She feared the government would never let her son go. But, she trusted everything will be in God's hand. Zubeidat wrote, "He talked to me, my boy. He was patient, but he was worrying. He asked: "Dad and Mom are they tantalizing you? Be strong, Mom. My wounds are healing, but my arm is broken."

Zubeidat feared he would be tortured during his time of imprisonment. If there was a way for her to get Jahar back, she would give her life in exchange. The mother wrote, "*they only wanted Tamerlan's life and now they're wanting Jahar's.*" His mother wished she was a bird who could fly to her only son and be next to him. She worried about his financial situation, and as a mother's heart worried, she asked her boy, "Can we send you money?"

Jahar told his mother to stay calm, "Do not worry, Mama. I do have money. Somebody opened an account for me. People send me lots of money here."

"How much money is it?" she asked.

"One thousand dollars."[48a]

Zubeidat was overwhelmed by the generosity of certain people for her son. However, there were people who would look at her family and conversely be inflamed and not support them. The Tsarnaevs were a "dysfunctional troubled" family. They were labelled as terrorists. The family insistently believed their sons were innocent and that the bombings were a set up. They were delusional people who thought their "kids would not be involved in anything." This was how the world viewed this family. Nonetheless, they are generally good people as described by family friends who knew them before the bombings.[50]

Through tears of disbelief and shock, Zubeidat only wanted the truth. Despite the shame the family underwent, many people were willing to help them. *She asked citizens to "forgive her" for saying "strong" remarks against them, saying "America took my kids away from me." She said Americans are not "bad" people because they are willing to help. The family is gracious for their support. She said, "It's not their fault that this happened to my kids."*[51] *Although the family suffered the loss of Tamerlan, the family did express their sympathy for the victims of the bombing.*[52]

As weeks went by, Jahar was healing. Due to his hand injuries, he had to learn how to write all over again. His mother told supporters he has thousands and thousands of letters to respond to; however, he cannot reply to everyone due to his hand injury. He has a scar going from the back of his ear and down his neck. Jahar experiences intense pain when he changes the position of his head up or down, making it hard for him to read or write.

Even though the world hated Jahar, there were supporters who had empathy for him. Many people thought about him every day. It is not popular to support a *terrorist*. Globally, people thought of this horrific event and the many lives that were changed. Those who had empathy prayed for Jahar's recovery. Others, questioned the intention to justify the magnitude of this transgression. It was unimaginable for some people to have a "love for the enemy" … for one such as Jahar who committed such a heinous act? He doesn't deserve this kindness or compassion. However, Jahar, had lost his way. Supporters put up prayer flyers displaying his face in public areas. They made videos about him and awaited updates on his health status. They perceived him as an impressionable young man who was misguided by his brother, who had influenced him negatively. Sometimes, they wondered how he was spending his time and were concerned with his emotional well-being. No matter what they believed, they were always concerned about him.

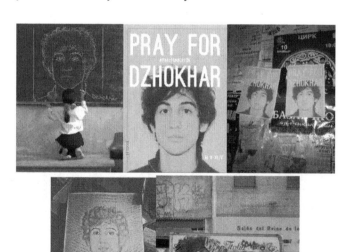

All images of Jahar are from "Dzhokhar is innocent," "Free Jahar, "Justice for Jahar" or "Pray for Jahar" *Tumblr* sites

The Boston Marathon Bomber

"I knew I had the image of the bad guy in the boat who was the real face of terror." – Sgt. Sean Murphy who captured the now famous photos of Dzhokhar bleeding and being arrested on the boat
– Time Magazine

BOSTON MARATHON BOMBING CASE

MONTHS HAD PASSED SINCE the bombings and Dzhokhar (Jahar) Tsarnaev's lawyers, led by Defense attorney, Miriam Conrad, had to sift through and read "terabytes and hundreds of thousands of pages" of documents, which had to be analyzed in preparation for the trial.[53] Tsarnaev's lawyers were overwhelmed by the amount of information they had to look through. They asked for the trial to be delayed until September of 2015. They even asked for a change of venue, but the Judge who oversaw the case, Judge George O'Toole, denied their request. The trial would stay in Boston.

The Prosecutors wanted a speedy trial because they had compiled solid evidence against Jahar and wanted to seek the death penalty.

HEADING THE PROSECUTION LEGAL TEAM:[54]

WILLIAM WEINREB – U.S. attorney and the deputy unit chief for the anti-terrorism and national security unit.

ALOKE CHAKRAVARTY – U.S. attorney in Massachusetts with a background in cases involving national security and human rights.

NADINE PELLEGRINI – U.S. attorney appointed chief of major crimes unit.

STEVEN D. MELLIN – Prosecutor with the DOJ criminal division.

The piece of crucial evidence the government held was a video footage of Jahar placing the deadly bomb that would kill eight-year-old child, Martin Richard. The video depicted a horrifying moment of Martin dying "right before your eyes." "It brought tears to our eyes," wept FBI agent Richard DesLauriers, who had viewed this video.[55]

On the other hand, Dzhokhar Tsarnaev's lawyers wanted more time to prepare for his defense, to investigate in depth his motive, his family background in the hope of saving his life.

THE DEFENSE LEGAL TEAM, defending Jahar's life was:

MIRIAM CONRAD – Lead Defense attorney was the Chief Federal Public Attorney of Massachusetts. Conrad worked as a crime reporter and defended Rezwan Ferdaus who plotted to attack the U.S. Capitol and Pentagon in 2011.

JUDY CLARKE – A renowned death penalty lawyer who defended monsters such as the Unabomber, Atlanta Olympics bomber Eric Rudolph and Jared Loughner who shot and severely injured U.S. representative Gabrielle Gifford.

DAVID BRUCK – Death Penalty appellate court, added on to Jahar's team later on.

WILLIAM FICK – Assistant defense attorney was present at Jahar court hospital hearing when he was injured.

Lastly, the fifth lawyer was TIMOTHY WATKINS, who was another assistant attorney.

Here is an interactive link online about Tsarnaev's family, associates and Tsarnaev's attorney. Click on the faces and read about them.
(http://gordondonovan.com/yahoo_news/boston_marathon_interactive.html)

THE LAWYERS LOVED JAHAR

Jahar was held in isolation at Devens, a prison medical facility. When he met his lawyers for the first time, he looked up and saw the two women who would be with him for some time in his cell. He was thankful to have company and to have someone close to him in the midst of his lonely days in isolation. Staring at them he smiled. Miriam Conrad had short brown hair and greeted him with her sunny smile and it brightened his day. Standing next to her was Judy Clarke. She was tall, had short light–brown hair, and she spoke softly. She cared for all her clients and treated them gently. The two women perceived Jahar as young and badly injured; they wanted to record and photograph his injuries.

Miriam was known as a terrorist sympathizer and Judy as an anti–death litigator. They began investigating Jahar's life and his involvement in the bombings; they both liked him.

When Jahar arrived in prison, he requested a Qur'an to read. But, he could not read lying down. He felt weak while trying to sit up. Jahar sat in bed and need to be supported by pillows on all sides, otherwise he would fall to one side. *(This was an update when Zubeidat received a call from one of Tsarnaev's lawyer. Supporters questioned its credibility. They interpreted it differently from what was written and thought his lawyers had helped him up by adjusting his pillows or surrounding him with pillows, so he would not fall on either side.)* Jahar sat for five minutes and was given the Qur'an. When asked about Dzhokhar, his lawyers said, "Dzhokhar is polite, and he has good manners. He is a "golden boy." He is a child. He loves to talk and smile."

Jahar interacted "well-enough" with his lawyers and that *"he is positive in spite of everything what has happened in his life."*

Jahar shared, "After all that has happened to me, everything is in God's hand." His lawyers told him he was very strong to survive such serious wounds from the two separate shootings. They were surprised when he smiled and answered them, "Allah was with me and it was not my time to die."

A couple months after Jahar's arrest, Zubeidat shared some news with the supporters who had given the Tsarnaev family support, hope and love. She shared with them how her son's wounds were healing. She said he could finally move his left hand which had been injured from gunshot wounds. His palm was *"full of metallic pieces."* He did not take any pain killers for his pain as his wounds healed.

In his small cell, Jahar prayed on his knees. He was practicing the Muslim's Five Pillars of Islam. He was observing the holy month of Ramadan. He did not eat or drink from 3 a.m. until 8:30 p.m. as he fasted and prayed.

Eventually, his lawyers Miriam and Judy visited with their client in a protective closed facility room and counseled Jahar. *(Tsarnaev's lawyers visited Jahar in prison when he was still healing from his injuries. When they first visited him, he was possibly bedridden. Tsarnaev family's supporters sent a message to Jahar supporters saying his lawyers were impressed by his behavior. The next prison scene is fictionalized to show an incident. It was known that Jahar was offered to have ear surgery on his left deaf ear, but he refused it because of fear. (See reference 56.) This is true. His lawyers also noted that he was fidgeting, a sign of psychological damage in the brain due to prolonged solitary confinement.)*

****

Jahar felt like tearing off the steel handcuffs and chains that were rubbing his wrists and legs. He sat in a chair, his face emotionless, and he rocked his body back and forth. He was getting weak from the effects of solitary confinement. The lawyers observed these effects overtaking his body. Jahar would fidget and assume a huddled position. Solitary confinement has been found to have a profound neurological and psychological effect on juvenile inmates. With no human interaction and touch, Jahar's brain ceased to capture normal activity. He needed social interaction. He became sensitive to sounds around him and he was often observed rocking back and forth.

The lawyers were very concerned. They told him, "You have been offered corrective surgery, because you are deaf in the left ear from the flash grenades."[56]

Jahar refused, shaking his head. "I am afraid. I don't trust anyone," he responded in a gentle voice. Images and feelings were tumbling in his mind as he sat listening to the professionals discuss *his* future. The unstructured, chaotic thinking required his attention... He *desperately* needed to find a way forward. Without resolution, the sustained torment was proving to be unbearable. The thoughts continued to echo... Jahar was afraid of the surgery because he feared what the doctors would do to him when he was under anesthesia. He feared they would try to hurt him. He had been traumatized by his interaction with the police after he was discovered hiding in the boat. He yelled for police to help him; he was bloody and dying. Instead, as he slowly got out of the boat, the police spat on him and it made him. Their actions hurt and confused him. But, he was not mad at them.

Death Penalty lawyer Judy Clarke, a mitigation specialist had compassion for Jahar. She sat at the table watching Jahar shake. Judy developed a close professional relationship with Jahar to learn more about her client. Jahar was rubbing his wrists where the handcuffs irritated his skin. Judy is known to be a mother figure to her clients who have been labelled as monsters in society. She has a motherly instinct to care for them. She wanted Jahar to trust her and she cared for his health and well-being in prison. Since Jahar was forbidden to have physical contact with his family and visitors, his lawyers (and prison guards) remained his only human physical contact.

Judy placed her hand on Jahar's back to calm him down. She said softly, "I care. I want you to have surgery because I want you to eat well." Judy meant it, for she saw how thin he was becoming. Jahar was fasting and was skipping both breakfast and lunch. He was starving himself; however, he was staying faithful in observance of Ramadan that month. Judy gently urged him to have surgery because his deaf ear was affecting the way he ate when he resumed eating.

Jahar sat in long silence, fidgeting with his hands. His shoulder blade muscles tightened, and then cramped as he tried to relax under the strain of his confinement. "No," he said finally. A close supporter of the family wrote: *"God gave him two ears, but he can hear from the right one okay. He was very calm."* (Perhaps, the loss of hearing in one ear would move him towards an internal need for restitution.)

Judy stared straight into his dark eyes. "Well, I'm not going to let you die." Jahar began to like Judy as his lawyer and he trusted her. He thought she was warm and had a humorous personality.[57] Sometimes, Judy made him laugh. He liked to tell light jokes and make people laugh too. Judy had the skill, sensitivity and compassion to understand Jahar's whole childhood and upbringing. Judy spoke to him, "Life in prison will be tough. You are looking to live the rest of your life in prison. We will provide you a reason to find new life and meaning here if you were to be sentenced to life." Judy was opposed to the death penalty for her client, so she fought instead for a life sentence for Jahar.[58]

****

Later, Judy confided her concerns to Jahar's sisters: Ailina and Bella that Jahar was not eating. She told them he is "getting thin and shaking a lot." Judy Clarke had defended many murderers and terrorists in her prestigious career, but Dzhokhar Tsarnaev was the youngest client she ever defended. Public Defender, Miriam Conrad had also defended terrorists. Both lawyers became concerned that the prosecutors were planning to make a decision regarding the death penalty before they could finish reviewing all the evidence. They called the process unfair. Prosecutors were already going after the death penalty while Defense worked on their defense arguments. Moreover, they were concerned with inaccurate information coming out based on the existing evidence they had.[59]

Meanwhile, Jahar grew weaker as another month went by. He learned the news that Tamerlan, his beloved brother had in fact died in the Watertown shootout with the police. The news was very hard for him to take. He stopped talking to his lawyers when he learned about his brother's death.

From Zubeidat:
Translation.
"Dzhokhar doesn't want to talk to them after he learned of the death of his brother. He can't eat or sleep. He grieves for his brother, and they call it "depression.""

By June of 2013, his lawyers claimed that Jahar was apparently very weak. "He is not eating well. He is sad. He cannot sleep. He grieves for his brother," they wrote to his family. He was extremely depressed. Jahar stayed in bed most of the time feeling miserable and depressed in both his heart and mind. He missed his family so much. It was summer time, and he was supposed to visit his parents in Dagestan, but he learned he wouldn't make the trip because he had not received his U.S. passport in time. Jahar had tweeted in March 2012, *"A decade in America already, I want out,"* because he mostly missed his parents.

JAHAR'S ARRAIGNMENT

Jahar hoped to see his sisters someday. On July 10, 2013, he went to his arraignment at the John Joseph Moakley courthouse located next to the waterfront in Boston. At the hearing, Jahar appeared in public for the very first time since the day of his capture by the authorities. The government charged him with 30 count indictment.[60]

15 – Charges for a use of firearm resulting in death.

7 – Charges for use of or conspiracy to use a weapon of mass destruction resulting in death.

3 – Bombing of or conspiracy to bomb a public place resulting in death.

3 – Destruction of or conspiracy to destroy property resulting in death.

1 – Interference with commerce by threats and violence.

1 – Carjacking resulting in bodily injury.

The front of the courthouse was a media circus. News media and camera crews from all outlets were there to report on Jahar's arraignment; however, cameras were not allowed in the courtroom to film the trial. Thirty surviving victims from the bombings also arrived and attended the Hearing. Outside the courthouse, a line of police stood to pay tribute to fallen MIT officer, Sean Collier.

Jahar stepped out of Devens for the first time. He was relieved to be outside in the warm sunshine. He rode in a white transport prisoner's van with the U.S. Marshals, and traveled the long distance to the courthouse. After three months in prison his hair had grown wavier and longer. His hair touched his shoulders. He did not care to comb it.

Inside the courthouse, Jahar sat in a holding cell in the basement waiting to present his plea. The courtroom was packed with strangers, the media and surviving victims. Nerves were getting to him. He explored around the small cell he was being held in. Jahar was bored of waiting. He had gotten up early that morning for the Hearing. He spotted a surveillance camera at the corner of the wall. Carefully, he stepped on the bench and gazed at the camera, patting down his messy hair and checking out his facial wounds in the camera's reflection.

Cameras were everywhere, everywhere he went. He was not used to them at first. There was a camera in his cell and another camera in the shower where he showered once or twice a week. He had to live with eyes all watching him. His privacy was violated. Before the bombings, he was a carefree kid, who was used to having his own way, and getting away with stuff. He could drive anywhere he wanted to. He could zip through his neighborhood, riding his skateboard, and setting off fireworks with friends at Charles River. But, here he was, stuck in a cell hold waiting…

Jahar thought he was going to get off easy with the plan. Unfortunately, he had to face the consequences and face the people he had horribly injured. Suddenly, Jahar stared at the camera. He quickly flashed his middle finger at the camera. He smirked and jumped down from the bench. He sat down, tight-lipped and biting his fingernails in the holding cell before his scheduled arraignment. A marshal watching the monitor cameras at the office saw Jahar flipped the bird. He was taken aback.[61]

The courtroom was packed with reporters, U.S. authorities, officers, agents, surviving victims, families of the victims, Jahar's friends and his supporters. Jahar's sisters entered the room. One of the sisters carried her baby. Jahar's lawyers, Miriam and Judy sat at one large table on one side of the courtroom. Jahar entered the courtroom with a swagger, led by U.S. Marshals. His feet were shackled. His wrists were cuffed too. He seemed impassive as the proceeding began. The U.S. Marshals took his cuffs off and he sat down between Judy and Miriam. Jahar wore an orange jumpsuit. A black t-shirt showed underneath his jumpsuit. The jumpsuit was too big on him. It made him appear younger than his nineteen years. Many reporters at the courthouse tweeted about Jahar's appearance. For example, they reported he had dark–brown circles around both of his eyes. He had a cast on his left arm. The left side of his face was swollen, and he had a visible scar below his throat.

A leaked court photo of Jahar's arraignment. July 10, 2013

Jahar's dark eyes glanced quickly at the people staring at him. He sat down and fidgeted, finding a comfortable position to endure the ten-minute proceeding. He rubbed his chin and played with the splint on his left hand.

A couple of his wrestling buddies were there to support Jahar. Later, they told reporters that Jahar does not usually fidget. Jahar was shocked to see many individual faces gazing at him. His isolation in prison for three months had made him fidgety. Judy patted him on the back to calm him down.

Jahar wiped his mouth and suddenly he heard a baby's cry. He immediately turned around and saw his sisters. He smiled at them, it was a lopsided smile. His two older sisters, Bella and Ailina were sitting there looking at him. One sister, Ailina, had a baby in her arms and he smiled at the baby. He turned back to the front, but he kept turning around to look at his sisters, smiling. Judy saw him doing this and she patted him on the back, so he would pay attention to the judge. Judge Marianne B. Bowler began the proceeding, "There are 30 victims and family members here today. We are here today for the purposes of arraignment."

Assistant U.S. Attorney William Weinreb read through the list of 30 charges, which included the use of weapon of mass destruction resulting in death. He said, "The maximum penalty is up to life in prison or the death penalty."

At that moment, one of sisters started to cry and Jahar turned to her and smiled. He tried to comfort his sisters and reassure them. Others in the room were disgusted with his smiles. To them, he almost seemed like he was smirking. Throughout the arraignment, he fiddled with the splint, smiled at the baby, and at his sisters, yawned and appeared not to pay any attention to the proceeding. This behavior really angered the victims because he never once glanced at them. He did not know the faces of his victims. He only knew the faces of his sisters. Jahar sent his two sisters, who were upset and crying all his love. The victims thought his behavior was discourteous and were outraged by his smirks and indifferent attitude towards them and this created a media sensation.

Judy asked, "May I recite the pleas on his behalf?"

"I would ask him to answer," said Judge Bowler.

Jahar responded with the plea of "Not Guilty" seven times. He stood up with Judy and Miriam and spoke his response into a microphone.

Throughout the proceedings, he was nervous. He clenched his hands when he responded with his plea of, "Not Guilty." Both lawyers placed their hands on his shoulders or back throughout the remainder of the arraignment. Judy attempted to reassure him that everything was going to be okay. Miriam had also done the same act of reassurance, to try to calm down Jahar's nerves.

"It was clear," a Jahar supporter wrote *"that they genuinely liked him."* He spoke loud and clear into the microphone, after each charge: "Not Guilty, Not Guilty," and "Not Guilty!" His throat injuries were causing a hindrance to his speech and it sounded like he had a Russian accent. After he said his pleas, he was released back into custody of the U.S Marshals. As he was being cuffed again, he stared at his sisters and blew them both a kiss. One of his sisters called out to him, "I love you, Dzhokhar." He left court appearing confident.[62]

After Jahar's arraignment, the police and surviving bombing victims and their families were outraged by Jahar's smirking and indifferent attitude. They felt he showed disrespect in court to the survivors. A federal marshal warned the survivors not to raise their voices or shout out any outburst to the defendant. However, the survivors were enraged. John DiFava, a MIT police officer walked out of the courtroom, saying the defendant is "not worth a tear." "I'd like to grab him by the throat, disgusted with the smug." He said, "The defendant looked "smug." He is a POS!"

Another victim walking on one crutch said she never saw the defendant's dark eyes gaze back to where many of the victims were seated. "I want him to rot in jail for the rest of his life and suffer the way he's made many other people suffer," she exclaimed.

A family member, Liz Norden, whose sons had survived but lost their right legs in the bombings, said she wanted to stare down the face of evil. "I actually felt sick to my stomach. He was smirking."

Ed Fucarile, a father whose son, Marc had lost a part of his lower leg, said, "He came out and he smirked at the families. The lawyers put their hands on his shoulders like it was going to be all right. I expected a lot more. It wasn't what I thought it would be."

DiFava said, "I didn't see a lot of remorse. I didn't see a lot of regret. It just seemed to me that if I was in that position, I would have been a lot more nervous, certainly scared." DiFava added: "I just wanted to see him. I wanted to see the person that so coldly and callously killed four people, one of whom being an officer of mine."[63]

Back at Devens, Jahar talked to his parents on the phone. They were concerned about what had happened to him in court after hearing the outrageous news regarding his arraignment. Jahar's "smirking" and "kissing" had made him appear indifferent to the proceedings. Newspapers ran the headline of Jahar's arraignment, it read: *"Smiling Assassin," "Punk!"* or *"Kiss This!"* Jahar told his parents the truth, "It's a lie!"

When he spoke with his parents, Jahar became upset with the way the media was portraying him. His smirks were just smiles. Jahar twitched when he remembered when a bullet from a burst of gunfire had entered the left side of his neck and exited out under his left ear. His jaw had been fractured and his neck had sustained a slashed knife wound. The injuries had left him with permanent nerve damage to both his left eye and mouth, leaving him deaf in his left ear. It affected the way he smiled.

In August 2013, the *Rolling Stone* magazine featured the Boston Bomber Dzhokhar Tsarnaev on the front cover. It was titled: JAHAR'S WORLD *"The Bomber, How a Popular, Promising Student was failed by his Family Fell into Radical Islam and became a Monster."* Editor Janet Reitman wrote and published a story centered on the family's struggles in America and Dzhokhar's education and upbringing.
Jahar's World:
(http://www.rollingstone.com/culture/news/jahars-world-20130717)

The cover of Dzhokhar on the magazine received a backlash and a firestorm controversy ignited. Some stores pulled the magazine off their shelves, but it did not hurt the sales. Instead, it doubled them.

Time Magazine released a video interview of Sgt. Sean Murphy, titled "Capturing the Real Face of Terror." Murphy had captured photos of Dzhokhar bleeding and of being arrested on the boat. He released the dramatic photos in response to the controversy revolving around the *Rolling Stone's* cover. "I knew I had the image of the bad guy in the boat who was the real face of terror."

Capturing the real face of terror video:
(https://www.youtube.com/watch?v=WM9itdQBeeM)

LETTERS FROM AROUND THE WORLD

Another heartbreaking note about Jahar conveyed, *"He is weak, but slowly getting better. He has no appetite and not sleeping well. He gets many letters from different people from different countries! He gets tired too soon and mostly is in bed. They bring him books that he orders himself. He is sad and looks depressed...."*

Later, another note revealed that, *"Jahar does receive a bunch of letters; that makes him happy..."*

Jahar received over one thousand unsolicited letters from people who believed in his innocence. Furthermore, he received letters from Christians urging him to repent of his sins and convert to Christianity.[65] People drew pictures for him, wrote him poems and told him about themselves. He was overwhelmed by the idea that many people all over the world were thinking of him and praying for him. There was a small window of opportunity to introduce Jahar to the gospel. So many brothers and sisters genuinely cared for him and wanted to share Bible scriptural verses with him even though they knew his religion was Islam. Jahar thanked all his supporters for their letters and cards. He had his mother convey to his supporters the following message:[66]

"He said if the supporters would not consider his request too selfish and rude he would prefer the Islamic literature mostly. He loved the book. Do not be sad and Dua is the weapon of the believer!" (*Dua* is a spiritual form of worship, a conversation to God.)

Jahar wanted to convey to non–Muslims that the *Dua* was his favorite book. He received many books from supporters. He told his mother to tell them…

"Send me religious books with positive texts, kind of Muslim soul supporting ones… Thank everyone who sent me books and support me and the family."

Jahar spent hours alone in prison reading many good books. He wrote to his parents, *"Got a lot of books and time flies by really quickly."* He added, *"Got a lot of wounds, but is not angry or has hate to anyone."*

It became clear to his Christian supporters that Jahar rejected Christianity. He proclaimed his faith. It was Islam. However, that did not stop us. We continued to pray for him and for the many obstacles he would be facing. He would soon face Special Administrative Measures which will be explained later in the book. We prayed about the pending death penalty that the government was seeking to impose on him and for the venue of the trial.

HAPPY 20th BIRTHDAY JAHAR!

(official group)
Djahar says thank you! HE SAID TO THANK ALL SUPPORTERS!!!;(;(;
(((((;(HE IS GETTING MANY MANY LETTERS!!!!AND CARDS!!!
Like · Comment · 2 hours ago via mobile ·

On July 22, 2013, Jahar celebrated his 20th birthday in prison. Many supporters wished him "Happy Birthday!" He received many birthday cards and many letters. He told everyone he appreciated them and that he loved them.

Jahar could read his letters with his attorneys beside him. He was thankful to everyone. The letters helped him, he said. He added he would have loved to write back to everyone, but it would be impossible for him to do so and he did not want people to get upset with him.

After this, the supporters never heard from him again. Here was the reason why.

HE WAS SILENCED

Dzhokhar's sisters, Bella and Ailina Tsarnaeva met with his lawyers for a scheduled lunch. The lawyers told them how they wanted to send him some family photos, so he could have them to remember good times with family. The sisters went through lots of family photos and gave them to Tsarnaev's lawyers. Miriam and Judy took a couple of them to show Jahar. Bella wrote to his supporters, lawyers *"took a couple of them to show Jahar, to bring him a little up."* They went to Devens to communicate with him and to pass him the family photos.

Upon their arrival, prison officials told the lawyers he is not allowed to have the family photos. This had a "chilling effect" on them. They were also made to turn away, consequently they could not visit with him. On September 6, 2013, William Fick, an assistant defense attorney went for a scheduled visit to meet with Jahar and he carried with him a folder containing some documents and photographs depicting family members. An officer spoke with Mr. Fick later and conveyed to the lawyer that his client was not authorized to see any pictures of his family.[67]

It was learned that Jahar had been put under SAMs – meant *Special Administrative Measure.* It was imposed upon him by the prosecutors and the government. SAMs are rules concerning how a detainee can correspond. Since Dzhokhar Tsarnaev was an accused terrorist, he was forced to remain silent. SAMs was placed to prevent a dangerous terrorist from communicating with anyone outside.

During Jahar's interrogation, he admitted to the FBI that he was committed to Jihad and hoped that others would be inspired to the movement. SAMs confinement prohibited him from having any media interviews and limited social visits with immediate family. He was locked down in his cell 24 hours in the day. He was to have no human contact. He had limited communication with his family and especially with his lawyers. SAMs also restricted his mail and meeting with other inmates. Lawyers became frustrated with these restrictions and they asked the Federal government to ease these restrictions on Jahar. During questioning at Beth Israel hospital, lawyers pointed out that Jahar had repeatedly requested a lawyer.

Lawyers argued, "Since his arrest, Mr. Tsarnaev has been in a highly secure federal prison. He is incapacitated and obviously could not engage in similar behavior now. Nor is there any evidence whatsoever of the existence of co-conspirators with whom Mr. Tsarnaev could arrange further terrorist or criminal activities, much less a "high probability" that he would make calls to do so, as alleged by the government."[68]

However, families of survivors did not want SAMs to be lifted. Tsarnaev's defense wanted to buy more time to prepare for their opposition to the enforcement of the death penalty in the case. Because of these SAMs restrictions they were still waiting for evidence from the government. The Federal government hindered the release of evidence that the Defense team needed to build their defense. Tsarnaev's attorneys argued in court papers that SAMs had created obstacles that had an effect on the team's ability to prepare and to get certain information from him that would defend him against the 30-charge indictment for using weapon of mass destruction.[69]

Jahar will live his life without pictures of his family. He hasn't seen his parents in three years since his imprisonment. He would never see his parents grow older. Jahar called his mother on a weekly basis by phone. He told her that he loved her and missed her.

A Complicated Case

"In an effort to elicit truthful info on an immediate basis, I told him Dzhokhar Tsarnaev's life was effectively over, whether he was still living or going away," – This was quoted by FBI special agent John Walker who searched Tsarnaev's friend, Azamat Tazhayakov's apartment for removing Dzhokhar's bag pack and laptop.[70]

DZHOKHAR AND HIS BROTHER Tamerlan had created carnage and destruction. Before Dzhokhar was caught, he wrote jihadi messages on the boat. This note revealed more about why the government feared he would inspire others to the movement. The message was written in pencil and there were streaks of Dzhokhar's blood running down the panels. The message was...the bombings were retribution for what the U.S. did to Muslims in Afghanistan and Iraq and called the Boston victims collateral damage in same the way Muslims have been in the U.S. wars. *"When you attack one Muslim, you attack all Muslims."* It also said, *"I don't morn for my brother. He is a martyr in paradise and I will soon join him there."*

There was more to this note: *"I don't like killing innocent people, "the U.S. Government is killing our innocent civilians... I can't stand to see such evil go unpunished." "We Muslims are one body, you hurt one you hurt us all,"* he wrote. *"Now I don't like killing innocent people it is forbidden in Islam but due to said (illegible) it is allowed... "Stop killing our innocent people and we will stop."*[71] *"The U.S. government is killing our innocent civilians but most of you already know that. As a M[uslim] I can't stand to see such evil go unpunished, we Muslims are one body, you hurt one you hurt us all...[t]he ummah {i.e. the Muslim people} is beginning to rise...know you are fighting men who look into the barrel of your gun and see heaven, now how can you compete with that. We are promised victory and we will surely get it."*

The Prosecutors feared that Dzhokhar's confession note would inspire others to a call to arms and carry out jihad violence that might further endanger the public. The Defense team wrote a 14-page motion document; they came back strong, arguing that, "The government has offered no evidence — and the defense is unaware of any — that Mr. Tsarnaev coordinated the offense conduct with others still at large or that he has any current desire, much less ability, to engage in communications that could instigate violence by others in the future."

And he was not attempting to recruit others to violence...

"There is no express call for others to take up arms," the attorneys argued, adding, "On their face, Mr. Tsarnaev's alleged words simply state the motive for his actions, a declaration in anticipation of his own death." Defense argued the intent of the note left behind was to explain his motivation behind the attacks if he should die. Meaning, Dzhokhar expected to die in the boat. He was bleeding to death and he wanted to explain and write a farewell message.[72]

COLD CASE: THE WALTHAM SLAYINGS

In May 2013, we heard the Tsarnaev brothers might again be involved in another unsolved cold case, the brutal Waltham murders on September 10-11 in 2011. The Boston Marathon case was becoming more complicated. In Brendan Mess' apartment, authorities found three marijuana dealers murdered. They were local friends: Brendan Mess, Erik Weissman, and Raphael Teken. They all had their throat slits. On their bodies was left a thousand dollars' worth of marijuana and $5,000 was left at the crime scene. Authorities have been trying to piece together the murders. They believe the killer and the victims knew each other. One of the victim's family believed that Tamerlan allegedly committed these murders.[73]

IBRAGIM TODASHEV

In May 2013, Ibragim Todashev, a twenty-seven-year-old Chechen native and former mixed martial arts fighter who knew Tamerlan Tsarnaev, was shot and killed in Orlando, Florida. Todashev was killed by law enforcement officers who had been interviewing him about the Waltham murders.

This case is still under investigation. A gun was pushed to Todashev's temple in an effort to make him sign a confession of the triple homicide. Todashev flipped out and knocked the agent to the ground with a metal pole, although reports indicated it was unclear what kind of object he had in his hand. The FBI has alleged that before he was killed, Todashev made statements implicating both himself and Tamerlan Tsarnaev in the Waltham murders – saying the crime was a drug robbery, and the murders were committed to prevent being identified by the victims.[74][75]

TAMERLAN TSARNAEV IMPLICATED IN WALTHAM MURDERS

On October 23, 2013, news uncovered that the late Tamerlan Tsarnaev was implicated as one of the participants involved in the Waltham murders. Tsarnaev's lawyers wanted access to the records that implicated his older brother to the triple slaying. While the lawyers requested these records, the government sought the death penalty for Dzhokhar. U.S. Attorney General Eric Holder had the definitive say on whether Dzhokhar received the death penalty or not. *Boston Globe* reported that Eric Holder should not seek the death penalty for Dzhokhar Tsarnaev, arguing, "…on the basis of his youth, lack of past offenses, and being under the influence of his older brother — all factors that would mitigate against a death sentence." Holder was a strong opponent against Capital punishment but had to make an exception in this case even though there was no death penalty law in Massachusetts.

DEFENSE SOUGHT WITNESS STATEMENTS FROM PROSECUTORS

On November 6, 2013, the Defense team filed another motion, "blasting federal prosecutors for trying to gain 'a tactical trail advantage' in their potential death–penalty case by refusing to turn over testimonies taken from Dzhokhar's parents and other close family members." The Defense said they "need to gather and place in context all available sources of information to depict Mr. Tsarnaev in all his complexity, to assist the Attorney General and possibly later a jury to see Mr. Tsarnaev as a complete human being who should not be sentenced to death."[76]

Laurel J. Sweet @ Laurel Sweet
#Tsarnaev is accused of showing "a lack of
remorse for the murders of three
#BostonMarathon spectators and MIT Police
Officer Sean Collier.
1/30/14, 11:36 AM

BOMBING SURVIVORS WANTED JAHAR TO SUFFER IN PRISON

Dzhokhar Tsarnaev was the most hated man in America. His attack was horrific. If his lawyers wanted the jury to see him as a "complete human being," it would be difficult to achieve. How can someone who was so nice before become so evil? Everyone wanted to see him suffer. There was a blood lust for him to die. A Boston victim who survived the bombings and who had lost a part of her lower leg called Dzhokhar and his dead brother, Tamerlan, *"F@#king bombers."*

The surviving victims were angry at him; they perceived he had a "lack of remorse." Marc Fucarile said, "I don't know where they got the nerve to ask for any of that. (Referring to the loosen SAMs restriction.) The people he hurt or killed don't get out…don't get fresh air. He's a coward, who detonated those bombs knowing those families were there. I think he should be suffering a lot more than he is because he doesn't understand the pain we go through every day."[77]

The following are statements documented in a variety of news articles when the Defense team fought to loosen his prison restrictions. Many inflamed, nasty, and rapid-fire comments were noted at the end of a single news article. People expressed a familiar theme of hatred toward Dzhokhar Tsarnaev. A sense of humanity should not be extended towards him.

"He should not get 'what he wants,' any more so than he gave to the people he harmed or killed. They did 'not want' that, either. He just needs to keep on sitting in jail."

"He needs the ultimate penalty for his vicious crime; death. If anything, he should have more restrictions while awaiting trial, not less. He is evil on earth."

"This piece of pig dung should not be allowed anything other than the bare minimum that must be furnished by law and should get the harshest punishment allowable under the law. The one possible exception would be to put him in a large cell full of hardened gang cons and turn off the cameras!"

"*This POS should have never been given a lawyer in the first place. Try him in a military court, feed him a bunch of bacon and ham then hang him on live t.v.*"

"*YES, he deserves his death! But he deserves a very Slow, Agonizing one. Let him feel it for hours, if not days. Let him cry and suffer. Sure, let the inmates have their bodily fun with him first. Then off to a horrible demise, Of course this would be more ideal, and justified. Just look at that Stupid, Pathetic, Dainty face of his. The big nose, curly hair, that look of idiocy in the eyes. The face of a Coward. A Loser. A Pathetic Skinny Boy. He should be tormented and put to death in a brutal manner.*"

A Christian organization was dedicated to seeing Dzhokhar Tsarnaev *receive* Christ. They believe Jahar needed to face the consequences for the crimes he committed. However, they wanted to *demonstrate* the love and grace of Christ. Many Christians adopted Dzhokhar and pray for him daily. "Christians United for Jahar" tweeted: "*As Christians, it's something we feel like we really need to do. We need to love and forgive him. No matter what he is accused of doing; he deserves to be treated as such instead of some unlovable subhuman animal. Let us not see in Jahar the face of a monster but of someone made in the image of God who can become our brother.*"

Pray for Jahar for he is a child of God.

We are to pray for our enemies.

God Loves Jahar.

Pray for the soul of Jahar.

May he be redeemed.

Tamerlan Tsarnaev

"I wanted to hug Tamerlan, but then we learned he was an adherent to some kind of radical Islam." —Naida Suleimanova, cousin

THE SKY WAS GRAY, again. Outside of his prison cell, Jahar stood inside a high walled concrete courtyard. He gazed at the surface of the earth, feeling disoriented. It was his only window to the outside world. He sensed it may be November or December. The weather was suddenly changing to cooler temps. He did not know what day it was or what was happening in the world outside. Living with SAMs restrictions had severe limitations; it is a harsh isolated environment. He hardly talked to anyone. *One more lap*, he told himself. Jahar tried to keep fit and ran in place inside his wire cage (like an animal's enclosure in a zoo) …back and forth he moved. He has been living in prison for nearly nine months. He spoke with his family once a week, but, they were not allowed to discuss the case.

His lawyers were working hard and keeping him updated. Jahar could not think about the death sentence over his head. Although a deadline date has been set for his lawyers to seek a change of venue, they had not yet decided to work on the request unless they knew he would be facing the death penalty.[78] *The Boston Globe* conducted a poll online asking readers whether they support the death penalty or not:[79] Recent poll said: "Yes" – 33% for death sentence. "No" – 57% for life sentence. Tsarnaev's supporters began a petition for the government not to seek the death penalty.

A petition website against the death penalty.

Jahar's life was like a hanging thread on a needle. By January, Holder would then decide if Tsarnaev receives the death penalty. Prison guards came into the courtyard to retrieve him and returned him back to his cell like a dog. They wore latex gloves as they snapped the cuffs on him, then walked him through endless corridors and electronically controlled gates. His head hung low as he shuffled back to his cell. The guards slipped off his ankle cuffs and closed the steel door behind him. Jahar put his hands through the meal slot. They unlocked his handcuffs and shut the slot door.

Back in his dingy small cell, Jahar crawled into bed. A crossword puzzle book he was working on was under the cover. He tossed the book onto the floor. By his bedside, he picked up a book, flipped through the pages and read for an hour. While he read, he ate candies and chips.

A guard sent Jahar a notification. More books had come in for him to read; however, prison officials had to send them back. The guard explained to Jahar that he is only allowed to keep five books in his cell. His own cell had once been turned into a miniature library. Jahar's supporters had been sending him many books that he had never seen or read. In addition to the Islamic books he requested, he received adventure books, Russian books, mystery and humorous books. This is Jahar's book list: **http://booksforjahar.tumblr.com/list**

Jahar got on the phone and talked to his mother. "My precious Mama, please tell supporters to stop sending books. They are sending them back." I have been reading a lot. I have been patient and make Dua (act of supplication). I read the Holy Qur'an. My wounds are healing. I love you."

PLEASE STOP SENDING BOOKS...JAHAR TOLD ZUBEIDAT THEY ARE STARTING TO SEND THEM BACK!!!

DJAHARS ALL WOUNDS ARE HEALING AND HE NEVER COMPLAINS!!! ALL IS IN ALLAHS HANDS MY GIRL! AS DJAHAR SAIS [sic] BE PATIENT MY PRECIOUS MAMA!!!;(;(;(;(;(;(;(;(;(I AM TRYING TO REMAIN PATIENT AND MAKE DUA;(;(;(;(

HE IS READING A LOT! AND HE READS THE HOLLY [sic] QUR'AN !!!ALHAMDULILLA!!!

Jahar thought about a time when Tamerlan was angry at him. Once Jahar drove home to Cambridge at the beginning of Winter break, two months before they allegedly bombed the marathon. Jahar was fish bowling - smoking weed with friends on campus inside his parked car with windows closed to get high. Later, he sold marijuana before going home. Tamerlan disapproved of his lifestyle. He checked inside the Honda Civic and found the evidence: pot and an empty bottle of vodka. The car had a foul smell of smoke. Tamerlan did not like his car smelling like weed.[80]

Jahar remembered becoming silenced and submissive. Tamerlan had rules in his household. Jahar could not accept his brother disciplining him regarding about his partying and pot smoking. Tamerlan reared Jahar at home, to teach him a lesson. He refused to let Jahar go back to school until he cleaned up his act. Jahar tweeted on January 6, 2013, "I need to go back to school, no freedom out here for a brother," with a hash tag *#lockeduptheywon'tletmeout.*

However, when Jahar returned to campus he failed to resist his physical urges. He smoked and drank. He earned money by selling marijuana, and he owned a gun.[81 81a 81b]

It never once occurred to Jahar that Tamerlan could even be an evil influence in his life. Tamerlan loved him very much and tried to protect him. Jahar described to his lawyers how Tamerlan would lose his temper around other people. He thought about the time he and his brother went to the Gold gym. On April 12, four days before the attack and they were there for training, to prepare physically for the jihad and their plan to set off the bombs. Before they went to the gym, they stopped at the mosque to pray. Tamerlan had shaved off his full-grown beard.[82] When they arrived at the gym, the manager asked Tamerlan to follow one of the gym rules, to take off his shoes. Tamerlan argued with the manager.

After all, Jahar glanced at Tamerlan annoyingly and obeyed the rules and slipped off his shoes. The manager told Tamerlan he was going to ban him from the gym. Tamerlan kept his cool. He was the first one in the ring. Tamerlan skillfully handled the jump rope, running in place and skipping.

Jahar noted how his brother was better at jumping rope. Tamerlan never missed a step. He was like an avid dancer, skipping, jumping... Jahar tried to jump rope like his brother, having difficulty, he missed a step. He tried to impress his older brother, but, failed. His large shorts were slipping down his waist every time he jumped. He dropped the jump ropes and watched Tamerlan exercise from the corner ring. While Tamerlan exercised, he glanced at Jahar and smiled. Jahar bounced on the boxing ring ropes, relaxed, and smiled back. Jahar idolized Tamerlan. He followed him around like a lost puppy. He wanted to do things to impress him. At the end of the day, he did a teddy bear hand stand.

But, they were both hiding a secret. No one knew they were planning an attack. Tamerlan was inspired by the jihad and its mission. He was radicalized and saved a terrorist song on his YouTube list, "I will dedicate my life to Jihad." At home, alone, while his wife Katherine was at work, he frequently visited jihad websites and supported violent Islamist activities.

Tamerlan was passionate about it. He could not tolerate the American government killing innocent Muslims in U.S. sponsored wars. *We Muslims are one body, you hurt one you hurt us all...*

Jahar read radical Islamic materials on his laptop, including a book by Anwar al–Awlaki, a U.S. born radical cleric who helped inspire terrorists' attacks. Jahar did not believe the 9/11 attacks in NYC to be an act of terrorists but rather thought it was an inside job.[83]

The Tsarnaev family emigrated from Chechnya, although the brothers never lived there. They spoke the language fluently and were proud of their heritage.[84]

Six days before the attack, Jahar tweeted a message to the media: *"If you have the knowledge and the inspiration all that's left is to take action."*[85] He was clear headed and ready to take action with Tamerlan.

Near dusk, the day before the marathon race the brothers went to take-out pizza for a late dinner. When they walked down Norfolk Street, a friend's neighbor yelled, "Hey, can I have a slice of pizza?" The neighbor, Malisha Pitt, calmed down her relative, and responded, "Stop harassing my neighbor." Jahar and Tamerlan laughed.[86] Jahar was hungry. They couldn't wait to take a bite of the pizza. That night they ate a quiet meal together. The bombs were already in their backpacks.

After they had finished eating, they went about their usual business. Jahar wore jeans that night and put on his hoodie. He grabbed his skateboard in his family's cluttered house and went outside. He cruised down Norfolk Street late that Sunday night. A neighbor, Ms. Nancy Aiguier who had seen Jahar on the skateboard one time said, "He made a lot of noise." Jahar rode several blocks down the street in Cambridge until another neighbor greeted him and complimented on his skateboard. "Yeah, thanks," Jahar answered.[87]

Everything seemed fine, Jahar thought, everything…

On Marathon Monday, April 15, 2013, they would accomplish their goal. They pursued their own selfish desires and did not care about anybody else and the unimaginable devastation that they were going to cause.

"He Seemed So Lost"

"One anecdote that wasn't in the article but that has been quietly
making its way around town, via one of his former nurses, is that
Jahar cried for two days straight after he woke up in the hospital. No
one in the group has heard this yet, and when I mention it, Alyssa
gives an anguished sigh of relief. "That's good to know," she says. "I
can definitely see him doing that," says Sam, gratefully. "I hope he's
crying. I'd definitely hope . . ." "I hope he'd wake up and go, 'What
the fuck did I do the last 48 hours?' says Jackson, who decides, along
with the others, that this, the crying detail, sounds like Jahar. But,
then again, no one knows what he was crying about."

— *A direct quote from Rolling Stone magazine - "Jahar's World" by Janet Reitman* [88]

JAHAR WOKE UP THE next day in his cell. The annoying lights turned on automatically like the movie, *Groundhog Day*, over and over again. It *was* another day. However, it was at heart a time of darkness and despair in his life. He thought internally in his head about his old life. Outside his cell, he could hear footsteps and voices, but no one was there. His mind was playing tricks. He had no idea what day it was. He never complained, reading more books than usual to keep his mind occupied.

Jahar thought about his cute auburn-haired niece, Zahara. *(Picture of Jahar with Zahara is from Tumblr.)* He tweeted on July 31, 2012, he had red hair once. Incredibly, his mom shaved his head and out grew his wild, curly dark hair! Jahar resembles his father when he was young man.

About a month before the attack, Jahar was baby-sitting Tamerlan's daughter. The little girl sneaked into his bedroom; he was teasing her to leave his room by making her mad. Here is the transcript of the video he taped of her:

"Why did you burp in my face?" He asked his niece as she played with Uncle Jahar. Two-year-old Zahara was starting preschool and talked in short phrases.[89]

"Thess is face," she babbled.

"You burped in my face," said Jahar, again.

"Ah…a burp here," she said and pointed to her nose.

"Get out."

"No go."

"Get out of my room," he teased her.

"No room go."

"Zahara, I said get out!"

"No out." Zahara was beginning to whine.

"Get out," Jahar growled.

"No…"

"I said look at me." Zahara stared at him fearfully. Jahar shouted, "GET OUT!" Jahar frightened her that he finally softened, enough teasing. "All right, give me a kiss." Zahara smiled and perked up. "No, give me a kiss."

"OK." She kissed Uncle Jahar.

"Atta girl," he praised her. "Now, get out!"

"No," she squealed.

Jahar kissed his niece over and over. She was his little princess. He would always let Zahara sit on his lap. They gazed at the computer screen and surfed the internet together. He taught her words. "My niece is the cutest in the world," he proclaimed on his Twitter account.[90] He missed her, and he will miss her growing up. He wondered if she would miss her Dad and Uncle Jahar's hilarious laugh. He loved Zahara the most. He wanted to become a father himself, and his goal within the year 2013 was to find a girlfriend and get her pregnant.

Jahar reminisced a year ago when he talked with his close friends about transferring schools, getting married, and asking a cute girl on a date. He recalled other memories: listening to music, going whale watching or setting off colorful displays of fireworks in the night at Charles River.

Jahar wanted to relive those memories...going out with friends to Five Guys for a cheeseburger, sucking helium out of balloons, playing video games with friends, meeting friends at a local basketball court, driving in his green Honda Civic going 120 miles per hour. He missed driving recklessly, steering the wheel with his knees and leaving his hands free to roll a joint. He missed going to the gym and exercising, watching his favorite television show, *Breaking Bad*, and chillin' with his friends.

Jahar remembered smoking in his car with college buddies Dias, Azamat and Robel. He had sent them a text message after the bombings.

Dias and Azamat were arrested for taking his laptop and backpack of fireworks out of his dorm room. The government accused them of obstruction of justice and conspiracy to obstruct justice. Robel was accused of lying to authorities. His friends had served time in prison and he wondered if they would resent him for ruining their lives.

Someday, Jahar would face the victims of the bombings. His lawyers told him the names of his victims and he learned about them and their injuries. He learned about the youngest victim who died, Martin, and the two women: Lingzi and Krystle, and the officer his brother shot, Sean. Again, he heard how many people lost their limbs and were now handicapped.

The thought of an afterlife and reward in eternal paradise or "Akhirah," was consumed in his teenage mind daily. This Islamic belief was stronger and more important to him than living every day on earth. When Jahar was younger, Tamerlan commanded him to read the Qur'an, to study books about religion. He had to listen to his big brother. At first, he suffered through the pains of learning and listening to him. As time passed on, he realized Tamerlan was the closest person in his life who would never give him wrong advice.[91] He admired his brother, obeyed him and learned about Islam until it consumed him.

Jahar shared his beliefs with his friends before the bombings that he no longer cared about his career goal of becoming a doctor. In fact, he could not stand the sight of blood. He had completely lost interest in continuing college. It was harder than high school, and his grade was plummeting. He got seven F's in all his classes. He told his friends he was disappointed going down this path in life.

"Everybody cheats," he told them, "It didn't matter if you are a doctor or engineer – everybody cheats. With religion and God, you can't cheat." The only thing that matters in life is God. It was the only thing he wanted to do.[92]

When Jahar slept in his dorm room in college, he would not get out of bed because he missed his parents and was not able to go to Dagestan to see them. He didn't know what his future would be. His future no longer belonged to him.

@fighting4jahar jahar himself said he felt like he couldn't get out of bed in the morning at college because he missed his parents and wasn't gunna be able to go Dagestan to see em an he felt he didn't know about the future I'm sorry ur don't wanna believe it and I kinda blame myself for not seeing him more and not knowing what he was goin through but it's true, his grades failed around that same time too so there's more evidence

A friend said Jahar didn't know about his future.

Jahar was failing in college in 2012 and was losing the support of his family. Before the bombings, Jahar was still searching and exploring what he wanted to do with his life. He missed his parents, his father especially. No one saw the pain he was hiding or the monster he would later become. His parents had divorced and were living separately. Jahar's sisters, Ailina and Bella lived near the brothers were not close at all to them. Jahar felt like the baby in the family and he was living in his brother's shadow. He idolized him, but, sometimes, he felt neglected in his own home. Although he had a lot of diverse friends, the paternal abandonment was affecting the way he thought of himself and he did not have self-worth. He tweeted this message on March 18, 2013. "People come into your life to help you, hurt you, love you and leave you and that shapes your character and the person you were meant to be."[93]

When Jahar became a senior at Rindge and Latin High School, the wrestling team was asked to bring a relative to the last match of the year. Cambridge had some students from broken families or parents working at nights, so each wrestler struggled to find a family member, a relative or a friend to walk out with them on the gym floor to receive a flower and a take snapshot picture with them. It would have been a night to celebrate their senior recognition and the support of family members. Jahar struggled to find someone to support him that night, to walk out on the gym floor so everyone could see who was special to him. He stood over Coach Payack's desk in his office to tell him there was no one.

Coach Peter Payack fixed his eyes on Jahar whom he called, "One of my guys." He loved Jahar like his own son. He wanted Jahar to be introduced to the families as the captain of the wrestling team. For three years, his wrestling teammates respected him. He asked Jahar, "Is there anyone who could walk out with you?"

Jahar peered down and thought. *No one.*

"Your father?" asked Coach Payack.

"No," said Jahar.

"Brother?"

Jahar shook his head no. "I have no one." It was sad for the one they called 'a beloved wrestling co-captain.' He had no one to walk out with him to receive his senior award on such a happy occasion. But, it was no problem for him. During senior wrestling night, one of the coaches walked him out instead and he received a flower and had his picture taken with the award. No one from his family showed up or came to his wrestling matches. No one even attended the milestone in his life, his high school graduation - a significant event, and the only person who showed up for that was the family's landlady.[94]

HE WAS LIKE A LOST PUPPY FOLLOWING HIS BROTHER

The Defense had portrayed Jahar as a follower, a lost individual, who went along with his brother, but vulnerable enough to be perhaps manipulated into believing his older brother's ideas regarding jihad.

Jeff Bauman, one of the survivors of the bombings who had lost both legs blamed the older brother Tamerlan for taking advantage of his younger brother. Bauman had no vengeance for the bombers but had developed a slight sympathy for Jahar and wanted to talk to him in prison to hear what he had to say. He wrote in his book *Stronger:*

"He wasn't a monster. He was a kid," he wrote. "I felt kind of bad for him, actually. Not as bad as I did for the victims, but a little. He was only nineteen, and when you're nineteen, you do stupid stuff... Sure, very few people do something that stupid or evil... but he was still just a depressed teenager acting like a jerk."[95]

Bauman also said: "I don't know, I'm just a weird person like that, I'm kind of sensitive, and, you know, I feel bad for people that hurt other people because it's just awful. I feel bad for them that they don't have, you know, that feeling of, kind of like love. You know, I wanted to ask him, you know, like what was the reason? What was the reason? Were you forced to do this? Like I just want to know why and then how he feels about it, how he knows that he ruined people's lives, and I want to talk to him, like see what he felt like."[96]

Manuel Matos who went to school with Dzhokhar said, "Even though I was angry that someone would do something to innocent people, I couldn't help feeling some type of sympathy. I thought what could possibly have happened to send him over the edge to even want to do something like that? Even though he's committed that crime, he's still a human being. I know personally, whatever I did I would not want to feel it's me against the world. Once you put a face to that bombing, everybody's against you. I don't think he woke up one day and said we're going to do this. I feel like someone convinced him to do it."[97]

Kaitlynn Cates, another bombing survivor, expressed compassion for the Boston Bomber and wanted to speak with him and ask him, "What were you thinking...all the people you hurt, what were you thinking?" Although Jahar pleaded not guilty she thought he did not have a fighting chance when she saw him eye-to-eye at his Hearing during his arraignment.

Cates said, "In July, I attended the first court hearing for Dzhokhar. I thought it would help the healing process, but it actually just made me feel sad for him. He seemed so lost." She has no hate for him but believes in forgiveness.[98]

As young as he was, Jahar cried. When he woke up in the hospital after his arrest he cried and cried for two days straight. He was lonely. There was no love there to be found. Jahar cried for the loss of himself, for the loss of his freedom, and even the loss of the family he will never see again.

Jahar sat in prison and recalled the night of the bombings.

It was late Monday night, April 15, 2013, after he and his brother had set off the bombs on Boylston Street. They returned home and watched the havoc unfold on the television in their living room. Nearly every channel was broadcasting the chaos and aftermath of people screaming and running away from the exploded bombs. Tamerlan was happy seeing the carnage of his achievement on all the networks, calling it the next big thing since 9/11.

"So what if a kid dies, God will take care of him," said Tamerlan to Khairullozhon Matanov, a twenty-three-year-old Russian speaking immigrant who worked as a taxi driver. Khairullozhon was Tamerlan's friend and he was at the Tsarnaev's apartment to invite the brothers out for dinner. He expressed his sympathy for the death of Martin Richard, the eight-year-old boy who was killed by the bomb. However, Tamerlan did not have sympathy for the boy killed. Khairullozhon said in reply, "This is bad. The public might direct this towards Muslims."

Jahar sat silently on the couch stroking Peep. The pale yellowish-brown cat purred on his lap. He loved the cat despite his allergies. He felt his eyes itch. After Tamerlan left the room, Khairullozhon sat on the couch and stared at Jahar with concern. "The bombing is going to be a big problem for Muslims because innocent people were killed," he said.

Jahar carefully hid his feelings from Khairullozhon. He gazed away from him, remaining indifferent. He replied, "For some people the bombings were a good thing, for others they were a bad thing."[99]

When Jahar returned to Pine Dale Hall dorm room after dinner later that night, he slept under the covers. Jahar moaned. He slept for hours until the late morning. A troubled overwhelming sadness came over him and his body shook as he slept on his side. He brought his knees up to his chest and hugged himself. Jahar thought about his life. It was all falling apart. He thought how he had to cover up and hide from his family and close friends.

THE DAY WHEN THEY WERE CAUGHT

The brothers could no longer hide. The day when they were caught all hell broke loose. Tamerlan was being tracked down. Before that fateful day, the FBI called him. They asked him what his reason for his return to his homeland was. In 2012, Tamerlan visited his father in Dagestan for six–months, including a trip to Chechnya to visit his relatives.[100] FBI had followed his travels and monitored the websites he visited, and had flagged him. Zubeidat told reporters that Tamerlan had been spied upon by the FBI for five years after his return to the States from Dagestan. "He only loves Islam," she told them. Yet, the FBI speculated he went to southern Russia to train with a jihadist group.

On the eve of the bombings, Zubeidat called Tamerlan. "I'm concern for your safety," said his mother.

"Mama, why are you worrying?" He laughed it off and hung up.

However, on his last day, Tamerlan called his mother in the morning before the shootout. He spoke tenderly, informing and warning his mother that the FBI had called him and that he should come in for questioning, "Mama, I got a private call from the FBI and I am under suspicion. I refused to see them. I told them, what do you suspect me of. If you need me, you should come to where I am."[101]

On Thursday, April 18, 2013, Tamerlan called Jahar around noon at school telling him to come home for dinner. His brother told him about the call from the FBI. Jahar was shocked by this news, left school that afternoon and returned to Cambridge. Horrified, he did not think his brother would ever be caught.

Suddenly, in the middle of dinner, Tamerlan received an unexpected call from the FBI requesting he come in for questioning again. The FBI claimed they needed his help identifying the suspects responsible for the bombings. Tamerlan became suspicious of the FBI's true intent in calling him. He hung up on the FBI, refusing to come in.

Jahar could never forget the look on his brother's face. Tamerlan was petrified with fear. "I'm taking you back to school," he told Jahar. Tamerlan did not want Jahar involved in anything that might go down with the FBI. The FBI was going after him. He wanted to protect Jahar. He had Jahar help him without telling him what he was going to get in to. They left in a hurry. Their dinner was still on the table. He called his mother again, and said, "Mama, the FBI called again. I am fed up with them. Dzhokhar is with me in the house. I'll give him a lift back home."

The brothers left the house. Jahar had no idea what he had gotten himself in to. Soon, the police came after them, and surrounded them in Watertown. The police started shooting at them. Tamerlan made a phone call to his mother during the fight, and in a different tone, he sobbed, "The police, they have started shooting at us, they are chasing us," he said. "Mama, I love you." Tamerlan called his wife and told her they were being chased and fired upon by the police.[102] Right after the calls, the brothers threw pressure cooker bombs at the officers. The police fired more than 200 rounds. When Tamerlan ran out of ammunition, he dropped his jammed gun and tackled the officers. Jahar escaped in the SUV, running his brother over as he careened down Laurel Street. He later abandoned the car and ran, and ran, and ran...

A Unique Case

"If he is put to death, then death has the final word, and I refuse to accept that. As devastating as that day was at the Boston Marathon finish line, a sense of city pride, hope, and love has proven to carry us out of that darkness since April 15, 2013. Dzhokhar Tsarnaev's execution will not bring justice; it will only continue the cycle of violence and death our world perpetuates. I hope goodness has the final say and that we can learn to heal together without seeking the death of another." – a comment about the death penalty coming from someone at the finish line, why the Boston Marathon Bomber should not be put to death

ON JANUARY 30, 2014, U.S. Attorney General Eric Holder authorized the federal prosecutors to seek the death penalty for Dzhokhar Tsarnaev.[103]

Christians 4 Jahar tweeted, *"Brothers and Sisters please pray. Jahar needs our prayers more than ever now. When praying for Jahar in reaction to the terrible news today, don't forget to pray for his family. I heard his mom is devastated."*

The shock of this news broke Zubeidat's heart. In Russia, she made a statement to the press. It wasn't easy to express her feelings. Zubeidat cried, saying: "The only thing I want to say is I want the whole world to hear that I love my son, my precious Dzhokhar, that's it. How can I feel about this? I feel nothing. I tell you one thing, that I love my son. I will always feel proud of him and I'll keep loving him. I love my son, my precious Dzhokhar. That's it please leave me alone. I have nothing more to say. I want to say a million times I love my son, I love my Allah, I love the prophet Muhammad, and I love my Dzhokhar."[104]

However, there was a flood of constant jeering and cheering going on the Pro-death penalty side on Twitter when the news broke out. A Tsarnaev hater said, "I'm generally against the death penalty, but I hope they fry this sicko." The surviving victims were split on the death penalty, but some strongly advocated capital punishment. Judy Clarke, Tsarnaev's lawyer was busy working out a plea deal to save his life.

A UNIQUE CASE

The Boston Marathon bombing was a very huge case and never had anything been interesting as these cast of characters...as Judge George O'Toole pointed out, *"Dzhokhar Tsarnaev's is a unique case."* Judge O'Toole ruled the case and the trial. Tsarnaev's trial connected other unsolved cases together: the unsolved triple murders in Waltham in September 2011 and the FBI shooting death of Tamerlan's friend, Ibragim Todashev in May 2013.

It was a case where the main instigator of the bombings, Tamerlan, had died and was far beyond the reach of the justice system. It was where friends of the accused bomber suspect and surviving bomber, Dzhokhar Tsarnaev, were arrested, implicated and jailed, all very young before their 20th birthdays. Over and above, it was a case where hundreds of bombing victims were injured and disfigured, and they had to live with the horrible memory of this tragedy. Some overcame their odds, but most had no mercy for this kid and wanted to see him to suffer in prison or die. The government was going to guarantee that every victim who wanted to have their day in court would indeed have their day in court. Boston criminal defense attorney Juliane Balliro said, "That's almost like 200 cases in a case."[105]

DEATH DURING THE DEAD OF WINTER

Jahar walked about with his head hanging low. He cringed and suddenly his weak body became ill. Never in his life did he think that his life would end in execution. He was going be put to death by lethal injection if convicted. The death sentence was announced during the dead of winter. At Devens, Jahar shivered as a snow storm brought in a foot of snow. Jahar had never felt extreme pain and deep sorrow in his life. When he received the news about the death sentence, he struggled to understand it. He felt numb and was dismayed. He had this sense of injustice. The government would not offer him a plea deal.

Not knowing what his future would be, Jahar prayed to Allah, leaving his own fate and faith to God. *(We don't know how Jahar might have felt when he received a death sentence, but this may explain his strong faith. Jahar was also still affected from his injures; this would explain why he rubbed his eye often.)* Jahar picked up his Qur'an, the black leather book with golden triangles on the cover. As he read the Qur'an his left eye began to bother him because of his injury. A tear oozed down the corner of his droopy eyelid and his left eye became blurry. It bothered him, and he rubbed it. The light was dimming in his cell. It was hard to read a book, so he had to squint to read. He brought the Qur'an up close to his face and tried to read. He was struck with how bad his left eye had become.

Eventually, the U.S. Federal government agreed to loosen prison restrictions for Dzhokhar Tsarnaev. Eric Holder agreed to modify the "Special Administrative Measures" imposed on him and his attorneys. These new rules allowed Tsarnaev to have other visitors. These people included a mental health specialist and a mitigation specialist who assisted in preparing for his defense against the death penalty.[106]

JAHAR'S SISTER VISITED HER BROTHER IN PRISON

Bella Tsarnaeva from New Jersey finally visited Jahar in prison. Jahar was delighted to see his sister. In the course of this desperate time, he needed love and comfort of family. He gazed at his beautiful dark-eyed sister from behind a glass partition. She wore a black and mahogany colored hijab. An investigator from the Defense team was seated next to her and a FBI agent had also joined them to monitor their conversation. They were present to gather information on the deceased older brother, Tamerlan, for mitigation purpose.

The siblings were only allowed to speak in English and not in their native tongue. Bella peered over at her brother. She was shocked at how thin he appeared. The left side of his cheek was still swollen. Jahar smiled crookedly. He noticed his sister's startled expression.

Bella became uneasy again and then asked Jahar about these special restrictions. She directed her attention to the FBI agent sitting next to them. The investigator, a member of the Defense team began explaining to Jahar's sister about the rules of "Special Administrative Measures" and how they affected his life behind bars.

Jahar nearly lost his temper when he tried to reassure his sister in his restricted situation. In an unbelievable moment of stress, he mocked himself over a sarcastic remark. The agent overheard his remark. However, the public is not made aware of the exact words of his "ill-advised comment" that was a "statement to his detriment." Prosecutors pronounced his alleged comment was damaging and would use this incriminating comment against him.[107]

However, in March 2014, the Defense made it clear that Jahar was only trying to be humorous when he made the "ill-advised statement" to his sister to comfort her gently over his situation being in tight restriction as SAMs. Defense made it clear that his comment did not characterize their client.[108]

FIRST TRIAL OF BOSTON MARATHON BOMBINGS

Jahar's three best college friends were Dias Kadyrbayev, Robel Kidane Phillipos and Azamat Tazhayakov.

According to the indictment, Dias Kadyrbayev removed a few items from Dzhokhar's dorm room, including the bombing suspect's laptop computer and a backpack containing fireworks. Azamat Tazhayakov and Dias then allegedly discarded the backpack in a dumpster outside of the apartment that they both shared. The backpack was later discovered by federal agents in a local landfill after the friends were interrogated. They both faced charges of obstruction of justice and conspiracy to obstruct justice. Robel Kidane Phillipos was charged for lying to the police regarding what he saw when he was with Azamat and Dias.

The first Boston Marathon Bombings trial ended in June 2014. This is a review of Tazhayakov's trial based on testimonies from witnesses. Azamat Tazhayakov, a Russian friend of Jahar, who was accused of obstruction of justice and hindering evidence was found guilty. After hearing the verdict, Azamat put his head into his hands and wept. His mother sobbed loudly in court when the verdict was read.[109]

The fireworks in Jahar's backpack contained red powder. The powder from the bombs was black. The fireworks were emptied of black powder. According to the American Pyrotechnics Association they believed the gunpowder from the fireworks could not have caused the blasts at the marathon. There was simply not enough firework gunpowder present to create this level of destruction. The powder could have been "a fuse or a starter device rather than the actual explosive device."[110]

At the trial, the prosecutors chose a picture of Jahar sitting on a couch with Azamat and his friends. The picture of the four friends was shown to the jury. The friends loved to hang out, smoke pot and play video games together. Jahar sat at the end of the couch. He had a disheveled appearance as if he had just woken up.

When Jahar was on the run from the police, he texted Dias to take anything he wanted from his room because he told them he was leaving. Jahar added a smiley face :-) at the end of the text which meant "marijuana." Dias, Azamat and Robel went to Jahar's dorm room to grab the pot. They saw a JANSPORT backpack containing some fireworks, but they had been emptied of black powder. Dias knew Jahar liked to play with fireworks with his friends for pure enjoyment. After seeing Jahar in the photos released by the FBI, Dias took the backpack from the room. It also contained Jahar's ethics homework, a thumb drive and a pair of black socks. Azamat never touched the bag. He only retrieved the headphones he loaned to Jahar to use. Dias rummaged through Jahar's things and took what he wanted. Among other things they took from the room: a baseball cap and an ashtray. They returned to their apartment to smoke and to watch a movie that Dias' girlfriend was watching, *The Pursuit of Happiness.*

Dias threw out the backpack when Dias' girlfriend, Bayan Kumiskali who stayed in the apartment, told Dias that it could be evidence. She did not want it in the apartment. She said, "Dias did not think it through" when he brought the backpack back with him. She told him to get rid of it.

Azamat agreed with the idea of tossing the backpack and thought it would help Jahar. Azamat did it because he wanted to stay out of trouble. Robel, who never touched the backpack, lied to investigators to distance himself being involved with the others in their attempt to dispose evidence. Dias got rid of the backpack, by placing it in a plastic trash bag and throwing it into the dumpster. It was retrieved later from a garbage landfill.

The backpack Dias retrieved contained a small jar of Vaseline. Dias said in Russian to Azamat he thought that Jahar used the Vaseline to make bombs. While they watched the news coverage of the bombings, they were utterly shocked when they realized it was Jahar who was being implicated in the marathon bombings. Azamat said, "How could he do this?" His Defense lawyer claimed that Jahar is "slick" and can "fool" his friends by having a stunning ability to deceive his closest friends. Azamat met Tamerlan once and did not like him. Tamerlan had given him a book on Islam but he never read it.

A couple days before the bombings, Jahar told his friends he knew how to make bombs in chemistry class over lunch, and he shared with them that he wanted to die as a martyr, "it was good to die as a martyr as you will die with a smile on your face and go to heaven." Azamat did not take his comment seriously.[111]

Jahar's ex-roommate, Andrew Dwinells, an electrical engineer major testified on stand. He said that Jahar seemed normal after the bombings, but he slept more. Although Andrew and Jahar were not very close friends, he said, "It can't be" that Jahar is a terrorist or could be disloyal to U.S. Andrew testified because Jahar's three friends asked him to unlock Jahar's dorm room to pick up the weed and retrieve other items that Jahar said they could take. Dias showed Andrew the text Jahar had sent to him. Andrew thought it was abnormal, so he texted Jahar to confirm this, though he never texted him back.

Alexa Guevara, a student at UMass-Dartmouth and friend of Jahar also testified on stand. She was friends with Jahar, Dias, Azamat and Robel. She told the jury how they had good times hanging out together playing video games, surfing the web and smoking pot. Together they went to Charles River months before the bombings and Jahar pulled out some fireworks and lit them. Alexa became emotional when prosecutors asked her if she thought Jahar could be the bomber when the FBI released his picture to the public. She wept and said she didn't believe it. Alexa then stated to the jury that Jahar never expressed Anti-American views.

JAHAR'S FRIENDS OR ACCOMPLICES[112]

STEPHEN SLIVA – arrested on July 21, 2014, at age twenty-one, pleaded not guilty and was arrested for heroin-distribution charges and possession of a Ruger pistol, which linked him indirectly to the shooting death of an MIT officer Sean Collier at Watertown a few days after the explosions. He pled guilty on December 19, 2014. Silva agreed to testify against Tsarnaev. He was released on December 22, 2015.

AZAMAT TAZHAYAKOV – arrested at age nineteen on April 20, 2013, found guilty during June trial of 2014 for assisting friend, Dias, to dispose evidence of Jahar's backpack. On June 5, 2015, he was sentenced to 3.5 years in prison and will be deported back to Kazakhstan in 2016 followed by 3 years supervised release.

DIAS KADYRBAYEV – arrested at age nineteen, on April 20, 2013, plead guilty for taking Jahar's backpack, laptop and disposing evidence. On June 2, 2015, he was sentenced to 6 years in prison, following 3 years supervised release.

ROBEL PHILLIPOS – arrested at age nineteen, April 20, 2013, found guilty during trial for 2 counts of lying to investigators. Defense claimed he was high on weed. He could not remember and was pushed by FBI to confess. Robel was lost and confused when confronted by the FBI. He spent 2 years in house arrest, but on June 5, 2015, Judge Douglas Woodlock sentenced him to 3 years in prison for lying for a week about what he knew and trying to distance himself from Tsarnaev. Attorneys applying for appeals, release in 2018.

KHAIRULLOZHON MATANOV, arrested at age twenty-three in May 30, 2014, was the fifth man arrested in connection to the Boston marathon bombings. He had nothing to do with the bombings, but he helped police identify the suspects. He was good friends with both Tamerlan and Jahar. He came to visit the brothers at their apartment the night of the bombings and invited them to dinner. That night he did not know the brothers were the ones responsible for the attacks. Khairullozhon was a cab driver who worked hard and sent money back home to his family and relatives in Russia.

FBI followed him for one year and then arrested him for lying to the FBI about whether he met the brothers at the restaurant or drove them there. He lied about the brothers' whereabouts after the bombings. He was also accused of deleting information in his computer knowing that the FBI would be visiting him and investigating his computer, which would reveal that he supported jihad.

He pled "Not Guilty" and there was no evidence ever found of his involvement with the bombings. Khairullozhon has no family in the States. During his imprisonment, he was severely beaten by guards after flooding his cell in protest after being labeled and harassed as a "Muslim terrorist." He has since then been moved to another correctional facility. On June 18, 2015, Judge William G. Young sentenced him to 2.5 years in prison for deleting computer records and for lying to the FBI.[113]

HAPPY 21st BIRTHDAY JAHAR!

On July 22, 2014, Jahar turned twenty-one, spending his second year in prison.

Bella and Ailina Tsarnaeva visited Jahar in prison to wish their little brother a "Happy Birthday!" The sisters were shocked again to see their little brother's appearance. He was becoming pale–skinned and physically underweight. He also had grown a slight scruffy beard on his chin.

However, Jahar was delighted and in good spirits to see his sisters on his birthday. Bella and Ailina shared with him the news of what his supporters were doing for him on his birthday. They wanted to do something nice for him. Because of SAMs he was not allowed to receive any gifts, letters or cards. He had "a big smile on his face" when he heard that people who cared for him would be doing acts of kindness and actions in his name. It would demonstrate that Jahar "inspires" supporters to do good deeds and acts of kindness, big and small. Supporters had given money to the hungry in the countries of Syria, Africa, Pakistan and Palestine in Dzhokhar Tsarnaev's name. All acts were documented in a humble scrapbook and given to the Tsarnaev's family. Jahar excitedly said to his sisters to include Tamerlan's name along in these acts of charity.[114]

From this day forth, may this be the start of something good. We prayed that hopefully he will engage in acts of kindness to people everywhere and be a kind person with a heart of gold like he was before the bombings. He loved to save people's lives when he worked as a lifeguard. He wanted to feed the hungry. He liked to help people who are disabled. He wanted to become a nurse. We prayed that he considers all the things that his supporters have done for him that he will inspire people everywhere, to help and to contribute to society.

We hoped he still has a part of his old-self who genuinely loved people. Jahar detested violence and would never have participated in violent behavior. Jahar would always be willing to drop what he was doing to help people and please them. However, we may never see this side of him again. He is now like all the other radicalized men who have been brainwashed by evil. He showed no signs. He has turned into a monster.

The government had stacked up everything against him:
- They denied him to have his trial moved out of Boston.
- He lost a bid for a request of copies of papers regarding the investigation case in Russia.
- Judge denied bid for info to the Waltham triple murders in 2011.
- Judge denied Hearing on media leaks.
- Worked on a possible plea agreement but failed to reach one. No plea deal.
- The trial was set for January 2015.

Prosecutors had brought up a concern that many witnesses and surviving victims were afraid or unwilling to testify against Jahar in the courtroom. Meanwhile, Jahar received many death threats. Many believed he may not receive a fair trial and that he deserved to die, but others saw him as a pathetic person. He garnered so much sympathy and hate. People wanted to know what he thought about what he did. Americans were curious to know how and why this attack came about. Therefore, this trial was a chance for us to hear how and why he became a terrorist.

Jahar's parents, Zubeidat and Anzor, live alone and were far away. They wished they could see Jahar more and show their support and love. However, they felt helpless. They could only write to him. They were not allowed to discuss the case together with him. Instead, they could only constantly reassure their love for him. Jahar loved them and missed them both very much. On the phone, they talked and laughed, recalling funny memories of Tamerlan and able to share their common love of him as they continued to grieve his death.[115]

Mama Zubeidat and young Jahar, pics from *Tumblr*

Jahar Appears

"I don't know how many rounds you shot into that boat. They couldn't kill him then, I'm not going to kill him now." — Juror no. 353 in the jury pool tweets Boston Globe's Milton Valencia

IT WAS JUST ANOTHER one of those pre-trial conference meetings.

In the John Joseph Moakley courthouse, Assistant U.S. Attorney William Weinreb, disputed with Dzhokhar Tsarnaev's lawyers over how much evidence each side needed to disclose to the other in Tsarnaev's trial. "Federal criminal trials should not be waged by surprise. Each side is supposed to have notice, generally, of what the other side is trying to prove," he said.

Tsarnaev's Attorneys David Bruck and Timothy Watkins sat at the counsel table. Defense feared the government's case against their client, Dzhokhar, was strong. No plea deal was offered. David Bruck, a death penalty defense specialist complained how their team was overwhelmed by the volume of evidence which included thousands of witness interviews, computer records and photographs of the bomb attack. Bruck said, "The government has more information about Mr. Tsarnaev than most of us have about ourselves. We need to put aside this claim of unfairness that the government is completely in the dark."[116]

Weinreb insisted, "You had plenty of time to work on the case, perhaps you had not used that time wisely. The rules governing discovery should be interpreted reasonably. The government needs reciprocal discovery from the defense in order for us to form our strategy."

David Bruck stared at Weinreb's stern face. He took a breath and swallowed, and explained to him slowly, "Our client's life had been seized by the government. The government has seized truckloads of evidence including all the contents in Dzhokhar Tsarnaev's dorm room and immigration files. It not only seized our client's but also his friends and entire family…

The only evidence in form of documents in our possession is provided by the government in the first place. Our team has very little evidence of physical items left, if the prosecution knew very little we had you probably would not file a Motion to compel."[117]

Judge George O'Toole at the bench sat patiently listening to the arguments. Weinreb turned to him and said, "Use your authority to order production of discovery."

Bruck said back, "It would not be possible for the defense to comply. We are hard at work halfway around the world. But, if the prosecution insists, we could get some stuff together, unrelated, and hand it over and let the government scratch their heads. However, this would be a waste of everyone's time." According to reporter Carl Stevens from *WBZ*, he tweeted – *"Defense spent 18 months gathering evidence, but they have given us nothing."*

Judge O'Toole seemed composed and did not want to rule on the evidence issue just yet. He said in other words, directing his words to Defense. "Have the Defense prepared both phases of the trial." Bruck said, "Yes, we indeed are ready."

Near the end of the meeting a *Boston Globe* reporter, Milton Valencia, tweeted that Weinreb wanted Tsarnaev at the last Status conference. "One last matter, the prosecution believes the defendant should be present at jury selection. He has not appeared in court since his arraignment nearly fourteen months ago."

Bruck replied, "I am confident that our client would not insist on being present."

Weinreb was insistent and demanded "I'm concerned if the defendant did indeed waive his right to be present at jury selection then issues could arise in the event of a conviction in this case. If the defendant did indeed waive his right to be present that this should be on the record."

Bruck glanced down at the table. He thought this was an interesting setup by the government. Now they demanded their client to appear in court. He nods his head, and said, "I'll discuss the matter with him." Reporter Valencia tweeted Bruck's reply, *"We'll certainly take that up with him."*

Two months later, on November 12, 2014, during the Ninth Status Conference, Judy Clarke, William Fick and Timothy Watkins were present at this meeting. Finally, at the end of the meeting, government's William Weinreb asked the Defense team again, "Is the defendant planning to attend the pre-trial conference for next month?"

Judge O'Toole said, "It is a common practice in my court for defendants to skip their status conference, but I expect that all defendants be present for their final pre-trial conference. I anticipate this is true of Tsarnaev as well."

Judy replied positively, "Yes, absolutely. It seemed to get everybody excited when the government asked a couple hearings ago that Tsarnaev be made to show up in court. We've just been following local practice and there's nothing wrong with the fact that Tsarnaev hadn't shown up so far."[118]

THE BOMBER WAS A REAL COWARD

Marc Fucarile, one of the surviving victims, sat in the gallery and had attended a couple of Tsarnaev's Status Conferences. Marc lost his right leg in the bombings. He remembered the bomb exploding, the screaming and yelling on that day. He could not move and knew he got hit. Marc had broken his spine and suffered shrapnel wounds throughout his body, had second–third-degree burns and partial permanent hearing loss. After forty-nine surgical procedures he was one of the last surviving victims of the bombings to leave the hospital. He thought Dzhokhar Tsarnaev should never be forgiven. "There's no forgiveness, never in a million years. They killed a little innocent boy; they killed a cop in his cruiser. This was something we did not choose to engage in. They're just complete cowards. If a guy is doing something wrong at work and something tragic happens, you forgive that. But not for what he did to [the Richard] family, their little daughter, Jane, and my son. She should not have to be dealing with that. My son should not have to be dealing with this. I'm OK with whatever happens to that guy," he said in an interview. "If you do this in our country, we should be able to kill you. The death penalty is too easy, but that's what we have. He should literally be stoned [to death.]"[119] Marc had said one time, "Personally, I'd love to torture him and do what he did to many people…"

Outside the federal courthouse after the hearing, Marc told reporters, "I'd like to have to see him face us that is why I come." He was upset that Tsarnaev had not attended one Hearing since his arraignment. He said, "Cause he's a coward, 'cause he didn't face us that day. He walked away. If he was a real man he could have stood there."[120]

600 DAYS LATER

Halfway around the world a father's voice cried out, "The Americans are going to harm my second son the way they did my oldest son." Anzor Tsarnaev told ABC News from Dagestan. He could not stay silent. There was anguished fear in his heart that the blood thirsty Americans will murder his only son. "We already know what's going to happen. Everything is in Allah's hand."[121]

Security was tight around the John Joseph Moakley courthouse in Boston on December 18, 2014. A news helicopter circled above the courthouse. Coast Guard boats patrolled the water. Boston police officers walked down the court entrance with bomb-sniffing dogs. Police snipers guarded the security area and beyond the courthouse. Various news reporters from all media outlets flocked to Boston to report the *"most significant trial this country has seen in recent times."*

On a cold winter day, the accused Boston Bomber suspect, Dzhokhar "Jahar" Tsarnaev rode into the city in a prison transport van. He was roused by guards in the early morning to attend a Pre-trial meeting, the final meeting before his trial. Jahar thought about this day, about waking up to face the world that would judge him. He could not bear the thought of seeing people or thinking what his future might be. He grew nervous. Jahar rubbed his eyes. It was 6:30 a.m. His tired eyes slowly began adjusting to the dawn light and he saw shadows of skyscraper buildings along the river. As the van drove into Boston he thought how much he missed his old life. Locked away for 20 months in a cement tomb, Jahar finally saw the courthouse ahead. The driver of the van released the sirens. The van screamed and passed through traffic. It had been a little over 600 days since Jahar was arrested, close to 608 days. He spent a week in the hospital treating his injuries, however, about

600 days in solitary confinement.

600 days of loneliness.

600 days of punishment.

600 days of staring at the walls.

600 days of breathing while others would rather see him dead.

600 days later, for the first time, he felt the cold fresh air of the outside world.

Jahar arrived at the courthouse. He was unsteady and needed help to stand on his own two feet. Both of his wrists and ankles were shackled. The U.S. Marshals pulled him out of the vehicle and steadied him. He was so young, so thin and small.

In a while, Jahar would confer with his Defense lawyers: Miriam Conrad, Judy Clarke, William Fick, and Timothy Watkins. He would also confront Judge George O'Toole and the Prosecution team led by Assistant U.S. Attorneys Nadine Pellegrini, William Weinreb, Aloke Chakravarty and Steven Mellin. Tsarnaev's lawyers had worked hard around the clock writing many dockets that were under seal. They had failed to reach a plea deal and to move the trial outside of Boston. Furthermore, they had coached Jahar on how to behave in court.

In exchange for his orange prison jumpsuit, he was given a soft, black cardigan sweater, a white dress shirt and green slacks. He was thankful to wear such nice civilian street clothes. It gave him a sense of normalcy. Jahar changed into his new clothes. He played nervously with the zipper on his sweater. Jahar looked ugly and gaunt. His hair was unkempt and curly. His face was still swollen from the injuries and his left eye was puffy and half–closed. And his left injured hand, thin and gawky, twirled the hairs in his beard. He grew a sparse beard on his chin that was also unkempt.

He rubbed his eyes and his nose again. Nervous but composed, he was about to face his fear. U.S. Marshals escorted Jahar into courtroom number 9 and all eyes locked on him. He fastened his gaze on Miriam and Judy and smiled at them. His feet were in shackles and he was seated between them at the counsel table.

Miriam placed her hand behind the back of his chair, and Judy touched Jahar's shoulder in a reassuring manner. Jahar peered down at his knees. He could sense that everyone was staring at him, including the Judge, the prosecutors and the government authorities. They had waited years for this day to stare him in the eyes. He feared what they were going to use against him.

Reporters were there sitting behind him tweeting away about his shocking appearance. Courtroom sketch artists began drawing his face. His sketch was published, and some people said his sketch resembled Abe Lincoln or Wolverine because of his bushy stand up hair. In court, Jahar touched his nose and face and he felt disoriented, so he slouched in his chair with his knees apart. A dozen families and surviving victims attended the pre-trial hearing. Bombing survivor Marc Fucarile who waited twenty months to see him finally, could not take his eyes off him.

Jahar appeared terrified. He had not yet adjusted to being around other people, locations and sights. Judy glanced at Jahar. She was so concerned about his health. She touched his shoulder again. Jahar gazed up at her and swallowed nervously. He blinked and if he wanted to keep focusing and not act oddly, he had to look into her eyes for strength. Judy patted him again to alert him that Judge O'Toole had questions for him.

Judge O'Toole stared at Jahar from his bench. He asked him whether he had waived his right to appear at previous hearings. Jahar answered in a clear voice, "Yes, sir." O'Toole asked him, if his lawyers had acted in his best interests. Jahar replied, "Very much" into the microphone in front of him.[122]

During the rest of the hearing, the team discussed a list of motions. Jahar sat slouching in his chair and played with his zipper sweater and then the note pad on the table. He watched Miriam take down notes. Cell-shocked and tired, his left eye was irritating him. He rubbed his left eye and a tear filled up his eye. He wiped the tear away.

Judy who sat beside Jahar took a water pitcher from the table and poured him a glass of water. Jahar took the glass and drank. It quenched his thirst. He listened to Weinreb and seemed dismayed when he spoke. He glanced down at his knees. Judy touched Jahar on the shoulder again with sympathy. In an impromptu moment, she asked Weinreb, "At what possibility of this trial that could end in a death sentence?" Hearing those words, Jahar's head jerked up slightly; he was freaked out about the death penalty. He *"grimace or might have been a smile"* under stress and fear.[123]

Miriam and Judy both acted motherly towards Jahar. His lawyers sat on either side of him like a "maternal cloak" caring for him like other mothers caring for their own child. Some reporters described their lawyer/client relationship to be like this: a "maternal cloak." The Defense lawyers acted as a protected cover for Jahar like an outer piece of clothing would do – like a cloak. They doted on him by talking to him, laughing with him, smiling at him, exchanging whispers with him and rubbing him on the back throughout the trial. They were kind to him as they worked through the legal procedures together. It seemed like they were his family now, since his own parents from Russia are banned from entering the U.S. It was impossible for them to attend his trial. His mother had felony shoplifting charges in the U.S. and could get arrested. Jahar's uncle in Maryland, Ruslan, had disowned his brother's family.

At the end of court, while Jahar was handcuffed, a woman supporting Jahar, Elena Teyer, stood up and shouted in Russian to tell Jahar that she and his mother were praying for him, "Dzhokhar, we know you're innocent. There are so many of us supporting you here. We are praying for you. We love you. We know you are innocent! Stay strong, my son." She conveyed to the FBI, "Stop killing innocent people. "Stop killing our innocent boys."

This woman was the mother–in–law of Ibragim Todashev, who was shot to death by the FBI in Florida and was a friend of the Tsarnaev's. The court deputies removed her from the courtroom. Outside, she told the press, "It's a very hard feeling for a mother when you can't help your own child. You feel hopeless," she said.

When Jahar heard the words in his native Russian language from that strange woman, he put his head down, and smiled slightly.

Outside the courthouse after the hearing, reporters caught up with Marc and asked him what they thought of Tsarnaev. Marc hesitated, possibly thinking about the early confrontation of Tsarnaev protestors declaring his innocence when he entered the courthouse and remembering Tsarnaev sitting in court appearing so pale and weak. He told reporters finally that, "I am grateful to be alive. They're all welcome to their opinion. There are supporters for him and there are supporters for us."[124]

JAHAR FACED 1,350 POTENTIAL JURORS

There was a call for a large pool of potential jurors because of the wide spread media coverage of the bombings, and many in Boston had attended the marathon and were victims of the lockdown when the police hunted for Jahar. Many people were affected by this tragedy. On January 5, 2015, 1,350 potential jurors were called in to become jurors for the trial. Lawyers were to select twelve jurors and six alternates. Jurors got their first glimpse at the Boston Bomber and they were *"transfixed by this shaggy–haired 21–year–old."*

Holly Bailey@hollybdc
Struck by how young Tsarnaev looks, even with a beard.

Jahar was frail when he entered the jury assembly with his attorneys without shackles to his wrists or legs. His left face was still puffy, and his left eye was not fully open, due to his injuries. People who saw the defendant gasped, immediately. Some were probably thinking: *Oh, my gosh! That's the defendant.* Even with a beard, he still looked so young. But, the government did not treat him as a wayward teen, but as a terrorist.

Jahar averted his gaze away from the prospective jurors. His demeanor was unlike the terrorist, Timothy McVeigh, who was mean-looking and defiant on his first day when he was introduced to his jurors. McVeigh committed a heinous crime in Oklahoma City on April 19, 1995. Jahar was a small child learning to talk on that day. McVeigh also received a death sentence and was convicted for discharging a truck bomb in front of the Alfred P. Murray building that killed 168 people and injured over 600. He was executed in 2001.

Jahar slouched in his chair. He was dressed in khakis and a dark sweater. He was nervous, scared and intimated to see the jurors face-to-face. Deep down in their hearts, they would decide if he should be put to death or spend his life in prison. He sat between Judy and Miriam at a counsel table and squirmed in his seat uncomfortably. He touched his facial hairs, rubbed his nose and fixed the collar of his sweater. His hair was also a bird's nest mess and his beard was long and untrimmed. Afraid of the direct confrontation, he stared down at his feet most of the time. He feared the eyes of all the jurors staring at him. They were either angry at him or had already decided his fate.

The Prosecution team sat at another table at the opposite end from the Defense team. For 1,350 jurors to attend and receive jury instructions there were six sessions. From Monday to Wednesday, two sets of groups of around 200 people arrived at the Jury Assembly room. The first group came in at 9 a.m. The second wave of potential jurors arrived at 1 p.m.

At the start of the session, Jahar lifted his head and scanned the first group of potential jurors. It was then he had to wonder who will let him live or who will let him die. He bit his fingernails nervously. He exchanged a few words with Judy. Suddenly, the Judge entered the Assembly. Judge O'Toole welcomed everyone. He introduced one-by-one the Prosecutors and they stood up. The Judge introduced Tsarnaev's lawyers in the Defense team and they stood up. Lastly, he introduced the defendant. "And the defendant is here," the Judge said.

Jahar stood up, had an inexpressive stare, looked to the Judge, but avoided eye-contact with the jurors. As the Judge talked about the possible death penalty in this case, Jahar listened. With his eyes downcast he seemed indifferent to the murders he was charged with committing.

While his lawyers sat still, Jahar stroked his chin as he leaned his head on his elbow. He paid attention to the Judge, but the ceiling was sometimes more interesting. He glanced up and gazed at the architectural design. (*It's true. He stared at the ceiling one time.*) He could not look at the jurors. In every session when Jahar stood up, all the people and especially people in the back row craned their necks to see him like he was a caged animal in a circus. Reporter Michael Hayes from *BuzzFeedNews* tweeted, *"Tsarnaev has appeared agitated and unable to sit still all week. His hair and beard a mess. His left eye, badly swollen."*

Another session introducing to another group of jurors was about to begin. Jahar exchanged a brief smile with Judy and Miriam as the Judge walked in. As they sat, Miriam kept peering down at Jahar's wriggling fingers. She seemed concerned. Jahar tapped his hand over his heart and drummed his fingers on his chest. Judy leaned over to him and whispered to him. Jahar stopped twitching, but it didn't last. The Judge opened with introductions and explained the trial. He introduced the Prosecutors, the Defense, and then lastly the defendant.

Each time Jahar stood up he completely avoided eye contact with the jurors. He stared down or over at the Judge instead. Midway through the proceedings, the Judge joked, "We're almost finished here now." The attorneys laughed, but Jahar stared down, still drumming fingers on his chair and under the table. By the fourth session of introductions on Tuesday afternoon, the Prosecutors and Defense Team and Jahar walked out to meet the jurors without Judge O'Toole present. There was a chilling awkward silence as they sat in front of the 200 prospective jurors.

For two minutes, Jahar stared fearfully at the jurors in awkward silence. Suddenly, the Judge came in late. He addressed them with a shout, "Good Afternoon!" followed by silent laughter from the jurors.

By the fourth round of introductions when Judge O'Toole motioned Jahar to stand, he needed encouragement from one of his lawyers, Miriam Conrad, to get to his feet. Miriam nudged him. Jahar was over–reacting at having to stand up over and over so the jurors could see him. Some jurors watched him nervously, others were interested, and some were even concerned for him. Some reporters said Jahar acted like a reluctant youth.

Laurel J. Sweet@Laurel_Sweet
For the third time in 24 hours, #Tsarnaev must listen as a room of strangers hears they might be tasked to order him killed.

Miriam and Judy likely talked with Jahar before the next session. Their conversation with Jahar must have been something like this: "Relax, it's almost over. The jurors are watching you and the media."

FOX 25 News Boston

Another shot of Tsarnaev on his way back to Fort Devins - fox25

The media was following Jahar since his pretrial hearing when the *Boston Fox 25* news helicopter recorded the image of him getting out of his prison transport van as he returned to Devens after the Hearing on December 18. Jahar was handcuffed and had swapped his street clothes for his regular orange jumpsuit. On his last day of introductions to jurors, he tried not to show his nervousness.

Jahar entered the jury assembly swinging his arms freely as he walked in this time. As he sat down, he was keenly aware that every juror and the media were watching him. Jahar and Miriam exchanged a smile and chatted briefly before Judge O'Toole proceeded with the introductions. Jahar appeared to be less fidgety but forgot the media. He raised his hand to scratch his face. He caught himself. He drummed his fingers under the table instead as observed, by *Yahoo* Reporter Holly Bailey. By the time he was introduced to more than 900 jurors, it was his third day.

During his fifth introduction to the jurors, he stood up quickly, with hands folded in front, he almost lost his balance. Judy caught his elbow and steadied him. While the sixth session, Jahar improved. Jahar and Judy walked in together, smiling and talking quietly with each other. By the last round of introductions, Jahar was accustomed to the jury instructions that he stood up quickly even before he was introduced and avoided eye contact again during the sixth session.

A couple bombing survivors attended the jury selection. They wanted to see the accused person who had injured them, so they could heal and move on with their lives. The bombing survivors were preparing for their day, for justice or vengeance against Tsarnaev. They could not even say his name. Only a few could bring themselves to face him in court. Some attended the trial, and some did not. Some couldn't decide what form of punishment he should receive. Others were outspoken. Liz Norden, the mother of two sons who had lost their legs said, "Capital punishment should be the easy way out for him." On the other hand, Marc Fucarile preferred Tsarnaev to be sentenced to life imprisonment.[125]

There was something oddly revealing about Jahar's reaction when the Judge read the charges against him and the death sentence. As he stroked his beard he "uttered something under his breath as the Judge read the death sentence." His lawyers had begged for a plea deal, but it was not happening.[126]

THE VOIR DIRE

Jahar Tsarnaev avoided the eyes of the jurors. Now it had come down to "voir dire," the process of screening hundreds and hundreds of potential jurors from the Eastern side of Massachusetts. The jury pool was the largest pool in Massachusetts. Since the government sought the death penalty in this case the selective jurors must be "death qualified jurors" to impose such a penalty.

Tsarnaev's lawyers quickly took him to the barber in Devens to have his hair cut and his beard trimmed. Jahar was also given very nice clothes to wear. His attire was a dark blazer, a sports jacket, some different colored light shirts, pants and shoes. Jahar stayed and slept in a prison cell in the John Joseph Moakley courthouse during the jury selection process. He tried the different clothes on and saw himself as quite a man who has grown up. He missed freedom. He missed his old life, his parents, family and friends.

It seemed like none of his family would attend the trial. However, his lawyers had contacted his relatives in Russia to determine if they would be willing to take the witness stand.

His sister, Bella, had her second child, and did not attend his trial. His other sister, Ailina, was arrested months ago and was charged with threatening the life of her boyfriend's ex-girlfriend with a bomb. She was no longer in custody and had remained out of the public eye. His Aunt Maret, the sister of Anzor from Canada did not attend either. She was not permitted to visit him in prison and the family did not rely on her.

He missed the closeness of family's like he had when he was a child. He missed the good times. When they arrived in Cambridge they were excited to live the American dream. He remembered when his family all sat on the rocks by the rocky shores.

A family photo was taken of him with his mother and sisters and Tamerlan. *(This photo is true. There is a photo of the family sitting on the rocks by the shore.)* The waves rippled at their feet. Jahar recalled his mother sitting on the rocks getting ready to pose for the camera. Tamerlan crouched on his knees and gave her a bear hug from behind. Jahar followed his brother's actions and also embraced his mother. The memory of this precious moment lingered in his mind. Jahar nearly broke down.

He received word that both of his uncles from Maryland would not attend. Jahar had not been in touch with his Uncle Ruslan for a long time. His other uncle, Alvi Tsarni said he would not have time to attend his nephew's trial. Jahar had to accept this situation regarding his family.

However, Jahar had to think positive. *"No matter where life takes me, you'll still find me with a smile."* He wrote that tweet one day on December 12, 2010. Jahar smiled when he thought of it, and the only people he would bond with and who would make him smile more were his attorneys.

Jahar
@J_bar
No matter where life takes me you'll still find me with a smile
RETWEETS 646   LIKES 651
3:12 AM - 10 Dec 2012

Judy had flown in from San Diego for the trial. After meeting the jurors that week, his lawyers met with him privately in a room to discuss matters. Potential jurors had filled out a long questionnaire. They said that most jurors had set it in their minds that the defendant was guilty. They strongly felt that they needed to weed out the too eager jurors who wanted to serve and the jurors who sought the death penalty for the defendant. One exalted juror tweeted on social media an obscene statement of exultation at the time of Jahar's arrest. In the meantime, they were also asking the appeals court to order Judge O'Toole to move the trial out of Boston or to suspend jury selection until he ruled on a third change of venue request.

The lawyers warned Jahar, "When you are in the room while we interview each juror, you may hear things that you may not want to hear. Many people were impacted by the tragedy. It will not be easy to hear these people decide whether you should live or die when we ask them this."

Since the government wanted him there to observe jury selections, Jahar had no choice. He shuddered and said weakly to his lawyers, "I can't look at them."

His lawyers believed he would be uncomfortable to sit and listen to jurors as they decided whether to impose the death penalty on him. He felt so much pressure and stress. *He is still very young,* they thought. They advised him to listen as much as he could; and they would keep him occupied with reading materials or note-taking.

Early Thursday morning on January 15, 2015, Jahar wore a dark blazer over a dress shirt. He neatly brushed his short hair and trimmed beard. The U.S. Marshals escorted him to the courtroom. He was nervous to meet the authorities, the prosecution team and the potential jurors. When he saw his lawyers were the only people in the room, he was relieved and glad to see Miriam, Judy, David and the other lawyers on his team: William Fick and Timothy Watkins. He also met the jury consultant working with his Defense team. He smiled at them and said, "Good morning." His lawyers greeted him and conferred with him.

Right away, Miriam said, "Come look at this." Jahar sat at a large wooden counsel table beside Miriam. The U.S. Marshals sat behind Jahar watching his every move. Miriam showed him something on her laptop. Jahar missed the internet and had been deprived of all electronic devices like his smartphone, the TV, radio and wearing his watch. Miriam knew his life in prison was gloomy and oppressed. She knew her client would be sensitively afraid to look at the jurors or the prosecutors during these serious proceedings. Therefore, she longed to nurture him by giving him warmth, her love, her support and to bring laughter to his pale face and lifeless world.

Miriam showed him a few comments, tweets or pictures on her laptop to get him to laugh and ease his tension. Jahar leaned in and stared at the screen for the first time. Whatever he saw on the screen, it was funny because they both were giggling. Jahar laughed and began chatting. He became a lively person, very animated and giddy as he spoke with his lawyers.

However, it ended too soon. Judge George O'Toole appeared with the Prosecution team Nadine Pellegrini, William Weinreb, Aloke Chakravarty and Steven Mellin.

Also, U.S. Attorney Carmen Ortiz, the leader of the prosecution team entered the room, and everyone hushed and became alert. It was her first day observing the individual jury questioning. When they walked in, Jahar's face became stern and he sat down quietly. Judy gave Jahar a yellow pad to take notes or to scrawl on. Miriam gave him her own pen. On the left side of the conference table sat the Judge and the prosecutors. On the right sat Jahar and his defense lawyers.

Judge George O' Toole addressed the first twenty jurors who were called in. They sat in the jury box. Reporters were present to tweet what O'Toole said. O'Toole explained about the death sentence, reminding them that this was a capital case and that the defendant was to be sentenced to death.

"Some charges are not punishable by death. A jury is never required to find death. The jury, and not the judge, is responsible for whether a defendant convicted of a capital crime will live or die," tweeted *Boston Justice's* J.M. Lawrence. Upon hearing these words again, Jahar gazed down at the table. The Judge finished his remarks.

Everyone rose to their feet as the jury took an oath. When they left the room, the lawyers shuffled papers inside a manila folder and reviewed the first candidate. One-by-one, the potential jurors were led into the courtroom and the lawyers and prosecutors began the voir dire process.

Some jurors had a personal connection associated with the marathon bombings. Several were forced to shelter from far and near the manhunt or knew friends who were injured in the bombings. One potential juror knew the officers who were searching for Tsarnaev during the manhunt. Another juror who lived near Watertown heard the gunfire shootings between the Tsarnaev brothers and the officers.

A second juror who had family and friends whose Watertown homes were riddled with bullet holes was interviewed. Someone else who was interviewed worked at a Watertown restaurant right in the middle of the media frenzy manhunt had customers coming into their eatery crying on the day of lockdown.

More jurors were interviewed, and some were distressed. A juror who knew Martin Richard came in, broke down and cried in front of the lawyers, prosecutors and Judge.

One juror's wife worked at the ICU at Mass. General who helped treat the bombing victims. The husband's wife said, "It hit my wife hard." Another juror had a business salon on Boylston Street where the bombs exploded.

One juror was a corrections officer inside Plymouth house of corrections where Tsarnaev's co-defendant Khairullozhon Matanov was imprisoned. One more was a sales manager for a company that develops emergency alert systems for terrorist attacks. His alert systems had been used during the terrifying shooting, takedown and capture of Tsarnaev in Watertown. Still, another had sponsored the marathon and had a co-worker who was near the finish line when the bombs went off, but luckily, he had not been not injured. Another potential juror who was dismissed in the early phase and did not go through the voir dire was an emergency room doctor who had treated Dzhokhar Tsarnaev at the hospital.

What a small world...

So on, and so on the interviews escalated. There weren't many who could serve and some still carried the terror and anguished emotions about the bombings. Reporter Alysha Palumbo from *NECN* tweeted, *"there is a persuasive sense that he did it in this community"* & *"such an explosive outrage."* Jahar heard everything. He bent down and stared at his pad; sometimes, he scribbled on it. Many had made up their minds already and believed he was guilty.

Until one break, midway through interviews, David and Judy were, *"clearly not satisfied how Judge O'Toole disinclined to speak about the charges their client is accused of"* from reporter Hayes.

Boston's Fox 25 reporter Gail Waterhouse tweeted, David spoke to the Judge, "Can you ask more specific questions on questionnaire over juror's feelings about the death of a child. Don't treat it like a murder charge, but someone who used weapons of mass destruction. We need to know what media the prospective jurors have consumed."

However, Judge O'Toole asserted, "The jury pool is fully aware that bombs were used in the crime. But, I don't agree that I need to ask them what specific media the jurors read."

With that answer, the voir dire continued.

As Jahar listened to each juror *"argued over his fate, Tsarnaev leans to side in chair, elbow a kickstand, his hand in face,"* observed reporter Valencia. He focused on hearing a young advertising account executive.

This juror sat up front facing both sets of lawyers. He jokingly said his friends thought it was cool he would have the opportunity to sentence Tsarnaev to death. Jahar appeared to be smiling at the joke, but both sets of lawyers glanced at each another. The death penalty was a very serious matter, not to be taken lightly. That juror was sent out the door.

JAHAR THE ARTIST

The voir dire continued the next day. Jahar reunited with his lawyers the following morning. He entered the courtroom wearing the same outfit he had on yesterday. He was very expressive as he talked with Miriam and Judy. Like his mother, Jahar spoke with hand gestures in the air. Miriam handed him a pile papers to read through and a yellow legal pad to take notes. He stroked his beard and read the papers.

The court session began after a delay. Judge O'Toole instructed the nine women and eight men in the jury pool to, "Be truthful. You will be doing a duty as a citizen and as a juror, no matter what your answers will be." Jahar glanced up and scanned the potential jurors occasionally. He stared at his pad, crossed his legs and began to draw. As the Judge talked, some perspective jurors glanced curiously over at Jahar.

Valencia reported that Jahar *"goes in between scratching at his hair, scribbling, writing and doodling on a pad,"* during the jury interviews. Jahar listened to each juror's interview. He sat forward if he was interested in a juror. Every so often, he leaned back, slouching in his chair like a bored teenager. Miriam would glare at him sideways and he would quickly sit up. Sometimes, he sat still with his face propped on his left injured hand, which rested on his chair arm.

"Hello Judge," said the Court camera guy to Judge O'Toole. "Can you move your seat closer to the juror, so you can be in the shot?" Everyone started laughing, except for Jahar. He just poured a cup of water for Miriam.

As the questioning continued, Jahar grew stressed listening to jurors talking about whether he should live for the rest of his life locked away in a tomb cement cell or be put to death by lethal injection. He wanted to remove his mind from the courtroom and start an art project. He began sketching on his legal yellow pad while the jurors were being interviewed.

Jahar loved to draw, and it helped turn his thoughts far away from the jury process. He thought his *'doodles were more artsy than most kids'* and he tweeted one day he could make *'bank as a tat artist.'* Jahar sketched many faces on the pad.

Later, in the middle of jury questioning when the jurors and attorneys were discussing the gravity regarding Tsarnaev's sentencing, Jahar showed Miriam a picture of what he drew, observed *WBZ's* Jim Armstrong. Miriam had provided Jahar comfort and he clung onto her like a child. Jahar seemed to say, *Look at my drawing.* Miriam thought in this precious moment of interaction with him, she could not help but have sympathy for this lost soul. She smiled when she saw the picture of faces that her twenty-one-year-old client drew. Armstrong tweeted, *"Tsarnaev is sketching, appears to be faces."* Miriam and Jahar whispered during the proceeding, and she gave him a new pen as observed by Valencia. When jury questioning was done for the day, Jahar got up and whipped his dark blazer off.

IN SEARCH OF AN IMPARTIAL JUROR

The following week, juror questioning continued. Day after day, Jahar listened to each juror as they were brought in. He sat back in his chair observing one juror. This one talked about Tsarnaev being on the front cover of *Rolling Stone* magazine. Reporter Sweet from *Boston Herald* tweeted Juror no. 59's reaction, *"I thought it was wrong."* The juror giggled.

The mention of the magazine came back to haunt Jahar. It brought him back to the days when he was a laid-back stoner. His lawyers showed him the magazine cover and he was never thrilled about it. He never wanted attention brought upon himself.

Juror 59 said, *"I already feel that he is guilty and be given the death penalty,"*– Valencia. A few jurors being screened were found to be biased against radical Muslims. It was difficult for them to be impartial. As these jurors left, Jahar turned away and he ceased to show any interest. They revealed their prejudices against him.

As other jurors were brought in again, Jahar's demeanor turned dark, *"He is guilty. His demeanor has darkened. He slumped in his chair and leaning on his left hand,"*– Sweet. "Guilty," said Juror no. 60 after seeing Jahar found bloodied and hiding in the boat. This juror watched the boat scene and was unsure about putting aside his opinion. "He should have been shot in the boat," declared the juror. Jahar stared down at the legal pad without writing a word. The juror said, "I don't think I can presume him to be innocent." Jahar twirled his curly hair and rubbed his forehead.

Juror no. 65 thought Tsarnaev was also guilty, *"I think I feel very strongly, I don't know if I could change my mind,"*– Palumbo. Armstrong tweeted that Jahar was leafing through the contents of a manila file folder. Some papers had photos on them. He flipped through them and put them back or studied them more closely. He slouched in his chair, rested his left hand, while looking at the papers. Perhaps he was reading the jurors' questionnaires.

However, he stopped reading to look down the table. Questions continued about his guilt and the death penalty. When it was time for a break, he leaped out of his seat and was escorted out of the courtroom.

After the break, another juror said, "We shouldn't have to do this."

"No one," said Judy, *"wants you to feel like you have to give a correct response,"*– tweeted Kevin Cullen from the *Boston Globe*. Jahar played with the pen in his hands. He hardly looked at the juror. "It's a sad thing…this trial," uttered the juror. Jahar rolled the pen between his fingers, but it dropped on the table with a loud noise. Miriam glanced at him. One day, Jahar picked up his pen and was twirling it around. Miriam placed her hand on his to stop his antics.

Jahar seemed depressed. Later, observed by Palumbo - *"he twirled around a block of post–it–notes, flipped them around in his hands.*

He picked up his pen again and started doodling on the pad as these questionings dragged on forever." Jahar became sick and had the sniffles and cough, so he could not focus on the proceedings. He blew his nose and threw the used tissues onto the counsel table as observed by reporter Sweet.

Throughout the screening Judge O'Toole asked the juror, *"Can you sentence someone to death?"* – Armstrong or from Valencia, *"Can you impose the death penalty on another human being?"* One juror was leaning toward death but had to see the evidence. "The government must prove guilt," said the Judge, "once you hear the story, there could be a change." The juror was insistent, and said, "I believe in an eye for an eye." Jahar was clutching onto his Dixie cup in his hands. However, the juror continued to say, "I could be swayed one way or the other."

The lawyers asked, "Could you impose sentence, life or death?"

"Yes," said the juror.

Jahar dropped the paper cup loudly. It had slipped from his hands. All heads turned to the table and stared at him. Jahar glanced shyly away. *Oops.* There goes another day of voir dire.

A TIME TOGETHER

It was an intimate moment of observation in a high-profile case. In courtroom 9 Jahar thumbed through a pile of folders and papers. He studied some of them closely. He sat in his usual seat in between attorneys Judy Clarke and Miriam Conrad. Also present in the room were the jury consultant, and the other Defense lawyers, David Bruck, William Fick and Timothy Watkins. It was one morning before the prospective jurors were all brought in.

Judy requested to have her glass of water filled. Jahar reached for the water pitcher and poured water into her glass. They were chatting lightly together. Jahar loved to chat, laugh and smile with his lawyers in the morning.

Jim Armstrong@JimArmstrongWBZ
#Tsarnaev is laughing, smiling, and chatting
with his attorneys as we wait....

It was a time he felt most comfortable. Miriam would place her hand on Jahar's shoulder or behind his back when they talked. They shared a laugh as they reviewed contents inside a big legal folder. *"...he seems to be most comfortable with her."*– Palumbo.

Gail Waterhouse@gailwaterhouse
#Tsarnaev appears to be more comfortable than
last week, speaking casually with lawyer, given
own pen & pad of paper to take notes.

It had been nearly three weeks since Jahar had stepped out of solitary confinement. Observed by Cullen he tweeted, *"Outside of his cell for half of the day his physical appearance is normal."* He could stand up and sit down easily.

Before the interviews, Jahar was unsteady when he stood up at the table because in his cell his movements were very restricted, and it had weakened his leg muscles.

The prosecutors entered the room and gathered at the left side of the conference table. They asked the Defense team to discuss with them how they would trade off during juror questioning. Judge O'Toole was running late in court, probably trying to check which jurors made the cut and who they could still interview. Both trial teams faced each other. It wasn't an awkward moment and they did not appear to be confrontational. Rather, they stared at one another and were joking with each other like school friends from law school. Lots of smiles and friendly rapport were exchanged. There would be plenty time for them to fight later during the trial. Both trial teams worked together over the paperwork, exchanging and sharing notes. Jahar slumped down in his chair casually. He appeared sullen. He hardly observed what was happening in the courtroom as the two trial teams talked strategy. He pulled a list from a file folder and began reading an official document. His left foot bounced as he stroked his beard.

One-hour delay into the session, lawyers from both sides were on their feet milling around in the courtroom. The Prosecutors were all on one side of the room laughing and talking about the Super Bowl, discussing Deflate-gate. The Defense, the dream team were huddling close together having an intimate conversation with their defendant. Miriam remained by Jahar's side. Death penalty lawyers David and Judy pressed close to Jahar. They were having a conference talk with him. They whispered into Jahar's good hearing right ear. Jahar listened. As he spoke, observed by Sweet, *"his long slender hands fluttered when he speaks."*

The teams received word that the interviewing session would begin soon. They returned to their seats. Jahar poured water into Miriam's glass. He was bored again. He slid back down in his own chair. Frustrated, he picked up a pen and drew on his own Dixie cup wrote reporter Sweet.

As Judge O'Toole and the new jurors appeared, Jahar showed no interest in them. Some jurors scrutinized Jahar, searching for a reaction from him as Judge O'Toole explained their role in his indeterminate execution. Jahar could not look at them but rested his head on his left injured hand.

SEEING GUILT AND SYMPATHY, DECIDING DEATH OR LIFE

Dzhokhar (Jahar) Tsarnaev was only nineteen-years-old when he allegedly blew up three Boston Marathon spectators with a homemade bomb as well as murdering a MIT cop. Jahar the accused murderer rarely regarded any jurors throughout the past three weeks of questionings. He sat back in his wooden chair and stared in other directions. Sometimes it was the ceiling. On the other hand, his lawyers always looked through intently at each juror, trying to decode their body language to determine if they were being honest in their feelings toward the defendant.

David Bruck suddenly asked a juror. *"When you came to court and saw Dzhokhar Tsarnaev, what did you think, what did you feel?"* – Armstrong.

"Objection!" exclaimed William Weinreb.

Judge O'Toole affirmed, "Sustained."

Defense lawyers began asking other jurors what they saw in the media that made them think Tsarnaev did it. *"What in media made you form an opinion?"*

"Everything," said one juror, *"the defendant killed four people."* – Cullen.

"I could sentence Tsarnaev to death," said Juror no. 83. *"I'm open to the facts. Obviously, he was involved in something,"* – Sweet. Juror 83 said the death penalty could be *"merciful, it takes away the burden of a person's soul,"* – Lawrence.

Another juror said Tsarnaev was guilty, based on the American media, but acknowledged that guilt or innocence had to be decided. After the trial teams interviewed 176 jurors, Jahar started sliding under the table. Judy gave him a playful slap on the leg observed reporter Sweet. One day, Judy asked an impartial juror. *"Would you give meaningful consideration in penalty phase that someone had a bad childhood?"* – Cullen.

"Object," said Weinreb again.

This juror thought the death penalty would be an "easy way out," but also thought life in prison would not be as bad as the death penalty, because it was not always "fair" that someone gets to live after killing someone.

Over thirteen days total of questioning jurors, Jahar sat silently at the table. *"His latest manner was playing with a pen,"* – Sweet. *"He combed his hair with a pen or fuzzing with his hair. Jahar slunk back in his chair, legs crossed as he began sketching on a pad rested on his knees."* He ignored a juror who was explaining to the lawyers about her view on death. She said she was torn on whether she could kill Tsarnaev. She said, "I have a teenage son. I can't help being a mother too."

Juror 224 felt the same way. As Jahar flipped a packed of post–it–notes, this juror could not put Tsarnaev to death. Jahar tossed the pad up and down with one hand. Miriam silently reached up and brought down his hand with the pad. The juror continued and said, *"His youth is one reason why I wouldn't want to put him to death. This kid is so young. I'm wondering if he made a huge mistake,"* – Waterhouse.

Jahar heard from one Christian juror who explained, *"I'm a Christian and believe life is a gift from God, and it's wrong to take that away from anybody,"* – Valencia. Jahar leaned on his arm and sat still. He had no reaction while listening to this Christian juror.

The juror continued to express her sympathy to the defendant, "I see the defendant is young. He could be under the influence of his older brother. I wouldn't vote for death." She said sadly, *"It saddens me that there is not even a chance of parole for him,"* – Valencia. It is too bad he must live his life with the decisions he made.

The Federal trial was postponed due to a huge major snow storm that blanketed the Boston region on February 1 and 2. Heavy snow, freezing rain and gusty winds, brought a great disruption to the city. The city closed down after two feet of snow had fallen. Jahar tried to stay warm in his small cell. He was fighting both a cold and a cough.

In his next appearance, Jahar shaved off his beard, leaving a bit of a goatee. When he appeared in the courtroom following the snow storm on February 4, he seemed so much younger than his twenty-one-years. The clean shave had restored his youthful appearance and brought a fresh softness to his features. *"Tsarnaev appears to have shaved the scruffy beard he had on his chin. Looked young before, looks younger now,"* – Bailey. His hair was neater, and he wore a dark-colored blazer and a button-down shirt. Jahar ran his finger over his clean shave. He acted like a college kid who woke up late for class. He slouched back in his chair and talked with his lawyers. He was energetic and alert. On the counsel table he saw Miriam's laptop and he suddenly felt an urge, a hungry desire to search on the internet, as observed by Laurel Sweet. Jahar's eyes *"hones in like a heat seeking missile"* when he caught sight of the Lunar New Year zodiac sheep on her laptop. The cartoon ram was taking a leap on the homepage of Google.

His Defense team had submitted a First Circuit Appeal Court to the Prosecutors, not the Judge to rule on Tsarnaev's bid to move the trial out of Boston. The court had interviewed more than a hundred jurors, and most of them believed Tsarnaev was guilty. Both teams of lawyers and Jahar worked, thumbing through paperwork. The day's session the lawyers would interview sixteen more potential jurors. Jahar clutched a tissue in his hand and quietly coughed into his suit jacket. He listened to his lawyers interviewing one juror who wore on her wrist a Boston Strong bracelet. "I live in Boston and this bracelet is everywhere," she said, observed by reporter Valencia. She would be open to the death penalty, "It would be an easy way out for terrorists who want to be martyrs. But, I don't know if that is the right punishment or not." Upon hearing her answer, Jahar glanced down from the table as she was talking.

Meanwhile that same day, the lawyers interviewed another young juror. Jahar was drawing circles on a pad with a pen. The pen was loosely dangling from his left hand. Jahar peered up from the drawing to glance at the young juror who was close to his age. His lawyer asked him about the death penalty. The juror said, *"It would be the way to go."* Jahar suddenly dropped his pen when he heard the remark. *"Tsarnaev sinks in his chair, flicks at his stubble, drums his fingers on the table. Another day, another vote cast for his demise,"* – Sweet. He was becoming more depressed.

Jahar thought and wished he was invisible. He was beginning to hide behind his lawyers and this was observed by reporter Armstrong. He tweeted, *"Tsarnaev continues to sit a foot or two back from the table, almost hiding himself from potential jurors, who can barely see him."* Jahar slumped in his chair and gazed up at the ceiling. Miriam whispered to him, "Sit up." Jahar sat up.

He acted busy and grabbed a binder on the table that contained juror questionnaires, observed by Bailey – *Miriam Conrad, one of Tsarnaev's attorneys – just whispered to him, and he sat up a bit and is now flipping through papers.* Perhaps he was thinking: *They are all saying 'guilty.'* The entire table waited to hear the one juror they were interviewing about her views regarding death. The juror said, "No one wants to be the person to put someone to death." Jahar gulped down a cup of water. "Capital punishment is not harsh enough. I think serving life in prison is harsher."

After a lunch break, Jahar seemed stressed after hearing over and over that jurors believed he was guilty and calling out his terrible fate as to whether he should live or die. He sat rocking the chair, by lifting the front legs of the chair and then letting the hind legs on the floor rock, *"rocking back and forth,"* observed by reporter Sweet. He did it often. One time he rocked back and forth, and Miriam shot him a glance. He stopped rocking.

He seemed badly damaged. Two years of solitary confinement may have dulled his senses and would account for his disconnection to the proceedings, his inability to react emotionally or his inability to view the jurors.[127]

As his lawyers interviewed a senior risk manager, he leaned his elbows on the table and was observed drawing on a piece of paper in front of him. Juror no. 333 seated in front tried to peek over at him. Juror no. 333 said, *"I feel pretty strong that he's guilty,"* – Valencia. Jahar threw his pen down and sank down in his chair. Defense hissed at the Prosecutors that she should be excluded. But the Prosecutors told her to continue. She then said, *"It's hard for me to imagine what evidence could be provided that could prove to me anything else. But, I could vote for a life sentence,"* – Valencia.

During another interview, a juror gave Jahar a bleak glimpse of his future life in prison. The juror said he could consider mitigating factors. He said he would rather have the death penalty than being stuck in a closet the rest of your life. Jahar's shoulders drooped. He seemed to be indifferent to with the thought of being stuck in a closet or having a lethal needle stuck in his arm.

Another juror walked in and sat down to be interviewed. The Judge and attorneys all listened to her as she spoke about her views, but Jahar again leaned back, out of her sight and looked away.

The Judge asked her directly, *"Could you vote for death? It's not a hypothetical, or an abstract question. It's a real one."* – Valencia.

The juror replied, *"If the evidence is there and you proved to me that's how it happened, yes, I would agree to the death penalty."* – Valencia.

Jared Pliner@JaredPliner
#Tsarnaev more eye-touching, looking at hand.
Judy Clarke usually glances over to see what
he's doing.

Jahar appeared detached and sullen. He rarely stared at the juror while sketching on a paper cup. The next day, Judy was by Jahar's side. She whispered in Jahar's ear as a new round of potential jurors walked in as observed by Bailey – *Judy Clarke is quite chatty with Tsarnaev today. Keeps whispering in his ear.* As they met each juror one–by–one, Judy kept on whispering into Jahar's ear. She was motherly and very kind to him by paying extra special attention to him as observed by reporter Palumbo. She told him to observe each juror. When he tensed up looking at them, she calmed him by placing her hand on his back.

One day, a juror said the death penalty was frequently discussed in Puerto Rico which had been plagued by violent crimes observed by Valencia. Jahar became agitated as the juror said the court needed to "send a message" by imposing a death conviction. Jahar feared death. He squirmed in his chair and looked over at one of his guards. *"He began messing with things on the table, it creates a ruckus. Judy saw his stressed. She returned her hand to his back to calm him,"* – Sweet. He settled down, feeling her gentle human touch and it comforted him.

One juror came in and got angry at Jahar, "I think the punishment should be death," he hissed. "So many lives were affected..." Judge O'Toole kicked the juror out of the room. It was high–pitched and intense, but Jahar kept his cool.

Juror no. 349 was in awe of being involved in this trial and recognizing Judy Clarke, a renowned death penalty lawyer who did big trials and defended infamous murderers like the Unabomber, Ted Kaczynski. This juror wanted to maintain his/her anonymity. Judy displayed her fondness for Jahar by showing the juror how much she loved her job defending people like him. Reporter Sweet observed Judy placing her hand on Jahar's back and giving him an *"affectionate squeeze."*

Jahar was always pleasant and cordial before the jurors entered the room for interviewing. He was like the water boy, keeping each member of his Defense team hydrated by pouring water and filling up their glasses. One time, observed by Sweet, *"he accidently fumbled while pouring a glass of water into a cup and the water spilled all over onto the console table. He even drenched his own dark suit."* He is human and can make mistakes.

Throughout the rest of the voir dire process, Jahar acted busy rummaging through papers in a folder or he focused on reading stacks of trial team documents. One time, he could not read and had a tear in his left injured eye. He wiped the tear away and rubbed his eye. He was forced to bring the paper close to his face. Maybe his left eye was getting blurry. At one point he amused himself by trying on Miriam's glasses to check out if he could see better with it!

The day wore on, and into the late afternoon the interviewing grew weary. One juror had to think hard if she could consider the death penalty. She had a hard time voting for it.

William Weinreb asked her, "Can you say, '*I vote for death?*'"

After a long pause, Jahar who was hiding behind Judy and out of sight sat forward. He peered down the table at her for several seconds. The juror said, "I find it extraordinary difficult to be the agent of that sentence of death." The lawyers cast an eye over at this thoughtful woman who struggled with such burdensome decision. She finally said, "I just think of myself as a person of peace."

In over 21 days the court heard 256 jurors. The voir dire was coming to an end. The Federal court had selected a pool of 70 qualified jurors. Lawyers would cut that down to 18.

On the second last day of the voir dire, Miriam Conrad conferred with Jahar on the next step of the process. When he left the courtroom, it was unclear if his lawyers would ever have him testify. It appeared there was something on his mind as he exited the courtroom. He stopped and tapped his hand on the witness box. After that, he was handcuffed again outside the room.

DZHOKHAR'S VISIBLE WOUNDS

Regarding Mr. Tsarnaev at the trial, he was described as a physically small and slight man. His injuries were noticeable. His left cheek was quite swollen. There was a scar down the back of his neck and down behind the left ear. The base of his skull and bones in his jaw and neck were shattered by bullets. His left eye was a little shut towards the corner. Mr. Tsarnaev could be seen flexing or rubbing his left hand where he was shot five times. There was a scar or raised bump on the top of his left wrist. He also had a broken arm. There was no rehab for him to regain his mobility and strength. This was why he was seen rubbing his hands often.

OBSERVING DZHOKHAR TSARNAEV

Artist Art Lien drew a couple pictures of Tsarnaev during the jury interviews. Check him out doodling and him chatting with his attorney Miriam.

View drawings: (http://courtartist.com/2015/01/observing-dzhokhar-tsarnaev.html)

During jury process, Mr. Tsarnaev sometimes leaned forward and buried his face in paperwork, or as one reporter commented, *"He is like a young man reading a book on a long train trip, oblivious to the scenery outside his window,"* from reporter Laurel J. Sweet.

Dzhokhar Tsarnaev's Trial

*Dzhokhar Tsarnaev's trial will revive memories of how those bombs
killed three people, blew the legs off 16 others and wounded 260 more.*
– "Boston is Eager to begin Marathon Bombing Trial, and to End It."
– By Katherine Q. Seelye, January 1, 2015

THE GOVERNMENT'S HEART HARDENED and for the third time, Judge O'Toole denied three requests from Defense for a change of venue. He remarked that "the process of interviewing prospective jurors in person...is proving successful," for the Boston Marathon bombing trial. Opening Statements for Dzhokhar Tsarnaev's trial will begin March 4, 2015.

On March 2, Judge George O'Toole gathered the attorneys together to discuss last minute issues before the Opening trial scheduled for March 4, 2015. Jahar walked confidently into the courtroom. He was very well dressed. He wore a sharp black suit and a burgundy striped dress shirt with open collar. Jahar had shaved but maintained a trimmed goatee.

Jahar nodded his head to Miriam. He sat down between his attorneys and immediately began talking and smiling with them with one arm draped behind him on the chair. Miriam talked with Jahar and he smiled happily. He seemed very amused with what she was saying.

When Judge O'Toole arrived, Jahar nearly hesitated to stand with his legal team when they were introduced. He was confused whether to sit or stand, so he did an awkward half–stand, but then he just stayed seated.

Judge O'Toole said, "There's a lot to address before opening statements. First issue is to hear the government's motion for exclusion of mitigating evidence in the guilt phase."

Both teams presented their arguments. The government did not want Defense to focus on the guilt phase involving Tamerlan, but rather to stay focused on Mr. Dzhokhar Tsarnaev's crimes. Defense argued that the Boston bombing wouldn't have occurred had it not been for Tamerlan who lead and negatively influence Dzhokhar.

Jahar sat still and emotionless, listening to his attorneys present their case against his brother. "We're allowed to prove that the defendant, a teenager, only 19 was greatly influenced by his older brother. The younger brother allegedly participated due to the domination by, love for, adoration for, submission to the older brother," Bruck explained from reporter Valencia. [128]

Judge O'Toole responded, "I would reserve the right to rule on this motion at a later date. Now, on some Defense issues which includes the writing on the boat."

Defense Attorney William Fick spoke: "The Government wants to bring panels from the boat into court as evidence. The cutouts could be prejudicial if they took it back and look at it for deliberations, it's divorced from context," – Palumbo.

Fick suggested bringing the boat to the courthouse and letting the jury view the boat in its entirety. "The evidence here really is the boat. It is powerful. The boat should be viewed as the boat. It's really quite striking, you can imagine Mr. Tsarnaev lying in the boat as one might lie in a crypt," – Armstrong.

"It's not really practical to involve the whole boat," objected Weinreb, "The boat is too big to haul in here. There are many photos of the boat. We have a heavy burden in this case to prove this defendant is guilty and that writing is an important part of that. Besides, the boat is covered with dried blood," – Kelly Tuthill from *WCVB*. "We don't want jurors climbing into the boat to read messages full of dried blood, broken glass and the message is hard to read. It's fair to say what the Defense really wants is for the jury to see a boat riddled with bullets to create sympathy for the defendant."

Judge O'Toole reserved his decision. "Maybe jurors can see the whole boat and cut out writings. I reserve my judgment. Perhaps I may want to visit this boat myself first before deciding."

There were other matters that were brought up during the meeting. The Defense listed it: the rumored video. David Bruck claimed, *"The video of Mr. Tsarnaev placing a bomb–filled backpack near little Martin Richard does not exist,"*– Sweet.

Lastly, the other concern was the autopsy photos of bombing victims. Miriam Conrad spoke up, "We want to keep autopsy photos of bombing victims out of evidence." From Tuthill – *"the photos are graphic and horrific."* How much should be shown? Government was sensitive about this and had taken steps to block out certain areas in the autopsy photos, only intending to show the jury what was important. They had respectively warned each victims' families about the photos. They would only be shown to the jury, the witness and the legal team. The defendant and victims' families would not be allowed to view them.[129]

At the end of the hearing, according to reporter Holly Bailey, Jahar looked worried, *"Judy Clarke gave him a supportive rub on his back. Beyond the doorway, Jahar could hear the jangle of chains and handcuffs call for him."* Laurel Sweet wrote Jahar appeared *"troubled and lost after today's hearing."*

JURY SELECTION FINAL – March 3, 2015

A court officer told the U.S. Marshals that they may bring, "Mr. Tsarnaev." Jahar entered the courtroom with Judy Clarke. He was well protected and guarded by a tight security team of seven agents, and two uniformed guards. *"Jahar stepped out; his hand smoothed down the front of his light collar shirt, paired with a brown tweed jacket and tan pants,"*– Sweet. Armstrong picked up the greeting: *"His legal team asked, "How are you?"*

Jahar answered, "Good, how are you?"

JAHAR THE LONE BOSTON BOMBER #2

The trial was expected to last until the summer arrived. Jahar's heart raced nervously. He found it hard to believe that the trial was beginning to happen. It seemed like yesterday he was in this same room for his arraignment. He remembered how frightened he was to meet a room packed with people and the media. After all these months, it was finally down to this. Jahar was more nervous than ever to face a room filled with the surviving victims. He tried to imagine it filled with people. He craned his neck and scanned around the room everywhere, everywhere except the reporters sat. Jahar turned away and felt uncomfortable seeing the media which sat in the five rows behind him, and in the overflow rooms. He just could not look at them. (This is true.)

Miriam noticed his fear and took him aside and talked with Jahar, sometimes smiling at him. He listened and spoke with her. It was a deep conversation, not serious though. Next, it was Judy and David's turn as they both conferred with Jahar. Judy showed him a sheet of paper and he listened to her explain the peremptory challenges.

Finally, sixty-four jurors made their way into the courtroom. Jahar's foot shook nervously as they all piled in. He checked out the jury. They all looked terrified, hoping they would not get picked to spend the next couple of months living and thinking about the trial. Jahar stood up and took a long sip of water as jurors continued to enter. Some jurors were too afraid to look at Jahar. When they all sat down in their seats, Judge O'Toole explained to the potential jurors how the process worked.

A prosecutor handed a form to Miriam and she reviewed the government's list of preemptory challenges. Jahar joined his team's discussion as the juror forms were passed back and forth. He read the list. Armstrong observed Jahar, *"sometimes he smiled, shrugged or pointed to his attorney who he wanted."* He held a yellow legal pad and wrote or drew with his right hand on his legal pad. Some jurors wanted to see what was happening, others stared at the floor.

Each trial team wrote down on a form the jurors they want excluded, using their preemptory challenges. Judy talked with prosecutors during this uninterrupted process of jury selection. Prospective jurors waited patiently as attorneys discussed who should or should not be chosen to ultimately decide the fate of Jahar. Prosecutors were smiling and seemed thrilled at the ones selected, but the Defense team, not so much.

Soon Judge O'Toole interrupted the process and asked to see lawyers at the bench, to check on the progress they were making in their juror selection. Later, they went back to their teams to work it more. More paper shuffling. Jahar sat silently, head down. Feeling the tension mounting, he drew on his legal pad.

Several jurors appeared stressed, sitting and wondering if they'll have to decide whether Jahar lives or dies. The Prosecutors and Defense teams were done with the list of the final jury selection.

Now, the Judge called out the selected jurors by number to the jury box. The chosen jurors didn't seem very happy. Jahar saw them closely for the first time. All eighteen jurors, mostly white and older were death qualified jurors and wanted to impose the death penalty. Only a couple jurors were slightly younger. There were ten women and eight men in the jury.[130]

THE TRIAL BEGINS – Day 1, March 4, 2015

Opening Statements began at 9:00 on a Wednesday morning on March 4, 2015. A bus filled with survivors arrived at the courthouse. The survivors attending the first day included Marc Fucarile and Heather Abbott who both lost limbs. Bill and Denise Richard, the parents of Martin Richard also attended. Other survivors included Officer Dic Donahue, Carolos Arredondo and his wife. Along with them came Liz Norden, the mother of two sons who each had lost a leg arrived in court. A Watertown police chief arrived as well.

In the John Joseph Moakley courthouse, there was a long line waiting to enter courtroom 9 for the start of trial. Two media overflow rooms fed live video from the courtroom. The courtroom and overflow rooms were packed with various journalists, some local and many from abroad. Main prosecutors William Weinreb, Aloke Chakravarty and Nadine Pellegrini set up a huge poster board display for the opening. The Defense team, Judy Clarke, David Bruck and Miriam Conrad quietly talked.

Court clerk Paul Lyness announced, "Counsel!" The room suddenly became silent.

Both Prosecutors and Defense took their seats. A Court officer announced, "The defendant, Dzhokhar Tsarnaev."

Jahar behind the closed court door held his breath as the U.S. Marshals opened the door to the courtroom. *"Dzhokhar Tsarnaev walked into the courtroom like he was walking onto a yacht. His standard uniform for trial: dark suit jacket, open collar,"* – Cullen. He kept his head down and strode out. The U.S. Marshals escorted him to the Defense table. He sat down between Miriam and Judy. He talked with Judy. Jahar smiled at Judy who patted him on the back. Miriam leaned over, chatted with him and touched his shoulder.

Many survivors and families sat in the gallery section behind Jahar. Some were staring at Jahar's back, others turned away from him. This was the first time the survivors laid eyes on Jahar. Unfortunately, no one from Jahar's family sat in court that day. Jahar stared forward, never looking back towards the gallery and at the survivors. Instead, he smoothed the back of his dark, long wild hair nervously.

Judge George O'Toole took the bench. First, his eyes scanned the entire packed courtroom. He raised his eyebrows in surprise. He had the legal teams meet him for immediate sidebar. An associate of the team sat next to Jahar. The Judge ruled on mitigation. The guilt and innocence phase of trial would allow evidence in Jahar's role, but not whether he was more or less culpable than his older brother.

The legal teams returned to their tables. "All rise for jury," the Court officer announced. Everyone, including Jahar, stood as the jurors entered. Jahar with a straight face looked up and down at the floor as they entered. A couple of the jurors stared right at him immediately. They ignored the crowd in the courtroom. Jahar tapped the top of the table with his fingers.

The legal teams stood up and were introduced. Only Jahar stayed seated. Judge O'Toole first announced that he denied the Defense's fourth change of venue motion. He greeted the jurors and asked if they avoided media reports. After that they were sworn in. They rose and raised their right hand. Clerk Lyness delivered them the oath of service.

Judge said, "The trial is officially under way," tweeted Bailey. Jahar stared down at the table. "As you know, this is a criminal prosecution." He explained to jurors about 'aiding and abetting.' He reviewed the indictment, including weapons of mass destruction, the killing and maiming of spectators, and killing of a MIT police officer. The Judge named the fatal victims.

The Judge said, "You should not question of punishment during the first stage of guilt of the trial. Defendant is innocent until proven guilty." The Judge concluded these words, tweeted by Patricia Wen from *Boston Globe*, *"The openings themselves are not part of the evidence. It is like the picture outside the jigsaw puzzle box. Jurors decide if they filled in each piece of the picture."*

Prosecutor William Weinreb stepped up and delivered his opening statement. Jahar watched and listened. Weinreb's statement was tweeted by Kevin Cullen from the *Boston Globe* and from other reporters as I have indicated.

GOVERNMENT'S OPENING STATEMENT

"Two years ago, Dzhokhar Tsarnaev, arrived at the Boston Marathon. It was a public event to enjoy watching international runner race and complete the marathon race to the finish line. Mr. Tsarnaev had a backpack and inside it was a homemade pressure cooker bomb. The defendant and his older brother, Tamerlan, walked around looking for places to put each of their backpacks with bombs. The defendant rounded the corner on Gloucester and moved toward the finish line. He had a backpack over his shoulder with a bomb. A bomb favored by terrorists. It is filled with thousands of pieces of tiny shrapnel to shred flesh, shatter bone, set people on fire and cause death. The defendant chose to put his backpack near a restaurant and a row of children including Martin Richard." –Cullen.

Denise Richard, the mother of Martin sat in the gallery listening to Weinreb's Opening. *"She stared at Jahar with a painful expression,"* – Sweet. Tsarnaev's security team maintained a low profile beside Jahar, surrounding and protecting him. Weinreb continued:

"He pretended to be a spectator, but he had 'murder in his heart'" – Armstrong. *"He stood there for four minutes watching before the bombs went off..."*

Weinreb gave a dramatic opening to the case, describing how the deadly bombs shredded peoples flesh and killed them. It was horrible to hear and to imagine that a beautiful day had been turned into a chaotic bloody war zone. People were maimed and had lost their foot or legs. Many lives fled in terror, others were destroyed. Weinreb talked how people *"sprang into action"* to help the injured, but Mr. Tsarnaev was caught on surveillance footage.

"He drove to Whole Foods in Central Square. After going to Whole Foods, he shopped for milk, even started to buy one, and then trading it for another type of milk. All caught on video. He believed he was a solider in a holy war against Americans and had won by killing those three spectators. Jury will see his own writing that he wanted to be a martyr. He left that note on the boat where he was captured. He believed U.S. government is the enemy of Muslim people" – Cullen.

Jahar sat and listened to his story and how his criminal act was all caught on video. He wasn't prepared to see what the government had compiled against him. Weinreb talked about how the Tsarnaev brothers went on killing and bombing cops in Watertown. Lastly, the opening statement ended when Mr. Tsarnaev was found bleeding and dying inside a boat stored away on Mr. Henneberry's property. He told the jurors he wrote a message in pencil on the inside of boat and that he had bombed the Marathon to punish America for killing Muslims. Mr. Tsarnaev killed his brother and Collier.

"He was killed by multiple shots to the brain. Campbell was killed from burned injuries and gaping wounds that drained virtually all blood. Martin's ribs were exposed, a hole blown through him with virtually no blood left. He died at the scene of his wounds. He did it because he thought it would help secure him a place in paradise. Mr. Tsarnaev is responsible because America needed to be punished for killing Muslims overseas..." – Cullen. End of prosecution.

...spoke Weinreb boldly, ending his remarks with this horrifying description of death and murder on Boylston Street.

It was a huge punch in the face. William Weinreb's opening blew the capsule off in the courtroom. Anger and revenge were settling in people's hearts for this senseless crime. There was heartache and sadness connected to the losses. Dzhokhar Tsarnaev, a heartless monster with no apparent remorse sat and listened to the prosecutor's opening and he could feel all his victims breathing fury down his back.

Next, Judy Clarke, defending Mr. Tsarnaev walked up front and spoke softly, opening her remarks with words of empathy for the victims. The following Defense statement was extracted from a court document.

DEFENSE'S OPENING STATEMENT

"We meet in the most tragic of circumstances, and horrific deaths, including the loss of 'precious' 8- year–old whose smile captured all of our hearts. And a very fine police officer whose lifelong dream was to protect and service. They committed the acts in April 2013 that led to the death and destruction, and they are inexcusable and for which Dzhokhar must be responsible.

For the next several weeks, we're all going to come face to face with unbearable grief, loss, and pain caused by a series of senseless, horribly misguided acts carried out by two brothers: 26-year–old Tamerlan Tsarnaev and his younger brother, 19-year–old Dzhokhar..."

"On Marathon Monday, Tamerlan Tsarnaev walked down Boylston Street with a backpack on his back, carrying a pressure cooker bomb, and put it down in front of the Marathon Sports near the finish line of the marathon..."

"If the only question was whether or not that was Dzhokhar Tsarnaev in the video that you will see walking down Boylston Street, or if that was Dzhokhar Tsarnaev who dropped the backpack on the ground, or if that was Dzhokhar Tsarnaev in the boat – captured in the boat, it would be very easy for you: It was him. Dzhokhar Tsarnaev walked down Boylston

Street with a backpack on his back carrying a pressure cooker bomb and placed it next to a tree in front of the Forum."

"You probably say, why a trial? He came to his role from a very different path than that suggested by the prosecution. A path suggested by his brother, paved by his brother. Unfortunately, and tragically, Dzhokhar was drawn into his brother's passion and plan – and that led him to Boylston Street... We will not sidestep Tsarnaev's role in this tragedy. But we have a different view of what happened.

What took Dzhokhar Tsarnaev from this, to this?"

Judy held up and showed two photos of defendant, one a wholesome teenager with his brother, to a killer walking side-by-side at Marathon 2013.

Judy held up a picture of eleven-year-old Dzhokhar beside Tamerlan. Tamerlan, age eighteen, had his arm around Dzhokhar.

Dzhokhar must be held responsible, but this was a path laid by his brother that led him to Boylston Street. We won't step side his responsibility for his actions. Dzhokhar must be held responsible. Writing in the boat reflect what defendant had read and heard but thinks that it needs to be read in larger context. He expressed he was jealous of his brother who achieved martyrdom and wished he could too. We ask you to carefully evaluate the testimony about writings, where they came from and how deeply rooted they may or may not be.

We the Defense attorneys conceding the first phase of the trial, finding guilt, but asking jurors to hold open their minds for second phase. None of you would be sitting here today had you not told us that you can remain open through this phase. Could you not keep an open mind?"

She asked the jurors,

"We will continue to hear from police, victims and more, and listen with heavy hearts. It's going to be a lot to keep your hearts and minds open, but that's what we ask. Tamerlan had a special kind of influence, a sheer force of personality. Dzhokhar, our defendant was drawn into his brother's passion and plan."

Judy finished her remarks and returned to her seat. The conceding of Dzhokhar Tsarnaev's guilt, "IT WAS HIM" brought out early in the trial shocked the government and the court. It was unexpected. Judy was most courageous to admit that her defendant admitted guilt but did not plead it. They would use the penalty phase to paint a more sympathetic portrayal of their client's life.[131]

A Full Court transcript of Opening Statements is online.
See reference number 132: [132]
Prosecution's Opening
Defense's Opening

PROSECUTION/GOVERNMENT'S WITNESSES

Testifying against Tsarnaev

THE GUILT PHASE

Victims' Impact & Witnesses Testimonies

"You just heard about the devastation, the loss, and the unbearable grief, and we're going to see it, feel it, and agonize with every witness who comes to talk about what they saw, they felt, and they experienced and what happened to them and to those that they love."
— Judy Clarke, Dzhokhar Tsarnaev's attorney

JAHAR RETURNED TO THE courtroom after a break. The Defense team would not be cross-examining any witnesses since they conceded to the defendant's guilt. They would listen to each surviving victim share their story of what they saw, experienced and where they were when the bombs exploded. Jahar prepared himself to listen. As he sat back in his wooden chair, he undid his top collar button.

The stories from victims' impact statements were horrific and riveting, terrible and heartbreaking. Throughout these testimonies, Jahar gazed down at the table, twiddling his fingers. This was a trial where every action from the beginning of the Tsarnaev brothers placing the bombs to the end was recorded and would play out like a story on video. The jurors watched the video from 2:49 p.m. on April 15, 2013 of the first bomb going off...at that instant, the second blast. Smoke wafted the air and a crowd of frightened spectators, shocked by the explosion were running away.

There was total silence in the courtroom. Like everyone else in the courtroom, Jahar, the accused Bomber was silent, staring at a monitor on the Defense table that showed the explosions. The survivors sitting in the gallery were stricken with sadness when they viewed the video. *"All you heard was screams sirens and screams like that,"* – tweeted Cullen who voiced Shane O'Hara's testimony. O'Hara was manager of Marathon Sports. A store near the first bomb explosion.

After hearing emotional testimonies from a couple of witnesses, Jahar strode back into the courtroom, half-cocky and angry after a break. Reporters weren't sure of his strange walk and behavior. He sat down again between Judy and Miriam without a single glance at the victims.

"Court clerk Paul Lyness just placed a big fresh box of tissues on the witness stand for an emotional testimony coming up," – Lawrence. Jahar sat back in his chair and stared at something on Judy's laptop as the court waited for the next witness.

The 3rd WITNESS: COLTON KILGORE who lived in North Carolina at the time went to see Mona DiMartino, his mother-in-law, run in the 2013 Boston Marathon. He stood near the store Lens Crafters when the first bomb exploded. He was holding a video camera and recorded the chaos. *"There were bodies flying around and I couldn't hear through my left ear."* Cullen – *"I realized it was much worse, must have been a bomb."*– Wen. The video captured smoke, shrapnel and ball bearings on the ground... Including his sister-in-law, Gina, who had an artery severed on her leg with blood pouring out. She was screaming and crying. Colton moved his camera, now filming his nephew, a five-year-old boy named Noah. The boy had shrapnel wounds to his leg. Noah was crying loudly. Jahar stared at the screen in front of him so he could sense the devastation of the bombs and how it impacted the children. He watched the little boy screaming and crying.

Colton had set the camera down to capture the continuing chaos. The video recorded the wounded on the ground. The sidewalk was flooded with blood and littered with tiny metal objects. In the distance, someone tried desperately to pick a blond woman off the sidewalk, but she hung limp. "A First responder slipped on the blood of some victims lying calmly in shock, others were screaming. "We're on fire!" someone yelled. The camera panned up to Kilgore who was screaming and distraught.
"What do you have here?" Paramedic called out.

"His leg," he answered.

"She's mobile, get her out of here," – Cullen.

"When Colton walked you could hear crunch of glass and metal as he steps through the bomb scene,"– Whitehouse.

In the courtroom, a courtroom artist saw Jahar acting fidgety and drew him playing with his shirt collar.

The 4th WITNESS: REBEKAH DIMARTINO was from Houston, Texas. Rebekah had lost a part of her leg because of the explosion. She was the mother of Noah who was crying when the bomb exploded near them. Rebekah told the court that when the bomb went off, *"My first instinct as a mother was where in the world was my baby where was my son? My bones were lying next to me on the sidewalk. I felt that was the day I would die,"* – Cullen. Rebekah heard her son, "Mommy, mommy!" She glanced over to her right and saw a young woman beside her – dead. It was Krystle Campbell. Rebekah took a tissue from the box to wipe her tears. "I could see them mouthing 'We have an amputee.' He said, *"This is really bad, but we're going to help you. I knew that if I wasn't going to die, I was going to lose my legs,"* –Bailey.

Rebekah explained she was put in a medically induced coma for a week. She was a patient at the Boston Medical Center Hospital for 56 days and underwent 17 surgeries on her left leg. She was the 17th amputation among the marathon surviving victims.

Rebekah went on to say to the court, "I lied down on the pavement and said a prayer. I said, *"God, if this is it, take me, but let me know Noah is OK,"* – Jenna Russel of the *Globe*.

Rebekah shared a family photo before the bomb and it showed Tamerlan standing close to her. The photo was shown on the courtroom screen monitor. The image was blurry, but Tamerlan's black cap could be seen in the photo.

Martin Richard's father, Bill Richard, leaned forward to see the image on the screen monitor. His face was resting in his hand. Jahar continued to stare at the monitor in front of him.

5th WITNESS: SYDNEY CORCORAN was nineteen years old and from Lowell, Massachusetts when she attended the marathon. She lived in Lowell with her parents and brother. Sydney was a sophomore at Merrimack College and studied psychology. She went with her mom, Celeste and her father, Kevin. Her aunt was running. They all went to the finish line to track her aunt's progress with their cell phones. Sydney said, *"Everything went up in smoke…I immediately lost my family even though they were feet away. I felt half of my right foot was gone. I started to limp I couldn't put pressure on it I grabbed a rail passed out,"* – Wen. *"Then I was immediately surrounded by men putting massive pressure on my leg. A man put his forehead on mine. He could see my eyes going white I was getting increasingly cold. I knew I was dying. I had a femoral artery break. I was bleeding out,"* – Cullen.

Sydney fought back tears as she told her story. Her mom, Celeste looked on. *"How can this be real?"* Sydney thought. *"Seconds earlier, it was all good in life. I didn't know where mom and dad were or if they were alive,"* – Bailey. Jahar stared straight ahead, not even looking at Sydney fighting back tears. In a photo, she pointed out where she had been standing. After the explosion, she had landed one foot from where she had been standing. Bailey tweeted Sydney's fears, *"I thought I was an orphan."* David Boeri from *WBUR* tweeted *"I thought my parents had been violently ripped away from this world and I was all alone."*

Her father, Kevin, was with Sydney when she woke up in the hospital. She was told her mother, Celeste, was okay, but both of her legs were gone. Cullen tweeted Sydney's anguish, *"I said, 'I don't care. I just want my mom.' Mom came in. Mom was wheeled into my room. We cried and held hands."* They were happy to be alive. Sydney had 7 or 8 surgeries. She had a hole blown through the bottom of her foot that turned into a scar, tweeted Palumbo. The foot was missing bone and tendon. There used to be a BB that was stuck in her thigh, but she had it removed, observed by Cullen. As the Defense team listened intently to Sydney's testimony, their client, Jahar, stared at the table. A female juror in the jury pool appeared to be tearing up at this very emotional testimony. There were no questions from the Defense team.

6th WITNESS: KAREN RAND MCWATTERS. She was also a survivor and has a prosthetic left leg. She worked with Krystle Campbell who died in the bombing. They had been close friends for eight years. Karen and Krystle went to the marathon together. Karen's boyfriend, Kevin, was running that day. Karen spoke about that awful day, *"Krystle and I stopped because we happened to get a good spot. A girl walked by and took a picture of us. We said to her, 'We're really not tourists! We're from here!'* Krystle and Karen insisted. *"It seemed like a good spot to stay and take pictures,"* – Bailey. Karen showed the court the picture of them. They were smiling. Karen identified herself and Campbell in a crowd photo at the finish line before the bombs. *"We were close to the stands, under the flags, across the finish line,"* – Cullen.

Right after that the bomb exploded near them. Whitehouse tweeted, *"Karen tried to drag herself over to Krystle her hands were burned by hot pieces of metal."* She was in excruciating pain but tried to get close to Krystle anyway. They put their heads together to talk. Karen recalled, *"We held our hands together. Krystle said her legs hurt, then Krystle's hand went limp and she didn't say anything else,"* – Cullen.

In one photo - the government submitted, Karen identified herself and Krystle. Their mouths were open, screaming. *"We were screaming, 'Help us or we're gonna die!' but truthfully, I didn't really think we were going to die,"* – Whitehouse. The photo showed a pool of dark blood where Krystle's leg was. The paramedics tied belts on Karen's leg. Karen ended up with Krystle's cellphone. That's why everyone thought Krystle was in the hospital, and Karen's family thought she was missing.

It was an emotional day of testimony. Tsarnaev's lawyers did not cross–examine any of the surviving witnesses. At the end of the first day of the trial, Jahar seemed particularly upset about something. *"Judy and Miriam patted Jahar on the back. He does not chat with her,"* – Whitehouse. However, David Bruck, his other attorney, *"slipped him a note as he quickly walked out of courtroom with his security guard,"* – observed by Sweet. Not sure what the note said or why Jahar was upset. It was only the first day.

A bombing survivor, Rebekah DiMartino wrote an Open Letter to Dzhokhar right after her testimony. She wrote that for the past two years she was scared to face Dzhokhar, but when she testified at the witness stand she wasn't afraid of him anymore and called him a coward. DiMartino wrote that he was a "nobody" to her and "officially he has lost." Dzhokhar is *"a little boy who wouldn't even look me in the eyes to see that. Because you can't handle the fact that what you tried to destroy, you only made stronger."*[133]

Day 2– March 5, 2015

Attorney David Bruck greeted Jahar with a warm smile the next day. The two men have not been seen interacting with each other. At the start of the trial, Bruck brought up the issue of surviving victim impact testimony. He exclaimed, "The extremely moving poised and articulate testimony of yesterday's Tsarnaev victims. It was the talk of the courthouse today! Bring reasonable limit on number of victims who can testify," reported by Wen.

The government responded that the presentation of victims had not been excessive at all, or beyond reasonable standard. Reporter Wen tweeted, *"I think the testimony yesterday did not go out of bounds,"* the Judge ruled.

Bruck pushed back on the Judge's remark. Jahar sat back, rubbing the left side of his face that suffered nerve damage. Bruck argued, "This makes those at defense table feel like we're in a fishbowl." The Defense team moreover wanted to remove the camera in the overflow room; the one that was visually focused on Jahar's face and was transmitting a live feed of his reaction to the crowded overflow courtrooms, - Bailey. Judge O'Toole said, *"I'll take a look into it,"* tweeted Cullen.

JEFF BAUMAN, THE 8th WITNESS who lost both legs from the bomb that Tamerlan detonated sat 15 feet away from Jahar. Jahar locked eyes with Jeff Bauman, and then looked away. He was the survivor who reported to the FBI that he saw the bomber. Jeff carefully climbed up the witness stand on his two prosthetics.

Jeff began to tell his story about seeing the bomber, Tamerlan, who seemed suspicious. *"He said he saw a guy who was hanging around, not seeming to be part of the crowd. "He was carrying a bag, looked like school backpack."* - Wen. Jeff said Tamerlan stared him down, but a friend turned his attention back to the race. Shortly after, he noticed an unattended backpack. But, the man...He didn't see him anymore. Jeff continued, "I thought it was weird. It's Boston. I didn't think the backpack was a bomb. Then a few second later – an explosion. Flash! Bang! I thought it was a bad firework." He saw his own legs, complete carnage. "This is messed up." Jeff thought he was going to die. *"Then something changed. 'I kind of had this second wind. I saw people trying to help me. Heard one guy yelling... I saw a guy in a cowboy hat. He was keeping me calm. I had hope at that point,' He means Carlos Arredondo, who ran to his side,"* – Cullen. *"My right leg was pretty devastated. The left leg was where most of my blood was coming out."* – Wen.

Jeff underwent three surgeries. "I saw him. I know what happened and I wanted to tell authorities exactly what I knew. I had breathing tubes and couldn't speak. We worked an hour on it. I wrote and drew to FBI, and then I could speak. I gave them a description of the bomber, *"he was taller than me, 6'2 athletic build. He had a black hat pulled down real low. He had aviator shades with a backpack,"* – Cullen.

When Jeff saw the picture of the suspect on the news, he was still hospitalized. "I was like, that's the kid I saw, that's him!" Jeff talked about his injuries, had burns on his back, cuts and scars on his arm. Every member of the jury focused their attention on Jeff and was interested in his story, but, Jahar gazed straight ahead the whole time.

Judy and Miriam appeared to soothe Jahar from the pain he had caused Jeff. However, Jeff smiled and struggled to step down from the stand. For a second, Jeff and Jahar's eyes met. Jahar smiled back and then lowered his gaze. He slipped down in his chair. Jeff walked right past the defense table, but Jahar did not look at him. Jahar stretched his back as jurors left. He placed both hands in his pockets and stared down.

Jahar returned to court and sat at the Defense table alone. Jahar's security surrounded him immediately. As he walked to his seat, he clutched his left hand that had been shot. *"He seemed to struggle to figure out what to do with his hands, and where to look. So, he started to look through paperwork as Judy walked over to consult with prosecutors,"* – Bailey. An unknown member of the Defense team moved up and sat with Jahar so that he did not sit by himself unprotected. Judge O'Toole and the jurors entered the courtroom. Jahar was slow to rise because he was still staring at the paperwork. Miriam alerted him, slapped his right arm to get him to stand up quickly for the jury. BPD officer Lauren Woods, later, took the stand.

"I knew something was wrong," said the 13th WITNESS LAUREN WOODS, A BOSTON BPD OFFICER. She had known the Richard's family since 2006. She met Martin when he was a toddler on Denise's hip. When the bomb went off, Lauren ended up tending the injured Lingzi Lu. Woods testified, *"Lingzi had been vomiting profusely…tried to clear her airway…so she was getting breaths. I briefly saw that her lower torso had extensive injuries, specifically to her legs…people working on her lower half. Did CPR. Her whole body was shaking. She had vomit in her hair. Debris in her hair. Her eyes kept rolling in and out,"*– Cullen. Officer Woods told Lingzi, *"Lingzi, stay with us, you're doing ok, stay strong."*– Valencia. There was a firefighter that took over, utilizing a pump that pumped air into her. Lingzi, the Boston University student died on the sidewalk. Defense had no questions. Jahar sat back in his chair, staring off and having no reaction to the testimony.

After lunch, when the jury entered, Miriam had to tell Jahar to stand. Jahar looked around the room, almost confused as if in a daydream, then he stood up. He was having side effects, feeling nauseous from the drugs that had been given to him before the day's court hearing.

15th WITNESS OFFICER THOMAS BARRETT told his horrific story to the jury. Officer Barrett got a bystander to help him tie the stump of a man's leg (Marc Fucarile) with the strap of her purse. He heard sobbing nearby. It was a little boy. He was three, named Leo. Barrett carried the crying bleeding boy and waved down an ambulance. Court showed the Forum surveillance video of Dzhokhar at 2:49 p.m. At the sound of the first explosion, the crowd peered to their left. Barrett looked that way, too. At 2:50, the second bomb detonated. A puff of smoke ascended. People's legs were ripped off; another woman was holding her insides and Barrett realized he couldn't help her.

In the video, Barrett was seen running across Boylston to the wounded outside the Forum. Marc Fucarile was on the ground, his leg blown off and Barrett was tying a tourniquet. *Someone yelled. "There's a child here!"* – Bailey. Barrett carried Leo, bleeding from his head. Prosecutor Weinreb froze the image of Barrett running with the screaming, bleeding child on a monitor in front of Jahar so he could stare at it and get that image into his head. Jahar stared at the frozen image of the crying Leo without having any reaction to it.

"Richard walked deliberately to the stand. Jahar stole a quick glance. As Richard is sworn in, Jahar stared at the table. Miriam turned and looks at her client several times," – Bailey.

16th WITNESS WAS BILL RICHARD, the father of Martin Richard who was killed in the second bomb.

The Richard Family went to the marathon several times. Bill's kids, Henry (10 yrs.) and Martin (8 yrs.) ran in youth relay weekend before the marathon in 2013. It was Jane's (6 yrs.) first time. The family was late leaving the house that day. Denise, his wife tried to find spots, so the kids could stand on the barricades. *"We left the corner to get some ice cream. Instead of Emack and Bolio, they went to Newbury to Ben and Jerrys,"* – Whitehouse. Bill remembered what each child ordered. *"I can remember details of the flavors if you want them, or I can keep that for myself,"* he said sadly, tweeted Whitehouse.

"I'll let you have your memories," prosecutor Nadine Pellegrini said with a warm smile. "Ever see this man with white hat on?" Nadine asked Bill. She pointed to the picture of Jahar.

"Til today, not in person," Bill answered back. "Just unlucky that day," reported Bailey. They didn't know Dzhokhar was the bomber who passed right behind them in a white ball cap. Until now, Bill had never laid eyes on Jahar. He did now, blankly. Jahar stared straight ahead. Bill said sadly with a smile.

When the second bomb exploded, Bill said, *"I was blown into the street and I remember getting up orienting myself,"* –Boeri. He said he had seen his son, Martin, fatally injured on the ground. Denise knelt beside him. She was hovering over trying to help Martin

"Henry walked towards me and we embraced. Henry had his hands on his head in disbelief. My pants were torn apart, leg burned. It smelled like gunpowder, burned hair. Henry asked, "Is this really happening?" "Yes" Bill replied. "You have to help me find your sister." – Cullen. *"Henry pointed Jane out. I didn't know the extent of her injuries. I knew she was scared,"* – Armstrong. Jane had landed next to the mailbox by a tree. She tried to get up, but she fell. Bill noticed her leg and he picked her up. She didn't have a leg. It had been blown off. Bill searched to find medical attention for her. When Jane was being tended to, he went back to find Denise and Martin. He knew Martin wasn't going to make it. Cullen tweeted, *"I told Denise I was going to be with Jane."* Bill went in the ambulance with Jane. Denise agreed. She was crying. That was the last time Bill saw his son alive. Bailey tweeted, *"I saw a little boy who had his body severely damaged by an explosion and"* pauses, swallow, *"from what I saw, there was no chance."* Cullen tweeted, *"I had to get back to help Jane. I grabbed Henry and got in Jane's ambulance."*

Bill ended his testimony by saying Martin was only eight-years–old when he tragically died. The survivors in the courtroom were crying as Bill testified how he had lost his son and how he had almost lost his daughter. The jurors had tears in their eyes. The press box had tears in their eyes also.

Jane had her left leg amputated below the knee. Henry had some cuts and scrapes and suffered temporary hearing loss. Denise had to have emergency surgery on her eyes. She nearly lost vision in one eye. Bill suffered two perforated eardrums and experienced some hearing loss.

David Bruck stood up and regarded Bill afterward, "Thank you, Mr. Richard, we don't have any questions for you." Bill looked down. – Armstrong. Jahar sat in his chair did not look to the witness stand. Bill doesn't cast an eye at Jahar. But then, Jahar with his hand on chin, briefly glanced at Bill as he left the witness stand.

Day 3 – March 6, 2015

On the third day of emotional testimony, bombing survivor victims and their families were chatting in the courtroom waiting for testimony to begin.

Finally, *"Jahar appeared and gives a slight (half–hearted greeting) smile to his attorneys. He stopped in front of Miriam who smiles motherly, as she readjusts his shirt collar,"* – Armstrong. Or *"She welcomes him like a doting mom, adjusting his collar,"* – Sweet. Jahar sat, fixed his collar and, stroked his beard and rubbed his eyes. *"His lawyers were fussing over him almost motherly. He fumbled through papers while stroking his trimmed beard. Judy puts her hand on his shoulder,"* – Sweet.

The 18th WITNESS, DANLING ZHOU from China gave an emotional testimony in court. She was Lingzi Lu's friend, also from China, who came to study at Boston University. Dangling wept recalling how Lingzi had been injured in her leg and on her thighs. Lingzi was screaming in terror. Danling was holding her own intestines, trying to keep them in her stomach, reported Cullen. The court saw the pictures of Danling sitting dazed against the Forum fence after the explosions. *"Zhou looking at photos of Lingzi's reaction to 1st bomb. She pauses to wipe tears from eyes,"* – Valencia. In the photo, Lingzi was lying down, hands to her face and shaking in pain. On a rail behind her hung a shirt stained with blood. The photo visually showed smoke was still lingering in the air.

Jahar slumped to the side of his chair, peering slightly downward on the computer monitor inches in front of him showing a dying Lingzi with her hands over her face. There was silence and sadness in the courtroom as Danling tried to explain her injuries when she woke up. *"Zhou tears up again and struggles to speak as she tells of learning of Lu's death while in hospital,"* – Bailey. "I told them to find my friend. I had tubes and couldn't speak. I was greeted by a Chinese ambassador when I woke up. I wrote on a piece of paper to communicate. Eventually I was told Lingzi passed away. That's her." A photo of Lingzi holding a blue cup of tea was shown to the jury. "It was a regular day," she exclaimed.

During the morning break, many people hung around in the hallway outside the courtroom with red, teary eyes after two testimonies observed Bailey. Before court began, the Richard family sat, their eyes fixed on Jahar when he was escorted back in. They were upset to see that Mr. Tsarnaev had shown no remorse or emotion toward the victims. Defense team had switched the seating. Jahar now sat between Miriam and David. Judy walked over and whispered something to Jahar. Whatever Judy was saying she used her hands to make her point, observed Bailey. Both Judy and Miriam treated him motherly, and Jahar was smiling and chatting with David.

Dzhokhar, We Caught You On Video

"We referred to them as White Hat and Black Hat."
Imel: suspects were referred to as white hat and black hat...didn't
know who they were. – Anthony Imel

"I HAVE SEEN THE explosions well over 500 times. It's been an interesting case," said the 21st WITNESS ANTHONY IMEL, who worked with the FBI's forensic audio and visual unit in Quantico, VA. He eventually spotted the "black hat and white hat" suspects in the video. *"Imel testifies he put 'several video compilations' together of Tsarnaev from bombing day,"* – Bailey. He said it was interesting that Dzhokhar wore his cap backwards. He had made no effort to conceal his face while Tamerlan wore sunglasses.[134]

First picture: Bombers identified as "Black hat" and "White hat" walking with backpacks. Photo credit to AP Photo/Bob Leonard.
Photographer Bob Leonard took snapshots of the bombers while taking pictures of the runners near the finish line. Photo is from Associated Press. The second picture is the first surveillance video footage released from the FBI of the suspects.

In the courtroom, Jahar touched his face, and watched himself and his older brother on the monitor in front of him. Both brothers carried backpacks. Yellow tracks traced Dzhokhar's footsteps and Tamerlan's were tracked in orange. In the video, it showed *"Dzhokhar following Tamerlan: that is the essence of the defense,"* – Cullen.

They were walking outside the Whiskey Bar. They traveled south on Gloucester toward Boylston Street. Shortly after, Dzhokhar stopped at the Forum, and Tamerlan continued to the finish line.

Dzhokhar stood outside and watched as crowds of runners passed by. He slipped the backpack off his shoulder and placed it at his feet. The jurors fixed their eyes on the monitor screens watching Dzhokhar standing outside the Forum.

Dzhokhar placed the backpack with the bomb behind Martin Richard. *"Tsarnaev is now making a cell phone call. His left hand is at his left ear. He is presumably calling Tamerlan at this point."* – Wen. Imel testified that he had Tamerlan's and Dzhokhar's cell phone information; the accounts had been set up a day before the marathon.

The people in court viewed the video of a crowd shot from The Forum Restaurant. Spectators were cheering, talking, eating and people passed through the crowd. Dzhokhar was watching the runners. Children and adults were all happy and cheering. Such joy on everyone's faces as Dzhokhar lingered by a tree.

In the video, the Richard's family watched the race. Dzhokhar made a 19–second call to Tamerlan at 2:49 p.m. on April 15, 2013. He hung up and the first bomb went off. In shock, suddenly, everyone focused to the left where the first bomb exploded. Dzhokhar hurriedly departed and glanced back to where he stood. Seconds later, the video shows a HUGE fireball explosion outside the Forum. It was a blinding burst of fire!

Watch the Surveillance video shown at the Boston Marathon bombing trial. (Warning! The graphic scene of the explosion is @ 7:55 minutes.) See reference number 134.

(https://www.youtube.com/watch?v=HqaGJ50Cz7o)

Everyone in the court gasped. Jahar watched the video feed in front of him. He cracked his knuckles and rubbed his face. During lunch recess, he had no expression to what he saw. He looked to the ground and then was escorted from the courtroom.[135]

Throughout the day, the government brought out their witnesses against Tsarnaev.

24th WITNESS WAS CAITLIN HARPER. She worked at Whole Foods Market in Cambridge in Central Square the day of the bombings. Harper said the store has many surveillance cameras. Dzhokhar Tsarnaev went to that store to buy milk after the bombings; he later returned it.[136] (Perhaps his brother yelled at him that he got the wrong kind of milk or he realized himself he had bought the wrong type.)

In the video, Dzhokhar went into the store to pick up milk. He entered the store without his white cap on. He lifted the milk off the shelf and read the milk label. He casually walked through the aisles and goes to check–out, paying $3.49 for the milk at 3:14 p.m.

Here is video of Tsarnaev buying milk. See reference number 136. *(https://www.youtube.com/watch?v=gSJpYhlPuHI)*

He left the store at 3:15 p.m. He started to leave in his car, but suddenly ran back and returned to the dairy section to switch the milk for another. Dzhokhar walked out of the store as if he didn't have a care or worry in the world.

25th WITNESS, GREGORY HOMOL, director of the UMass-Dartmouth Fitness Center. Homol testified Dzhokhar swiped his gym card on April 16, the day after the bombing at 9:05 p.m. Video showed Azamat Tazhayakov walking with Jahar to the school gym, showing how Jahar acted totally normal the day after the bombings.[137]

Here is the video of Dzhokhar going to the gym. See reference number 137.

(https://www.youtube.com/watch?v=QmUkvZGvW2w)

27th WITNESS: FBI SPECIAL AGENT STEVE KIMBALL. Agent Kimball identified two social media accounts. The first account was Jahar's Twitter account – "*J_tsar.*" Kimball later found a second account belonging to Dzhokhar Tsarnaev under the name *al_firdausia*, which was his twitter account directed toward his Muslim beliefs. Kimball reported that Dzhokhar's avatar was the holy city of Mecca. *Ghuraba* was the screen name; it meant "stranger." In court, Jahar saw his tweets now staring him in the face. A few of the tweets that he saw included:

"Listen (a shaheed iA) the Hereafter Series, you will gain an unbelievable amount of knowledge."

"Dear Muslim brothers and sisters follow me for some Islamic insight."

On March 10, 2013, he tweeted, *"I want the highest levels of Jannah, I want to see Allah every single day for that is the best of pleasures."* The prosecutors picked these specific tweets to reflect that as a teen he had developed an extremist thinking already absorbed in Awlaki's lectures.

Kimball also reviewed selective *J_tsar* tweets for the jury. In 2012, *J_tsar* tweeted a menacing tweet like *"I shall die young"* (read in Cyrillic) which could reflect Dzhokhar's desire to die of martyrdom. On the day of the 2012 Marathon, a year before the doomed 2013 Marathon he tweeted, *"They will spend their money and they will regret it and then they will be defeated."* His *J_tsar* account had about 1,100 tweets.

Another tweet dated, April 15, 2013 at 5:04 p.m. said, *"Ain't no love in the heart of the city, stay safe people."* That was sent about five hours after the bombing. Some, not all Dzhokhar's tweets seemed dark. If we were only reading his tweets, but didn't know him in person, he seemed to have an extremist frame of thought. It's as though he was not the person everyone knew. At the end of the day, Jahar stood up slowly. He talked with one of his attorneys. Before he left, he stopped to rap the witness box with his hand.

Day 4 – March 10, 2015

Jahar entered court smiling with his attorney Judy Clarke. He seemed very much at ease and shared a laugh with Miriam Conrad. FBI Agent Steve Kimball retook the stand to be questioned by Defense Attorney Miriam Conrad about *J_tsar* account. Miriam asked Kimball, "How did you select 45 tweets you presented to jury?" His answer was that he had no part in the selecting process and that it was done by the prosecution team. Miriam began to discuss that some tweets came from American and Russian rap songs from artists Eminen and Lil Wayne. She asked him, "Did you know *"I shall die young"* is from a Russian rap song?" It sounded as though Agent Kimball had not investigated further the source of the tweets. *"Agent says his job was to study what he was given, not look deeper at meaning/links in the Twitter account,"* – Wen.

Miriam dismissed the tweets as being neither pro–jihadist or threatening. She showed jurors that Tsarnaev's tweets were typical of a 19–year–old who was into music like other kids his age. His tweets were sometimes funny, and he tweeted about girls, cars, homework, sleep and food. For instance, his post *"Come party at my house,"* on September 11th was a quote from a *Comedy Central show.*

Miriam asked Kimball, "You don't know what the slang phrase *"cooked"* means, referring to the *"LOL. Those people are cooked."* Tsarnaev was responding to someone else's tweet on the night of the bombings: *"MelloChamp and they what "god hates dead people?" Or victims of tragedies? Lol those people are cooked."*

Kimball fidgeted, and tried to guess. "I assume, like, crazy?"

"It means high," responded Miriam. Defense claimed the *"Those people are cooked"* tweet was a slam at the Westboro Baptist Church who were protesting the bombings or protesting the Marathon victims' funerals. Tsarnaev meant those people picketing were cooked, not the bombing victims. [138] [138a]

"Do you know who Key and Peele are?" *"Conrad trying to show that Tsarnaev was just a kid tweeting. FBI agent looks nervous and is fumbling on stand;"* from Bailey who observed *"Conrad was very, very sassy."*

"No," said the agent.

"Key and Peele are the lead performers of a *Comedy Central* sketch show," said Miriam. "Do you know what *"LOL"* means?"

"Laugh out loud," he answered correctly.

"You said the picture [that forms the background of the second twitter account] was a picture of Mecca," said Miriam, towards the end of a on the edge and lengthy cross–examination.

"Yes, to the best of my knowledge," answered Kimball.

"Did you bother to look at a picture of Mecca?" Miriam shouted back.

"No."

"Would it surprise you to learn that it is a picture of Grozny?" The picture on the account was not of Mecca – the FBI had misidentified it. It was in fact a picture of the Akhmad Kadyrov Mosque in Grozny in Chechnya.

This was an embarrassment for the FBI, as Miriam pried into their investigation into Tsarnaev's tweets. Kimball admitted that he did not know that several of the tweets the prosecution had chosen to show Tsarnaev's radicalization and violence were lyrics from pop songs such as the Lil Wayne song, *"The Block is Hot"* and the tweet, *"I shall die young,"* when read in Cyrillic.

In one last shot, Miriam asked, "Did you know where *"they will spend their money and they will regret it and then they will be defeated"* is from the Qur'an?"

"No." Kimball replied. Miriam said although it was tweeted on the day of 2012 Marathon, it conveyed no reference to the Boston Marathon. Government was only drawn by the date of the tweet.[139]

28th WITNESS WAS OFFICER TOM BROWN, a Boston police bomb technician. Officer Brown's task was to clear the scene of any explosives near the Watertown boat. There were six bomb technicians combing the area. Officer Brown noticed a note written inside the boat. Inside the hull of the boat was a message. It was written with a pencil and the message was splattered with bullet holes and blood. "Do you see the person?" asked the prosecutor.

Officer Brown pointed. "He's got a dark jacket on."

"You saw him bloodied?"

"Correct." – Cullen. He pointed to Jahar at the defendant's table.

"When Brown pointed at Tsarnaev he looked down. Miriam smiled at him," – Valencia. He wrote in pencil, between bullet holes and streaks of blood these words, "I'm jealous of my brother who... ha...ceived the reward of jannutal Firdaus (inshallah) before me (then next word is blocked out due to bullet hole...) I do not mourn because his soul is very much alive. God has a plan for us all...mine was to hide in this boat to shed some light on our actions. I ask Allah to make me a shahied to allow me to return to him and be among all the righteous people...in the highest levels of heaven...to bear witness that there is no God but Allah and that Muhammad is his messenger...US Government is killing our innocent civilians... We Muslims are one body, you hurt one you hurt us all...Now I don't like killing innocent people it is forbidden in Islam but due to said (hole) it is allowed. All credit goes (hole)"

Tsarnaev's attorney David Bruck crossed examined Officer Brown. Brown admitted he witnessed Mr. Tsarnaev being removed from the boat. The bullet holes appeared to come through from the outside to the inside of the boat. None of the bullet holes went out. Jahar did not have any weapons or any bombs on him when he was arrested.

Officer Brown said blood smears showed the writing was done before the blood stains set. Jahar appeared grave and somber as he recalled the spray of a hundred bullets firing into the boat at him. He was traumatized when he was shot in the neck, hand and legs. His proclamation – the note, pierced with bullet holes, and him nearly being killed brought back terrifying fear and sadness. He put his head into his arms and peered down observed reporter Wen.

The Backpacks, Cell Phones & The FBI Web Page

"Tsarnaev brothers hunt got 24 million hits in 24 hours."
– The FBI web page, FBI agent James Eppagrard

AFTER LUNCH, JAHAR CAME back into court. He appeared pale when he returned to his chair. At this moment, he drew closer to his attorney Judy Clarke, where she engaged with him in a lively conversation. *"Jahar had a usual low–key demeanor, tho' seemed part somber after testimony about boat writings,"* – Wen.

The Defense attorneys had heard from over 29 witnesses called by the Prosecution in four days. The trial would now be focusing on dry technical testimonies from FBI special agents who worked on the case and had collected 450 pieces of evidence from the bomb scenes. They were analyzing the evidence, seeing if they could piece the bombs together. A specialized FBI plane was used to take GPS–based pictures to dot the pieces of evidence collected at the crime scene. About 100 pieces of evidence were photographed and documented at the Forum scene.

Jahar sat still, looking bored as discussion about the evidence continued. He only took a glimpse at the screen showing graphics of the crime scene. Suddenly, after a couple of agents testified, the Prosecution wheeled in about fifteen boxes of evidence into the courtroom. It woke Jahar up and he sat up! He seemed very interested in the cartloads of evidence rolling past him. As it passed, Jahar eyed them curiously as Judy and Miriam leaned over to him and whispered…

Jahar watched as carts with multiple boxes passed him. Without delay, Judge O'Toole made a surprising announcement that there was no afternoon court. He told the jurors, "Your day is over." Judge dismissed the court before lunch and sent the jury home. He stressed that he and the lawyers had work to do. He planned to investigate the Watertown boat where Jahar had hid for eighteen hours on April 19, 2013. As the Judge exited, Jahar rushed out of his seat to leave the courtroom but took his seat again as evidence was taken out of the boxes. He watched until the guards came.

THE SHREDDED BACKPACK – Day 5 – March 11, 2015

A protester stood in front of the courthouse, and he wanted Dzhokhar Tsarnaev dead. His sign read: *"Death penalty for murder."* Jahar appeared in court the next day in a black suit and blue V-neck T-shirt. He smiled and chatted with his attorneys as he walked in. *"Jahar, only 21 years, looked increasingly thin and tired,"* – Sweet. Each day in court, he appeared depressed. He would rather have been hanging out, talking and laughing with friends and playing video games instead.

On the stand was the 34th WITNESS FBI AGENT SARAH DELAIR. 576 pieces of evidence were brought to court and were packed inside the boxes. Agent DeLair wore a pair of latex gloves. She opened a container to remove the shredded remains of a backpack. It was the one Jahar allegedly dropped behind Martin Richard. It was a black and white backpack, burst and torn almost beyond recognition. (Jahar's backpack was gray-white.) She held up a torn black fabric – part of the backpack, found in the middle of the street in front of the Forum. A brand label of the word "Fox" was identified from the shredded remnant recovered from Boylston Street.

View backpack:

(http://bostondefender.org/wp-content/uploads/2015/03/3090.pdf)

Agent DeLair ripped opened another evidence bag and the court could hear the crinkling noise of the bag opening when she removed the pressure cooker. *"Agent now opening up a bag and pulls out a large metal silver curled–up object and says part of pressure cooker,"*– Wen. She showed a picture to the jury that the pressure cooker – a size of a cereal bowl was found on Boylston Street in front of the Forum Restaurant.

Another evidence bag contained wires. This wire could be found in a car radio and was used in the bomb's detonating mechanism. Jahar settled back in his chair, lightly stroking his beard. She also removed from the sealed evidence bags: BB's encased in paper, shards of metal, a zipper, pieces of black material, small nails, and some duct tape.

"Judy Clarke wants her to go back at backpack, and so she puts rubber gloves back on," – Valencia. Judy asked about the shredded paper in the backpack. "Can you see there are pieces of paper in there? Was this submitted for fingerprinting?"– Bailey. The pieces of paper felt like Styrofoam type.

Agent DeLair answered, "I don't know."

"But the lab had it?" asked Judy.

"Correct," she answered. – Cullen.

Judy pointed to other evidence at one of the bomb scenes, including fragments of cardboard boxes. She called up a close–up photo of charred cardboard and duct tape beside what appeared to be a red flag. "It went to lab?" She asked.

"Yes," answered Agent DeLair.

"Found outside Marathon Sports?" asked Judy.

"Correct," the agent answered. – Cullen. Judy wanted to have the fingerprints on the evidence identified to discover who had packed the backpack.

View charred cardboard:
(http://bostondefender.org/wp-content/uploads/2015/03/3093.pdf)

THE CELL PHONES

Jahar stared at a monitor in front of him as 35th WITNESS FBI AGENT CHAD FITZGERALD, cell phone analyst testified about cell phone data he pulled up for the case. Jahar scratched his head with his pen as he listened to his technical lecture about how cell phone signals locate a cell tower when one makes a call.

Prosecutors have alleged the Tsarnaev brothers made a call on the phone before detonating the bombs and subsequently after the bombings. Jahar activated a pre-paid T-Mobile phone the day before the marathon attack, April 14, 2013 under the name "Jahar Tsarni." First call was made at 2:49 p.m. Tamerlan's phone placed a call to Jahar's phone at 2:51 p.m. At 2:53 p.m. Jahar's T-Mobile cell called Tamerlan's phone and they were both in the same cell phone zone, not far from Public Garden. At 3:14, Tamerlan made a call in Cambridge near Whole Foods. (This was while Jahar was in Whole Foods buying milk and later switching the milk. Tam probably did yell at Jahar and sent him back to buy the right milk.) There were more phone calls from Tamerlan in the Cambridge area on April 16. On April 17, Tamerlan's phone stayed in and around Boston all day. The day after the bombings, Jahar went to UMass–Dartmouth and used his cellphone around there. On April 18, on Thursday, records showed Jahar and Tamerlan phones being used in Cambridge.

THE FBI WEBSITE

36th WITNESS WAS FBI AGENT JAMES EPPARD in charge of public affairs. Agent James Eppard worked on the *fbi.gov* website. On Thursday, April 18, 2013, the FBI held a press conference at 5 p.m. to release the images online of the bombing suspects. Eppard declared the web page the FBI dedicated to the Tsarnaev brothers hunt received 12 million hits in 24 hours according to reporter Bailey. They designed poster size pictures of Dzhokhar and these were released by the FBI.

In court, Jahar saw a poster picture of himself featured on a monitor. He leaned forward in his seat, studying it in detail. Eppard said, *"He was still being sought, so additional posters were created to aid in his capture,"*– Cullen. As the FBI Wanted poster popped up on a screen in front of him, Jahar leaned way forward in his chair, putting his face right in front of TV screen and he saw himself, a wanted fugitive! Bailey tweeted, *"This might be 1st time Tsarnaev is seeing some of this stuff."* After the viewing, Jahar seemed lost and not well. He appeared pale. He sat back with Judy and Miriam. They talked with him. They asked him if he was okay because he appeared disoriented.

The Murder Of Officer Sean Collier

"I told him to be safe, and left. Never saw Collier alive again."
– John DiFava, chief of the MIT Police

MIT POLICE OFFICER DAVID SACCO, THE 38th WITNESS felt uncomfortable when he dispatched Sector 12 – Officer Sean Collier – to respond to banging noises in the area but didn't hear back from him. Sacco tried to contact the sergeant, "Based on that call, I dispatched sector 1-2, meaning Sean. We didn't get any response." MIT Officer Henniger told Officer Sacco through radio he would check on Collier. Suddenly, a radio transmission was sent, "Get me help here!" The court heard Henniger's cry, "Officer down! Officer down!" reported Cullen. By then, at 11:15 p.m. Collier had died of multiple gunshot wounds.

The courtroom was quiet after hearing his testimony. The jurors appeared fixated. However, Jahar looked stoic, head tilted and listening, reported Valencia.

39th WITNESS MIT POLICE SGT. CLARENCE HENNIGER saw Officer Collier had been shot in temple on the right side. "There was blood everywhere. I observed a wound to the head, the temple. I observed a wound to the neck. Blood all over the car, his body," said Henniger. Henniger checked for a pulse; it was weak. He shouted, "All units respond, officer down!" He screamed, "GET ON IT!" Officer Collier had been shot in the head, neck and hand. Later, Officer West responded to the scene. They both pulled Collier out from the car. *"It was hard to get his body out because his foot caught between gas and brake pedal. Once we had him out of the car, West said, "Hang in there..."* – Wen. They did CPR. Officer West said, "Hang in there." Sean was unconscious. 'Who did this to you?' Henniger asked, reported Cullen. No response. In the gallery, Collier's father was apparently upset as he listened to the details of his son's execution.

Collier's gun around his waist was tampered with and was covered in blood streaks. *"He pulls out a black holster & refers to it as having a "triple retention" feature. It has 3 ways of preventing anyone from grabbing gun,"* – Wen. The Tsarnaev brothers had tried to take his gun, but they were unsuccessful in their attempt to extract the weapon. Henniger explained that there was a release button that one needed to press. Prosecutor Weinreb brought Henniger the holster and Jahar shifted in his seat. He leaned forward interested in how this release worked. Jahar watched Henniger demonstrate with a fake firearm how to unlock the gun from Collier's holster.

A surveillance camera captured the shooting of the officer. It was on top of a 20+ story building on MIT campus. *Here is the MIT Surveillance video. See reference number 140.*

(https://www.youtube.com/watch?v=DPNwoxAiy1A)

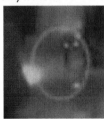

At 10:23 p.m. a yellow circle highlighted the two suspects as they walked towards Collier's cruiser. *"Two figures in shadow, walked near back of cruiser. "They were there for some time."* – Bailey. *"Close up of video shows an arm extend, muzzle flashes, and Sean's brake light flashes,"* – Cullen. It wasn't clear who shot the officer in the video. The blurry video showed a cyclist riding on a bike by the patrol car at night. The suspects quickly disappeared around the corner building where originated from. The cruiser's brake lights flickered, on and off. In court, Jahar was unable to sit still, watching the video of his crime play out right in front of him.[140]

Jahar peeked up and saw the next witness. The 42nd WITNESS WAS NATHAN HARMAN. Nathan was a MIT graduate student who was riding his bike past Sean Collier's cruiser during the murder. After 10 p.m. Nathan followed his usual route home.

Nathan's voice quavered nervously as he spoke *"That night, he noticed parked MIT cruiser. When I went by, the front door was open, and someone leaning into the driver's side door."* – Wen. Nathan saw a man *snapped up behind the driver's side door and looked startled.* – Wen. Straight away they saw each other.

"Did you get a good look at his face?" asked a prosecutor.

"He looked younger – I assumed MIT student. He was normal height. Thin." – Wen.

Nathan told the jurors that when he turned around he said the assailant's sweatshirt was dark, but he couldn't see more. He said he was a white male.

"Any facial feature?"

"I remember thinking he had a big nose. He looked startled."

"You see him in courtroom?"

"He's right there; he has a blue shirt on." – Cullen.

Nathan pointed to Jahar who sat up uncomfortably. It appeared that Jahar was leaning into the car trying to get Sean Collier's gun. Defense claimed Tamerlan had killed the cop. Nathan continued riding on his bike and laughed, *"I just startled him. I only saw one person, not a second person."* – Wen. Defense took note that Nathan only saw Dzhokhar because Tamerlan was squatting, reaching over to get Collier's gun out. *"Harmon remembers Tsarnaev in a knit cap, government shows picture of defendant with a white pageboy cap on head,"* – Bailey. Nathan was shown a photo of a person wearing a dark Adidas hoodie and a white brimmed hat. "Yes, that's the clothing I saw that night. Definitely could be that person," he said, reported Wen. Nathan's hands suddenly shook nervously as he held his coffee on the witness stand. He took a sip. Jahar sat less than 15 feet away from him. Defense did not cross–examine Nathan. He left without looking at Jahar.

Judge O'Toole called it a day. Judy lightly stroked Jahar's back, comforting him and easing his tension and surprise. It was an awkward encounter for Jahar seeing this witness again. As he left, Jahar gave his team a reassuring smile.

Day 6 – March 12, 2015

Every day since the first day of the trial the Bombing survivors and families have been in court. Jahar entered with the U.S. Marshals. He sat in his usual spot next to his attorney Judy and sometimes he talked with her. This day he seemed joyless. He wore a black suit and a denim dress shirt, though the collar was upturned. He paged through paperwork, talking with Judy. She whispered to him to fix his collar as he flipped the pages in the binder folder.

The next couple of witnesses were from the Massachusetts State Police force. The 43rd WITNESS WAS MASSACHUSETTS STATE POLICE TROOPER MICHAEL CASHMAN. He found the Tsarnaev's green Honda Civic abandoned in the middle of the road on Laurel Street in Watertown. He traced the Honda back to the same car that had driven off after leaving the murder scene at MIT. As the government brought up witness after witness, the court had heard enough about the senseless murder of Officer Collier. A medical examiner, 45th WITNESS, DOCTOR RENEE ROBINSON was getting ready to testify regarding Collier's autopsy. *"As Robinson takes the stand, Judy Clarke stands up and gently pushes down the monitor in front of Tsarnaev so that he can't see,"* any of the gruesome autopsy photos of Sean Collier. - (Bailey). Jahar listened as Robinson described Collier's gunshot wound to his head. His brain had been destroyed. "The barrel of the gun was close to the skin," she said, reported Bailey. She showed the pictures to the jurors only. One of the jurors stared at the photos and broke into tears, reported Valencia.

Jahar had now seen himself in several surveillance videos. His latest capture on video of him was on the night of April 18th when the brothers made a stop at a Shell gas station to get gas and some snacks. Tamerlan had already kidnapped Dun Meng and had stolen his SUV. Jahar went to the cooler case and the snack aisle in the store filling his arms with junk food: Red Bull soda, chips, Doritos and candies. Suddenly, Dun Meng bolted from the car and ran across the street. Tamerlan ran into the Shell store telling Jahar to get moving. Jahar nearly sprinted out the door without paying for the items; however, hesitated, and dumped the snacks on the cashier counter and told the clerk he had to run. Jahar was capable of killing, but not of stealing. In court everyone was struck how much of this crime had been captured on video.[141] When Jahar left the courtroom he *"bangs his fist off the witness box twice,"* as observed by Garrett Quinn from *Boston Magazine*.

Here is the video of Jahar grabbing some junk food and the carjacked victim escapes. See reference number 141.
(https://www.youtube.com/watch?v=yj8zwPWXqWg).

The Chinese Carjacked Victim

"He told me, 'you know I'm serious so don't be stupid.'"
— Dun Meng aka "Danny"

DUN MENG'S EYES GLANCED nervously at Jahar as he was sworn in. THE 48th WITNESS WAS DUN MENG, the carjacked victim who escaped from the Boston Bomber, Tamerlan. Jahar gazed up at him. Meng stared back at him intensely. He shook with fear when he remembered the older brother pointing a gun at him. Jahar returned the look. Meng wore glasses and spoke with a Chinese accent. *"Meng is from China and came to the U.S. to study transportation engineering. He got his master's degree in 2012."* – Wen.

In court, Meng shared his story about what happened that night on April 18, 2013 when he drove home from work. "How close was the gun?" Prosecutor Steve Mellin inquired.

"Very close. I feel totally shocked. 'What is this?'" – Cullen. Meng said in court. Meng described how a tall man quickly opened his SUV door and jumped in pointing a gun at his head. He had simply pulled to the curb of Brighton Avenue to answer a text message when it happened. He thought the man, who arrived in another car, was only asking him for directions.

Abruptly, the conversation changed… *"He pointed the gun to me."* He pulled out the magazine of the gun, and showed him that it was loaded with bullets, he said, *"I'm serious, don't be stupid. Do you know the Boston Marathon explosion?"* Meng was terrified of him, said, "Yes." The man replied, *"I did it, and I just killed a police officer in Cambridge,"*– Cullen. Meng could not believe it. While the man pointed the gun at Meng, he asked for his wallet and money. Meng gave the man all he had. Reporter Armstrong tweeted Meng's fear, *"Terrified, the whole world everybody is looking for them at the time."*

The man was Tamerlan and he told Meng, *"I'm Muslim, Muslim hate Americans."* Meng said to him, *"Chinese are friendly to Muslims."* – Cullen. Tamerlan asked Meng for his bank card and PIN code. Meng told him the PIN code was his girlfriend's birthday. Tamerlan asked him where the girlfriend was. He told him she was in China, reported Wen. When Tamerlan probed him with questions, Meng's hands were shaking as he drove nervously into a dark street. Tamerlan asked, "Do all white people look the same?" The reason was because he did not want Meng to remember him. Meng replied he wouldn't remember his face, reported Cullen. *"He felt 'safer' if he said he doesn't remember anything,"* – Wen. Meng feared they might get rid of him later.

Upon arriving at Watertown on Dexter Street, a green Honda sedan drove up behind them. It was the same car that had pulled up beside the SUV when he was carjacked. Tamerlan stopped the car and ordered Meng move to the passenger seat. As Meng sat in the front passenger seat; Tamerlan and another man opened the trunk of the SUV and transferred some packages into the SUV. Meng heard them speak in a language he did not understand. He was too afraid to see what they were loading. Instead, he checked out to see what street they were on.

"Why trying to remember name of the street?" asked Prosecutor Mellin. *"Meng testifies that he started looking around, trying to remember the name of the street. 'Feels like it might be useful,'"* – Boeri. After they finished loading Tamerlan took the driver's seat, and the defendant, Mr. Tsarnaev joined in the backseat right behind Meng.

"Point him out?" asked Prosecutor Mellin.

"That gentleman over there." Meng pointed at Jahar.

"Wearing a black coat?"

"Yes," – Cullen.

Meng said the defendant talked with his brother. They drove in Watertown for ten minutes until they stopped at a Bank of America ATM.

"Tsarnaev then left the car and knocked on the window and asked me for PIN code. He knocks at front pass window," – Wen. Meng gave Tsarnaev the PIN code. He went to the ATM machine.

Here is the video of Tsarnaev at the ATM machine. See reference number 143.

(https://www.youtube.com/watch?v=mfwZw6EyTwk)

While Meng stayed in the car with Tamerlan, he thought of escaping. Meng clarified it was Tamerlan who told him they both had guns. But, he indicated Mr. Tsarnaev never claimed he had a gun. The defendant returned with the money, and he talked to Tamerlan in a language he didn't understand. They drove off. When they drove, *"past Waltham police department then made a U-turn, Tamerlan asked can your car go out of state…like New York? And do you have GPS?"* – Steve Cooper from *7 News in Boston.*

Meng said he didn't have GPS; however, he lied. He had GPS in the car. He was afraid they would get rid of him. The SUV needed gas, so they stopped at a gas station, but the lights were out. It was closed. *"Around that time, Tsarnaev spoke for one of the first times, and asked if Meng if he could connect his IPhone music in the car,"* – Wen.

Tamerlan asked Meng how the radio worked and nervously tinkered with the radio controls. They drove back to where the green sedan was parked in Watertown. Mr. Tsarnaev went back to the sedan to retrieve a CD. As soon as he got back in the SUV, they played the CD. "The music," Meng described it in court, "it sounded very weird, religious." It scared the heck out of Meng. It made him nervous thinking the brothers were going to kill him.

Suddenly, *"Tamerlan makes a U–turn, and they end up somehow driving east towards Boston again. Meng's roommate calls his cell,"* – Armstrong.

Tamerlan asked who was calling as it came through the car system. Meng did not pick up but soon a text message appeared, and it was in Chinese. Meng's friend texted, 'Where are you? It's dangerous outside,' reported Cullen. *"Tamerlan examined the Chinese text message and asked what it said. Meng told him, "He asked me how to spell 'no' in Chinese,"* – Bailey.

At that moment, Meng showed him an English to Mandarin dictionary app on the phone and showed Tamerlan how to text and he typed no in response, reported Cullen.

However, the boyfriend called back five minutes later. Tamerlan became nervous and pointed the gun at Meng, and said, "No, you have to answer the phone," insisted Tamerlan.

In court, Mellin asked, "Where gun pointed?"

"At me. My head," replied Meng." – Cullen.

Tamerlan warned Meng, "If you say one word in Chinese, I will kill you," – Boeri.

Meng complied that he will answer in English, and Tamerlan said, "Just say you are safe. You will stay at a friend's home tonight." – Cullen. Meng answered back in English which was weird because the friends always spoke in Chinese. His roommate was surprised asking him in Chinese, "Why are you speaking English?"

Meng said to his friend, "I gotta go, we can talk later."

Tamerlan told him, "Good job, boy. Good job," – Cullen.

On the road back to Boston they saw lights coming from a gas station on Soldier's Field Road. Meng was excited and thought about escaping. Mellin asked, "Did Tamerlan ever yelled, threatened his younger brother? Threaten him with a gun?"

Meng said, "No. I didn't think so." At Shell gas station, Mr. Tsarnaev got out of the car and tried to buy gas with a credit card. He asked Meng for his zip code, but it was cash payment. Tamerlan told him to put 50 dollars of Super in the tank. The defendant went into the store to buy gas and junk food. Tamerlan had the gun in his pocket.

Meng thought this was his opportunity to escape. He thought if they went to New York with him there would never be another chance. He decided to take this chance to run away. He counted down 1,2,3,4. Meng unbuckled his seatbelt and opened the car door. – Cullen. He could feel Tamerlan trying to grab his left hand. As Meng ran away, he felt the wind around him and he heard Tamerlan shouting a word. – Boeri.

"What word did Tamerlan say?" asked Mellin.

Meng said, "He said f***. Can I say that?" asked Meng.

"You have now," said Mellin. (Laughter)" – Boeri.

Meng dashed into the street and prayed that the next gas station was open. It was opened, and he begged the store attendant to call 911. Meng sheltered behind the store attendant and hid. Seconds later, the police arrived quickly to attend to Meng.[142]

Here is the video of the carjacking victim asking for help. See reference number 142.

(https://www.youtube.com/watch?v=bUENGGnGSXk)

The jurors were all engrossed in Meng's carjacking testimony. Jahar slouched to the left side of his chair, not looking at Meng. As Meng walked off the stand, he glanced back to see if Jahar was looking at him. Jahar was not, reported Valencia. As the jury left, Jahar folded his arms and watched them leave, reported Cullen. His lawyers gave him another back rub and he walked out with his guards. Laurel Sweet tweeted, *"And as he so often does, he paused to playfully rap the witness box. He disappeared out of the court, whipping off his suit coat as soon as he's in the hallway, like always."*

Laurel J. Sweet
@Laurel Sweet

With another back rub for the road, #Tsarnaev saunters to his guards. And as he so often does, pauses to playfully rap the witness box.

Right after lunch, Jahar returned to the courtroom. He loved to chat and smile with Miriam and Judy. He was a foot taller than Miriam and sometimes she had to lean over to whisper to him, and he peered down at her and would smile. Judy also leaned towards him, whispering, observed by Bailey.

Back in court Meng told police the two men looked Middle Eastern. He was shown a photo of his shot-up SUV. "That's my car," said Meng. Jahar saw the photo and did not flinch. Meng never saw if one of the brothers had another gun besides the one Tamerlan carried. Moreover, he said Tamerlan had threatened to kill him. Prosecutor Mellin asked if the first words the defendant asked him was if he could connect his iPod to the car. Meng said yes. Prosecutor Mellin asked who was the one loading packages into his car. Meng said both were loading packages. Mellin asked who asked for your pin, took out your money and tried to fill gas twice. Meng said, "Dzhokhar." Mellin asked if Dzhokhar ever told him he had a gun. Meng said no, as reported by Wen.

Eight hundred dollars was withdrawn from carjacked victim Dun Meng's account. Dzhokhar tried to withdraw $800 again but was rejected because he withdrew too much of an amount, reported Cullen. The money was recovered when the police arrested Dzhokhar in Watertown. Jurors watched again a video of Dzhokhar wearing his Adidas sweatshirt and light cap swiping a card and accessing a ATM bank machine in Watertown.[143]

At the end of the day, Jahar stood up and stretched. He watched the jury leave the room. Judy talked with him one last time before he returned to Devens. He smiled and said goodbye to his Defense team for the weekend and later rode back with the U.S. Marshals to return to his world of isolation, the jail cell.

The Shootout With Police In Watertown

"I could see them ducking down behind the Mercedes, come in and out of fire." How many rounds? *"It felt like hundreds."*
– Sgt. John MacLellan

Day 7 – March 16, 2015

A NEWS POOL REPORTER counted *"at least a hundred and ten bullet holes"* on the Slipaway II boat, – Wen.

Inside a raw mill warehouse the jurors were lifted on a forklift to view the infamous damaged boat where Tsarnaev almost died. Jahar watched them passively from under a white tent. Judge O'Toole felt the jurors needed to see the boat where Jahar hid from flying bullets. His Defense wanted the jury to see the full boat to enhance their imagination the environment their client was in when he wrote his confession note. Prosecutors thought it was unnecessary, that the viewing of the boat riddled with bullet holes would provoke sympathy for Jahar. *"Most of the bullet holes are clustered toward the middle of the boat,"* – Boeri. *"Mr. Tsarnaev was sitting alone and unshackled during boat viewing. Surrounded by US marshals. Described as 'awkward,'"* – from *Fox 25* reporter Jessie Grossi. Jahar *"sat at a table with tablecloth, just watched jurors look at the boat,"* – Cullen. He watched but had *"little reaction"* to jurors viewing the boat, – observed Palumbo.

In court on Day 7, Jahar wore what *"looks like a new jacket, Kenneth Cole style, with an olive shirt,"* – Valencia. Grossi tweeted, *"Dzhokhar Tsarnaev is usually chatting and smiling while waiting for the judge. Today not the case. Interesting."*

Jahar knew these next witnesses were serious. His confrontation with Watertown cops had left him frightened and disheartened as he fled from them. Grossi tweeted, *"Dzhokhar Tsarnaev and his defense team are all looking down. They are not speaking as we wait for the Judge and jury."* Boeri tweeted, *"Jahar smiled to lawyers and looked at notes while waiting for the Judge."*

The court began with testimonies from police officers involved in the Watertown shootout with the Tsarnaev brothers on the night of April 18, 2013. The first Watertown cop who arrived on scene after the midnight hour at 12:41 a.m. had locked eyes with Tamerlan, the driver of the SUV. Tamerlan had gotten out of the vehicle and began shooting at Officer Reynolds. "Shots fired! Shots fired!" shouted the government's 52nd WITNESS OFFICER JOSEPH REYNOLDS. Officer Reynolds got out, used a driver's side door as a shield and exchanged gunfire with Tamerlan, reported Cullen. They exchanged fire for eight minutes. Unexpectedly, Reynolds saw Sgt. John MacLellan had run to a side yard. He ran swiftly to meet him. They used a small tree for cover. Reynolds saw Tamerlan and Dzhokhar, *"I could see two men. I could see muzzle flashes. I saw a wick burning. It was thrown toward myself and it landed and exploded,"* – Cullen. *"Three more pipe bombs lit and were thrown at them. Two more exploded. A larger bomb came through the air,"* – Cullen. When Reynolds saw the bomb coming at them, he yelled at Sarge to run. He grabbed him by the shoulder. The bomb exploded right above them with a huge blast that left Reynolds' ears ringing. It set off car alarms. The police were showered with debris, reported Cullen.

JAHAR THE LONE BOSTON BOMBER #2

In the dark night, the police could see two suspects moving: one of them was big, and the other one looked skinny. 53rd WITNESS WAS WATERTOWN POLICE SGT. JOHN MACLELLAN who was with Reynolds in the midst of the gunfire exchange. They recognized the big guy as Tamerlan, and the skinny one as Dzhokhar.

"MacLellan says two suspects had different styles of throwing explosives. 1 threw like a baseball. Other threw like a hook shot," – Boeri. MacLellan thought it was fireworks initially or M-80's being thrown because the first bomb wasn't that powerful. He also thought the brothers "fired hundreds of shots. Knows it was at least dozens," – Boeri.

Tamerlan stood at a driveway of a house and exchanged gunfire with the 54th WITNESS, WATERTOWN'S SGT. JEFF PUGLIESE. Then Officer Reynolds started shooting at Tamerlan; he had a good shot: "Had a good visual. I dropped down to one knee" yet "Reynolds did not know what Dzhokhar Tsarnaev was doing at this point – as Tamerlan lets bullets fly all over Laurel Street in Watertown," – Cullen. Tamerlan charged towards Reynolds and fired at him six times, but Pugliese chased Tamerlan and tackled him from behind. Pugliese, who fired at Tamerlan, ran out of bullets in another magazine. Meanwhile, Tamerlan's gun jammed and he threw his gun at Pugliese in frustration and ran, reported Wen. Pugliese chased him down, tackled him and brought him to the ground. Tamerlan was bleeding. Reynolds ran to assist Pugliese who was struggling to arrest Tamerlan. They finally pinned him down and put handcuffs on him. Tamerlan was still moving around, so Pugliese put his foot on his back, reported Cullen. "He was wrestling with us. He's a big kid. We couldn't get control of him," – Sweet.

As they wrestled, Reynolds could hear an engine starting, and the SUV approaching them head on. Reynolds shouted to Pugliese and others, "Get off, get off, he's coming back toward us!" Reynolds pulled his gun out and tried to shoot Dzhokhar. It missed Dzhokhar and it hit the windshield.

Pugliese tried to pull Tamerlan out of the way of the vehicle's path, but Tamerlan was run over by the vehicle. He was stuck in the rear wheel and was dragged. Pugliese tried to pull Tamerlan off the road though he couldn't. *"When SUV tried to escape, it struck my parked cruiser, and I tried to shoot him, but not successful,"* – Wen. *"Jahar got loose and kept going down Laurel,"* – Cullen.

Officer Reynolds pointed at Jahar at the table. He said, "It was him. I tried to shoot him, but not successful. Others did shoot. He ran over his brother."[144] (Officer Dic Donohue was struck by friendly fire. He was sent to Emergency. He nearly died; however, he amazingly recovered.)

Pugliese said he rolled onto his back, *"felt the breeze of the vehicle on my face,"* – Cullen. He tried to pull Tamerlan away from being struck...instead Tamerlan bounced under the Mercedes SUV driven by Dzhokhar. Pugliese stood up, demonstrating in court and if front of the judge how he had gotten out of the way of the SUV. *"Tsarnaev looks carefully, but no visible emotion."* – Wen. The Watertown police were finally able to get Tamerlan's hand behind his back. The Boston EMS arrived; they cut Tamerlan's clothes off, rolled him over, and saw there was a trigger device on his body. The prosecutors showed a picture of Tamerlan's blood on the street, a pool of blood in the middle of Laurel where Dzhokhar had run him over. MacLellan pointed out that Dzhokhar had plenty of room to pass without striking Tamerlan. In court, Jahar had some reaction when the officers said he ran over his brother.

Tweet: The blood of Tamerlan #Tsarnaev pools in front of the cruiser. Dzhokhar hit as he dragged his brother to his death.

56th WITNESS WAS ANDREW KITZENBERG who ran up the flight of stairs to the second floor of his house to take pictures of the gunfire and the crime scene. Kitzenberg said, *"I could see gunfire, I could see them crouching, I could see them going into backpacks on the ground. I see the men going back to a green sedan that had its doors open, grabbing things from it,"* – Palumbo. He also said the Mercedes SUV made a U-turn to face the police. The defendant floored the car and drove towards the officers. Dzhokhar drove off down Laurel and eluded the police, reported Cullen.

An hour before daylight, police officers quickly formed search teams with K-9 officers. Leading the manhunt search was 58th WITNESS STATE TROOPER FRANK HUGHES with the Massachusetts State Police. Major Hughes cordoned Laurel Street off as a crime scene. They walked down many streets, *"Then went house to house in the neighborhoods searching for suspect at large,"* – Wen. The teams went door to door about an hour before sunrise. By 6 p.m. the next day, the shelter-in-place order was lifted. Immediately after the lockdown, Watertown police received a 911 call from a gentleman from Franklin Street in Watertown. David Henneberry claimed to have seen the suspect in his boat. They put up a perimeter around that boat. *"I believe every type of law enforcement agency in the area was there,"* –Wen.

Trooper Hughes pointed to the man wearing a dark jacket at the defense table and gave him a prolonged stare of recognition. *"Jahar appeared to look in Hughes' direction as he identified him as the man he saw being taken into custody from the boat,"* – Palumbo.

"I saw him travel by me on a stretcher." Hughes recounted. It took authorities an hour and a half to capture Mr. Tsarnaev from the time of his discovery in the boat to his actual arrest. Timothy Watkins, Defense attorney stood up to question Hughes about "flash–bangs." Hughes said it disorients the person. "They produce bright light that blinds them," Hughes explained, reported Wen. Defense attorney Watkins asked Hughes about the multiple flash bang grenades thrown into the boat. "Yes," said Watkins, "there were several thrown into the boat, right?"

"They were done over time," replied Hughes

"Watkins asked, "And there was never a reaction from the defendant?"

"Not that I know of, no," answered Hughes, tweeted Armstrong. The monitors in the jury box flashed on and a photo appeared. The jurors peered down and stared at the screen. In a dark night scene, "Jahar in his Adidas sweatshirt and his face and body all bloodied, comes out of the wrecked boat...

Dzhokhar surrendered to police.
Photo taken by ex-Mass. Police Sgt. Sean Murphy. Photo credit to
Associated Press. Photo from *Tumblr*.

One hand is slightly raised in surrender." – Wen.

Watkins continued to ask if there was a concern if Tsarnaev was armed. Trooper Hughes said 'absolutely.' Hughes saw Tsarnaev carried past him on a stretcher with a blanket over him. However, he did not see blood on him, reported by Cullen.

The Slipaway II Boat & The Ruger Gun

"Just being stupid. I wanted to show it off."
– Stephen Silva, showing off the gun to Jahar

Day 8 – March 17, 2015

HENNEBERRY FOLLOWED THE TRAIL of blood and saw more blood on the front side of his boat. He said, *"Just kept fixating on the blood,"* tweeted *Boston.com* writer Hilary Sargent. 59th WITNESS was the owner of the Slipaway II, DAVID HENNEBERRY, of Watertown. His boat was a 1981 Seabird that was stored in the backyard and covered with a zippered boat wrap for the winter. On the morning of April 19, there was a shelter in place. At 6 p.m. the advisory was lifted, and he noticed there was something wrong with the boat. *"Went to look at boat when shelter in place lifted at 6 p.m. Put the pads back up. I just thought it had come loose in the wind,"* – Cullen. Getting a ladder, he climbed to put the pads back up, but immediately, *"I noticed a lot of blood, on the deck of the boat inside,"* – Palumbo. *"I just kept fixating on this blood." "I could see his boots, or shoes. Black. I could see his pants. Tan. Hooded sweatshirt pulled up over his head. Lying on his side,"* – Cullen.

Henneberry got down from the ladder and called 911. Henneberry was calm on the witness stand. He had a gray mustache and wore glasses. The jurors saw Mr. Henneberry's boat, ridden with bullets. Most bullets were at mid-deck. Some of the holes were at the bow and stern. No one could believe how Mr. Tsarnaev had survived all those bullets. The jurors saw more photos: Jahar's writing written in pencil and streaks of his drying blood turning light-brown and fading away on the boat. Jahar's writing was located on the top left and on two wooden slates. He wrote "Stop killing our innocents…"

View boat: (http://bostondefender.org/wp-content/uploads/2015/03/3036.pdf)

THE RUGER GUN

They were very close friends since 8th grade middle school in Cambridge. They graduated from Rindge and Latin high school in June 2011. As friends they hung out, smoked weed, drank, talked and listened to music. They even jumped a ledge near a reservoir at Swampscott. They did the typical teenage stuff together; however, sadly they faced one another in court today.

The government called its 60th star witness against Tsarnaev, STEPHEN SILVA, age twenty-one, *"arriving cuffed and in gray prison garb. He shoots an angry stare at Tsarnaev as he walks past defense table,"* – Armstrong.

Stephen glanced over at Jahar, *"who is now sitting forward in his seat, kind of hunching his shoulders,"* – Armstrong. As Stephen was sworn in, the old friends stared at each other reported Cullen. Stephen was imprisoned for gun and drug charges. He pleaded guilty in federal court. *"Stephen gave the Ruger gun to Jahar, the gun was used to murder Officer Sean Collier and to shoot at the officers at Watertown cops,"* – Cullen. How did that happen? Stephen would testify against his old friend. It was awkward. *"Tsarnaev looking at Silva while he's testifying. So far more engaged,"* – Wen.

Prosecutors showed a graduation picture of Jahar and Stephen back when they were friends.

View Stephen and Jahar:
(https://media.justice.gov/video/usao/ma/150317/Exh%201179%20-%20Silva_and_Jahar_1.png)

Their relationship had been very close. Stephen said, *"We were best friends back in the days. I called him Jizz. After high school, I went to college in Tampa. Jahar went to UMass–Dartmouth. Texted and phoned each other,"* – Cullen.

To make money Stephen worked as a lifeguard at Harvard pool and sold weed with Jahar. At seventeen, they both worked together selling grass in high school. They sold a quarter pound. Stephen also got pot in Tampa.

In court, Jahar paid close attention to his old friend, *"Tsarnaev body language different hearing Silva compared to boat owner. Moves in chair more, sits up more. Looks toward Silva,"* – Wen.

Late 2012, Stephen's brother, Steve, a business partner, was robbed of a large quantity of pot, - Cullen. For protection, a friend named Howie asked Stephen to hold his firearm, a P–95 Ruger.

The gun was concealed in Stephen's ceiling panel in his apartment. Later, he told Jahar about the gun. *"It wasn't much of a reaction, he just acknowledged it,"* – Cullen. Stephen and his friend, Nicholas, went to meet two buyers in a car, asked to see the money for the marijuana. Nicholas pointed the gun at the buyers after Stephen got the money from them. *"They were kind of shocked. Later, told Tsarnaev about the gun. 'He just laughed,'"* –Valencia.

At a New Years' Eve party, Stephen showed off his gun to his friends. *"Just being stupid. I wanted to show it off,"* – Cullen. In January, Jahar asked to use the gun, *"'Why?' He said he wanted to rip some kids from URI,"* – Cullen. Dias, a friend from UMass-Dartmouth, came with Jahar. They smoked weed. Stephen took the gun out and handed it to Jahar. After Jahar handled the gun, Stephen tried to hand it over to Dias. Except he did not want to touch it, reported Cullen.

Stephen *"Gave the gun to Jahar in Feb. 2013. Didn't take it at the first time he showed him. A few weeks passed,"* – Cullen.

"Prosecutor: "Why not pick it up on that day?

Silva: "He told me he didn't want to drive back with that…on him…he already had marijuana on him,"– Cullen. Stephen expected to get the gun back within a couple of weeks although they still hung out together. Stephen gave him the ammunition. He remembered, *"Dzhokhar Tsarnaev asked for ammo, telling Silva he needed 'food for the dog,'"* – Cullen.

Afterward, Howie, the person who loaned Stephen the gun wanted the gun back. Stephen asked Jahar to return the gun, but Jahar kept making excuses, saying, *"oh, I was in rush. I couldn't bring it."* – Valencia. (By this time, the gun could have been given to Tamerlan.) So, Stephen told Jahar he loved him and left. He tried to talk to Jahar before the Marathon. No answer. Jahar's phone had been turned off. He tweeted instead.

Stephen said he had never met Tamerlan Tsarnaev before, reported Cullen. *"After seeing photos of the Tsarnaev brothers, 'I was in a huge state of shock, disbelief, paranoia' disposed of his phone,"* – Whitehouse.

Stephen was the first close friend Jahar had seen since his capture. He described Jahar as a very good student, with a high GPA. However, in college he struggled the first year.

Jahar had said to Stephen one time that, *"American foreign policy tend to be hostile toward the Middle East, persecuting Muslims…trying to take over,"*– Cullen.

Stephen admitted he only had been to Jahar's house only once. During the summer of 2012, he needed a place to stay and he met Jahar's sister-in-law, Katherine and her daughter, Zahara. Stephen slept on the top bunk. In court, Jahar listened deeply to Stephen. The jury saw a picture of Jahar's bunk bed, computer and black flag with white writings on it that hung on his wall, along with another picture of Jahar with the Islamic flag. *"Stephen has serious somber demeanor in testifying. He seemed to have lost weight since arraignment this past summer. He has been in prison since,"* –Wen

During cross–examination, Miriam Conrad questioned Stephen on the witness stand. He said he didn't see Jahar get angry often. He only got mad when he called him a "Russian refugee." Jahar was proud of his Chechen heritage. Stephen's eyes darted to Jahar as he answered Conrad's questions. In the *Rolling Stone* interview about Dzhokhar, he used the name "Sam."

Stephen said Jahar never talked to him about religion. He never saw anything that would make him think he could act violently. Stephen told FBI he *"felt 150% that Tamerlan" influenced Jahar,* – tweeted Boeri, and Tamerlan had *"built the bombs."* Miriam asked Stephen some questions: *Miriam:* "You said he was one of the realest and coolest kids you knew." *Stephen:* "Yes," – Cullen.

Miriam: "Was he violent? Even though trained as boxer and wrestler, you never saw him fight?" *Stephen:* "No, I never have seen him violent," – Armstrong.

Miriam: "He was humble?" *Stephen:* "Yes, he was," – Armstrong. *Miriam:* "You never heard him say he had resentment about America?" *Stephen:* "No," – Boeri.

Miriam: "You guys smoked weed, went up to Swampscott to jump off cliffs, chased girls?" *Stephen:* "Yes," – Armstrong.

Miriam: "Didn't you tell the government you used peer pressure to get Jahar to smoke weed?" *Stephen:* "I can't recall."

Miriam: "You were friends for 6 or 7 years and you never went to his house until that one time?" *Stephen:* "Yes."

Miriam: "Did he tell you, 'you don't want to meet my brother?'" *Stephen:* "Yes." *Miriam:* "Did you ask him what that meant?" *Stephen:* "Yes. He said his brother was very strict, very opinionated. Since I wasn't a Muslim, he might give me a little s#it for that," all tweets from Cullen.[145]

Miriam: "Did he complain his brother was keeping him on a short leash?" Government objected," – Boeri. Miriam continued, "Did he ever say he couldn't let car smell like weed because of his brother?" Government objected again," – Cullen. Miriam wanted Stephen to talk about the fear that Jahar had of his older brother, but the government objected. Stephen said he would never have loaned the gun to Jahar if he knew it was for his brother. Personally, he felt bad that the gun was used to kill Officer Collier. As the U.S. Marshals led Stephen away, he sadly looked at Jahar. *"Silva's eyes soak in Tsarnaev's for what may be the very last time in their lives."*

Forensic Evidence & Cyber Detectives

"It's lined with BB's. It was full. It's an improvised grenade used an elbow pipe because when it's tossed it will not roll away, it will stay where it lands."

–Mass State Police Trooper, Robert McCarthy.

Day 9 – March 18, 2015

TAMERLAN BUILT THE BOMBS. He was the mastermind. *"The remote–control transmitter & other items found in a Tsarnaev backpack left in Watertown,"* – Armstrong, could explain how the bombs were remotely detonated. 69th WITNESS WAS BRIAN CORCORAN JR., a special agent with the FBI bomb technician found the transmitter in a computer bag on the ground on Laurel St.

Inside the bag there was a piece of modified electronics, but he said it was not an explosive.

The other items Corcoran found was Tamerlan's diploma from Cambridge Rindge and Latin School dated June 8, 2006.

It also contained a Samsung laptop, a Russian document with Tamerlan's ID, a HTC cellphone from T–Mobile, a hard drive and a laser pointer.

There was another bag found, a dark messenger shoulder bag which included a mini thumb drive, a lighter and a UMass-Dartmouth pencil.

Behind the driver seat of the defendant's Honda sedan, a plastic Tupperware bomb was found.

63rd WITNESS WAS MASSACHUSETTS STATE POLICE TROOPER ROBERT MCCARTHY who discovered the Tupperware bomb filled with green wire fuses inside. These green wires were seen on the pipe bombs; they must be lit for the bombs to detonate.

In the trial, a pipe bomb lined with BB's was shown to jurors. The BB's were glued to the metal with *"glued-like epoxy stuff."* – Wen. The second bomb shown was an elbow pipe bomb because when tossed *"it will not roll away"* where it lands. – Cullen

The brothers did a lot of damage to many homeowners' properties in Watertown during their confrontation with officers. A car parked in the driveway was hit by a pressure cooker on Laurel Street. It was a "Fagor" brand pressure cooker. In court, jurors saw a pressure cooker imbedded in the rear side door.

After the shootout the Mercedes was brought to the Watertown Police Department. The 64th WITNESS WAS MASSACHUSETTS STATE POLICE TROOPER MATTHEW HESS, a crime scene investigator who took photographs of the SUV and marked the bullet holes. The jurors viewed a photo of a SUV with bullet holes in the windshield. A dozen bullet holes marked the passenger side.

Driver's side of the car showed more bullet holes.

65th WITNESS WAS MASSACHUSETTS STATE POLICE crime scene investigator, PATRICK MOYNIHAN whose job was identifying Dzhokhar's fingerprints and palm prints. He found 10 of Dzhokhar's fingerprints on the outside of the carjacked Mercedes, and 3 from Tamerlan. Inside the SUV: 2 prints from Dzhokhar and 7 from Tamerlan. Dzhokhar's prints were also found on a magazine for the Ruger found in the vehicle, reported Cullen.

This is what happened to Dzhokhar when he abandoned the vehicle.

"... Dzhokhar fled from the pursuing police. He had abandoned the SUV and smashed the evidence: the cellphone, GPS and ATM card. He hid them between concrete blocks. He was shot in the hand and leg and was bleeding as he fled on foot. Frantically, he looked from house to house down the

street, bleeding and searching for a place to rest and hide. It was after midnight and all residents were asleep. He could no longer run or leave a trail of blood behind him."

62nd WITNESS WAS FBI SPECIAL AGENT JESSICA ULMER. Ulmer found Tsarnaev's blood on a garage door and a car on two neighbors' properties. Furthermore, she found broken glass and blood on someone else's back door. At another, they found broken glass and blood leading to a bathroom, as well as cell phones and Dun Meng's debit card, reported Valencia. The two iPhones, black and white and the card were found smashed behind a shed under loose slate and cinder blocks at a house at 63 Franklin Street. The defendant must have been trying to find a place to hide and was bleeding until he found refuge in the boat.

"Dzhokhar awoke in the boat. His wound was deep, and he suffered pain in his leg. Ignoring the pain, he wrote busily with a pencil in his right hand he had found in the boat. He began etching jihadi messages on the inside hull and beam of the boat. It was a chilling confession."

61st WITNESS WAS FBI SPECIAL AGENT MICHAEL NEALSON. He processed the Slipaway II crime scene on Franklin Street in Watertown. Two slats about 3–4 feet long, Tsarnaev wrote in CAPS, "Stop killing our innocent people and we will stop."

66th WITNESS WAS D.J. FIFE, a physical scientist for the FBI. He went to collect fingerprints at Beth Israel Hospital of the suspect. He collected the 20–dollar bills in the wallet taken from the ATM. He saw people treating Tsarnaev at the hospital, including removing, ripping and cutting his bloody clothes off him so they could be processed as evidence, reported Cullen. In court, Jahar stared expressionless at his torn-up gray/yellow/blue Adidas sweatshirt hoodie he wore on the night when he was captured. Court artist Jane Rosenberg's sketched him in court staring at the screen monitor. He's probably thinking, *oh man, that was my favorite sweatshirt*, because he was seen wearing it often.)

View the ripped Adidas sweatshirt:
http://bostondefender.org/wp-content/uploads/2015/03/3058.pdf
View Rosenberg's court sketch:
https://cbsboston.files.wordpress.com/2015/03/tsarnaev-day-9-
jahar.jpg?w=625&h=352&crop=1

75th WITNESS WAS FBI SPECIAL AGENT MATTHEW RIPORTELLA. Agent Riportella went to a firing range in New Hampshire where the brothers had practiced shooting on March 20, 2013, a couple weeks before the attack. Riportella obtained their records and the surveillance video. Dzhokhar was seen wearing the same Adidas sweatshirt. They rented a glock 17 and s glock 34 – 9mm guns as well as 9mm ammo. They spent an hour there. *"...video very damaging to defense: Jahar trained to shoot,"* – Cullen.[146] *Here is the video of the Tsarnaev brothers visiting the gun range before BMB. See reference number 146.*

 *(https://www.youtube.com/watch?v=HHEcj2B12PI)*

78th WITNESS WAS WATERTOWN POLICE OFFICER MIGUEL COLON. He arrived at the Watertown scene around 12:45 a.m. *"I tried to get the suspects' attention by pointing my spotlight on them,"* – Cullen. He was shot at in response. They hit his spotlight and his door. Colon saw the SUV head his way moments later. *"Saw Jahar ducked to his right, leaned over dashboard as he drove past and dragged brother. Colon jumped into his cruiser to and followed,"* – Cullen. His cruiser chased the SUV with Dzhokhar behind the wheel. Colon said there was room for him to pass on both the right and the left sides of the Honda. Dzhokhar exited Laurel Street.

Defense Tim Watkins cross-examined Colon, suggested something could have blocked the far end of Laurel near Quimby. Was it blocked by police perhaps explaining why Dzhokhar did a 3-point turn to flee Laurel St? *"The defense has repeatedly tried to suggest Jahar didn't escape via Quimby because other cops were there,"* - Cullen. Officer said there was no police road block on Quimby. Government rebutted the defense's theory that east of Laurel Street had been blocked by police cars. Instead, Government defended its theory that Dzhokhar did a *"3-point turn to turn car around to go towards police"* - Ward. Dzhokhar had enough room to get around the cruisers without hitting Tamerlan. Defense was done with Officer Colon, but *"Jahar fidgeted in his seat,"* observed by *Fox 25's* Grossi.

Day 10 – March 19, 2015 – CYBER DETECTIVE

71st WITNESS WAS FBI SUPERVISORY SOCIAL AGENT, KEVIN SWINDON. *"This FBI agent likely to help introduce evidence pulled out of Tsarnaev's laptop, why gov't says shows Tsarnaev's secret radicalization,"* - Wen.

A proof of Dzhokhar's radicalization was his searches on the cyber internet. Here were some files investigators found on his Sony VAIO laptop:

- YouTube clips named "Allah, The Prophet of Mercy and War", "Tour of Jannah Paradise."
- YouTube clips named "Jihad is the way", "Call for Jihad," and "Muslims has supernatural experience with Jesus."
- "Join the Caravan" pdf files. (These files refer to Abdullah Yusuf Assam - father of Global Jihad calling on Muslims to rally to cause of all Muslims.)
- Files of Music from Al Makdisi, Nasheed. Tsarnaev listened to chanting music to Islam.
- The Hereafter Series (Anwar al-Awlaki preaching jihad).

- *Inspire* Magazine produced by Al Qaeda, "Make a Bomb in the Kitchen of Your Mom." This magazine described a small group called the "mujahidin" whose efforts are to strike back at the enemy by 'making an explosive device to damage the enemy.'
- Movie poster: *And Allah Selects the Martyrs.*
- Tsarnaev wrote in Modern World History class for Ms. Otty, "The Predator War."
- Laptop had numerous files re: writings of Anwar al-Awlaki, (who was killed in U.S. drone strike and highly influential in radical recruitment.) In an external hard drive, investigators found CompleteInspire.PDF and many back-issues of Inspire until 2011.

  View Inspire magazine: (https://www.justice.gov/sites/default/files/usao-ma/pages/attachments/2015/03/23/exh_1142-91-01.pdf)

JAHAR'S RESUME

Jahar sat quietly staring at all the files on his screen. He seemed interested in his own files including his resume. The people in court also saw his UMass–Dartmouth student resume. Jahar characterized himself as *"responsible, hard worker, great swimmer, social, nice, can enforce rules, very enthusiastic, reliable, people person, certified as a Lifeguard/First Aid and CPR/AED as of 5/8/2010, and quick learner."* Also, he was skilled in CPR. He had received his CPR certificate on June 18, 2011.

View resume: (https://www.justice.gov/sites/default/files/usao-ma/pages/attachments/2015/03/23/1142-150.pdf)

Day 11 – March 23, 2015

DEFENSE CROSS–EXAMINED SWINDON ABOUT TSARNAEV'S LAPTOP

Defense attorney William Fick crossed–examined Swindon about Tsarnaev's laptop, saying this was a 'representative sample.' Although there were hundreds of thousands of files on the Sony, the defendant had saved a lot of homework assignments. Swindon picked a homework assignment about drones, *"Fick shows assignment about drones. You're aware there were other homework assignments, but you just picked this one,"* – Cullen.

Fick argued the FBI expert was cherry–picking only the extreme jihad and al–Qaeda files and not showing Tsarnaev as a typical teen. *"'151 sub files out of half a million?' defense attorney Fick asks, calling FBI investigators' choices 'fly speck' out of total,'"* – Lawrence. Dzhokhar had other music instead of Jihad music and writings that the FBI missed like Jay Z's *"In the Heart of the City."* – Cullen. William Fick also mentioned among the top 16 search terms by Tsarnaev there was nothing about *"jihad"* or *"Islam."*[147]

Tamerlan had used the computer while visiting Russia the first seven months of 2012. It was possible that he connected to the internet while there. *"Swindon acknowledges lot of the material on the Sony laptop of Tsarnaev was also a found on his brother's Samsung."* – Sweet. TruCrypt encryption software was not included on Jahar's Sony Vaio. (Suggesting: Tamerlan was secretive, not Jahar), – Cullen. Also, from Sweet, *"On the Samsung hard drive of Tamerlan Tsarnaev, a file titled, 'Blast effects of explosions.'"* Fick made the FBI agent Swindon aware that in *Inspire* magazine it advised potential terrorists to use encryption software. Agent Swindon was not aware of this, reported Cullen. Defense was able to break into Tamerlan's computer. His password was *"Allahu-Akbar"* followed by a number – the defense claimed it was a *"weak"* password. "Allahu-Akbar," Fick said, 'with a hint of mockery.' He translated the password code. It meant, "That's Arabic for *'God is great.'"*

Jihad 101

*"...lone terrorists don't tend to travel, sending communications and
transferring money, and don't set off trip wires to detect them.
They aren't likely to set off "spectacular" attacks..."*
– Dr. Matthew Levitt

72nd WITNESS WAS TERRORIST EXPERT DR.
MATTHEW LEVITT, a counterterrorism and intelligence expert for
the Washington Institute. Levitt wrote an expert paper for the
Tsarnaev case. For purposes of analyzing the Tsarnaev jihadi
collection, Levitt stressed, "I have to take the evidence at face
value." Levitt's testimony explained the reason why jihadists waged
war through terrorist attacks. He first basically explained the global
jihad movement is an idea. The jihadi movement is made up of lone
offenders. It's "terrorism to go" which means the terrorist has no
office or training camps to learn to defend, to unite or to build these
attacks. Everything he wants to know is sitting on his computer in
Mama's basement, just as the Tsarnaev brothers had discovered.
First hand, lone wolf terrorists don't travel, don't send
communications or transfer money. They terrorize the society by
making people afraid.

Terrorists have this extreme sadistic ideology that killing
innocent people is praise-worthy. It is *"a personal obligation to serve
the cause."* – Wen. Levitt explained to the jurors that for instance, *"if
you want to be a good Muslim, killing people is not only okay, it's
accepted."* Levitt said, *"This movement has begun a 'twisting of Islamic
concepts' to encourage acts of terrorism,"* –Wen. This killing of
innocents is an extreme radical religion, a radical Islam.

The brothers believed that if Muslims were being persecuted, then Muslims killing nonbelievers was justified. That was what Tsarnaev wrote in the boat: *"We Muslims are one body, you hurt one you hurt us all."* Jihadists believe also that killing nonbelievers is done in the name of Islam. Levitt said that "all religions have the capacity for extremism" so believers would kill so they would become martyrs. Martyrs engaged in this behavior would be rewarded into the highest levels of heaven.

THE BOAT MESSAGE

The Watertown boat message was aimed at the American public to explain what had been done. Dzhokhar wrote, *"God has a plan for each person. Mine was to hide in his boat and shed some light on our actions. I ask Allah…"* This was his testimony, a way of taking the weight off from his older brother Tamerlan's role. This confirmed the defendant had been radicalized in his own independent way. The message was similar to those in the global jihad movement, "Join the Caravan." Dzhokhar's word indicated that he was asking for Allah to make him a martyr. *"Shaheed"* is martyrs, killed in act of jihad. The Tsarnaev brothers hoped to be crowned a martyr for God by carrying out the Boston Marathon Bombings. *"Levitt said it "is traditional" to state one's true intentions "on the death bed" to reap the maximum rewards in afterlife,"* – Sweet. This is the *"Jannutul Firdaus"* reserved for the pious and the martyrs, who would enter the highest levels of heaven, reported Cullen. The terror attack was motivated by religious extremism with the intent to punish the United States for their mistreatment of Muslims in the wars. *"Expert said the Jihadist movement has a "foundational idea" there is a war between Muslim Ummah (nation) and the West,"* – Wen.

The banner that hung-over Dzhokhar's bed, *"Levitt says, the banner is a symbol used by many jihadis. It's not inherently radical, but used by many radical organizations,"* – Boeri.

Levitt tried to decipher Tsarnaev's boat note. He explained the language had been taken from extremist Muslim materials he got online.

"Levitt compares another boat writing to an Inspire magazine article "we Muslims are one body, you hurt one, you hurt us all," – Palumbo. The jury was shown a side–by–side of Tsarnaev's boat note and a passage from *Inspire* magazine: *"We Muslims are one body, you hurt one you hurt us all,"* draws on Ummah, reported Cullen. Levitt read the quote from *Inspire* which was similar to Tsarnaev's boat note, *"We say that whoever terrorizes us, we will terrorize them."* The theme of victory in Dzhokhar's message, is the common theme of all jihadis, said Levitt. Boat message read: *"we are promised victory and we will surely get it"* – *Inspire Magazine similarly reads: "Victory is on our side,"* – Palumbo.

Throughout this testimony Jahar sat still with his arm slung back over his chair, staring ahead at the video screen in front of him.

Day 12 – March 24, 2015 – TSARNAEV'S RADICALIZATION

Defense attorney David Bruck asked Matthew Levitt if it was possible, *"couldn't someone put this content on his devices and also have harangued him and contributed to his radicalization? Levitt: Yes."* – Armstrong. However, *"Levitt: "We are all products of the totality of our experience...I can't get into defendant's head. Tsarnaev was radicalized,"* – Steven.

Defense suggested that Tamerlan pressed him strongly with his beliefs, brainwashed his brother. *"Levitt said he doesn't care if someone else downloaded material onto Tsarnaev's laptop, what matters if that he was influenced by them,"* –Wen. Levitt also said that hours of listening to *"Hereafter Series"* by Anwar al-Awlaki could be a *"gateway drug"*, a pathway toward violence and visions of paradise." – Wen. Awlaki even talked about hell, reported Cullen. Levitt described the powerful leader's voice, *"Awlaki proved to be a seductive voice."* – Wen.

Anwar al-Awlaki who started *Inspire* was a very effective communicator, having spent much time in the U.S. He was later killed in a U.S. drone strike. Many Muslims and those descended from war-torn countries can be drawn to the jihad's history. Awlaki had a seductive voice and many people became captivated when they listened to Awlaki. They would *"follow him into his expressly violent lectures"* on Islam. - Palumbo.

Bruck asked, *"How long would it take someone to learn those slogans and statements?"* Levitt replied, *"One could learn them quite quickly. Radicalization has no one model and can happen very quickly."* - Cullen. *"Bruck suggesting Tsarnaev had a rapid conversion, and boat confession not part of long-term radicalization process,"* - Wen. Levitt believed that Tsarnaev was radicalized not only through influence or from talking with his brother…that he learned it himself. He was a self-radicalized jihadist.[148]

Searching For Bomb Clues In Pine Dale & 410 Norfolk Street

"It almost looked like a construction site. There were tools everywhere, lots of debris." Derks says they seized entire drawers, lots of tools found to try to match tool marks, also several rolls of packaging tape. – Christopher Derks

DZHOKHAR LIVED IN PINE Dale Hall at UMass-Dartmouth. His dorm room was ransacked for bomb clues after he was apprehended. The FBI confiscated everything in the dorm room including an empty pizza box. When Dzhokhar's identity was aired on national television the SWAT team proceeded to Pine Dale to search for him, but he was hiding in the boat. The SWAT encountered the dorm room door decorated with colorful cut out turkeys, a lily pad and a little green frog. The big lily pad had Dzhokhar's name on it and his roommate's name was on the little frog. It was in a shape like Kindergarten name tag cut-outs on the door, and these name signs had been designed by the residence assistant of the dorm. *View the door: (http://bostondefender.org/wp-content/uploads/2015/03/1230-6.pdf).*

As Jahar attended his trial he was about to revisit the old dorm room where he slept and stashed his grass. In court, attorney Miriam Conrad showed the jury how Dzhokhar's name was spelled wrong twice: DZHOKHAR was misspelled "D-Z-H-O-K-A-R." The FBI investigators who cleared the room found no firearms in Jahar's dorm room or ammunition.

Jahar sat in the courtroom and leaned forward to the monitor to examine the documents of everything recorded of his life as student at UMass-Dartmouth. They were all laid out before him.

Jahar had a UMass swipe card and the 79th WITNESS MARK PREBLE, the UMass-Dartmouth Vice Chancellor of Administration & Finance began showing the jury his swipe card entry data:

View swipe card: (https://www.justice.gov/sites/default/files/usao-ma/pages/attachments/2015/03/24/exh_1180b.pdf)

"Now looking at UMassD swipe card data for Tsarnaev. Shows on 4/17/13 around 5 p.m. (two days after bombing) he swiped card, but no entry made," – Wen. *"Last entry by Tsarnaev into his dorm was at 4:02 p.m. on 4/18/13,"* – Armstrong.

The jury also read a letter from Tsarnaev to UMass-Dartmouth, *"he's asking to keep his financial aid despite his dropping grades,"* – Armstrong. Jahar was doing so poorly in school he was informed by UMass in his second semester that he would lose his financial aid. He claimed the breakup of his family was upsetting him. His report card showed that he did failed many of his courses. In Fall of 2011, he received two F's in chemistry. The following 2012 Spring semester reported 2 D's, one in Economics, the other in Human Ecology. There was also two F's in Reading & Writing and in Finite Math. Fall 2012 semester his grades clearly dropped more with three F's in Psychology, American Politics and General Psychology, and one D in Writing and Reading. His GPA at the end of the Fall semester: 1.09. His Spring 2013 semester was marked incomplete. In January 2013, in his letter to UMass–Dartmouth he made an appeal, explaining that he wanted to stay in school to one day help his family members who were being terrorized by Russian soldiers. Jahar wrote: *"This year I lost too many of my loved relatives. I was unable to cope with the stress and maintain school work. My relatives live in Chechnya, Russia."*

His appeal was denied.

View Jahar's report card: (https://www.justice.gov/sites/default/files/usao-ma/pages/attachments/2015/03/24/exh_1180e.pdf)

View the letter: (https://www.justice.gov/sites/default/files/usao-ma/pages/attachments/2015/03/24/exh_1180c.pdf)

Jahar saw a diagram of his old dorm room, number 7341 in Pine Dale Hall. In the courtroom, jurors could access an interactive program on their monitors that showed all the evidence and exhibits collected for this trial. They could click on the item and the jurors could learn about it and view more photos.

AGENT KIMBERLY FRANKS, THE 80th WITNESS was a FBI Washington Supervisor who searched Tsarnaev's dorm room at UMass–Dartmouth. Franks found a box of BBs on a desk shelf. *"Govt has not yet explained who built bombs but is now showing Jahar had in his possession the BBs that were part of bomb,"* – Cullen. *"Also found in Tsarnaev's dorm room drawer: receipts from Dick's Sporting Goods for a Smith & Wesson BB gun."* – Armstrong.

Jahar watched Franks removed a box and BBs from an evidence bag on the witness stand. Jahar's friends had told the *Boston Globe* that he liked to play with BB guns and liked to light fireworks for fun. The jurors saw a box near the window sill, containing a tube of fireworks called "Big Snow."– Wen. *"The next photos show a black coat found on the dorm room chair, that jacket is in an evidence bag that Franks IDs,"* – Palumbo. That dark coat was the one Tsarnaev had worn to the marathon. Jahar's famous white hat was also found on his dorm room bed. It was a Polo hat with a giant navy-blue pony on the front and a number 3 on the side. They saw other evidence from the bombings: a thumb drive and a photo of two cell phones, *"The iPhone is badly smashed. Franks holds up both in an evidence bag,"* – Wen. At the foot of Jahar's bed on the floor was a bag containing a book titled, *Soldiers of God,* written *"by Robert Kaplan about how Soviet invasion of Afghanistan led to rise of Taliban,"* – Cullen. Franks pulled the famous white hat out (a Polo Ralph Lauren hat) and placed it on the witness stand. At the end of the day, *"Tsarnaev, standing for the jury, watches quietly as his hat is repackaged on the witness stand. But, he lingers too long and is given a stern gesture by his security team to get moving, drawing a quick look of irritation from Tsarnaev,"* – Sweet.

Photo Images and Exhibits of Tsarnaev's Trial are at this website. Website: https://www.justice.gov/usao-ma/tsarnaev-trial-exhibits

Day 13 – March 25, 2015 – THE HOME ON 410 NORFOLK STREET

The floors creaked, and the walls of the house were so thin that Derks could hear other people talk next door. While the 81st WITNESS FBI SPECIAL AGENT CHRISTOPHER DERKS and his team worked to search through rooms in a house on 410 Norfolk Street for bomb clues, they stumbled upon a strange room in the back of the kitchen. This was the home Jahar Tsarnaev grew up in with his family. After his parents had split up and were back in Russia, Jahar went and set up residence at the college. Ownership of the apartment shifted to Tamerlan and his wife (Katherine) and their daughter, Zahara. *"Apt had 3 bedrooms – one w/ a woman's belongings, second w/ child's belongings and third w/ bunk beds. "Small," Derks says of the apt,"* – Bailey.

As a child, Jahar shared the small bed room with his older brother.

The messy, crammed room had a bunk bed, desktop computer, their piled-up clothes and belongings and a black and white flag with Arabic writings.

The jurors saw Dzhokhar's ID and U.S. citizenship papers when he became a citizen during college, reported Wen.

Although Jahar lived in his college dorm, the Defense strategy intended to show the property belonged to Tamerlan. After the search, Derks found two boxes for the IPhones, a tube of gun lubrication, gun–cleaning brushes, a box of BB's, a bull's-eye type target, two small bottles of super–glue, a jar full of small carpet nails and Christmas lights all balled up on the floor of the house, according to reporters Wen and Cullen.[149] Also found, *"Derks now holding up for jury a dusty glass pickle jar full of nails, metal found in closet of Tsarnaev apt. Half empty, it rattles,"* – Bailey.

Now, the jurors saw the strange room behind the kitchen. Derks described the room, *"It almost looked like a construction site. There were tools everywhere lots of debris,"* – Cullen. They seized entire drawers, found lots of tools and several rolls of packaging tape. He also discovered a hobby fuse, a top of pressure cooker lid, a roll of gorilla tape, a wire cutter in the kitchen area. Derks shared, *"The thinking was these tools could be used in the making of a device…so we took everything,"* – Cullen. Jahar viewed the monitor showing his brother's apartment.

The government seized everything from the apartment and brought them into the courtroom inside several bins and bags. *View tools (http://bostondefender.org/wp-content/uploads/2015/03/3066.pdf)*

FBI Agent Derks rummaged through a bin full of wires and tapes and identified them for the jurors. *"Duct tape, Teflon tape, clear packing tape – multiple rolls of tape seized from various locations in the Cambridge apartment,"* – Whitehouse. BB's were found scattered on the floor, in addition to a soldering gun. Gorilla glue, a gun-cleaning kit, top of a soup can, battery charger for a remote-controlled car, a BB gun, and a tube of clear silicon caulking. Derks found a book with Russian writings. *"FBI agent pulls out a folded, dried–up piece of paper, which is breaking off in pieces. Defense wants to enter as exhibit,"* – Wen.

"It is notebook paper, fringe still on part of the side, written in what appears to be a foreign language," – Armstrong, which translates *"Kalmullah.com," "Prophet Series"* and *"Anwar Awlaki."*

Miriam picked up a notebook, but Derks said quietly, "Put on rubber gloves please," to prevent contamination of the evidence. "Sorry," she said. There were six notebooks with writings in a foreign language and in English. One of the notebooks had a Bunker Hill Community College logo on it; that was where Tamerlan went to school briefly.

View notebooks: (http://bostondefender.org/wp-content/uploads/2015/03/3155.pdf)

"Conrad asks agent if he recalls seizing Russian airline ticket for Tamerlan from apt. He does. US object. Overruled," – Lawrence. This Russian plane ticket dated July 17, 2012 was used when Tamerlan returned from Dagestan, and where he tried to join some extremist Muslim groups. She wanted to admit it as evidence; however, the Government objected, and the Judge overruled it. *View plane ticket: (http://bostondefender.org/wp-content/uploads/2015/03/1219.pdf)*

INSIDE TAMERLAN'S WALLET

Defense showed the jury the inside contents of Tamerlan's wallet. Tamerlan had Home Depot receipts and a Target receipt showing he had purchased two backpacks, one $39 and $59 at a Watertown Target on April 14, 2013, a day before the bombings. Other receipts showed a $40 purchase from Stateline Guns, Ammo & Archery in Plaistow, NH on April 11, 2013. There was also a MoneyGram receipt transferred for $900 sent to his mother in Russia on April 13, 2013. *–Reported by Wen & Cullen.*
View wallet: http://media.justice.gov/video/usao/ma/150325/Exh%20948-563.JPG)

TAMERLAN CAUGHT ON VIDEO BUYING BACKPACKS

On April 14, 2013, surveillance camera at Watertown Target caught Tamerlan alone exiting after purchasing two backpacks for $106 on the afternoon before bombing. Dzhokhar was not with him. One Ful brand #069100374, another was Jansport #069100253. The FUL backpack was used to conceal the bomb that exploded at the store Marathon Sports. However, Tamerlan did not buy the FOX brand, the label found at the Forum explosion site. Dzhokhar's backpack remained a mystery.[150] – *Reported by Wen & Cullen.*

View Tamerlan caught on video:
(http://bostondefender.org/wpcontent/uploads/2015/03/3096.pdf)

View receipts:
(http://media.justice.gov/video/usao/ma/150325/Exh%20948-575.JPG)

View GPS: (https://www.justice.gov/sites/default/files/usao-ma/pages/attachments/2015/03/26/exh_1152-7.pdf)

View Fagor pressure cooker:
(http://media.justice.gov/video/usao/ma/150319/Exh%20948-306.JPG)

82nd WITNESS WAS FBI SPECIAL AGENT CHRISTIAN FIERABEND. GPS was found in the Mercedes SUV; it showed that Tamerlan visited Macy's to purchase "Fagor" brand pressure cookers. The pressure cookers used on Boylston Street were 6 quarts and the ones on Laurel Street 4 quarts. On January 31, 2013, a 4-qt. and 6-qt. pressure cooker were sold in Saugus. In early February, Tamerlan made a stop at a firework store in Seabrook, New Hampshire and purchased 3 lbs. of black powder. On March 17, 2013, a 6-qt. was purchased at Square One Mall in Massachusetts. The GPS map showed stops at three Walmart stores in New Hampshire on March 6, 2013. These stops were matched to receipts. In Manchester, New Hampshire two boxes of BBs were paid for in cash. There was another same purchase in Amherst, NH. No video footage of these Walmart or Macy purchases were recovered.

86th WITNESS WAS FBI SPECIAL AGENT HEIDI WILLIAMS. She examined Text messages from Dzhokhar's Sony VAIO laptop. On December 25, 2012: *"Doing something with Tamerlan, I'll hit you up in a bit bro."* January 2013, he texted: *"Come May I'm out," "There's one other option, highest level of heaven," "I got a plan, I'll tell you later about it,"* and *"I'm really down for that jihad life."* Another text exchange mentioned a name *"Tima"* being very influential in Jahar's life. Tima could have been Tamerlan's nickname. Jahar tweeted, *"I've been sober for a month. I love Tima for that."* Kevin Cullen tweeted in court, *"Tsarnaev is bragging about being sober in months leading up to bombings can't help defense narrative of stoner following radicalized brother. But defense loves Tamerlan being described as a "role model" in those texts."* In a text dated, January 28, 2013, Jahar told a friend that he, *"for now read a lot of Islamic literature."*

Day 14 – March 26, 2015 – EXAMINING BOMB EXPLOSIONS

On Day 14 of the trial, people sitting in the gallery stared at Jahar searching for any clues. He never gazed back as he exited the room. An observer described Jahar during the proceedings said he would often slouch down in his seat. He seemed like a bored student, fidgeting, stroking his goatee, "has a mixture of physical discomfort, guilty, embarrassment, and the gravity of knowing just how obviously inexcusable of what he has done."[151] He also looked sick, increasingly skinny, unhealthy and pale. When he stood up, his suit hung off him since he started wearing it. His body language was tough to read.

87th WITNESS WAS DAVID MCCOLLAM, a chemist for the FBI.

He and his team analyzed more than 300 pieces of evidence from the bombings. McCollam said explosives were classified into two groups – low & high, reported by Cullen.

HIGH	LOW
Explosives react faster than the speed of sound	React slower than the speed of sound
TNT, dynamite, nitro, military grade explosives	To fuel flares, fireworks, black powder, road flares, kitchen matches
Need a shock wave, detonator, a black cloud, carbon	Need a chemical source called an oxidizer, which supplies oxygen, a white cloud.

Both residues from the Boylston Street bombs and Watertown blasts were all low explosive, firework type material. They found big pieces of metal fragments with black residue that they scraped off to test. McCollam said his team found "pyrotechnic flash powder" at the Boylston Street and Laurel Street sites.[152]

"Again, FBI chemist says he can't say where the bombs were built, but gov is strongly hinting Tsarnaev apt in Cambridge," –Bailey. Explosive containing pyrotechnic residue was tested and found on a latex glove in the family CRV vehicle and Honda Odyssey. The tool drawer, the hobby fuse had explosive residue on them. The soup can lid also tested positive for nitroglycerin. *"No explosive residue found in FBI tests of Dzhokhar Tsarnaev's dorm room at UMass, FBI chemist testifies on cross."* – Lawrence.

HOW PARTS OF THE BOMB WAS MADE

THE 88th WITNESS WAS FBI SUPERVISORY SPECIAL AGENT EDWARD KNAPP

From reporter Cullen & Bailey complied.

- Parts were made from toy cars using the electrical fusing system.
- A strand of Christmas lights, lightbulb sets off "low explosive charge."
- RC car's controller was connected to the Christmas tree bulb; sets off the bomb.
- Toggle switches that required being flipped on to activate the devices.

BOMB REMNANTS FOUND AT BOMB SITE ON BOYLSTON STREET

First Bomb at Scene A – at Marathon Sports – "Ful" brand
– Found remnants of a heavily–damaged "toggle switch" to "arm" the device.
– Found hobby fuse that ignited the IED, covered with electrical tape.
– Found backpack, "Ful" brand. Found zipper.
– Pressure cooker lid was found some distance away.
– Found circular pieces of cardboard.
– Found BB's, found Christmas tree lightbulbs.
– RC car, transmitter/receiver, battery, etc.; items were found at Scene A.

Second Bomb at Scene B – at Forum Restaurant – "Fox" backpack
– Found a battery pack & hobby fuse, also shreds of a "Fox" backpack.
– Found no toggle switch at the 2nd blast site, but it may not have been needed.
– Found RC car speed controller.
– A used brand of receiver was found there in reconstruction.
– BBs and circular cardboard were found at both blast sites, also small nails at 2nd blast site.

BROTHERS GOING SEPARATELY PLANNING AND BUYING

The Government showed a receipt for the T–Mobile. The defendant had purchased a pre-paid cell phone a day before the bombings. Dzhokhar bought the phone at 6 p.m. on April 14, 2013, in Cambridge. Next, the government presented the receipt for the backpacks his brother Tamerlan purchased two hours before Dzhokhar bought the cell phone at 4:06 p.m. on the same day.

THE MATERIALS TAMERLAN PURCHASED TO MAKE THE BOMBS

The FBI obtained records from NitroRCX dated February 8, 2013. This was the company that made remote controlled model cars. Also, on Feb. 8, Tamerlan bought AA batteries online and a 1 Rally Monster truck. On April 4, 2013, Tamerlan bought more batteries and gear for a radio control car from Amazon. Tamerlan purchased a new transmitter/receiver for radio-controlled cars for about $70 from "RC Cars of Boston" in Malden. On April 11, another receipt for a shoulder holster was found in his wallet.

View purchase:
(http://media.justice.gov/video/usao/ma/150325/Exh%201431.jpg)

BOMB MOCK-UP

In court, Agent Knapp had put together a mock-up of the 3 pressure cooker bombs, 2 pipe bombs and a Tupperware bomb. All along Knapp's demonstration, Dzhokhar exhibited interest, reported Cullen. Knapp showed how BBs were taped inside and a model car control inserted inside a pot. On top of that he added fake gunpowder. He demonstrated how to flip a switch to turn toggle on to complete the circuit. He showed how they fit in the backpacks. *"It is pretty heavy,"* – Knapp said while carrying one. – Bailey. The jurors passed around the mock up pressure cooker to feel and inspect it. During cross-examination, Defense Timothy Watkins asked if the cardboard disc pieces inside the pressure cooker bombs went out for fingerprint analysis. Prosecution objected, but the Judge allowed the question. Knapp finally said, "Yes." Defense wanted to prove that Tamerlan had been to one to build the bombs, pack the bombs and put them into the backpacks.

HOW TO MAKE A BOMB

Dzhokhar slouched in his chair watching the monitor and listening to Agent Knapp read the *Inspire* magazine article on how to build a pipe bomb. The jurors listened as Knapp read the article the step-by-step how-to on making a pipe bomb, how to handle Christmas tree light, also how to make a low explosive.

The magazine instructed to place the bomb in a crowded area, and to conceal or camouflage the shrapnel with cardboard. These remnants were found at Scene A and B on Boylston. "This is an explosive device so take care in preparation and wear gloves," *Inspire* said, "Final advice, put your trust in Allah and pray for success."

JAHAR MOMENTS

"As Jahar exited, he pressed his right palm on the top of the witness stand where Agent Knapp stood." – Sweet

"While Jahar returned back in the courtroom he appeared to try on someone's eyeglasses very briefly." – Bailey. He probably needs glasses! *"Jahar looked animated – it's rare – chatting with his lawyer, Judy, as they wait for the start of afternoon testimony."* – Cullen

"The court goes to a 15-minute break. In the jury box, a sleepy juror succumbed again. Even Jahar has noticed the juror. "Clink, clink, clink," the sounds of the handcuffs, Jahar heeded to the "clink, clink, clink" of the Marshals' jailer keys and trudged out." – Sweet

"During sidebar, several of the older female jurors stared at Jahar, beginning to wonder about him." – Sweet

Three Deaths On Boylston Street

"Martin was 53 inches tall and 69 pounds... He was 8 years old."
– Chief Medical Examiner, Dr. Henry Nields

AUTOPSY PHOTOS WERE SHOWN to the jury, witness and attorneys only. No one in the gallery or media could view them. Jahar listened to the graphic testimony. He stared down at the defense table and did not observe the medical examiner. Autopsy photos were not shown to him.

Behind him his lawyers were moving around a monitor. He turned back, checking to see what they were doing and somehow, he glanced at the monitor briefly. He caught a diagram of the autopsy, but not the photo. Defense attorney Judy, quickly put her hand on Jahar's shoulder and told him to turn around. He turned around.

Jurors reacted to the autopsy photos became very emotional. Some jurors cried, wiped away tears. Others glared at Tsarnaev angrily. Others became upset, winced or glanced at the photos.

The mood at the Defense table around this time of the trial seemed very gloomy, even Jahar took it in, appearing subdued and was not talkative with his lawyers.

KRYSTLE CAMPBELL, 29

"She passed away from blast injuries to her torso and lower extremities. It was a "homicide,"– (Cullen), said 89th WITNESS MEDICAL EXAMINER DR. JENNIFER HAMMERS.

Krystle Campbell:
(http://media.justice.gov/video/usao/ma/154021/1601-28.bmp)

Memorandum: Krystle Campbell was dearly loved by her friends that she was a bridesmaid seventeen times. She was honored with a peace garden in Medford that will include benches, walkway, five fountains and a flagpole symbolizing the marathon finish line. Each fountain would be marked with a bronze memorial plaque that would be shaped like compass points to commemorate the four who were killed.

Campbell's would point east because she lived east of the garden; Sean Collier's to the north because he was from Wilmington; Martin Richard, to the south toward his home in Dorchester; and Lingzi Lu's to the west in China.[153]

LINGZI LU, 23

"The cause of death was blast injuries of the lower extremities," said Lindstrom. "Death was homicide. She died within "seconds to minutes" and it was very painful injuries,"– (Wen) said 90th WITNESS DOCTOR CATHERINE LINDSTROM, CHIEF MEDICAL EXAMINER. Lingzi was killed by the second bomb, the one carried by Dzhokhar.

Lingzi Lu:
(http://media.justice.gov/video/usao/ma/150422/1607-05.jpg)

Memorandum: Lingzi Lu was shy, sweet and bubbly. She was quiet and well-behaved. She focused on her studies and was an "A" student at Boston University. She became a well-known student in mathematics and statistics. Before her death, she finished her qualifying exams. She passed those exams with flying colors. She died before learning about her exam results.

Day 15 – March 30, 2015

91st WITNESS WAS MICHELLE GAMBLE, an FBI crime scene photographer who went after the bombings to Boylston Street to photograph evidence and the bodies of victims, reported Wen. She also put together the compilation videos and photos of the Tsarnaev brothers for the entire investigation. One video showed Dzhokhar standing behind children and on the phone 19 seconds before the second blast. The backpack was at his feet. Prosecutor William Weinreb suggested to the jury that Tsarnaev was perhaps targeting the children, but Attorney Miriam Conrad argued that the backpack was not put directly in back of the Richard's children, but at other people around them. The Richards were not the target, reported Bailey.[154]

When the court took a short morning break, *"Jahar stood up. He nearly stepped over one of his lawyer's luggage, as the top Marshal sternly beckoned him back to custody,"* observed reporter Sweet. Then as he left, Judy, Miriam and David gathered together. They all had very serious and sad looks. They knew what was about to come next. The prosecution would rest on their last witness, focusing on the youngest bombing victim, eight–year–old Martin Richard.

MARTIN RICHARD, 8

"I'm struggling here with how much to say. I'm choosing to omit some of the most graphic details. Suffice it to say, Martin Richard had extensive and terrible injuries to many of his internal organs as a result of the explosion,"– (Armstrong), said 92nd WITNESS WAS CHIEF MEDICAL EXAMINER DR. HENRY NIELDS.

Martin Richard:
(http://i.huffpost.com/gen/1181699/images/o-MARTIN-RICHARD-MEMORIAL-SERVICE-facebook.jpg)

Memorandum: Martin Richard was a nice combination of his Dad and Mom. He was innocent and very well behaved. He was curious and a joy. He loved the simplicity of life.

Jahar slouched in his seat. He showed no emotion to any of the graphic autopsy testimonies. In the courtroom Martin Richard's parents, Bill and Denise had not seen these photos. Bill wrapped his arm around Denise as they tried to listen to the horrific detailed autopsy description of their child's murder. The jurors listening to the testimonies were wiping away their tears, glancing at the photos or glaring at Jahar. While one of his lawyers, David Bruck, studied the autopsy photos, Jahar held his stares straight ahead, reported Valencia. Prosecutors asked how old Martin was at the time. *"He was eight–years–old."* – Cullen. Denise wiped her wet eyes with a tissue. [155]

The government presented 92 witnesses over 15 days in the guilt phase of the Boston Marathon bombing trial. "The government rests," William Weinreb declared. Judge O'Toole stated after, *"May be some temptation to talk about things...the time will come, but it is not now."* – Cullen. At the Defense table, the attorneys had a look of anxiety, realizing they *"have a mighty hill to climb,"* – (Cullen), with only a small number of witnesses to present for the guilt phase.

DEFENSE'S WITNESSES TESTIFYING FOR TSARNAEV

"Tamerlan", "Tamerlan" And "Tamerlan"

"The bombs didn't build themselves, did they?"
– William Weinreb, prosecutor asking fingerprint expert.

JAHAR TSARNAEV RETURNED TO court, and he immediately began conversing with Judy. His Defense team was at the table going through files and preparing their case. They all looked very somber today. Everyone was waiting in anticipation to see who the Defense would present as witnesses. Defense would try to prove that Tamerlan was the mastermind of the bombings and not Jahar. For a few seconds, Jahar was alone at the defendant table while his lawyers met with Judge O 'Toole. There seemed to be an argument going on between Tsarnaev's attorneys and the government. After the sidebar meeting was over, the jurors entered, and the Defense brought in their first witness.

A book was found under the couch in Tamerlan's apartment in Cambridge. The evidence was in the possession of the FBI. Defense's 1st WITNESS WAS FBI PHOTOGRAPHER MICHELLE GAMBLE. The first evidence presented by Defense was a book about home wiring, titled, *Wiring: Complete Projects for the Home.* Miriam asked Gamble if the book was submitted for fingerprints. Gamble said, "Yes." Gamble was also involved in the search for evidence in Jahar's dorm room in UMass–Dartmouth.

Miriam asked if vacuum samples were taken from his room. The FBI agent said she believed they were. As Gamble finished and left the stand, the Defense team called for a sidebar to argue against the government. The jurors were released for a short recess.

Everybody was tense, including the Defense and government that Jahar was led out from the courtroom. He stretched out his back and left. They entered a court docket: *"Tsarnaev motion to dismiss certain counts based on insufficient evidence."*

After a short break, Jahar returned as his Defense continued to present their case. In the gallery, Bill and Denise Richard watched him. When the jury entered again Jahar made eye contact with them, but none of them would look at Jahar. The court and media were clueless as to how many witnesses the Defense would present or who these witnesses were. Their list was under seal.

Jahar had his face up against the monitor in front of him as he read his own tweets on the *j_tsar* account. 2nd WITNESS WAS GERALD GRANT JR., a computer forensic expert. Grant was a *"federal public defender in Western District of NY who has expertise in digital evidence, computers, telephones, and cell tower location–plotting,"* tweeted Bailey and Armstrong, respectively. On the stand he explained Tsarnaev's posted tweet on April 16, 2012 — which was the day of the 2012 Boston Marathon, not 2013, the doomed marathon. Tsarnaev wrote *"they will spend their money...and then they will be defeated."* The prosecution claimed this tweet expressed extreme Jihadist views.

(From *http://bostondefender.org/wp-content/uploads/2015/03/3126B.pdf*)

Defense disputed prosecution claims that Tsarnaev showed any intent at radicalization. They highlighted the tweet on April 15, 2012 at 4:58 p.m. a day before the marathon, Tsarnaev tweeted: *"get breakfast or go back to sleep...always a tough one"* was posted the day before the marathon.

This tweet, the Defense hoped would remind the jury that he was just a teenager. Two hours later, April 16, 2012, around 8:30 a.m. another few tweets were posted from Dzhokhar about sleep and breakfast, reported Wen.

"*Now defense matching these tweets with Tsarnaev's entry-key times at Maple Ridge Hall, his freshman year dorm at UMass-Dartmouth. Computer specialist said records show Tsarnaev apparently entered this UMass dorm at 10:56 a.m. on 4/16/12,*" – Wen.

"*Defense now showing tweet from marathon day 2012. "Yea summers gonna be amazing." Grant says this was posted from a computer,*" tweeted Lana Jones from WBZ. Defense attempted to prove that Tsarnaev had no radical intent toward the event a year ago by showing that tweet, "*Defense now shows a tweet at 12:46 p.m. on 4/16/12 from a computer, when runners would have been crossing the finish line,*" – Palumbo. Dzhokhar made no mention of the marathon in his tweet posting.

Grant's presentation about cell phone towers was technical. Jahar seemed to lose interest, scratching his curly hair. Grant created a map "*with plot points, again based on cell phone log data, to tell where a phone was at any given time*" – Armstrong. Defense stressed that Dzhokhar could not have used cash to buy the two pressure cookers at Macy's in Saugus's Square One mall on January 31, 2013 at 8:30 p.m. Data showed at 9:03 p.m. Dzhokhar was texting from his phone at UMass-Dartmouth. Defense asserted that Dzhokhar used his meal swipe card on January 31, 2013 at 6:54 p.m. So, it was not possible for him to be in Saugus. Bailey tweeted, "*According to Grant, Tsarnaev was specifically eating at Wendy's at UMass that night.*"

Defense pressed on, emphasizing that the older brother Tamerlan was the one purchasing bomb components. It was not Dzhokhar because he was at school at the time of the purchase.

Another receipt showed Tamerlan had purchased BB's from Wal-Marts in New Hampshire on March 6, 2013. At a Wal-Mart in Amherst, he purchased the items at 3:22 p.m. He purchased more BB's from another Wal-Mart in Manchester, about 13 miles away at 5:34 p.m. But, data showed that Jahar's phone was in the UMass-Dartmouth area on that afternoon on that day.

The Government's prosecutor Aloke Chakravarty attempted to poke holes and asked if Grant had analyzed Tamerlan's phone. Defense objected. Chakravarty asked abruptly, "Are you aware of an outbound text to Tamerlan?"

"Grant says he's unaware of that call, but that it wouldn't surprise him. Prosecution then points out that the Tsarnaev brothers texted each other day of pressure cooker purchase, and had a 4-min. phone call," – Boeri. Dzhokhar had sent a text to his brother on the day the pressure cooker were purchased.

Chakravarty persistently asked Gerald Grant if he knew who purchased the BB's, if there was video footage of Tamerlan making such a purchase, or if he knew what vehicle was in New Hampshire that day. Miriam had to "whisper yell" with her colleague Tim Watkins to "object" Chakravarty. Chakravarty started to ask Grant if there were other communications between the Tsarnaev brothers like emails, phone calls or texts. *"Did you also analyze Tamerlan's cell phone? Objection, sustained,"* – Armstrong. "In fact, on April 14 --" Chakravarty got cut off by Defense.

Watkins: "Objection." Judge: "Sustained."

Chakravarty could not stop asking, "Did you see anything in your research showing Tamerlan made the BB or pressure cooker purchases?"

Grant answered, "No, sir."

Defense tried to show that Dzhokhar could not have purchased the bomb components in Saugus and then driven back to UMass according to his cell phone records.

At the end of the day, the jurors left the courtroom. Afterward, Jahar and his lawyers, relieved from the cross-examination of their first witness Gerald Grant, shared a laugh. They seemed a bit more confident. Jahar smiled and talked with his attorneys. His lawyers reassured him and talked with him, and then he was taken back into custody. The Defense case solely centered on who orchestrated the attack and created the bombs, magnifying the role of the older brother as the leader, and the mastermind. Jahar would hopefully be viewed as just an adherent, devoted to the cause and as a lost college student, reported Wen.

Day 16 – March 31, 2015

On the morning of March 31st, the second day, the Defense attorneys Miriam Conrad and David Bruck paid Jahar a visit before the start of testimony. As soon as the lawyers returned to the courtroom, *"Tsarnaev pads in quietly like a cat."* His current appearance was quite shocking, looking pale and underweight. He did not look like the picture of him in *Rolling Stone*. His face was thinner. One eye was half shut and his face – swollen. On the second day of Defense testimony, Jahar shared a whispered conversation with Judy. As he stood for the Judge and jury, *"Tsarnaev is looking over paperwork so gripping that he didn't stop looking at it as he stood."* – Bailey.

The 3rd WITNESS WAS MARK SPENCER, a digital forensic consultant. He began his testimony about how the brothers had 5 million+ files and folders on their drives, not counting deleted (but recoverable) items, plus all the deleted space and zip files. He had examined two laptops: Tamerlan's Samsung and Dzhokhar's Sony VAIO. Spencer had also examined the HP desktop from Tsarnaev's apartment in Cambridge.

Tamerlan's laptop and HP in Cambridge had the username of "Umar." He had googled a word search for *"Ruger p95"* on March 4, 2013. *"More searches on 4/10/13 and 4/11/13 from Tamerlan Tsarnaev's computer: "gun stores in Salem," "Boston marathon,"* – Bailey. This is the pistol that was used to murder Collier and used in the Watertown shooting. Even though Tsarnaev borrowed the Ruger from Silva, the gun was also used by Tamerlan. *"Next on Tamerlan's laptop: Searches for "radio transmitter," "oscilloscope,"* – Armstrong. *"From Tamerlan's computer search history for 4/7/13: "fireworks firing system," "detonator,"* – Stevens. These searches were entered before 2013 bombing.

Spencer had analyzed Dzhokhar's Sony laptop. It had the user name of "Anzor." It had no searches involving the Boston Marathon before the bombings, tweeted Adam Reilly, 89.7 *WBGH* radio. From Patricia Wen of *Boston Globe*, she reported *"Tsarnaev's laptop only looked up Boston Marathon in connect w/bombing, (must be after the bombings). His top sites were Facebook & VK (Russian social media)."* His Facebook had 1,378 hits and the Russian media site had 1,275 hits. He had also used Google and watched videos on YouTube. Besides that, typical for a teenage boy, *"The 10th most visited website on Tsarnaev's computer? A porn site,"*– Boeri. *"Basically, the Defense stake to make its case that Tamerlan was searching for guns and bomb components. And Dzhokhar was cruising on Facebook, cars and girls before being led astray by Tamerlan,"* – Cullen.

On Tamerlan's computer, Spencer found mp3 files of Sheikh Anwar al-Awlaki videos on the external drive, including copies of complete *Inspire* magazine—which illustrated how to make bombs. He had extreme jihadi images copied from a jihadi website, including sections on how to construct a bomb. None of this was on Dzhokhar's computer.

However, a complete *Inspire* on Tamerlan's computer dated December 21, 2011 was transferred to Dzhokhar's laptop. Spencer traced the origin of the *Inspire* file where it was created. The file was on Tamerlan's computer and a month later, *"the Inspire file was copied on a thumb drive and uploaded to Dzhokhar laptop early morning of January 21, 2012. It was the same day Tamerlan went to Russia,"* tweeted Boeri. Defense wanted to show that Tamerlan had arranged to transfer all his radical content onto Dzhokhar's computer right before he left for Russia.[156]

After cross–examination, Spencer agreed that, *"Dzhokhar's Sony contains numerous searches for Boston Marathon bombing after event and jihad,"* tweeted *Fox 25's* Bob Ward. On April 11, 2013, two days before the bombings, Jahar had conducted a search on *"The Call of Jihad."*– Cullen. On February 2, 2013, Dzhokhar's computer also showed a search for Jannah Al-Firdaus. *"Jannah al–firdaus"* refers to the ultimate (highest) level of heaven. Finally, Chakravarty claimed that a month before the marathon on March 18–19, 2013, Dzhokhar had removed songs and homework from his hard drive and had replaced it with Jihadi propaganda and al-Awlaki files. Chakravarty showed Dzhokhar had already become radicalized.

The court was dismissed for morning recess. Jahar stood. He frowned. He probably was thinking about how the government had found all his searches on the internet. The first phase of the trial was drawing to a close. Jahar exhaled and put his hands in his pocket. He rubbed his eyes and walked out of the courtroom.

4th WITNESS WAS ELENA GRAFF, a fingerprint examiner for the FBI. Graff was called last minute by the Defense to testify about the fingerprints on the bomb components and tools in a large bin found in the Cambridge apartment. Graff had analyzed over 800 fingerprints in this case. The Tupperware bowl filled with firework powder found at Watertown, carried 2 of Dzhokhar's prints and 6 of Tamerlan's fingerprints. From the pressure cooker lid recovered in Watertown, Graff recovered only one print: Tamerlan's.

Graff also recovered Tamerlan's prints from his high school diploma and his travel documents for Russia. "I found Tamerlan's prints on those," said Elena Graff. A receipt for the purchase of bomb components was found inside a car at Cambridge. *"Receipt from "RC Cars of Boston": Graff found three prints. Tamerlan's,"* – Reilly. *"Jar of nails. Prints collected. ID'd to Tamerlan,"* – Ward.

Several items were found in the Cambridge apartment: a two–page letter in Russian was analysed for prints. Graff identified 10 prints and they all belonged to Tamerlan. The caulk gun: one latent print found – identified to Tamerlan. Graff also found one latent fingerprint that belonged to Tamerlan on two rolls of tapes as well as dozens of prints on several notebooks. No prints from Dzhokhar were found on any items. However, Dzhokhar had left prints on the storage container bomb in the carjacked Mercedes: 2 for Dzhokhar, 6 for Tamerlan.

EXAMINED BY GRAFF, TAMERLAN'S FINGERPRINTS FOUND ON:
Source: Tweet from Eric Levenson@ejleven

Radio transmitter	Several Jars of nails	Pliers
RC transmitter receipt	Caulk gun	Rolls of plumber's tapes
Tamerlan's high school diploma	Duct tapes	Tamerlan's notebooks
Tamerlan's Russian passport	Wires	Gun cleaning equipment
Pressure cooker lid	Soldering gun	Wiring instruction manual

Cardboard from inside the pressure cooker bombs and the backpack in shreds.

Defense investigated a junk drawer of tools seized from the Cambridge apartment. Most of the tools had Tamerlan's prints on them. Dzhokhar's prints weren't on any of the bomb components or tools. *"Jahar leaned forward in his seat and listened with interest in all this fingerprint testimony. It did have an effect of resurrecting the dead Tamerlan in the courtroom,"* – Wen. Tamerlan's prints were found in half–dozen notebooks, on gun cleaning equipment, pliers, duct tape, wires, on *The Sovereign* newspaper – (a radical publication) and on a wiring book found under the couch.[157]

FINGERPRINTS GATHERED AT BOYLSTON STREET

Graff said she examined over 500 objects, only 6 objects produced prints.

Scene	Marathon Sports – Scene A	Forum Restaurant – Scene B
Who	Tamerlan sets bomb.	Dzhokhar sets bomb.
Prints Found	Found 4 prints, 3 palm prints & finger prints.	Found 2 latent palm prints, 1 print found on 2 pieces cardboard.
Remnants	Found burned pieces of cardboard.	Print found on shredded backpack and cardboard.
Who's Prints?	Prints identified to Tamerlan's, none Dzhokhar's prints.	Prints identified to Tamerlan. No evidence was found of second blast site with Dzhokhar's prints.

Weinreb got up to cross-examine the witness. He asked, "Hundreds of items from scene A & B were tested for both brothers' prints? You found usable prints on only two pieces of cardboard? And outside Forum, only single print of Tamerlan?" Graff explained how cardboard and paper were porous items and could retain prints. So, yes, was her answer as to how she found those prints, reported Bailey. "The bombs didn't build themselves, did they?" asked Weinreb. "No," responded Graff.

"The backpacks didn't carry themselves?"

Watkins objected, but the Judge, sustained.

Weinreb asked Graff, "Then where are all the other prints?"

Graff answered, "Fingerprints are very fragile, they are easily destroyed,"– Armstrong. Dzhokhar's prints could have been destroyed or could have evaporated after the explosions. Weinreb suggested, "The person may have worn gloves, or the prints were smudged, or the fingers were too sweaty? Then no prints left?"

"Yes," reported Cullen.

"If someone who didn't live in a resident full time would you expect to find their prints?"

"No," she answered. Weinreb asked again, "You found Tamerlan's prints on the objects in his own apartment?"

"For the most part, yes." – Cullen.

"The bomb found in back of the abandoned Mercedes in Watertown, you found both Dzhokhar's and Tamerlan's?"

"That is correct," reported Cullen. Elena Graff, the fingerprint expert stepped off the witness stand.

THE DEFENSE RESTS

The Defense announced they had no more witnesses, but they wanted to introduce some photos before they rested their case. A few jurors smiled that the first phase was almost complete. However, Weinreb objected to the evidence and Judge O'Toole ordered a sidebar. Music filled the room. Immediately, Jahar turned to attorney David Bruck and talked with him. During sidebar, many jurors observed Jahar, wondering. Jahar was tapping his left knee in time with the rhythm of the Jazz music. He hadn't heard music in a long while. He quickly turned sideways and glanced at the jury staring at him.

At sidebar, Judy talked with Judge O'Toole about the photos. Still, the Judge would not allow defense to show the pictures without witnesses. He called for a break.

The lawyers got together with Jahar as the jury left. Judy rubbed Jahar's back to give him some hope. She filled him in on what might happen next. Later, he was led out of court.

Over recess Tsarnaev's Defense team laughed while the government attorneys talked and smiled in their corner. Afterward, lead prosecutor William Weinreb secretly crept in, chatting with the Defense team.

After the break, Judge called another sidebar. Jahar returned and security made sure Jahar was not sitting by himself while his lawyers argued their point. An older woman from the team sat with Jahar. Prosecutor Mellin brought out a large law book on federal procedure. Judge O'Toole read the book with the attorneys. A court reporter typed their conversations. Suddenly, Judge announced a lunch recess to resolve legal or procedural issues regarding the photos, and whether Defense would be allowed to show them. Jahar shrugged his shoulders as he left.

After lunch, there was another sidebar. Another recess was called as the Judge retreated to his chambers. Lawyers were grinning, and it was *"madness"* observed reporter Sweet because *"Jahar was getting his exercise. He exited the court with his security guards."* After a while, Jahar returned, smiling and chatted with Judy. They viewed Miriam's laptop screen with David Bruck. The Judge returned, and the court had another sidebar. After the sidebar, the jurors entered. A Court officer shouted, "Quiet, in the courtroom please!" It had been two hours since Defense announced they had no more witnesses to call.

Judy Clarke stood up and declared, "At this point, we rest," reported Cullen. No photos. What did these last photos show? Defense had the Judge look at the photos, and it served his notice to know about them. The Defense seemed quite pleased, despite failing to have these photos shown. "The evidence is concluded," said Judge O'Toole. All the attorneys turned and smiled as the jury exited the room. Jahar stared down as they left, as observed by Bailey. He left the room thereafter. In this guilt–phase which brother masterminded the bombings? Jahar was pretty good at playing poker face. He had an expressionless face that hid his true feelings. No one truly knew who Dzhokhar Tsarnaev really was.

Closing Arguments & The Verdict

"I think what it really shows is that, overall, he bought into his brother's plan and his brother's actions and, as the boat writing suggests, was convinced they were right."
– Judy Clarke

TSARNAEV'S PUNISHMENT HAD ALREADY begun claimed survivor Marc Fucarile, who had been badly injured and who lost his leg at the marathon while he supported a friend who ran the race. He told NBC, "He looks like he's been staring at a wall for a long time, so it's actually kind of rewarding, you know, to see him not looking the healthiest." On April 6, 2015, the 17th day of the trial, the first phase of Dzhokhar Tsarnaev's trial neared an end. Outside the courthouse a line of anti-death penalty protestors stood, holding anti-death penalty signs. All public seats in Courtroom 9 were filled as assistant U.S. Attorney Aloke Chakravarty prepared to deliver the closing. Many survivors, survivor's families, members of the public and reporters swarmed to the courtroom.

Jahar swaggered into the courtroom. As usual, the victims and survivors in the room stared at Jahar's cocky swagger as he entered, but he never regarded them. He walked with his head down and took a seat between Miriam and David. Jahar was seen having an animated conversation with attorney David Bruck. He drew something for David on a pad of paper and showed it to him. Immediately, *"Judy whispers to Tsarnaev, who nods and then grabs a file. He's flipping thru paperwork now,"* – Bailey.

Later, Judge O'Toole entered with the jurors. He gave further instructions regarding the written copy of 30 counts against Tsarnaev and talked about the history of federal laws. The eighteen jurors paid close attention, yet Jahar sat slouched in his chair with his head hung down.

After the Judge delivered the instructions the government's Prosecutor Aloke Chakravarty went first with his closing argument, followed by Defense's Judy Clarke and ending with a rebuttal from Prosecutor William Weinreb. THE FOLLOWING EXCERPTS WERE EXTRACTED AND SUMMARIZED FROM THE DOCUMENTS REFERENCED #158 AND 158A.

PROSECUTION'S ARGUMENT & EXCERPT SUMMARY

1. **He chose to destruct.** Prosecutors argued the defendant was a holy warrior and wanted to punish America for what they did to his people.

PROSECUTOR ALOKE CHAKRAVARTY: *(Excerpt found on Page 4, begin line 1– 14.)* The defendant chose Patriots Day as the day to terrorize the country and to target civilians.

2. **He was guilty.** Prosecutors argued the defendant was guilty, and that he should take responsibility.

PROSECUTOR WILLIAM WEINREB: *(Excerpt found on Page 49, begin line 13 through Page 50, end line 9.)* Defense pointed that Tamerlan was the "real criminal" and that Dzhokhar went along with him to commit the murders, but prosecutors argued that the defendant should take full responsibility and find him guilty.

3. **He led a double life.** Prosecutors argued the defendant kept his Jihadi life a secret.

PROSECUTOR ALOKE CHAKRAVARTY: *(Excerpt found on Page 34, begin line 10 through 13.)* Chakravarty said that *Inspire* magazine taught the defendant to be careful and to keep his Jihad life a secret, *"To the outside world he showed one face and inside he harbored another."*

4. **Brothers were partners.** Prosecutors argued the brothers were partners and were not individuals who had different roles.

PROSECUTOR ALOKE CHAKRAVARTY: *(Excerpt found on Page 35, begin line 16 through Page 37, end line 17.)* Both brothers handled the bombs and evidence showed they both transported, placed and exploded the bombs on Boylston Street and in Watertown. Although Tamerlan made purchases for bomb material and backpacks, Dzhokhar was in on it as well. He bought the SIM card for the phone and took the gun from Stephen, so he can give it to his brother. They were both partners.

PROSECUTOR WILLIAM WEINREB: *(Excerpt found on Page 54, begin line 13 though Page 55, end line 15.)* Both brothers needed each other and helped one another what they needed to do or to get it done. Tamerlan kidnapped Meng. Dzhokhar took Meng's ATM card to get his money. Both brothers had making bomb instructions on their computers and Dzhokhar spent time at his brother's home.

5. **He had Jihad material.** Prosecutors argued the defendant had access to Jihad materials and was studying them.

PROSECUTOR WILLIAM WEINREB: *(Excerpt found on Page 58, begin line 24 through Page 59, end line 19.)* Weinreb said the defendant had read and absorbed Jihad teachings. He had terrorist writings, songs and video lectures on his computer, iPods and his thumb drives. The defendant had listened and studied these materials for over a year. These teachings convinced him and because of it he believed it was right to murder people.

6. **He was a believer in violent extremism.** Prosecutors argued the defendant made deliberate choices to kill people...He made political choices and was angry.

PROSECUTOR WILLIAM WEINREB: *(Excerpt found on Page 53, line 18 through Page 54, end line 12.)* The defendant was a true believer of violent extremism. He tried to kill three officers by attempting to run over the officers. He was willing to run over his brother. He was committed to act out with violence.

JAHAR THE LONE BOSTON BOMBER #2

PROSECUTOR ALOKE CHAKRAVARTY: *(Excerpt found on Page 46, line 15 through 23.)* Chakravarty argued the defendant teamed up with his brother to terrorize the area. He chose to help his brother with his plans and planned to murder.

7. **He was angry, and he sent a message.** Prosecutors argued he made political choices and was angry and sent a message to America that Americans are destined to lose the fight against violent extremism.

PROSECUTOR ALOKE CHAKRAVARTY: *(Excerpt found on Page 32, line 16 through Page 33, end line 13.)* When people were searching for Dzhokhar, he hid in the boat. He was angry and etched a message into the boards on the slat. *"Stop killing our people and we will stop."* He was negotiating the stop of the killing of his people using anti-American political message.

DEFENSE'S ARGUMENT & EXCERPT SUMMARY

1. **Dzhokhar followed Tamerlan.** Defense argued he was not an equal to his brother, Tamerlan and he was not the leader. Tamerlan led and Dzhokhar followed.

DEFENSE JUDY CLARKE: *(Excerpt found on Page 5 line 11–13 and Page 15 line 7, end line 11.)* Dzhokhar would not have done this if not for Tamerlan. Who was leading and who was following? Clarke argued that Tamerlan bought the pressure cookers at Saugus while Dzhokhar was at UMass–Dartmouth. Evidence showed that he was on his phone in school.

(Excerpt found on Page 20 line 12 through Page 21, end line 11.) Tamerlan, the leader, influenced Dzhokhar to read Jihad magazines. He transferred complete *Inspire* magazine from his Samsung laptop to Dzhokhar's missing thumb drive, Patriot, to his laptop. It was done on the day when Tamerlan left for Russia on January 21.

2. **Tamerlan was to blame.** Defense argued that Tamerlan came up with most of the terrorist bombing plans, bought the bomb

materials and carried out the murders. Dzhokhar did not do these crimes independently.

DEFENSE JUDY CLARKE: *(Excerpt found on Page 6 line 1 through Page 15.)* Tamerlan did the research on building the bombs on the internet. There was evidence (receipts) that he built the bombs from the fingerprint expert's testimony. Tamerlan's prints were on most of the tools. Tamerlan murdered Officer Collier and was squatting and bending trying to retrieve Collier's gun out of the holster. He led, and Dzhokhar followed. Tamerlan also led all the talking to Dun Meng while Dzhokhar followed Tamerlan's orders. Dzhokhar *"fully participated in these events if not for Tamerlan, it would not have happened."*

3. **Dzhokhar did typical teenage stuff.** Defense argued that the secret Twitter account he had showed no signs of violence, and he had it only for two days because he lost interest in it. The most prominent stuff he had in his life was Facebook and his Jahar Twitter account.

DEFENSE JUDY CLARKE: *(Excerpt found on Page 16 line 18 through Page18, end line 23.)* Clarke felt government "cherry–picked" Dzhokhar's tweets showing that he was radicalized by jihadi propaganda. But, Clarke pointed out these were quotes from rap songs. Dzhokhar had tweets of "a typical teenager" going about his daily routine. He mostly used Facebook and VK. Clarke said, *"This is a kid doing kid things, this is a teenage doing kid things."*

4. **Dzhokhar Tried to Express His Actions.** Defense argued that the boat message was not what a violent jihadist would write. He did not write "Death to America" or "Curse to America." Defense explained he knew it was wrong to take innocent lives and that it was because he bought into the plan and bought into the beliefs and did this when he was only 19. He was living a teenage life and flunking school.

DEFENSE JUDY CLARKE: *(Excerpt found on Page 22 line 13 through Page 23, end line 13.)* Clarke said the boat writing was this *"19-year-old's attempt to write about why they did what they did."* Dzhokhar wrote, *"I'm jealous of my brother who has received the reward of paradise. He's gone."* Clarke remarked, *"He didn't write this "message to the world,"* but, rather *"tries to explain what they did. He knew it all along that it was wrong to take innocent lives, and he says that. But he expressed the very twisted belief, that his actions would make a difference."*

DID DZHOKHAR WANTED TO SAY SOMETHING?

Dzhokhar sat very still throughout the closing arguments, until Prosecutor Chakravarty walked up to Dzhokhar and glared directly at him. He yelled at the defendant's face, "making a statement on 'An eye for an eye. You kill us, we kill you.'" Suddenly, Dzhokhar became a little fidgety. He was moving his hands around nervously. He seemed he was affected by some of the things that the prosecutor was saying. Although one observer felt that he acted like a kid in class trying to raise his hand to answer, the prosecutor was reprimanding him instead. For the most part he was poised with his head way down during the admonishment.

At the end of prosecution's closing, Dzhokhar showed no emotion whatsoever. He seemed slow to react. As he stood, he fidgeted, stretched his hand and then put his hands in his pockets. He exited the courtroom with his head down. When he returned from break, he looked very somber.

At the end of closing by defense, Judy asked the jurors to "hold your minds open to what more there is to hear, to what more there is to learn, and to what more there is to understand…we are not asking you to go easy on Dzhokhar. We are not asking you to not hold him accountable and responsible for what he did." Judy empowered the jury: "Dzhokhar Tsarnaev stands ready, by your verdict, to be held responsible for his actions."

Read the Full Transcript of the Closing Arguments of Tsarnaev's Trial [158, 158a]

JAHAR SEEMED GUILTY... AND HE FELL INTO HIS CHAIR...

On April 7, 2015, Day 18 of the trial, Jahar was being uncuffed outside the courtroom. Everyone could hear the cuffs' chains rattling outside the doorway. Jahar finally appeared, entering quietly. He seemed *"drawn"* and *"exhausted"* tweeted Bailey. Perhaps he had been up all-night thinking about what the prosecutors said about him in their arguments. Weinreb's rebuttal got him thinking, *"Yes, he was a young man with a young man's interests and beliefs and habits. That's the side that he revealed to his friends. But he was also a true believer in violent extremism. That's the side that he kept mostly hidden."* Jahar thought about how he had to cover up and hide his thoughts and beliefs from his family and closest friends. He was tired, and it was all affecting him. Jahar talked softly with attorney David Bruck. As he spoke to his attorney, *"his voice sounded hoarse, tho hard to tell if that's normal,"* tweeted Bailey again. Perhaps he was up all-night crying in his sleep, but his lawyer had probably told him to remain unemotional in court.

This was the first day of deliberation. None of the jurors regarded Jahar as they entered. However, Jahar glanced over at them for they would decide his fate soon. Judge O'Toole gave the jurors some instructions, and afterward they filed out to begin deliberation. Jahar's eyes scanned each one of them, hoping, hoping... After the hearing, Jahar left the courtroom in custody.

At the end of the day, at 4 p.m. the defense attorneys and the prosecution team gathered in courtroom 9 as the Judge checked in with the twelve-member jury. Jahar entered court and smiled at Miriam and Judy. Bailey tweeted, *"Miriam asked him, "So, what have you been up to?"* For the past seven hours, he had been in the jail cell, waiting. He chatted with Miriam and turned quickly around to scan the (nearly empty) courtroom gallery.

The only people in the room were his lawyers and reporters. As the jury entered, Jahar observed them closely. There were no smiles on the jury's faces. The jury – seven women and five men – had deliberated for about seven hours. The Judge said the jury members sent two notes with questions but would receive answers the next day. Tsarnaev's attorneys reassured Jahar. *"Jahar gets a precious few moments of movement, but his expression is one of seriousness,"* – Sweet.

On Day 19, April 8, 2015, the prosecutors and the Defense team were in their respective groups. Reporters were in the room waiting for the verdict and it could happen today. *"As Jahar entered, his eyes were trained on the ground. He slid into his seat, but he stumbled and fell into his chair,"* observed Sweet. Miriam laughed at Jahar when she saw him fall. She patted Jahar on the back and checked on him. She must have said: *Are you okay?* Judy greeted Jahar with a pat on the arm. Judy would say: *Hello Jahar, it's all right. Don't be afraid.*

Immediately, they laughed and talked. Jahar seemed very shy at this point and must may have been feeling so guilty in his heart. Today, he wore a casual suit jacket over a blue V–neck and white T–shirt. He stroked his goatee, and Miriam leaned closer to him to talk with him. He seemed to have lost his courage and looked nervous, contemplating about his uncertain fate. After a pep talk by Miriam, he sat up. Judge O'Toole began answering the jury's questions after they arrived. Jurors asked: *"Whether a conspiracy can be over a period of days or just one event."* –Wen. The Judge said a conspiracy can be limited in scope or over a long period of time. The second question asked: *"What is the difference between aiding & abetting; is there difference between the two?"* Judge answered: *Aiding and abetting is one concept, one thing – that he must help and share knowledge of criminal act, but act committed by someone else."* – Wen. Soon after, the Judge told the jury to get back to work.

VERDICT REACHED

The mood at the federal courthouse suddenly changed with word that a verdict had been reached. The news revealed that it had taken the jury about 11.5 hours to decide on a verdict. They went thru 30 counts, 17 of which carried the possibility of death penalty. Bombing survivors and family members flocked into the courtroom to hear the verdict. It was a packed house. The defense lawyers took their places in the courtroom. They did not appear nervous. Their focus was on the penalty phase. The Court clerk, Paul Lyness, called for the U.S. Marshals to get Mr. Tsarnaev. Jahar came in with a downward gaze. *"He is greeted by attorney Judy, who touched his arm, leaned over and whispered to him quietly."* – Bailey. Jahar smiled at Judy. He adjusted his jacket collar, and nervously swept his left hand through his dark curly hair. For the first time, Jahar sat between Judy and his other lawyer, William Fick. Miriam Conrad was absent. Judy and William both placed comforting hands on his back. Jahar appeared worried, *"looking down, each hand grasping the other. His lawyers Judy Clarke and William Fick tap him on each shoulder. They sit."* – Valencia. They flipped through the verdict form.

Clerk Lyness reminded everyone, "You are to maintain complete silence, no reaction to these verdicts, no outbursts, no photography or video recording allowed." Again, he said, "All rise." Judge O'Toole and the jury entered the room at 2:05 p.m. The jurors wore grave faces, and some avoided looking at Jahar. However, *"Tsarnaev shyly looks up as the jury enters,"* – Sweet. Jahar took a long stare at the jurors as they slowly took their seats. Only twelve deliberating jurors entered the jury box, while the other six sat on the side. Clerk Lyness asked for the Defense to remain standing. "Have you reached a verdict?"

"Yes," said one juror, a restaurant manager, who was the forewoman, handed the clerk the verdict slip that was 32 pages long containing 30 charges. Jahar stood along with his attorneys, while everyone else was seated. He crossed his arms. The Judge opened the envelope with the verdict sheet. He flipped through pages of jury slip, reading, while everyone remained silent. Jahar scratched his head. He was on pins and needles, waiting to learn his fate. In the gallery, parents of Martin Richard were present and waiting to hear the verdict. Bill Richard, placed his arm on his wife Denise's shoulder. Rustling sounds of the court verdict slip, pages flipping, were the only unwelcomed noise in Jahar's ears. Jahar clasped his hands in front of him, and then dropped them to his sides. He glanced towards the jury again and gazed down as the Judge skimmed over the last sheet. Finally, Judge O'Toole said, "You may announce the verdict." Clerk Lyness began reading:

(All verdict tweets were from Reporter Alysha Palumbo of NECN.)

"Count 1, conspiracy to use a Weapon of Mass Destruction – GUILTY." Count 1 – "Yes," Death to all 4 victims. "Count 2, use of a Weapon of Mass Destruction (Pressure Cooker Bomb #1); aiding and abetting – GUILTY." Jahar did not react to the first count of the verdict. He peered down and rubbed his face. "Count 3, Use of Firearm (Pressure Cooker Bomb #1) in relation to use of a Weapon of Mass Destruction; aiding and abetting – GUILTY... Count 4 – Use of Weapon of Mass Destruction (Pressure Cooker Bomb #2 near Forum Restaurant – GUILTY. Count 5... GUILTY..."

Judy whispered to David. They looked unhappy. They pretty much knew this was coming. They must now try to save Jahar's life in the penalty phase. The verdict form was on the defense table and Jahar read along. He crossed and uncrossed his arms. "Count 6, Conspiracy to Bomb a Public place – GUILTY... Count 7, Conspiracy to Bomb a Public place with pressure cooker #1...GUILTY. Count 8, Use of Firearm in a (Pressure Cooker #1) in a Public place at Marathon Sports – GUILTY."

Jahar stared at the floor. He lifted his head up and tried to stare straight ahead. As Clerk Lyness announced each verdict: "Guilty... Guilty," it smashed onto the ground like dropping stones. The entire room continued to stare the back of Mr. Tsarnaev's head. *"So far GUILTY on Counts 9, 10 and 11, including deaths of Lingzi and little Martin..."* Jahar looked down, with arms still folded. He appeared pale. Everyone in the *"room continued to look for any reaction from Jahar, but he was giving them nothing,"* reported Bailey. The survivors listened to the words guilty over and over. Kevin Cullen tweeted, *"You could hear pin drop in courtroom throughout that long recitation of the verdict. Tsarnaev did not react, just read along the verdict slip."* "We unanimously find the defendant Dzhokhar A. Tsarnaev, GUILTY," Lyness repeated and continued, *"Count 16, Use of Firearm (Ruger handgun) during Conspiracy to Use a Weapon of Mass Destruction – GUILTY."* This guilty count was for the murder of Officer Sean Collier. Although the prosecution admitted they did not know who pulled trigger; they said both brothers were responsible for his death. The jury agreed. *"Counts 17 and 18. GUILTY."* Jahar still had his arms crossed, eyes to the ground. No reaction to the verdict. *"Count 19, Carjacking, aiding and abetting, 1 Carjacking and aiding and abetting causing serious bodily injury to Officer Dic Donohue – Yes, GUILTY."* This was the Officer in Watertown that had been hit by friendly fire, but government argued officer wouldn't have been shot had Mr. Tsarnaev not been fleeing. Jahar was being held responsible for Donohue's shooting. *"Count 20, Use of a Firearm (Ruger handgun) during carjacking and aiding and abetting – GUILTY."*

Adam Reilly@reillyadam
#Tsarnaev's arms folded tightly around his
midsection, like he's sheltering himself.

It was a gesture Jahar had never made before and was observed by the media. Milton Valencia from the *Boston Globe* tweeted, *"Tsarnaev has hands wrapped around front of him, lower chest area. First I have seen him like that."* Jahar had wrapped his arms around his lower chest area, like he held himself. It was the first time anyone had seen that. Later, it was interpreted that he could be doing the SALAT, an act of prayer by Muslims. *"Counts 21...22...23...24...all GUILTY. All in relation to using firearm and weapon of mass destruction in Watertown." "On Count 25, GUILTY..."* Jahar quickly glanced up toward the jury and lowered his gaze. *"Count 26, Use of a Firearm (Ruger handgun) in relation to use of a Weapon of Mass Destruction in Watertown – GUILTY,"* relayed Clerk Lyness. Jahar kept reading the jury form on the table. *"Count 27, Use of Weapon of Mass Destruction (Pipe Bomb #2) on 4/19/13 in Watertown – GUILTY."* Jahar rubbed his face and stared at the ground. He calmly turned the page on the verdict form as he read on.

Outburst was not allowed. So, survivors and families were silent. They nodded their heads with approval. The twelve jurors were still standing, listening to the guilty verdicts. Many glanced over at Jahar. Steve Cooper of *News 7* tweeted, *"Jurors almost seem proud of their verdict ...standing tall shoulder to shoulder."* They had a serious look on their faces, clearly focusing and glancing at Jahar, deciding if he should face execution or not. One juror, a younger male glared at Jahar who showed no reaction to the verdict. This juror thought about the death penalty as *"merciful, it takes away the burden of a person's soul." "Counts 28 and 29, GUILTY, all carrying the pipe bomb, the weapon of mass destruction and the ruger gun in Watertown."*

The last "GUILTY" echoed in the room condemning the doomed convict. *"Count 30, carrying WMD, gun and pipe bomb in Watertown. GUILTY."* He was found guilty on all 30 charges. Seventeen of those counts are punishable by death.

Then Clerk Lyness asked, "Madam Foreperson, is that your verdict?"

"Yes," the foreperson replied. – Wen.

"What say you all?" the clerk asked.

"Yes," the jurors responded together. – Valencia.

Judge O'Toole asked the jury if the verdict was as they reported. "Yes," they replied reported Bailey. The Judge ordered Dzhokhar and the Defense team to take their seats. Dzhokhar Tsarnaev was now the convicted Boston Bomber. Judge O'Toole told the jury that they would now proceed to the death penalty phase. Dzhokhar was guilty of crimes that called for capital punishment. They would decide if he will live his life in prison or be executed for his crimes. The Judge had some last words for the jury. Jahar tried to stare at the Judge as he spoke. Overwhelmed, he looked numb. Palumbo observed Jahar, *"Tsarnaev leans back in his chair, playing with his hair, squirming a little before looking at the jury before they leave."* After all is said and done, he glanced at the jurors once and kept his head down.

"Many people kept asking if Mr. Tsarnaev had a reaction during the verdict when it was read. There was nothing, no clue, only offering a few hints, there and there," – Armstrong. Some hints were this: as the Judge spoke he collapsed in on himself, head dropping, and shoulders slumped forward. The only sign that he may have been impacted by events was when Judy quickly turned to Jahar before he was being escorted away by security. She acted very motherly towards him, concerned that he was upset, so *"Judy Clarke whispers to Tsarnaev, who offers her a weak smile,"* – Bailey. He seemed a bit sad. He shrugged his shoulders slightly as Judy leaned over to talk to him. The second he could leave the courtroom, he zipped out quickly through the side door, followed by his security team.[159]

SURVIVORS AND FAMILIES WELCOMED THE VERDICT

As Denise Richard wiped a tear from her eye, Jahar left the courtroom as he always did, looking straight ahead. Bill Richard embraced Prosecutor Nadine Pellegrini. Outside the courthouse, many survivors welcomed the verdict and thanked each of the jurors for making Dzhokhar Tsarnaev accountable for the terror attacks. This is what certain survivors said:

"Today's verdict will never replace the lives that were lost and so dramatically changed, but it is a relief, and one step closer to closure." – *Survivor Jeffrey Bauman*

"I think it is great! And not surprising to me at all — the case was a slam dunk!" – *Survivor Marc Fucarile*

"Nothing can ever replace the lives that were lost or changed forever, but at least there is some relief in knowing that justice is served and responsibility will be taken." – *Survivor Heather Abbott*

"Guilty like we all knew he would be. Great jurors." – *Survivor Sydney and Celeste Corcoran*

The Richard family would like to thank law enforcement and DOJ for their efforts in this matter. Richard family had no comment on verdict. Respect the family's privacy, especially their young children at this time. – *The Richards*

"Sean Collier gave his life doing what he was born to do - serving and protecting all of us as a police officer. Sean was more than a police officer to us, though. He was a caring, fun, loyal, and protective brother and son. While today's verdict can never bring Sean back, we are thankful that [Dzhokhar] Tsarnaev will be held accountable for the evil that he brought to so many families. We want to thank the jury for their service and for rendering this just verdict." – *The Colliers*

HOW SURVIVORS FELT ABOUT TSARNAEV

"If he showed any remorse, personally, I wouldn't have bought it. I would be more frustrated if he had shown it," said Karen Brassard from New Hampshire who had been ten feet away from the bomb. She had been injured in the attack. When she saw Jahar at the arraignment she was angry at him. She did not feel he had any remorse for what he did, and he had not been manipulated by his older brother. "He was all–in," she said. "I won't lose sleep over him being put to death."[160] [160a]

Rebekah DiMartino who penned the Open Letter to Dzhokhar shared, "I feel like he doesn't really care. I think the death penalty is ultimately what he wants. So, I don't know — life in prison alone with your thoughts — I think that might be ... I don't know. I'm glad I'm not the jury." Rebekah had testified during his trial: "I'm really glad I did it," she said, when she saw Tsarnaev from the witness stand. It took away her fears and it gave her a sense of peace, and closure. Rebekah said Tsarnaev never glanced at her. "I just got so sad because here is this kid, essentially. He was 19 then, and is 21, I think, now, and he's facing either the death penalty or life in prison," she told ESPNW.com.[161] "He's completely wasted what could have been a beautiful life. I just can't comprehend how people have that much hatred in their heart, and I just kept looking at him, thinking, Man, what if that was my son?"

Should We Kill Dzhokhar?

"If the goal of our justice system is to seek revenge against criminals, then Tsarnaev should be executed. But if the goal is to seek justice, then spare his life." [162]
— Pope Francis

MEANWHILE, ZUBEIDAT TSARNAEVA SENT a message soon after the guilty verdict was read against her son. The mother of the Boston Bomber, Dzhokhar Tsarnaev was angry. "I will never forget it. May god bless those who helped my son. The terrorists are the Americans, and everyone knows it. My son is the best of the best," she posted in Russian on VKontakte, a social media site.[163]

The Boston Globe published an article on April 9, 2015. It was titled, *"Many Debate Death Penalty For Tsarnaev,"* by Patricia Wen and Laura Crimaldi.[164] The State of Massachusetts banned the death penalty and capital punishment was abolished in 1947. BG's article focused on an ESL teacher, Robert Granich, at Ashfield Middle School in Brockton. He said his students were interested in discussing Tsarnaev's punishment. Granich wrote on a white board "WHAT SHOULD HAPPEN TO JAHAR?" In the class of mostly adolescent internationals students, a majority supported a sentence of life imprisonment and believed he had been negatively influenced by his older brother, Tamerlan. It was heartbreaking to know some were sympathetic to Jahar and did want him executed while others believed he should be punished with death.

On a white board, the students wrote their thoughts about the death penalty for Tsarnaev.

One student wrote:

"HE SHOULD BE KILLED BECAUSE HE KILLED THREE PEOPLE & THEY ARE DEAD AND A BUNCH ARE INJURED SO THEY SHOULD GIVE HIM THE DEATH PENALTY."

Another student wrote, begging,

"HE STILL HAS A FUTURE. HE IS TOO YOUNG TO BE DEAD. DON'T KILL HIM." (With a sad face.)

Dzhokhar would pay for his part. He was in ways paying for the sins of his dead brother. Tamerlan took the easy way out. Dzhokhar would suffer for the rest of his life. Defense team admitted that Tamerlan gave birth to the bombing plans, bought all the bombing materials and his fingerprints were found on most of the bomb components. Defense expressed their doubts that their client could meet the high standards for a federal execution. In the next phase, the penalty phase, the Defense would portray a more sympathetic portrait of their client, his life, his family, his brother's influence and his motives. We could only pray that Dzhokhar who sat in the courtroom and heard from many witnesses and saw horrifying videos of the bombings would come to fully understand the horror and tragedy he had caused and be willing to repent. The only way for him to be spared from the death penalty was for him to express deep regret for his criminal actions and to plead for mercy. All through the trial, Dzhokhar had shown no reaction or betrayed his emotions to anyone. Why no emotions? Was he proud? He may never show remorse because his murderous act was a righteous deed done in the name of Allah. To the Jihads, the brothers were celebrated as brave heroes. If Dzhokhar exhibited remorse it would be seen as a sign of weakness in his faith. Tsarnaev's team did not want him to testify; it would be too risky to put him on the stand. But, Dzhokhar would be allowed to make a statement at the end.

FAMILIES SPOKE OUT OPPOSED THE DEATH PENALTY

The Collier Family objected to the death penalty. Sean Collier's sister, Jennifer L. Lemmerman, did not believe in the death penalty. She said, *"I can't imagine I'll ever forgive him for what he did to my brother, to my family, and I'll have to live with that for the rest of my life, whether he is on this earth or not. But I also can't imagine that killing in response to killing would ever bring me peace or justice. Just my perspective, but enough is enough. I choose to remember Sean for the light that he brought. No more darkness."*[165]

The Richard Family also objected to the death penalty – They explained, *"...We are in favor of and would support the Department of Justice in taking the death penalty off the table in exchange for the defendant spending the rest of his life in prison without any possibility of release and waiving all of his rights to appeal. We understand all too well the heinousness and brutality of the crimes committed. We were there. We lived it. The defendant murdered our 8–year–old son, maimed our 7–year–old daughter, and stole part of our soul. We know that the government has its reasons for seeking the death penalty, but the continued pursuit of that punishment could bring years of appeals and prolong reliving the most painful day of our lives... As long as the defendant is in the spotlight, we have no choice but to live a story told on his terms, not ours. The minute the defendant fades from our newspapers and TV screens is the minute we begin the process of rebuilding our lives and our family..."*[166]

Jessica Kensky and Patrick Downes, both survivors who had lost limbs in the attack also asked the federal government not to put Tsarnaev to death.

SURVIVORS FOR THE DEATH PENALTY

Liz Norden, whose two sons, JP and Paul, both lost a leg in the bombing, called for the death penalty, declaring, *"I want to see justice for my boys."*

Adrianne Haslet–Davis, a dancer, who lost her lower leg called for the death penalty.

Kevin and Celeste Concoran both called for the death penalty. Celeste lost both of her limbs in the attack. Her daughter, Sydney Concoran, had her foot severely damaged when the bombs went off. She also called for the death penalty.

Katie Timura, who was standing near the Richard family when the bombs went off, said, *"I'm hoping that justice is served. I don't think he deserves to live anymore. I don't think he represents anything that we stand for."*[167]

The second phase of the Tsarnaev's trial would mainly focus on the defendant's life. In the penalty phase, Tsarnaev jurors would have to choose which punishment he deserved, to sentence him to life in prison or to put him to death by lethal injection.

PENALTY/ THE SENTENCING PHASE FOR TSARNAEV
PROSECUTOR'S OPENING STATEMENT

Unconcerned, Unrepentant And Untouched

"Dzhokhar Tsarnaev was and is unrepentant, uncaring and untouched by the havoc and the sorrow he has created."
– AUSA Nadine Pellegrini

Day – 1 – April 21, 2015

IT WAS A LATE start on this first day of phase 2. Death penalty protesters gathered at the federal court on opening day of the sentencing trial for Dzhokhar Tsarnaev. Back in courtroom 9, Bill Richard watched the prosecutors set up three large easels. He and his wife, Denise, smiled and talked with others. They had publicly asked the government not to seek the death penalty. Conversely, Liz Norden, who had attended each day of the trial called for the death penalty.

Mr. Tsarnaev had been convicted of the murderous bombings on April 8, two weeks ago prior. After a lengthy conference, lawyers emerged in the courtroom. *"The convicted Boston Bomber Jahar Tsarnaev walked slowly into the court. His walk was not his usual cocky strut. He was looking down and had little expression on his face,"* – Palumbo. Valencia tweeted, *"Tsarnaev has a suit and v–neck shirt, bluish. Keeps head down as slumbers to his seat."* His hair had grown longer and wavier. The public stared at him as he sat down.

Armstrong tweeted, *"Miriam Conrad walks up to Tsarnaev, pats him on shoulder, whispers with a smile, "how ya been?"* She shook his hand, and he laughed. After the greeting, Judy pointed something in a document out to him. He read it carefully. Miriam and Judy both whispered to him about it. He placed the paper on his lap and studied it further. Perhaps he was reading the opening statement or maybe it was the obscene photo of him in his holding cell. As his lawyers chatted with him, the government prosecutors gathered on their side of the courtroom were being very serious. Reporter Bailey observed Jahar, *"Tsarnaev seems to be asking a lot of questions about whatever paperwork he's looking at."*

Soon after, the penalty trial began; Judge O'Toole and the jury entered the room. Jahar eyed each one of them. The Judge gave the jury instructions, and presented an overview of the charges, "We are now about to begin the penalty phase of the trial," he declared. "The sole issue for your consideration is punishment," Judge O'Toole stated, "It is imperative that you keep that promise you made months ago, that you will consider the death penalty and life in prison."

EXCERPTS OF PROSECUTOR'S OPENING STATEMENT

AUSA NADINE PELLEGRINI delivered the Opening Statements of phase 2:

"HE IS UNBEARABLE; INDESCRIBABLE... – *(Excerpt found on Page 3, line 4 through Page 4, end line 14.)* Pellegrini opened her statement describing Dzhokhar's crimes as "unbearable, indescribable, inexcusable and insensitive." The murders he committed were deliberate and cruel.

"Why is the death penalty the appropriate and just sentence? – *(Excerpt found on Page 6, line 20 through Page 8, end line 1 and on Page 10, line 5 through 15.)* Pellegrini believed he deserved the death sentence because the answer would be demonstrated in his actions.

Dzhokhar's character and actions of carrying the bomb, and subsequently exploding it "created death and destruction" and horror. He created a risk of death for everyone and "twisted the marathon into something cruel and ugly." His actions and decisions reflected a political statement of his own beliefs, and to others who were drawn to those beliefs.

"HE IS CALLOUS AND INDIFFERENT TO HUMAN LIFE. – *(Excerpt found on Page 11, line 6 through Page 12, end line 24.)* There was nothing that would explain his cruelty, callous and indifferent to human life. But, how could he have detonated a bomb and left it behind children and walked away? Dzhokhar faced troubles of his own, growing up in a dysfunctional family or carrying a troubled family history, but that would not justify the murder a child. Dzhokhar's "cruel character" (indifference) originated from his own beliefs and motivations. Evidence showed that it was his fault and that he was willing to cross the line, forgetting his own humanity.

"HE IS UNREPENTANT, UNCARING, AND UNTOUCHED – *(Excerpt found on Page 13, line 17 through Page 14, end line 1.)* Dzhokhar was an unrepentant and uncaring person who remained untouched by the havoc and the sorrow that he had created. He crossed the line into radicalization and killed people for his own personal glory and for the reward.

HE IS DESTINED TO BE AMERICA'S WORST NIGHTMARE – *(Excerpt found on Page 16, line 22 through Page 17, end line 7.)* Dzhokhar's destiny was determined by himself. His decisions, his actions and his beliefs made him who he was to become. He was America's worst nightmare. "He is a man whose heart was full of rage and whose mind was dead set on the path that he took."

HE IS AN UNREPENTANT KILLER – *(Excerpt found on Page 17, line 8 through line 24.)* Dzhokhar remained unrepentant. He knew his victims were innocents, but he murdered them anyway. After he was charged for his crimes and in custody, "there was a video camera…Dzhokhar Tsarnaev was alone…and once more, just as he had done on the boat…" There was a video shot that showed him flipping the bird to the camera in lock up. "He had one more message to send. THIS is Dzhokhar Tsarnaev!" declared Pellegrini.

Pellegrini ended the Opening with the image of Jahar giving the middle finger to the camera (images from *Boston Magazine*) while lock up at the federal courthouse where he was being arraigned on July 10, 2013. The rumor of his middle finger cursing was real. Pellegrini revealed the demon in the defendant. *Voila! This IS HIM!* She chastised him publicly.

A transcript of Pellegrini's Opening Statement.[168]

In the picture, Jahar was in jail in his orange jumpsuit giving the camera the middle finger. The government announced this conveyed his true feelings towards his victims and his case. The picture was shown to illustrate that he had no remorse.

Bill Richard, partially deafened by the bombings, listened through headphones. His eyes squinted at the image. At the defense table, Jahar could feel every eye on him. He did not flinch. "He remains the unrepentant killer that he is…" Pellegrini repeated to the jurors. Jahar stared at the defense table and twiddled his fingers. Defense could hear everyone gasp in the courtroom as the photo of Jahar giving the camera the middle finger was shown. *Watch Tsarnaev's jail cell surveillance video in Reference number 169.* [169]

(https://www.youtube.com/watch?v=XlEkjknGPcA)

The government insisted on the death penalty. The obscene photo of nineteen-year-old Jahar quickly flashing his middle finger garnered world-wide attention and made to the top of the evening news. The government had showed this powerful image of the "unrepentant" Jahar, to ensure that the jurors would not feel sorry for him. Some jurors were shaking their heads. Jurors' minds already have been made up regarding Jahar.

There was no plea deal. Government was sure he would be found guilty on all counts and they would not drop the death penalty option. This was a huge blow to the defense. Did Judy and Miriam know what was coming? How could they explain Jahar's action who seemed really callous and showed disregard for his victims?

The next day, on April 22, Tsarnaev's lawyers called the GOVERNMENT'S 11th WITNESS, U.S. MARSHAL GARY OLIVEIRA to the stand. He worked at the cell block in the courthouse. He testified that he sat in the marshal's office monitoring the cameras. Oliveira was deputy marshal in charge of operations on July 10, 2013, when Jahar was being held in Cell 4 awaiting arraignment. It was about 11:23 a.m. when Jahar stared straight into the camera. Oliveira said he witnessed Mr. Tsarnaev extend his middle finger to the camera. Defense wanted the jury to see a whole two-minute video clip of Jahar in the holding cell, not just a freeze frame of his obscene gesture. The court viewed the video of Mr. Tsarnaev being placed in the cell. He entered in an orange jumpsuit. He had a brace on his left hand. They removed the handcuffs and the chains around his waist. *"In video, he sits down, scratches his head repeatedly. He walks to camera, seems to look for his reflection,"* –Armstrong.

Defense showed another clip of video, *"In full video, Tsarnaev gets on bench, fixes his hair, throws a peace sign and then throws a finger, all in a matter of seconds, gets down,"* – Valencia. Miriam suggested that Mr. Tsarnaev used the camera lens as a mirror to see if his unkempt bushy hair looked okay. We guess he wanted to appear neatly combed for the court since some prison cells don't have mirrors, and probably was his first time seeing his own reflection. Mr. Tsarnaev made a face into the camera and checked his facial injuries. His left eye was swollen.

The Defense wanted to put into evidence the 2-minute video which showed Jahar as a teenager with a wounded face and fixing his hair. The flipping of the middle finger was an act of provocation and it lasted only a few seconds. Defense wanted to depict him as a "teenage brat." He was not angry or defiant, but rather just a bored and frustrated prisoner. That he was flipping himself off. We don't know how much damage this footage did to the Defense. Miriam tried her hardest to show that Mr. Tsarnaev was more like a typical rebellious nineteen-year-old teenager with behavioral issues and that the gesture was not a defiant message to the U.S. When she finished she sat down next to Jahar and they gave each other a smile.[170]

Broken Hearts & Wounded Lives

"The government encouraged the families of those victims to talk so they can get the jurors to get the full humanity of the victims in order to motivate them to give Tsarnaev the death sentence. To kill him…Dzhokhar Tsarnaev not only killed Sean Collier or put a bomb next to Lingzi Lu, but he also killed their families."
— WBUR's David Boeri and The Boston Globe's Kevin Cullen

"THE STORY OF THE Boston Marathon bombing is not about Tamerlan and Dzhokhar Tsarnaev. The story of the Boston Marathon bombing is one of tragedy of their making, but it is more than that," stated attorney Judy Clarke during her closing statement. The Defense team emphasized their deep sympathy for the family members who spoke of their heartbreaking loss and their pain. A couple of survivors testified and shared with the jurors their anguish at losing their limbs. 1st WITNESS to testify was victim CELESTE CORCORAN who lost both of her legs when the second bomb exploded. After the bomb explosion, Celeste recalled how her feet felt weird and how she was in intense pain. The EMT's wrote #1 on her chest and ordered the aid workers, "She needs to leave now. Get her out of here!" Celeste remembered thinking she wanted to die. The pain was too much. "I don't know if it was the mom in me. I can't die. I have to be there for my kids. I have to be there for my husband." Immediately, *a doctor with a clip board said, "Celeste, we need you to sign this because we need to amputate both your legs,"* – Cullen. She quickly scribbled her name because she wanted the pain to stop. Celeste wiped tears away as she recalled the moment she was told she would lose both legs. When she realized her daughter, Sydney was alive, *"I just started crying because it was the second time I almost lost her. Most heart wrenching thing, for a mom, to see your child in pain and not being able to go to them,"* – Cullen.

Up next, the jury heard from family members of the deceased. They were broken-hearted over losing their loved ones. The 3rd WITNESS WAS WILLIAM CAMPBELL III, Krystle's brother. He expressed how his sister, "Krystle Campbell was the centerpiece." Krystle's father, 4th WITNESS, WILLIAM CAMPBELL, JR. spoke about his daughter, *"She was the light of my life,"* – Bailey. The Campbell family described Krystle as very popular with many friends. She was a kind person. She was the maid of honor in many weddings and coordinated these special events. Krystle moved in with her nana when she was ill and cared for her. "She could put anyone in a good mood," said her father. *"Since Krystle died "nobody filled" that role,"* – Wen. William who resembled his sister with the same smile and same eyes spoke about the time when he learned that Krystle was among the victims. At first, nurses told him his sister was okay, and would recover. Hours later they learned that there had been a mistake; his sister was in fact dead. Krystle's ID had been confused with that of her friend Karen McWatters who was at the marathon with her. William shared how he felt when he learned the news, "I had a hard time dealing with her death; my family was horrified." Krystle's father, William Jr. took it hard. He cried, "Krystle was already dead. It wasn't her," he choked. "I passed out on the floor…" He described that day, how it was the worst possible thing a parent could go through. He shared how he missed his daily hug from Krystle the most. She never left the house without hugging her dad.

Day – 2 – April 22, 2015

"Sean was someone that was a moral compass…it was black and white, what's right and what's wrong. He would always choose the right thing…Right down to a bug. You can't kill a bug. You got to put it outside," – Cullen, said the 6th WITNESS ANDREW COLLIER who was the older brother of Sean.

The deceased Sean Collier had always wanted to be a police officer. He was the kid who would chase the other kids around making siren noises, telling them they were breaking the law.

Andrew shared, "It was really after his death we found out how many great things he was doing for people. He helped the MIT Outing Club. He emailed and contacted parents a week after saving a baby. When we did get together it was like we were never apart. I really felt like we were getting closer and closer." But the death of Sean made him very sad, "I think of him every day. It's still a huge loss." 7th WITNESS WAS JOSEPH ROGERS. He was Sean Collier's stepfather. Joseph talked about a time when Sean was caught drinking. When the Sox won World Series in 2004, Sean went to a party, and engaged in underage drinking. Boston cops told him to stay there, and he did. Other kids would have run away once the cops turned their backs, but Sean later said getting caught was God's way of teaching him a lesson. Regarding Sean's death, *"Sometimes it still feels like a dream. We were taken to see his body. He had a hole in the middle of his head. My wife hasn't been able to work since his murder. Sean's mom, her hands were covered with her son's blood when she was taken to see his body. It has been a terrible two years. There's somebody missing. Thanksgiving, Christmas will never be the same. It's all gone."* – Bailey. Sean's death had also been felt throughout the MIT community.

8th WITNESS WAS MIT POLICE CHIEF JOHN DIFAVA. DiFava had been the one to hire Sean Collier. He said, "What made Sean a police officer was not the uniform, not the badge, it was his character. Sean engaged with students, faculty, everybody…" *The atmosphere of the department has changed greatly…an atmosphere of sadness…great loss,"* – Cullen.

Broken hearts were painfully felt by the family of Lingzi Lu. Lu's parents in China could not come to testify, so Lu's aunt testified in their stead. 12th WITNESS WAS HELEN ZHO. She shared, *"Her mom cannot get out of bed for two days. She was so upset by her death,"*– Wen. Lingzi came to U.S. in August of 2012. Helen said she helped Lu get her apartment ready when she came to Boston University to study. It was hard for students to come to study in America. Family members in China helped her with financial assistance for her travel and education. Lingzi was an only child.

Lu's aunt said, *"When I picked up Lu at the airport early, they wanted dim sum, but places closed. We found a greasy basement place to eat,"* – Wen. The jurors laughed at this. Lingzi was an only child because China forbids more than one child per family, to control population growth. *"Lu was center of the family life, particular close to her grandfather who taught her Chinese calligraphy. Grandma braided her hair,"* – Wen. She had big ambitions and wanted to work on Wall Street in pension planning. She was a very diligent, smart, hardworking...a bubbly, innocent girl. Her notebooks were so neat they looked like textbooks. Her grandfather wrote a biography in memory of Lu, *Boston Remembering a Chinese Girl*, which contained portions from her diaries. Lu's aunt described her as "a beautiful nerd" who one time took a half-hour nap while taking a test. In *"chinese culture, parents take care of children, children take care parents: "For the parents, that's extremely sad. That's it, she's gone."* – Valencia. Lingzi's mom buried her daughter in a pink bridal gown with a tiara, like the princess she was and the bride she would never be. Her mom touched Lingzi's hand in the casket and said Lingzi had beautiful porcelain hands. The family decided not to return her body back to China because she had planned to live in Boston. Lu's aunt expressed, *"How she died and why she died, it just felt like she was part of Boston, part of the city. Just felt she should be here."* – Cullen.

Many survivors who became amputees shared their stories how their lives forever changed. 10th WITNESS was survivor ADRIANNE HASLET, the dancer who had lost a leg, but miraculously went back to dancing using a prosthetic leg. She shared, "I knew right off the bat it was a terrorist attack, though I don't know why," when the bomb went off. She was injured. She recounted, "*I wrapped my arms around my husband and said the next one's gonna hit, the next one's gonna hit!* "– Cullen.

"*I was covering my mouth out of disbelief, shock, and unknown. I saw a lot of smoke and heard screams,*" – Wen. "*I crawled along the broken glass, shredding my forearms with broken glass. I could feel the broken glass and my foot dragging...*" – Cullen.

Adrianne cried as gave her testimony. She was taken to the Boston Medical Center. "*I kept screaming I was a ballroom dancer.*" – Valencia. Adrianne lost her left leg below the knee. Her husband, Adam, had suffered constant ringing in his ear, a blown artery in his foot and lost chucks from both calves.

Day 3 – April 23, 2015

On the third day, the jurors heard from a couple more of the surviving victims. 13th WITNESS was survivor MARC FUCARILE. Jurors saw a chilling video of Tsarnaev, wearing a white hat, and walking right up in front of the Forum Restaurant where Marc was standing with Paul and JP Norden.

Tsarnaev walked swiftly away, the bomb exploded shortly after and Marc was thrown into the air. "*Oh sh*t, he's still on fire! I need to cut his pants off,*" *someone said. Marc undid his belt buckle; he was burned by it.*" – Cullen. His right leg had been instantly severed by the blast. Ninety percent of his body suffered burns. His face was also burned, and he had to be treated with skin grafts. Marc explained what a skin graft was. "*Cheese grater. They slice your skin off then spread it out using almost like a pizza dough roller.*" – Cullen.

Marc still suffered pain in his left foot. He explained how the prosthetic caused him great pain, due in part to the burns on his legs. *"For treatment he takes 24 pills in the morning, 22 pills at lunch and 26 pills at night,"* – Cullen. Also, a large BB had lodged itself in his heart. He had 60+ surgeries so far and was being treated at Walter Reed Medical Center in DC.

14th WITNESS WAS HEATHER ABBOTT who was the last survivor to testify. When the second bomb went off, she said, *"I was catapulted through the doors of the restaurant that were open. I landed... in puddle of chaos on the ground. People were running in herds by me, through the restaurant, away from where the bomb was. I felt like my foot was on fire...I looked at it like it had flames coming out of it,"* – Cullen.

Heather was rescued, and a tourniquet was tied around her leg which was in extreme pain. The EMT called her parents. They tried to save her foot three times. The surgeon informed her that she had a choice to make. The recommendation was amputation below the knee. Regarding her decision to amputate, *"It was probably the hardest decision I've ever had to make," she said,"* – Bailey. Heather started a foundation to help those who suffered limb loss like herself. It would be called the "Heather Abbott Foundation" where people could go and be fitted with customized prostheses.

The Stare Downs & The Chilling End

".... there's Tsarnaev's lack of remorse — opening day, the prosecutor's final shot of Tsarnaev locked up, giving the security camera the finger. From his blood–scrawled justification in the boat after the bombing to this day, the message has been: Screw you, society. Tsarnaev may take the stand to beg for mercy, but only if he now feels or at least can fake remorse." – CNN's Robert Blecker [171]

JAHAR'S FACE LOOKED ALMOST the same as it did in the jail cell video clips of him flashing his middle finger. Except before the bombings, his face had appeared youthful and gentle. Years later his features had grown sharper, more defined, mature and his appearance was scruffier. The beard along the jawline on his chin made him look very pinched and pointy. The formal clothing and the paleness of his face had made him aged more. Jahar had lost weight and was apparently worn out from the trial and solitary confinement. It had all taken a toll on him.

Jahar was uncomfortable at showing any type of emotion towards the victims. Occasionally, he stole a glance, but mostly put his head down or looked straight ahead. The surviving victims had their day in court to confront in person, Mr. Tsarnaev, the Boston Bomber. They seemed ticked off that he hadn't shown any emotion during anyone's testimony. Here were some moments: When victim Gillian Reny stood at the stand, she glanced at Jahar as she awkwardly waited to be called. Jurors watched Jahar like a hawk as he sat at the defendant's table while his lawyers were at sidebar. Jahar peeked over at Adrienne Haslet-Davis for a moment out of the corner of his eye as she took the stand. Despite Jahar's shy peek, when Adrienne left the stand she stopped behind the defense table and gave Jahar a good long furious glare for several seconds. Jahar would not gaze up. His lawyers leaned in to protect him.

After a break, Marc Fucarile rolled up to the witness stand in his wheelchair next to the door where Jahar would enter. Quickly, Judy talked to security and three officers were positioned between the witness and defense table in the courtroom. As the court waited for the Judge and jury, Jahar was brought into the courtroom. He passed right in front of Marc. Marc glared and stared intently at Jahar, while security surrounded Jahar. Jahar avoided eye-contact but finally peered over at Marc as he was sworn in. Jahar sat very still. There was tension in the air.

16th WITNESS WAS MICHELLE GAMBLE, A FBI PHOTOGRAPHER

"Gamble has brought in a roll of heavy paper the same size as the grate to show where Tsarnaev was in relation to Richard family," tweeted Boeri. It was made of tyvek material. Gamble measured a distance of 3.5 feet between bomb explosion and location where Martin Richard stood. Defense did not like this demonstration.

"Gamble created an exhibit synching sound from a video shot at Atlantic Fish Co. with soundless video shot from the Forum," tweeted Reilly. On the sound video there was a lot of screaming. The court heard, *"Oh my god what the hell was that?" "Something blew up!" "More horrible screams...and then the second bomb explodes."* At this moment the Defense team, Miriam and Judy leaned across Jahar, for an *intense–looking exchange,"* - Reilly.

THE LAST WITNESS

17th WITNESS WAS STEVE WOOLFENDEN, and he was the last witness to testify against Tsarnaev. Steve and his then three-year-old son, Leo, went to the marathon to watch his wife Amber run in the race. He was supposed to meet friends at a bar on Boylston. At that moment he realized they were on the wrong side of the street. When the first bomb went off, *"I was in shock and disbelief...we needed to get out of there, took a 180 turn, but we didn't get that chance. The bomb exploded,"* – Cullen. Steve remembered the intense heat. His first instinct was to check on Leo. Leo, his blond-haired boy was alive and screaming, *"Leo was crying and screaming uncontrollably. He was saying, Mommy, Daddy, Mommy, Daddy,"* – Boeri. His head was bleeding on the left side. At that instant, Steve discovered his leg had been severed... *"He put a belt around his leg to stop the bleeding, but when he went to unbuckle his son from the stroller, his fingers were numb,"* – Bailey. He tried to comfort his toddler son in the stroller. *"A bystander asked if he was ok. Woolfenden asked him to take Leo to safety. He did but first applied another tourniquet,"* – Whitehouse. A police officer took his son to safety. At the hospital, he immediately told a nurse that he was separated from his son, and he needed help to find his boy. Amber finally came and informed him that Leo was safe at Children's. Steve went into surgery Monday night and next remembered waking up on Wednesday. He lost his leg below the knee. His son, Leo was discharged and had a laceration on the left side of head, one centimeter in length and suffered a skull fracture.[172]

THE CHILLING VIDEO

It was an eerie, powerful video to watch. (This video was not shown to the public.) *"Video paused to show Tsarnaev walking right past Woolfenden as first bomb went off. He was trying to back up stroller when 2nd bomb went off,"* – Bailey.[173] The people in court and the jurors viewed another video of the bomb explosion taken from a surveillance camera from the Forum Restaurant.

Steve did not see Jahar as he departed right near him. Soon, the second blast occurred. *"Stroller is right next to where Martin Richard was blown back. You can see his mother Denise tending to him as Steve looks at Leo,"* – Whitehouse. In the video, Denise Richard was tending to her son, Martin, as Steve checked on Leo. *"Such powerful video, as you can see Woolfenden grab a blanket from stroller, to wrap around his bloody leg & frantically trying to help son,"*– Wen. As Steve testified on the stand, he wiped tears from his eyes. His tears stained his sleeve. He spoke softly and glanced over at Jahar as he answered questions.

At some point amidst the chaos, he became aware of a little boy with his mother beside him. It was Martin Richard. *"I saw Martin's face. And I could see – I could see a boy that looked like he was fatally injured,"* – Reilly. *"I saw his hair had been singed. I saw that his eyes were rolled in the back of his head, and his mouth was agape,"* – Boeri. *"I could see the top part of his torso. I saw an immense amount of blood... I was really, really terrified,"* – Reilly. Denise was pleading with her son, *"Please"* and calling his name many times, but no sound uttered from his lips. Steve put his hand on Denise's back. Martin's mother turned and asked Steve Woolfenden if he was okay – and he said that he was, reported Cullen. She desperately turned her attention back to Martin.

So, *this* was the government's rumored video featuring the death of Martin. Defense had thought this video footage did not exist. Perhaps it was because they already had viewed the one that Anthony Imel had compiled and presented. However, the government had saved the actual rumored video and now had the defense team in a corner.

In the video close-up, *"Jury looking at Forum video again, zoomed in on Martin Richard's body as his mother stands above him. He's dying,"* – Bailey. Martin's body writhed on the ground as Denise leaned over him. She drew closer to his lifeless face. Denise looked anguished and in shock. The whole court had witnessed this child's horrible death right before their very eyes. Martin's left arm flailed up in agony and suddenly it dropped dead. It appeared he was reaching out for his mom. He did not die instantly. *"Many jurors looked stricken,"* – Bailey. They cried seeing the death of an innocent boy. The video clip ended with Denise drawing back from Martin and putting her hand to her mouth in grief. In court, Steve was excused from the stand. The government rested. Jahar could not watch the video. He didn't need to because it had affected him. That was why he kept his head way, way down the whole time.

At the end of the court day, Jahar stood slowly with hands crossed in front of him as jurors filed out observed reporter Cullen. Yesterday, he offered a weak smile to his attorneys at day's end. However, this day, when *"Miriam offered him a smile, he gave her none,"* – Bailey. He had a straight-face as he talked with her briefly.

Judy touched Jahar on his left elbow to check to see if he was okay. Security asked for Jahar to leave. Jahar stared down at the floor. He brushed past his lawyers, ignoring them. His head was down. He did not look back as he headed through the side door out of the courtroom. Both lawyers seemed concerned. Judy quickly followed him. She motioned for him to stop in the hallway, so they could talk. Did Jahar give up on his lawyers? Or did the video have an effect on him and he finally realized the cruel devastation he had inflicted on others, and did he now feel ashamed about it?

DEFENSE'S OPENING STATEMENT
Dzhokhar Will Be Severely Punished

"We are asking you to punish Dzhokhar by imprisoning him for the rest of his life. If there's one thing to remember it's that Dzhokhar will be severely punished either way."
— *Attorney David Bruck*

Day 1 – April 27, 2015

ATTORNEYS DAVID BRUCK AND Tim Watkins walked into Courtroom 9 to fight for Dzhokhar's life. At this point, Mr. Tsarnaev, who had done the inhumane, would be redrawn with flesh, bones and a heart. His victims found it hard to believe he even possessed a soul. However, his attorneys who had spent two years in close contact with him would attempt to humanize him by sharing with the jurors his story, his life, and his home life. They would address several mitigating factors such as his age, his immigration status, and him idolizing and following his overbearing brother. The attorneys, Judy Clarke, Miriam Conrad, David Bruck, Tim Watkins and William Fick were in the front courtroom checking their computers and setting up a large TV screen in front of the jury box.

"Announced by the Marshals' secret door knock, a very somber Jahar makes his entrance in contrasting shades of blue," – Sweet. Jahar wore a tight blue V-neck shirt and black suit jacket. The courtroom instantly hushed at his entrance. Jahar appeared, a thin skeleton of a man. Bailey tweeted, *"Courtroom is totally silent. Appears Tsarnaev has shaved a bit. Chin beard a little trimmed. Very pale, dark circles under eyes. He does not look toward the gallery as he takes his seat in court."* Jahar was soon encircled by Miriam and Judy, his maternal cloak and they sat on either side of him.[174]

He sat down and smiled at them. *"He's smiling broadly. He looked almost elated,"* – Reilly. His courtroom demeanor was different. He didn't appear to be nervous. While Jahar talked with Miriam, David Bruck focused on giving his opening statement. Momentarily, Judge O'Toole and the jury took their seats. Jahar glanced at the jury who would ultimately decide his fate: a future behind bars or by execution.

DEFENSE'S DAVID BRUCK BEGAN HIS OPENING STATEMENT: Bruck's "Opening" was extracted from a court transcript document. The link to the document is reference number **#176.**

EXCERPTS OF DEFENSE'S OPENING STATEMENT

"Punish Dzhokhar by imprisoning him for the rest of his life." – *(Excerpt found on Page 33, line 15 through Page 34, end line 12.)* Bruck opened his statement telling the jurors that Dzhokhar would be severely punished either way. His older brother was dead. Only he, the 19-year-old younger brother was left to take the punishment. He asked the jurors to make the best choice, that there was no point in hurting him more because he was already hurting, knowing that he had done could be undone. Two choices for his punishment: one punishment was quick, to put him to death or the other was to lock him up for the rest of his life.

"Tamerlan had power over Dzhokhar." – *(Excerpt found on Page 36, line 3 through line 15.)* Tamerlan's motivation to commit this attack was so much stronger than Dzhokhar's. Their personalities were different. Tamerlan had "the fanatical emotions and ideology" that drove the plan. "If Tamerlan had been in the picture, would Dzhokhar have done this on his own? No one would say Tamerlan forced him to do it. When Tamerlan said it was time, his little brother went with him. When he did, Dzhokhar was all in. He drove this plot."

Page 39 line 23–25, *"Jahar's radical internet activity was a faint echo of Tamerlan's. Tamerlan's computer shows his obsession. He was consumed by Jihad."*

"Young brothers tend to look up to older brothers." – *(Excerpt found on Page 40, line 19 through Page 43, end line 20.)* By comparing the two computers side–by–side, it showed who drove the plot and lead and who just followed. Tamerlan was the "fuel" of the plan and he would "pull his younger brother in." The brother's relationship was dynamic and intense due to their culture being a nuclear family. Dzhokhar grew up in the North Caucasus region of central Asia and it is a culture in which the eldest brother can yield tremendous power and influence. When a father can't fulfill his role, the eldest brother can assume that role. He rules the family. As a teenager, Dzhokhar went online to better understand his roots. He read all about the history of terrorism/uprisings in the Chechen region and learned about the patriarchal culture.

"Dzhokhar portrayed himself as independent to his friends, but Dzhokhar did not defy Tamerlan to his face, not ever." – *(Excerpt found on Page 42, line 23 through Page 43, end line 10.)* Dzhokhar would smoke pot with his own friends, but he would not defy Tamerlan, not to his face. He supported his older brother. *"Culture is what's bred in the bone...In a family like Dzhokhar, turn your back on your older brother and you're no one." (Page 43, line 6–10.)* "No one is going to claim that Tamerlan forced Dzhokhar...but when Tamerlan decided it was time, his little brother went with him." – *(Excerpt Page 36, line 3 through line 15.)*

"Dzhokhar's parents emigrated to Cambridge in 2002. Nothing worked out..." – *(Excerpt found on Page 45, line 22 through Page 48, end line 16.)* When the family arrived in Cambridge in 2002, they had high hopes for Tamerlan, but he was failing at school. He took up the sport of boxing, though he did not keep it up. Both parents were diagnosed with severe mental health problems. Anzor became sick and Zubeidat started dressing in all black, covering her head with a hijab, and becoming more and more radical in her thinking. Tamerlan was the answer to all the family's problems. He was planning to go to Harvard. He was the person everyone looked up to and Tamerlan loved and adored his mother very much. Dzhokhar Tsarnaev grew up an atmosphere of maternal delusion. However, Tamerlan failed at everything and dropped out of school. His boxing career crumbled, and he became a stay-at-home dad absorbing extremist ideas he found online.

"Parents are gone. Now Tamerlan is in charge." – *(Excerpt found on Page 48, line 17 through Page 50, end line 17.)* Both of Dzhokhar's parents had left the U.S. and returned to Russia under duress. At that time Dzhokhar was a young teenager going to college and he was left with Tamerlan as his only guide. Tamerlan stepped in and took charge of raising Dzhokhar. *"He had to take direction from the most powerful adult–and in 2013, the only powerful adult in his world."* – (Excerpt found on Page 50 line 15–17.)

Jared Pliner tweets Apr 27, Bruck: Dzhokhar a "lost teenager" who was raised to take direction.

Dzhokhar grew up in an unrealistic atmosphere, full of unrealistic expectations and disappointment. *"Dzhokhar was a lost teenager without any real motivation to do anything on his own. He was raised all his life to take direction from the most powerful adult in his life, Tamerlan"* – *(Page 50, line 14–16.)* ...Dzhokhar really was what he appeared to be – a lost and misdirected teenager.

"Dzhokhar was loved by his teachers and appreciated by his friends." – *(Excerpt found on Page 49, line 2 through Page 50, end line 17.)* Dzhokhar was quiet and did well in school. Everyone liked Dzhokhar. "He was a good kid," "He was the quiet, helpful kid for his relatives' children," "Did his homework," "Loved by his teachers, appreciated by friends," and he "didn't beat anybody up." *"But no one said any of that about Tamerlan. When people who knew Tamerlan heard that he'd bombed the marathon, it kind of fit. But, people who knew Dzhokhar were stunned"*– *(Excerpt on Page 49, line 20–23.)*

The government believed Dzhokhar was a fake. A good kid who was not being sincere. When did this fakeness start? College? High school? Was he fake when he was 8? Was he faking it when he started the Al-Firadus Islamic Twitter account because after seven tweets he had lost interest in it. This evidence showed that he really was a lost individual with little motivation of his own that he and needed a spark of influence and inspiration in his life.

"Do you remember that still photo of Dzhokhar with his middle finger?" – *(Excerpt found on Page 50, line 18 through Page 52, end line 1.)* Bruck brought up the middle finger incident and said to the jury that he could almost hear them gasp at the obscene gesture. Bruck explained how Dzhokhar was acting immature when he flashed a peace sign, then the middle finger at the camera. However, he was also using the camera to fix his unkempt bushy hair. Bruck noted his sneer, Dzhokhar's facial expression when he flashed his middle finger. He had been shot in the face and his face had been slightly twisted by the wound.

"If sentenced to life, this is where he'll be. Supermax, ADX, in Colorado." – *(Excerpt found on Page 52, line 2 through line 25.)* Dzhokhar would be securely locked away at Supermax, ADX and would never be heard from ever again. He would grow up to face the lonely struggles ahead while society would be protected from him. Dzhokhar would never see the world outside, not even the Rocky Mountains. He would only have a narrow cell window that looked out to a patch of sky. Dzhokhar might feel regret for what he did, but no matter how much he might mature his last chance came when he was 19 and he would never be given another chance. He would be in Supermax, forgotten, and there would be nothing for him.

"He was only 19." – *(Excerpt found on Page 53, line 8 through Page 54, end line 19.)* Dr. Jay Giedd, a medical doctor was called as a witness to discuss the development of the teenage brain. Many people at Dzhokhar's age do things that leave people saying, "What was he thinking?" Bruck summed up over the that last few years, modern science wanted to understand how a teen's mind works. The answer had to do with the different parts of the brain, maturing at different rates. *"Teens are like cars with powerful engines and faulty brakes. All teens are impulsive."* Bruck asked the jurors to take into account Dzhokhar's youth as a mitigating factor when imposing the death penalty against him. Dzhokhar was 19. He was still at an age too young to buy a beer, an age where people make horrible self-destructive decisions. No one under age of 18 should be given the death penalty. Dzhokhar could have controlled himself and he knew what he was doing. But he was, still only 19.[175]

DEFENSE'S WITNESSES TESTIFYING FOR TSARNAEV

Resurrecting Tamerlan

Tamerlan stood up and "fired up and very hot." Assaf says of Tamerlan, "You can see his face like tomato red, shouting 'This is not Islamic. It is wrong. You should not say that!'"
— Loay Assaf

DEFENSE'S FIRST STRATEGY WAS to bring back the dead Tamerlan into the courtroom and lay it out as if he was on trial. They called on people who knew him and how he had rubbed them the wrong way. Interesting to note was Tamerlan's personality and how he first began as a good boy, but later grew up to become an angry man. In life, he struggled, trying to achieve his goals and fulfill his dreams. When he attended high school, he claimed he had not 'one single American friend.' Tamerlan felt the world he lived in was treating him unfairly and obstacles were placed as he pursued his goals. He tried things and if things did not work out, he got angry and frustrated or gave up and tried to find another way that would lead to his own happiness, desire and obsession. It was an obsession that would eventually preoccupy his mind and ultimately lead to his demise.

"He was a solidly built boy," stated the 8th WITNESS, ROBERT PONTE. Robert Ponte was a former music teacher at Cambridge Rindge & Latin HS who had taught Tamerlan how to play the piano. Ponte said, *"He was polite, he was respectful, but he was a little isolated. Kept to himself." "I don't recall him smiling in my presence"* – Valencia.

Tamerlan did not have adequate training to join the Jazz piano group, but he wanted to involve him in a jazz ensemble class. Tamerlan wanted to do it even though he didn't have a piano at home, reported Wen. He had only one semester of piano. He would use the piano lab at school whenever he could. Ponte told him it wasn't going to be easy. Tamerlan appreciated that warning and he had tried to keep up.

However, *"Tamerlan had difficulty keeping up with piano practice. Ponte told Tamerlan if he didn't keep up, wouldn't let him play in spring concert. "I can't put you on that stage if you're not ready,"* – Valencia. *"He didn't yell at me, but he glared at me. I won't say I was ever nervous but not being able to read him I was uncomfortable,"*– Cullen. Tamerlan eventually withdrew from the class and earned a "C." Tamerlan also failed to keep up with jazz ensemble. From that point on, his interests in activities went downhill.

Later, Tamerlan found his path to Islam. 1st WITNESS FOR THE DEFENSE WAS LAITH AL–BEHACY. He was an owner of a Middle Eastern food store in Cambridge. Tamerlan visited his store on the day of the bombings to grab some cookies and chocolate, reported Wen. Al-Behacy asked him about the bombings which he saw broadcast on the news. Al-Behacy joked, "So you're not the one who did it?" Tamerlan replied, "No." In Fall of 2012, Al–Behacy was at the mosque where he was comparing the prophet Mohammed to Martin Luther King. Tamerlan was there and he got upset. He did not like what he had just heard. He rose before the small man. Tamerlan had strong muscles and had an intimidating presence. He interrupted, shouting, "You shouldn't do this. You can't compare the prophet with a kaffir, non–Muslim."

Afterward, he called Al-Behacy a hypocrite in Arabic. Another interruption in the mosque was when 2nd WITNESS LOAY ASSAF a member of the Muslim American Society gave a speech at the Cambridge mosque. Tamerlan interrupted Assaf twice while he was preaching. *"Interruptions can be considered a distraction – a void prayer said the iman,"* – Wen.

Assaf was advocating for immigrant Muslims to celebrate Thanksgiving when Tamerlan stood up and shouted, *"This is not Islamic, this is wrong, you should not say that!"*– Bailey. Another incident occurred was in January 2013 and Assaf was paying tribute on Martin Luther King Day, declaring King to be a "great man" and "he had a cause and fought for just cause." Tamerlan stood up, "fired up and very hot," face and started shouting. Assaf said, *"You can see his face like tomato red, shouting, 'This is wrong. I remember you from last time!'"* – Cullen. Others at the mosque told Tamerlan to sit down, but he left instead.

Shouting, speaking loudly and getting angry at the accused was the way Tamerlan interacted with others when he took offense to what they were saying. He was finger jabbing and screaming at people too. 3rd WITNESS WAS ABDERRAZAK RAZAK, an owner of a Middle Eastern food store in Cambridge. When Tamerlan entered his store, he saw a sign in the window that said the store was selling Halal turkeys. Tamerlan began shouting at Razak and jabbed his finger at him. *"Tamerlan asked me why we were selling turkey. He yelled at me, said, 'This is not right. Not right to sell turkeys,'"* – Wen, recalled Razak. He demonstrated to the jurors how Tamerlan jabbed a finger at him, screaming, and then how he waved his arms. Halal meat had been slaughtered in accordance with Islamic traditions, but Tamerlan was still not happy.

Tamerlan's attitude was very opposite from Dzhokhar's which was observed by 4th WITNESS ROBERT BARNES. Robert went to school with Dzhokhar at Cambridge Rindge and Latin. *"Barnes is asked about Dzhokhar's personality. 'More reserved,' Barnes says. Was he angry, a bully? 'No,' "*– Bailey. Dzhokhar was unlike Tamerlan. Tamerlan greeted Robert with a playful punch one time. Robert also told of a story about a German exchange student named Albrecht who visited the pizza shop where they were eating. Albrecht did not greet Tamerlan. Tamerlan took offense and got angry at him.

One time when Albrecht overheard Tamerlan and Robert's conversations about U.S. foreign policy, he stood up and challenged Tamerlan's statements, reported Wen.

At the time, Robert knew Tamerlan was critical of U.S. foreign policy, had visited Russia and *"was wearing 'longer garments, a robe' and had a beard,"* – Bailey. Albrecht, believed that women were not treated well in Islam. This angered Tamerlan, who got "up in Albrecht's face." Tamerlan was very passionate about Islam. Tamerlan who was much bigger than Albrecht started poking him in the chest. Albrecht became scared and asked him to stop. They went outside and continued to argue.

"WHERE'S MY FAMILY?"

Dzhokhar scoped out the courtroom after lunch break. There was no sign of his family arriving from Russia. He had been waiting to see his family come to court, but sadly he had not seen his sisters. His lawyers told him five of his relatives from Russia would be coming to testify on his behalf.

"WHAT CAN I HOPE FOR?"

Jahar sat alone at the defense table staring straight ahead. He must be thinking: Supermax or death. No, what's behind curtain No. 3 to hope for. – tweet from Laurel J. Sweet

ON TAMERLAN'S PHONE

On Tamerlan's phone, there was a preserved video clip showing his little daughter, Zahara, climbing a ladder at a playground. In court, everyone heard Tamerlan's laugh and he said in a playful voice, "She looks like a monkey."

Tamerlan and Zahara

"A monkey!" his daughter shouted. She slid down a slide. "Allahu Akbar," Tamerlan cried, laughing as his daughter going down the slide. Dzhokhar was transfixed. This was the first time anyone in court heard Tamerlan's voice, the voice of Dzhokhar's late brother, resurrected from the dead.

TAMERLAN'S INFLUENCE

Defense argued that Tamerlan had influenced Dzhokhar or had brainwashed him to become interested in Jihad. 5th WITNESS WAS GERALD GRANT JR. who was with the federal defender's office and was a computer forensic consultant. He examined the email accounts of both Tamerlan and Dzhokhar. There were 23 emails between the two brothers originating around January 2011. While Dzhokhar sent him photos of cars, Tamerlan (was in Dagestan) was consistently sending Dzhokhar radical extreme Jihad propaganda while he was in school and influencing him to look at the Jihadist material, reported Wen.

Tamerlan visited Russia for six months and had sent several emails to Dzhokhar in 2012. One email featured a religious figure preaching. He wrote, "Watch this, it's interesting" referring to a YouTube video. Tamerlan sent another email to Dzhokhar and his wife, Katherine with another video attached dated April 28, 2012. Another email was sent on May 2, 2012, from Tamerlan to Dzhokhar, *explained he needed to spread Islam,*" – Cullen. While still in Russia, another email from Tamerlan to his younger brother stated, "I am educating myself more and more about Islam."

Grant showed another email from Dzhokhar to Tamerlan. Dzhokhar wrote, "I miss you...hope everything's all right. I can't get through to you when I call." This was indeed telling how Dzhokhar yearned to contact his brother so much. Tamerlan never responded back to Dzhokhar about the photos of the car or with a comment. Dzhokhar loved him, but Tamerlan had abandoned him and was busy learning more about Islam and continued to send him radical Islamic messages.

Dzhokhar wrote a response after watching a jihad video: "Thanks, it's interesting." Tamerlan was slowly converting Dzhokhar. Tamerlan sent many of these types of emails with attached videos jointly to Dzhokhar and his wife, Katherine. He educated them about Islam religion and politics. Tamerlan wrote another email to Jahar, referring to him as a "pious brother." He sent Dzhokhar a video of a lecture by a cleric, "Why Pray to Allah?" reported Cullen. Defense showed how Tamerlan had influenced Dzhokhar and subsequently helped Dzhokhar become a fervent believer.

It was indeed sad knowing how alone Dzhokhar felt and how much he needed his family's love. He needed someone to be a good role model for him. He did not have anyone and was forced to do things on his own.

Tamerlan not only had influenced Dzhokhar, but also influenced his wife, Katherine. The 6th WITNESS WAS JUDITH RUSSELL who was Katherine's mother. Katherine married Tamerlan; they had a daughter, Zahara. Judith said Katie, as she called her, was "independent-minded." *"She was into music and jazz club and ballet, and went to Suffolk University,"* – Wen. Her daughter met Tamerlan through one of her roommates. The relationship became serious. Later, Tamerlan cheated on her. *"The family tried to advise her not to go back to him...we weren't happy with her choice in the relationship,"*– Cullen. They broke up but then got back together. "They weren't really a good match," said Judith. Other members of the family tried to talk Katherine out of seeing Tamerlan. "It didn't work. Soon after, Katherine began researching and exploring Islam," stated her mom. "She was not religious as a child, but all of a sudden became interested in Islam. She liked the religion."

7th WITNESS WAS GINA CRAWFORD, who was Katherine's friend. Gina shared, *"I knew she was really becoming serious about it (Islam) when she became pregnant and started covering. She had been reading Koran,"* – Cullen. Gina believed Tamerlan had put that idea in her head.

Tamerlan tried to encourage Katherine's mother, Judith, to also read books about Islam, but she had no interest in it. She knew Tamerlan went to Russia: *"Tamerlan went to Russia in 2012, said to see family, and, "I thought it was pretty selfish, because it was a vacation basically,"* – Valencia. When Katherine became pregnant she started wearing a headscarf. "I had no problem with her adopting Islam because there's nothing wrong with Islam. I didn't like the whole package. It seemed like Katherine was giving up a whole lot to be with Tamerlan," said Katherine's mother.

From Drinking To Obsessing Jihad

"Extremist violent jihad was the proper path." –Tamerlan

Day 2 – April 28, 2015

JAHAR'S RUSSIAN RELATIVES WERE flown into Boston to testify. Soon, Jahar will see his family. He had not seen his aunts and cousins for many years. *"Jahar walked in slowly, with his head down, a dour expression to match his dark ensemble,"* – Sweet. When Jahar entered the courtroom, everyone fell silent. He sat at the defendant's table deep in conversation with his attorneys, Judy and Miriam. Later, Judge O'Toole and the jury entered court. As the 9th WITNESS ROGERIO FRANCA took the stand, Jahar twice turned to Judy and whispered to her about Rogerio. Judy whispered back in return. Jahar remembered meeting Rogerio before.

Assisted by a Portuguese interpreter, Rogerio relayed how he had moved to Allston from Brazil in 2006 and quickly befriended the neighborhood's Russian community. When asked if he knew Tamerlan had a younger brother, Rogerio replied, *"I saw Dzhokhar twice before today, when he would knock on my door looking for older brother,"* – Valencia. Rogerio became friends with Tamerlan Tsarnaev. He said, "Tamerlan used to drink alcohol and smoke weed with the group. I learned a lot from them." He became friends with Ibragim Todashev and Khairullozhon Matanov. "Sometimes we go to the bar."

The jurors viewed a photo showing Tamerlan and Rogerio in his kitchen: Rogerio said Tamerlan lived a few blocks away. *View photo:*
(http://bostondefender.org/wp-content/uploads/2015/03/3226A-C.pdf.)

He never visited Tamerlan's apartment. "Tamerlan was at my house a lot. He used to smoke weed in my basement. Most of the time he was drunk, most of the time he was high. So, I could never have a talk like that friend," reported Cullen.

Bailey tweeted, *"One day, Franca, says he came home and found Tamerlan selling drugs in his bedroom. Saw weights and baggies."* He told them to get out. They left. "Tamerlan kept smoking weed at my house after I asked him to stop. He was angry at me for asking him to stop smoking pot. He was also drunk a lot."

11th WITNESS WAS JOHN CURRAN. Curran, a retired boxing coach met Tamerlan and initially thought, "He was kind of charming" and was "eager to participate" in boxing, reported Valencia, but, *"My problem with him is he didn't listen to the coaching instructions. He fought with European style, straight up. Tamerlan was reluctant to pick up American style."*– Cullen. *"Most boxers, American boxes, bend their knees,"* – Bailey. Curran showed the jury a photo of Tamerlan in his boxing gear. His father, Anzor was beside him, standing proudly by his side. Tamerlan's father was very proud, supportive, encouraged by his son's ability. Tamerlan trained hard when his father was there, but less hard when he was not there reported Valencia. *View photo: (http://bostondefender.org/wp-content/uploads/2015/03/3264.pdf)*

John Curran recalled seeing Dzhokhar twice in his gym. He pointed at the defendant, and Jahar gazed up at him. Curran described Dzhokhar back then, *"He looked like a puppy following his brother,"*– Wen.

Dzhokhar was ten–years–old and he had a close relationship with Tamerlan. Jahar saw the photos presented in court. *"Jahar stroked his beard as he stared at the brother he crushed and the father who left him crushed,"* – Sweet.

Tamerlan participated in the Golden Gloves boxing competition and it allowed non-citizens to compete. In 2009, he won and was supposed to go to nationals in Salt Lake City and compete. However, he got the flu, and became too tired to fight. Rules changed in 2010 and foreign athletes no longer allowed to advance to nationals. *"He thought I could pull a rabbit out of a hat and make it possible for him to go. Asked him to but couldn't."* - Valencia. They parted ways and saw each other less.

View photo:
(http://bostondefender.org/wp-content/uploads/2015/03/3240.pdf). Curran recalled, *"I saw Dzhokhar twice as a young boy. He might be in the ring, rolling around or bouncing off the ropes,"* – Valencia.

Young Jahar images from *Tumblr*

12th DEFENSE'S WITNESS WAS KENDRICK BALL. He worked as a personal care attendant and owned a boxing gym in Worcester. He said one-time Tamerlan objected to wearing protection when he fought, he would rather act like a tough player spitting up blood in a spit bucket. Ball's thought about Tamerlan: *"He stood out and different from everybody else. He had a trench coat on, tight fitting jeans, and boots that looked like aluminum foil."* – Cullen.

13th WITNESS WAS BRANDON DOUGLAS. He was involved in wrestling and mixed martial arts. Brandon said he met Tamerlan at a local gym in late 2008. At first, Tamerlan showed self-control, but later he became a very dangerous competitor because he hit fast. He began to change. He was intense when he talked politics. "There was insanity to it." He stopped wearing his "flashy" clothes and shiny alligator shoes. He started to grow a beard.

FUNNY, THE GOVERNMENT WAS GETTING BORED OF DEFENSE'S PRESENTATION

Defense lawyers wanted to show a clip of Tamerlan's boxing victory. However, Prosecutor Steve Mellin objected. He said, "This is cumulative." *(Guess he's bored hearing about "Tamerlan." Let's get to the defendant's story!)* But, the Judge allowed it and so the jurors saw a clip of a boxing match. *"End of clip shows the two boxers waiting for announcement of winner, and Tam named winner, and his hands go in the air in triumph,"* – Wen. The crowd cheered as the theme music from "Rocky" played.

Next, Defense wanted to introduce a photo when Tamerlan wore "flashy" clothes! But Prosecutor Steve Mellin stood up again to object. However, the Judge allowed it. Mellin said after, "It's fine, you're honor. I give up." Everyone laughed. Showing the picture was worth it. The court saw a picture of Tamerlan dressed up in fashion style jeans, white shirt, jacket, with a huge scarf around his neck and looking at his cell phone, reported Wen.

View photo:

(http://bostondefender.org/wp-content/uploads/2015/03/3242.pdf)

Prosecutor Mellin asked, "Do you know the defendant?" Kendrick Ball responded, "No." As Defense moved to call the next witness, the government immediately objected because the testimony was "cumulative." Every witness that prosecutors cross-examined knew nothing about Dzhokhar. It was an interesting strategy by defense shifting focus from Tamerlan to Dzhokhar. Several jurors gazed at Jahar, wondering when they would hear his story.

Defense showed a recent surveillance video from Wai Kru gym, *"Video shows Tam taking far more initiative at ring & younger brother looking very lax and disinterested (sort of like in court sometimes),"* – Wen. Dzhokhar was wearing gray shorts, watching from the side. Jurors watched a video footage from April 12, 2013, four days before the attack. Tamerlan was warming up, getting ready to enter the boxing ring.

Tamerlan, Dzhokhar and a third man were featured in the video. Dzhokhar was *"lazily bouncing off the ropes like a little kid,"* or *"mainly loiters at the ropes."* He was disinterested in whatever his brother was doing. Tamerlan was hopping, stretching and rolling his neck, and then he urged his younger brother to follow him.[177]

Defense wanted to demonstrate to the jurors that Dzhokhar did exactly what his older brother told him to do. Dzhokhar walked funny across the ring, stretching, twisting and rolling his body just like his brother. He leaned on the ropes in a corner of the boxing ring, acting relaxed and bored. Tamerlan threw some hand wraps at Dzhokhar's face. He told Dzhokhar to roll the wraps. Tamerlan often borrowed items from the gym without asking. That day, the gym's General Manager emailed the owner to express his disgust with Tamerlan's behavior. It was the same day when Tamerlan got angry at the owner when he refused to follow rules to take his shoes off. Except, Dzhokhar complied and removed his shoes.

Here is the Surveillance video of Defense's Exhibit Tsarnaev brothers at Boxing Gym. See Reference number 177.

(https://www.youtube.com/watch?v=-3h3DBLtYdE).

LANDLADY'S SON REMEMBERED THE TSARNAEVS

14th DEFENSE'S WITNESS WAS SAM LIPSON. Sam Lipson met the Tsarnaev family in 2002. His mother, Joanna Herlihy owned the 3-unit home on 410 Norfolk St, Cambridge. Joanna rented the three-bedroom apartment to the Tsarnaev family. The apartment was small for the family of six. *"Lipson said his parents speak Russian and he speaks some, and so his mother thought good for Lipson to meet this Russian-speaking family,"* – Wen. Defense asked Sam Lipson the following questions and this is how he answered.

Defense: What was Anzor like?

Lipson: Jahar's father, Anzor, was very strong, a tough man who worked late at night outside in the cold. He was also very warm and hospitable. Anzor worked in Cambridge fixing cars on streets, in alleyways or in established garages. – *from Wen & Cullen*

Defense: How did Anzor change?

Lipson: Over time, Anor had lost weight and his *"muscular build was diminished."* He later became less energetic and he had *"appeared to be in pain."* Lipson recalled that Anzor became more withdrawn and less happy He became sick and was also burdened.

Defense: What was Zubeidat like?

Lipson: Jahar's mother was a very lively, excitable person. Anzor was quieter, but Zubeidat loved to talk.

Defense: What were the changes in Zubeidat?

Lipson: Zubeidat began to dress differently. She covered herself in Muslim traditional, simple and darker clothing. She used to wear colorful clothing and dresses.

(Photos are from Tumblr.)

Defense: What was Tamerlan like?

Lipson: Tamerlan was *"Very strong, muscular...Kind of smooth, slick,"* – Bailey. He was older than Dzhokhar and was more mature. He was charismatic. Tamerlan grew a beard and grew more distant.

Sam Lipson knew Tamerlan had gone back to Dagestan and also knew the parents left the States and returned back to Russia in 2012. He did not see Dzhokhar around much even before college. Sam said the interaction between himself and Tamerlan was almost nonexistent and Tamerlan became more withdrawn.

Defense: What was Dzhokhar like?

Lipson: "Sam has a faint smile about him as he identifies Dzhokhar," – Valencia. Sam met Dzhokhar when he was eight. "He was very sweet skinny kid...a little shy," – Cullen. Sam would recall walking in and he would be racing off on his bicycle. Dzhokhar seemed "cheerful" and would wave or give a cheerful greeting. He last saw him in 2012.

Sam testified both parents were optimistic when they first arrived in the U.S. They became more anxious and pessimistic over time. Zubeidat would speak of her fears and concerns mostly, and how things weren't working out. Lipson admitted he did not know the Tsarnaev's sisters very well.

DZHOKHAR HAD A LITTLE FUN PLAYING A GAME IN COURT

While Tsarnaev's attorneys and prosecutors were called into the Judge's chamber, Dzhokhar sat alone at the defense table waiting for court session to begin. An associate sat with Dzhokhar and they both appeared to *"play some sort of game using pens and paper,"* tweeted Bailey. Dzhokhar was smiling and giggling. Whitehouse tweeted, *"They appeared to be playing tic tac toe or dot to dots."* Suddenly, Clerk Lyness came out of the Judge's chamber and spoke to the U.S. Marshals. They took Dzhokhar out of the courtroom before the trial could resume. Dzhokhar left the courtroom and went back into lock up.

Day 3 – April 29, 2015 - MORE BORING JIHADI GIBBERISH

On April 29, the third day of defense, the day had been spent mostly focusing on Tamerlan and less on Dzhokhar. It became boring. After the FBI reports, jurors who were trying to stay awake examined a notebook page with Russian handwriting on it. Several notebooks FBI confiscated by the FBI were shown as evidence shown in court on March 25. The notebook paper contained handwritten religious verses. Defense began translating the foreign language. This document had the verse, *"Fight them and Allah will punish them with your hands."* – Cullen. The writing continued, *"Without Allah you have no guardian and no helper among those who believe they are faithful to the covenant that they made with Allah"* and *"March forth, whether this is easy for you or burdensome, and fight on your path toward Allah."* On another page was written, *"Muslims...are like one body."* Defense did not know who wrote them, but there were lots of Islamic quotes. They believed these notebooks were Tamerlan's and showed how much he adored Allah and was consumed by Jihad, reported Wen. One page said, *"The one who endures the blows of the sword will be glorified and his work will be rewarded."* Another page said, *"Someday I want to stand before the One for whom I fought so much."*

Another verse said: *"Once Madzhahid begins the Jihad, he goes until the end. His motto: victory or heaven."* – Cullen. Defense guided the jurors, so they could develop a deeper understanding of Tamerlan's mindset, his religious fervor and to show that he was the mastermind and Jahar was his follower. During Defense's presentation there were very few marathon survivors in court...lots of empty seats.

Judge O'Toole interrupted, "How many more of these readings?"

Miriam Conrad responded, "There are eight of these notebooks." When she said there were eight more notebooks to go, the Judge called for a morning break.

After the break, Jahar talked to Miriam and Judy, gesturing a lot with his hand. *"He poured more water for himself and Judy. He spilled a bit, smiles as he wiped it up,"* – Bailey. Jahar's demeanor had not changed much in court. He still did not look much at witnesses. He only glanced up at them.

Defense continued to read Tamerlan's notebooks and interpreted the quotes. *"Oh Allah, free us completely from our attachment to life on earth,"* and *"O Allah, free all Muslims who are held captive by the kafir."* – Cullen. In translation these quotes talked about Allah, the unbelievers, victory, and having the mujahideen faith. The last passage in the notebook read: *"He is Allah the one and only Allah,"* followed by his daughter's name written over and over again: *"Zahara, Zahara, Zahara and Zahara."* Those were his last four words in the notebook. – Cullen.

TAMERLAN'S JIHADI OBESSION

- Tamerlan's Samsung laptop contained al-Awlaki lecture audio files on CD.
- Files on Dzhokhar's laptop originated from Tamerlan's laptop.
- Tamerlan downloaded many "Jihadi" YouTube videos.
- Tamerlan's computer searched for bomb components: i.e. radio controllers, Ruger P95 gun.
- Tamerlan's laptop had security software – True Crypt.
- Tamerlan's laptop had wallpaper showing many images of death and fighting in Syria.
- Tamerlan's laptop had a collection of malformed images of dead children and adults.
- Tamerlan had images of battles, masked men in the forest, jihad recruitment tapes, children dying and suffering, and people of Muslim nations.[178]

- Tamerlan had messages on his desktop, from the Qur'an: *"The one for who Allah stands will not perish."* And *"Fight them, Allah will punish them through your hands, will belittle them and will grant you a victory over them and will heal…the believers."*

Court showed a photo of Tamerlan with a gun, dressed as a Jihadist. "I have this rage deep down in me," said Tamerlan over treatment of Muslims.

Photo of Tamerlan:
(http://bostondefender.org/wp-content/uploads/2015/03/3306C.pdf)

15th WITNESS: FBI 302 REPORTS created after interviewing a witness who could not be in the trial.

In a nutshell: This witness told the jury what happened and provided deeper insight into the terrorist brothers:

- Tamerlan wanted to join the mujahideen fighters and thought they were brave.
- Tamerlan went to Russia with the intention of fighting jihad in the forest. A relative suggested Tamerlan was naïve, "he just watched a lot of videos on the internet." Tamerlan was consumed by Internet content on Kavkaz Center. Afterward, Tamerlan told his relative during his visit to Russia, *"You have convinced my head, but my heart still wants to do something."* Tamerlan felt that jihad was mandatory and immediately began pestering people for radical Islamic hookups.
- Dzhokhar said he was tired of America, wanted to visit Russia. Dzhokhar was very quiet and often just listened rather than saying much.

A Story About Two Brothers

"So prior to lunch we learned two things about the Tsarnaev brothers: Tamerlan wanted to die and Dzhokhar is allergic to cats."
– Laurel J. Sweet, reporter

THE DEFENSE WAS WINDING down its portrayal of Tamerlan as the bitter Tsarnaev seed, the troubled charismatic, yet aloof man, who was filled with rage, and had carried a profound deep obsession to become a jihadist fighting alongside the mujahideen fighters. His heart grieved for a cause. He fought it until his death. He was the brother that wanted to die. The Tsarnaev defense attorneys would finally present the story of their client, Dzhokhar, the younger brother. Their strategy was to paint a softer portrait of Dzhokhar, a calmer "young pup," who tagged alongside his older brother. They sought to spare Dzhokhar from the death penalty by presenting different stories of how he and Tamerlan behaved when the medics treated their wounds after their capture by authorities.[179]

16th WITNESS WAS PARAMEDIC MICHAEL SULLIVAN from Boston EMS. Tamerlan had not died yet after the shootout with Watertown police. Sullivan transported the injured Tamerlan from Watertown after he had been run over by Dzhokhar on Laurel Street. On April 18, 2013, Sullivan treated the injured Tamerlan en route to the hospital. Armstrong tweeted Sullivan's testimony, *"We headed to trauma center at Beth Israel; I tried to bandage his head wound and abdominal wound (his intestines were coming out)."*

The paramedics tried to talk to Tamerlan, but he was pale, sweaty, and looking around reported Wen. The cops locked him in handcuffs since he was in custody. He wouldn't talk or answer them. Suddenly, Tamerlan fought back when the paramedics tried to get an IV into his arm to treat his shock with fluids. *"Sullivan: Whenever we tried to touch him, Tamerlan got combative, fought us. He lifted himself up, yelling, screaming, resisting,"*– Armstrong.

"He was yellin', loud, like a 'Rrrrrrrr!' type of…." – Reilly. The *"Rrrrrr"* sound was coming from Tamerlan. He was trying to free the restraints that tied him down. The paramedics tried to keep him flat, but he wouldn't remain still so his blood pressure dropped further. They couldn't save Tamerlan. He resisted and fought them as he died.

In court, Jahar looked down, no expression on his face.

The jurors remembered Dzhokhar walking down Boylston Street and placing that deadly pressure cooker bomb beside spectators that included children… Flashed images of death and mayhem that followed. They remembered him buying milk after the bombings. They saw him on a blurry surveillance video with Tamerlan at MIT campus, walking up next to Collier's cruiser and shooting Collier in the head as they tried to steal his gun. They remembered him kidnapping Meng and watched surveillance video footage of him gathering snacks at a gas station store where Meng eventually escaped. They remembered Dzhokhar throwing pipe bombs at police officers in Watertown. They remembered the bullet-ridden boat he hid in and the anti-American message he scrawled on the interior of the boat. He was bloodied, injured and dying after the shootout with police. He surrendered in the boat, and the police finally arrested him. Now, it all came down to this scene. After hearing the name "Tamerlan" for three days, the jurors wondered what they would hear about Dzhokhar when he was rushed to the hospital on the night of April 19, 2013, clinging onto life.

17th WITNESS WAS LAURA LEE a Boston EMS paramedic who was with Dzhokhar in the ambulance on the night of his capture. *"As Lee took the stand, Jahar glanced her way, then quickly back at the table. No real reaction to testimony about brother's last moments,"* – Bailey. Lee said they heard the gunfire at dusk. It was when they were preparing their equipment. She was at the scene where Jahar was hiding in the boat. She heard flash bang grenades go off, calling them "less lethal" tools. "We hid between the houses, so we were safe," recalled Lee. They waited for two hours until it was clear.

"They had suspect in custody and we were escorted down to where he was." Reilly tweeted, *"He had a wound along the jaw, here, that was open. It looked like one of the fragments had probably gone off."* Lee's role was to tend to Tsarnaev's gunshot wound. He was stable and awake at the time, reported Cullen. *"Hair was all matted...Had a wound along the jaw...Cheek looked a little deformed... Eye was damaged, rolling back in his head,"*– Bailey. She told the jurors that someone had uncuffed him—so that they could insert an IV into his arm to receive treatment. Defense wanted to show the difference between Tamerlan and Dzhokhar. Dzhokhar did not resist. After Lee investigated his airway, and found a pulse, the paramedics started the IV. Dzhokhar was losing consciousness. *"When Lee spoke loudly to Tsarnaev, he was able to open his eyes, keep them fixed. She asked diagnostic questions. He answered all of them," –* Reilly. Dzhokhar took deep breaths and moved his legs. Lee said, *"I was worried about the bullet fragments as well," – Armstrong.*

Government asked, "He was able to respond to all those questions? Any allergies? Date of birth? etc."

Lee responded, "He said he was only allergic to cats, not any medications. We went to Beth Israel Hospital."– Cullen.

Government asked, "Was he ever combative?"

Lee explained, "Mr. Tsarnaev had a possible gunshot wound on his leg and he got mad and loud—"

Watkins objected, hoping she would not explain further. Government objected, therefore Lee continued, revealing that while the paramedic in the ambulance was applying a tourniquet on his leg, Dzhokhar became angry and it made him upset. She explained, "It was uncomfortable for him," reported Wen.

"Tourniquets are painful?"

"They can be,"– Cullen.

"Aside from that, was he compliant?" Lee replied he was compliant and that he answered all her questions. Government asked if Dzhokhar ever tried to get out. Unlike Tamerlan, Dzhokhar stayed put with seat belts strapped on. When they arrived at Beth Israel Hospital Dzhokhar asked the paramedic where his brother was. They told him he would find out soon. Cullen tweeted, "Government asked, "What was the question he asked you?"

"He said, 'Where's my brother?'"

"And you didn't answer?"

"No. They said, 'You'll find out soon.'"

"Someone other than you said that?"

"Yes.'"

Here is a note about Jahar's cat. *(Katherine Russell, Tsarnaev's wife took care of Peep the cat after Tamerlan died. But the cat missed Jahar and Tamerlan and it later died. Peep would go around the house, meowing and looking for the brothers. The cat only obeyed Tamerlan and it did not want to be held. Katherine brought the cat back to the breeders. Peep was Jahar's best friend and part of the family. However, Jahar discovered he had become allergic to his own cat. He tweeted on December 24, 2012, "Living with this is cat is straight torture. I'm not a cat person anymore.")*

Jahar@J_tsar 9 Nov 2012

We're best friends already, fuck my allergies tho

Jahar's cat "Peep." Jahar is allergic to cats.

Jahar @J_tsar 2 Jun 2012

i neva had allergies on cats before i met my cousins cat, it was ugly and sick and i made fun of it, straight asshole jokes. Now im allergic

Jahar @J_tsar 2 Jun 2012

i still have mad love for cats tho

Beloved Kid, Dzhokhar's Childhood Days

"I always knew I was going to have a good time if I hung out with Dzhokhar." – Alexa Guevara, friend of Dzhokhar.

THE DEFENSE'S 18th WITNESS was Dzhokhar's former teacher at Cambridgeport School, CATHERYN CHARNER-LAIRD. The next defense witness held the attention of the jurors.

Charner-Laird taught Dzhokhar in 3rd and 4th grade in 2002-2003. [180] Armstrong tweeted, *"When asked if she sees him in the courtroom, she says yes, stares lovingly at him."* She smiled and would gaze fondly over at Jahar as she talked about having him in her class. Jahar noticed her and returned her smile. *"Dzhokhar seemed more interested in Charner-Laird's arrival on the stand. Looked closely at her before quickly looking away,"* - Reilly.

Dzhokhar was nine. Charner-Laird had him in 3rd grade in 2002. *"Normally would have been in 4th grade but didn't know English very well. His teacher described him as "Incredibly hard-working...cared a lot about his studies...always wanted to do the right thing,"* - Bailey.

Dzhokhar was learning English at the time. English was his second language. He was a very quiet boy. *"I remember how hard he worked. It's not easy to come into a classroom and not know how to speak the language,"* – Boeri. *"Charner-Laird smiles as she talks about him…he never seemed to stop or give up,"* – Whitehouse.[181]

Charner-Laird told the jurors she never had a discipline problem with him and that he was never a troublemaker. She smiled when she recalled what a nice boy Dzhokhar was. "I do remember he was always playing soccer at recess…that's a way he could connect with other kids," – Whitehouse. "His math skills were definitely probably above grade level at that time."

"Do you remember most students?"

"Yes," – Cullen.

"He was smart? Disciplined?"

"Yes."

"Did the teacher meet Jahar's parents?"

"I don't remember specifics…I do remember they very much wanted him to be advanced degree. He was doing well." – Cullen.

During cross-examination, prosecutors showed that Charner-Laird only knew the young boy and not the young man Dzhokhar was now. "Even though it's been quite a while, you remember Dzhokhar?"

"Yes."

"You had him eleven years ago…when people have their whole lives ahead of them?"

"Yes." No more questions.

As the court learned about Dzhokhar's childhood and school days, the gallery section reserved for victims and survivors remained pretty much empty.

Another Cambridge teacher who had also taught Dzhokhar came to testify. The 19th WITNESS WAS TRACEY GORDON, who had taught a combined 5th/6th grade classroom. According to Gordon, his parents had wanted him to be promoted academically. *"Dzhokhar essentially skipped 4th grade. Came up to 5th early in the school year,"* – Boeri. He skipped a grade because he had caught up academically. Gordon testified, *"He was an outstanding student in terms of being just a very kind and hardworking and dedicated person, beyond his academics...,"* – Cullen.

The jury saw a photo of Gordon and her 5th grade class. In the photo, *"Jahar is so tiny than the other kids. He is sitting in the front row, smiling, wearing red t–shirt, khakis and sneakers. Tsarnaev is wearing what looks like a red Spider–Man shirt. In court, he leans forward and studies photo of his younger self,"* – Bailey.

View photo of tiny Jahar.
(http://bostondefender.org/wp-content/uploads/2015/03/3416.pdf)

Gordon remembered him because he was an outstanding student who was also very kind and hardworking. He was socially friendly, really smart, and a very kind, lovely person. She shared that she doesn't remember all her students, but Dzhokhar comes through... *"Tsarnaev was also a person "that you enjoy being around,"* – Boeri. He was "very respectful to all kids and adults." The teacher remembered meeting Dzhokhar's father, Anzor, at a parent teacher conference.

"Did you know he was foreign?" asked the Defense. Gordon replied, "Yes," and said he spoke English very well. Jurors saw more photos of Dzhokhar at a farm school in Athol, where kids would spend a few nights working at the farm.

View Photos: Jahar working at the farm school.
(http://bostondefender.org/wpcontent/uploads/2015/03/3407.pdf)
Jahar is in the kitchen.
(http://bostondefender.org/wpcontent/uploads/2015/03/3408.pdf)

"How was he in participating?" inquired the Defense. Gordon recalled that he was always happy to try new things. He was an enthusiastic person willing, to go to farm school and excited to both learn and participate. Defense showed more photos of young Dzhokhar. At the Defense table, *"Tsarnaev leans forward and puts his hand on his chin, studying old photos of himself back in 5th grade. Hasn't looked at his old teacher,"* – Bailey. One photo showed Dzhokhar watching a group of dancers with fellow students, and he was following along. Gordon was asked if Dzhokhar participated in activities.

Gordon said Dzhokhar was "easygoing." She said, "Sometimes kids at this age are self-conscious. Jahar was eager to try whatever school had to offer. I wrote he'd be a great candidate next year for peer conflict resolution. Jahar didn't have any particular alliances. He really was outgoing in a way that he would befriend anybody and help anybody in need. I thought those would be helpful skills," – Cullen. However, the Program failed to develop, and Dzhokhar went to another school in 7th grade. – Cullen.

As attorney Miriam paused to go over her notes, Tracey Gordon gazed sadly at Jahar, but he did not look at her. Miriam slipped in a question, "What was your reaction to hearing Jahar was involved in the Boston Marathon bombing?" Government objected; Judge, sustained the motion. Gordon stepped down after the government prevented her from responding to the question, and *"what she thought when Jahar was arrested."* – Cullen.

The 20th WITNESS WAS BECKI NORRIS *"the middle school principal of the Community Charter School of Cambridge,"* – Cullen. She smiled warmly at Jahar as she took the stand. Jahar stared at Becki Norris as she was sworn in. *"She met Jahar in summer of 2005 when she was his adviser. She made home visits."* Norris continued, *"When I first met him, he was really shy and quiet. I spoke Russian so I would practice my Russian with him,"* – Bailey.

Since Dzhokhar was Norris' summer advisee he had applied to get into her school. His family participated in a lottery for admission, and he got accepted. Norris taught him 7th grade math, science and 8th grade algebra II. Norris commended Dzhokhar, *"'He was really bright. Algebra II is usually for 10th graders, he was in 8th. Well behaved kid.' Teachers loved him,"* – Cullen.

Norris said, *"He wasn't a rebel. If you asked him to do something, he would do it,"* – Armstrong. Furthermore, Norris was concerned about his academic performance, "If homework only partially done, "I'd say, 'Dzhokhar, I know you can do better.' Next day, it would be perfect," – Bailey. Jurors saw Dzhokhar's report card from 8th grade. He had *"A's"* in all his courses except for Spanish where he got a *"B"*.

"Teacher Norris smiles broadly as she picks Tsarnaev out in courtroom," – Lawrence. It was clear that his past teachers were very fond of him and they would still smile warmly at him in court. As Norris identified Tsarnaev, Miriam said, "I guess he's changed a little since you saw him," – Bailey.

Norris replied, "He looked a little different than in middle school. I ran into him once in High School." The court saw a photo of Dzhokhar.

View Jahar's 8th grade school portrait.

(http://bostondefender.org/wpcontent/uploads/2015/03/3413.pdf)

Miriam asked, "What else about Dzhokhar? Was he a good player?"

Norris' husband was a soccer coach. "He was one of the best," she answered. "He was little and fast and could get in between people...was very coachable." Norris went to the soccer games and watched Dzhokhar play. Even her husband remembered Dzhokhar as well and, "really loved him too, just like I did." – reported Cullen.

Miriam asked, "Was he full of himself?"

"Not at all. He always came off as quite friendly and humble."

In January 2007, Becki Norris was on maternity leave. She showed the jurors a picture of Dzhokhar smiling and holding her ten-day-old baby daughter.

View photo at:
(http://bdc.w.o0bc.com/wp-content/uploads/2015/05/tsarnaev-850x478$large.png)

Norris said, "Only a couple of the boys wanted to hold her. I thought they would break her. But Dzhokhar was one of them who wanted to. He was happy," – Cullen

View Photo: Defense showed another photo of young Jahar getting a second-place trophy in soccer league.

(http://bostondefender.org/wp-content/uploads/2015/03/3421.pdf)

Her husband had presented the trophy to Dzhokhar. They had pizza after losing a soccer championship game. "He was a pretty tiny kid," – Cullen, said Norris.

"Do you know his family?" asked Defense.

Norris met his mother, Zubeidat, who was thrilled to know that Norris also spoke Russian. Norris said, "Spoke Russian to her. Made appointment, came over. She was very friendly with me. I met Ailina. She fed me. She told me she was studying to apply permanent makeup, this cosmetology thing, offered to do it for me. She said, 'We'll be good friends,'" – Cullen

"What is this event called 'Round Table?'" asked Defense.

"It feels like a mini defense of what you'd do for grad school. His parents did not come to round table. Perhaps they were out of town or country," – Cullen. The "Round Table" displayed a portfolio of one's work and there was a panel of judges who assessed the portfolios.

Norris said Dzhokhar attended 9th grade for just a few days. He missed a day, then came back and told her it would be his last day. Norris explained that the school had a uniform dress code; he was supposed to wear black pants, but he only wore blue. She sent Dzhokhar home to change pants. Dzhokhar's mother was angry over the change in the dress code and contacted the school, reported Cullen. She complained Dzhokhar didn't have clean pants, didn't have money and was going to pull him out of school to attend Rindge and Latin instead. Norris was upset, recalling, "I didn't want him to go. I didn't think he wanted to go." I told Dzhokhar, 'Your mom likes me, let me call her,'" tweeted Cullen. Norris offered to call Zubeidat Tsarnaeva; however, Dzhokhar, who was fourteen at the time, said out flatly, "No. Don't call her." – Boeri.

"Why?" inquired defense.

"I don't remember," responded Norris.

"What was your impression of him for the future?"

"He was one of our top students and top athletes," replied Norris. – Boeri. "We get students into good colleges…I thought that would work out for him. Thought he'd get a full ride." – Cullen.

One day, Norris and her husband ran into Dzhokhar on Cambridge Street. Norris said, "We're so excited to see him. We asked how school was when he was a sophomore or junior in high school. He said he had a *"D"* in chemistry. I was shocked. I tried to encourage him and said, *'Dzhokhar, you're so much better than that.'*" Norris regarded Dzhokhar as one of the top handful of kids she really treasured. "You don't forget them. He connected really well. He was just a great kid." – Cullen. Norris smiled at Jahar as she left the witness stand. *"But, Jahar did not look at Norris as she left the stand. She smiled sadly at him,"* – Bailey.

Becki Norris wrote a compassionate letter about Dzhokhar, her beloved student. She posted the letter on her Facebook page. She showed the world her love for him by saying, "I still love him" and that he needed love. He needed people who would care about him despite what he had done. Are you one of them?

This is her letter.[182]

*"This is Dzhokhar, holding my daughter at 10 days old. He's known to many as the younger (and surviving) Boston Bomber. To me, he was a beloved advisee and student. Over the past two years, I've discovered the painful truth that **when you care deeply for someone, that doesn't stop even if they do unfathomably horrible things.** We humans are really good at holding two irreconcilable ideas in our psyches at the same time. Yes, he did the unforgivable. And yes, I still love him. And – this one is hard to fathom, I know – **he still needs love (He is a human being who still needs love.)** I testified on Dzhokhar's behalf in court today, during the penalty phase of his trial. He was already rightly found guilty. I testified to help the jury see why he might be spared the death penalty. I also hoped to show him, **in spite of what he's done, that someone cares about him as a person.** Dzhokhar made eye contact with me several times today, and we smiled at each other each time, as he heard me saying why I cared. I don't expect to ever see him again. I will hold onto those moments, and I hope he does too. I don't expect anyone to understand this, but I ask you to try. Ask yourself what you would think or do if someone you loved and cared about walked far, far down a deadly path. Ask yourself about what we, as a civilized society, do. There are no easy answers here. But my wish is that something good will come from all of this when people stop and think hard and ask, "What would I do? What would I believe? What *do* I believe?"– Becki Norris*

Norris agreed with the defense's argument that Tamerlan was the mastermind. She said, *"I knew [Dzhokhar] was a really compliant kid, and I knew he cared about pleasing people in authority. I couldn't imagine him planning this, but I could believe that he was impressionable."*

Although Ms. Becki Norris cried while hearing stories about the victims, she felt sad when she heard people label Dzhokhar as *"evil," "inhuman,"* and *"monster."* After her testimony she said, *"When I stood up to exit the courtroom, I looked one last time at Dzhokhar. And then I walked to the door, flooded with grief at the realization that I would never set eyes on the child I loved again."*[183]

21st WITNESS WAS RACHEL OTTY, who taught Modern World History in 12th grade in 2011 at Cambridge Rindge & Latin School. Tsarnaev wrote a paper in her class in which he criticized U.S. Foreign policy. It was titled, "The Predator War." Dzhokhar didn't talk a lot in class. Otty said, *"There were pretty big personalities in the class and Dzhokhar didn't strike me as one of those personalities,"* – Boeri.

22nd WITNESS WAS BRENDAN KELLS, a history teacher at Cambridge Rindge & Latin. Kells also moderated Model United Nations club. Kells met Dzhokhar in 2010–2011 at Model UN conference. Dzhokhar was involved in Model UN.

JAHAR'S COLLEGE FRIENDS TESTIFIED

"I knew his sister and immediately thought he looked like Ailina," said TIARRAH DOTTIN, THE 23rd WITNESS, who was one of Dzhokhar's friends from Cambridge Rindge and Latin school. She met Dzhokhar in her freshman year in high school. Tiarrah was also friends with Ailina. She knew the Tsarnaev family while growing up, starting as far back as in elementary school. *"'Tsarnaev was more of an acquaintance' in HS, Dottin says. Said hi in the halls,"* – Reilly.

Tiarrah said, "I saw him at parties that high school kids threw. Drinking, lot of people, hanging out," – Cullen. Tiarrah decided to attend UMass–Dartmouth because it was the cheapest school she got into. – Cullen.

Bailey tweeted, *"'It's a small school.' Dottin says of UMass. Tsarnaev was there too, in the dorm next door."* Tiarrah said five kids from Cambridge Rindge and Latin School went to UMass–Dartmouth together, "Jamie, Robel, Stephen and Jahar and myself."

"How did five of you become close?" asked Defense.

"We hung out," she said. – Cullen. The friends bonded because they attended the same high school and knew each other for a long time.

Tiarrah spoke nervously as she testified. Jahar did not look at her. It was tough for her to be here to testify. *"Five kids from Rindge & Latin got tight at UMass–Dartmouth. We hung out, we drank together, we played video games,'"* – Reilly. The jury saw photos of the Cambridge friends chillin' at college.

College pictures are from *Tumblr*.

She called those nights "Bro Nights," reported Cullen. She was joined by other Rindge grads: Robel Phillipos, Stephen Silva, both of whom were associated to this case. "I was one of the boys hanging out," she recalled. Defense attorney Timothy Watkins asked, "Why are those nights important?"

Tiarrah replied, "I enjoyed having people I knew from Cambridge...and us being so close together." – Cullen.

Tiarrah suddenly began crying because their friendships were very close and had meant a lot to her.

In the next photo, the guys were seen playing video games, and the ladies playing beer pong. Jahar leaned toward the monitor to see the pictures taken of himself and his friends in a college dorm room. Jahar saw himself sitting on the top of a bunk bed.

"Standard operating procedure for bro nights?" asked Watkins.

"Yes," replied Tiarrah," – Bailey.

Tiarrah cried when she saw the next photo. It was from a school-sponsored road trip to Providence, RI. It was a picture of her and Dzhokhar hugging each other at a Providence nightclub. It was getting difficult for her to testify while Jahar sat nearby, her once close friend. Tiarrah said the friends often ventured into Providence to go to clubs. But, she didn't expect to see Dzhokhar at the club. The photo was a selfie. Dzhokhar was holding the camera. She was excited to see him and placed her arms around him and smiled. "We had been drinking. I said, 'Jahar! Let's take a picture!'"

Tiarrah's face filled with sadness at the memory. She stared up at the ceiling trying not to cry. She recalled how generous he was. He had offered her rides in his car, especially to Target. Tiarrah glanced at Jahar, who stared blankly straight ahead. She then spoke of how they grew apart. "Did you still see Jahar?" asked Watkins.

"Yes."

"What happened?"

Tiarrah explained she didn't see him as often, but when she always saw him she would be, 'excited.' 'I'd hug him,'" – Cullen, she said. By sophomore year in college, the Bro Nights drifted apart. The friends got together less. But, she would always be excited to see Jahar.

"What did you think when you realized Jahar was Boston Marathon bomber? Government: Objection. Sustained. Judge says no," – Cullen. The Defense was interested on asking their witnesses what they thought of Dzhokhar after the bombings. Defense asked for a sidebar. However, Prosecutor William Weinreb started cross-examination, asking Tiarrah a series of questions. She answered that he never talked about politics, and he never expressed anti-American beliefs. She didn't know Dzhokhar was a Muslim. "When you knew Dzhokhar in college, was he his own person?"

Tiarrah answered, "Yes."

"What was his character?"

"He was loyal, fun, laid back."

"Was he friendly?"

"Yes. To everybody,"– Reilly.

Weinreb wanted to know if the defendant was easily pushed around or if he wasn't a follower. Tiarrah answered, "No" to both questions. Weinreb wanted to ask how close they were and if she had ever confided in him. She replied they were close friends, but they did not confide in each other. – Armstrong. Weinreb asked her more questions regarding Dzhokhar's radicalization: "Would he share what he was thinking?"

"No."

Weinreb asked her, "Somewhat private?"

"Yeah."

"Did you know he was watching al-Awlaki lectures?"

"No," – Cullen. Weinreb nodded. This was the confirmation that he sought to pry from this current witness. Dzhokhar had kept private all his Jihadi beliefs, even from those closest to him, including his own family. He finally asked, "He kept private from friends that he was listening to jihadi propaganda and songs?"

"Yes," she responded. – Cullen. Tiarrah still upset, stared at Jahar for a long time before she left the stand, but he did not return her gaze. Tiarrah wept when she returned to her front seat. A man came and put his arm around her, trying to comfort her.

Next up was the 24th WITNESS, ALEXA GUEVARA, who was a close friend of Dzhokhar. She admired him affectionately. She went to Rindge and Latin High School and was an acquaintance of his. They both were the same age, twenty-one. Armstrong tweeted, *"She looks intensely, lovingly at Tsarnaev as she takes her seat. She keeps looking at him, sympathetically."* Jahar appeared uncomfortable yet glanced at her briefly. Alexa told her story that she didn't know Jahar very well in high school, but met him at college when her friend, Tiarrah, introduced him to her. Alexa also knew Azamat Tazhayakov and Dias Kadyrbayev, other friends of Jahar who were charged with hiding evidence in connection with this case. She was one of the witnesses who testified in Azamat's trial.

"You see him here?" asked attorney Miriam who directed questions at Alexa. *"Alexa was watching Tsarnaev, identifies him, 'he's sitting right in front of me,' she says, with a faint smile. He glanced at first, but no longer,"* – Valencia. Alexa seemed nervous, about to become emotional. A tissue box was in front of her, but she did not reach for it yet.

Miriam asked, "Was there a particular food that Jahar liked to order?"

"Domino's. He liked cheesy bread." Alexa recalled his love of Domino's cheesy bread and chocolate lava cakes. "He always offered to share before he ordered." – Cullen. Alexa said this while looking at Jahar. She hung out with Jahar and "the boys" watching them play video games or watching television together. "I always knew I was going to have a good time if I was hanging out with Dzhokhar," she said with a giggle. – Armstrong.

"Can you describe his manners?" asked Miriam. She thought about the question, and it brought tears to her eyes. She grabbed a tissue. While Alexa described his manners, she began to weep.

"Alexa describes Tsarnaev as 'Very approachable, very kind, very accepting of what anyone had to say,' She gets choked up," – Whitehouse. Alexa added nervously, "I never saw him fight with anyone. Jahar was way more respectful than other boys. He could be flirtatious but never in a way that would make you uncomfortable. He knew when to stop," – Wen.

"How did he make you feel?"

"Really happy. I felt at ease. Like I could relax."

Jahar would not make eye contact with Alexa. Alexa's eyes kept wandering back to Jahar. He ignored her. Alexa sniffed as she described the most heated fight she ever saw Jahar engaged in. "I used to hear Jahar argue with Dias about who was the best rapper. He liked Kendrick Lamar."

Interested in that detail, Miriam asked, "Tell us what happened."

Alexa said, "The boys used to argue, but get over it." (Alexa and Miriam smiled; but there were no jurors smiling. They sat there stone-faced and unsympathetic.) Alexa teared up, she never recalled Dzhokhar being political or radical. "We would get together to drink, smoke some marijuana as a group of friends," – Armstrong. She began crying heavily.

"She cries looking at Tsarnaev, who does not look her way. 'Help yourself to tissues,' Miriam Conrad tells her," – Bailey. She continued to describe Dzhokhar as having many friends and that he loved cars. *"'Was he loud?' 'No. He was a floater. Friends in different groups.' Loves cars. Dias and Azamat had a BMW. Other bud had Camaro,"* – Cullen. Armstrong tweeted, *"He likes fast cars. But he had a 'typical college start-up car' which was often broken down."*

Alexa told Miriam how she played a word game "Ruzzle," a scrabble-like app with Dzhokhar, "Once we started it was like every day between classes all the time," – Boeri.

"Who was better?" asked Miriam.

"Me," said Alexa. Jahar remained unemotional as he listened to his closest friend testify about how they played games. Alexa teared up again, talking about their plans. "He encouraged me to go to art school."

"Why?"

"Him and Dias saw me sketching one day...they thought they were really good," – Cullen. Dzhokhar told her she *"'had talent, and shouldn't let it go to waste,' Guevara recalls, weeping. "It made me feel really good,"* – Reilly. Alexa said Dzhokhar wanted to transfer to UMass Amherst to study marine biology. He encouraged her to go to art school. "He made me feel good about myself because he believed in me," recalled Alexa. She did not know much about his family. He was private when it came to his family. He never talked about Tamerlan either. Nevertheless, he raved about how he loved his little niece, Zahara, who he said was *"super cool."* He once showed her a picture he had of Zahara on Instagram.

Picture of Jahar with Zahara is from *Tumblr*.

"Tell us about how funny Jahar was? He was corny?" asked Miriam.

With tears streaming down her face, Alexa responded, "he was really corny. You could tell he was not taking himself too seriously. Would laugh at himself." – Cullen.

"Why are you crying?" Miriam asked, but the government objected. The Judge overruled. With that cleared, Miriam again asked Alexa why she was crying.

Alexa sobbed, "because I really miss the person that I knew. He was a good friend, a supporter and he was there for me," reported Wen.

When Alexa talked about missing him, Jahar put his head down, hand to face, and looked away. He shifted uncomfortably in his seat. Miriam patted Jahar on the back. Three jurors who cried before seemed to be emotionally moved with what she shared. The other jurors were stone-faced, but one juror bowed her head and clearly wept.[184]

"Were you aware of a trip Jahar took to NYC?" asked Miriam.

"Yes," she said. The jury viewed a photo of Jahar with his friends in Times Square in 2012. She said she saw Jahar and the friends: Azamat and Dias over spring break. *"On March 16, 2013, she met up with Jahar, Dias, Azamat and others & went to Charles River near BU Bridge. Purpose? 'To set off some fireworks'"* – Wen. They met in Cambridge, about a month before the bombings. "We went for a walk along the Charles River. Jahar went to his car, took out a backpack, and there were fireworks inside. *"He lit one, didn't work. Second one worked. They were 'whooping and happy' It was like a 'giant sparkler' and Tsarnaev jumped through it,"* – Bailey. Alexa described the fun they had that night. They were laughing and jumping together. The fireworks: "It was like a giant sparkler and Jahar jumped though the sparks." – Wen. It would be the last fun, happy moment that Jahar, his friends and Alexa would share together.

Firework photo of Jahar is from *Tumblr*.

"Really?" asked Miriam, sounding very delighted to hear something so captivating about the young Jahar.

"He was being really silly," she said.

"Is that typical for him?"

"Yeah."

"When was the last time you spoke to him?"

"I spoke to him was about two weeks before Marathon Monday and I didn't notice anything different." Defense was done questioning her. Since it was near the end of the day, there was no time for cross. Alexa would return later.

Alexa tried to make eye contact with Jahar as she stepped down from the stand, but he did not return her gaze. As she walked out of the courtroom, she broke down in loud gasping sobs. Everyone in the courtroom was startled by her emotional reaction and they could hear her sobs from the hallway. The Judge and jury heard her crying and left for the day. Jahar stood up, fixed up his collar on his jacket. His head down, he was escorted out by his security guards.

Alexa Guevara sketched this drawing to illustrate her feelings towards Dzhokhar. It's called, "GARDEN OF SECRETS." It portrays Dzhokhar who was once this golden person who glowed with life, love and innocence in her life, but has now become vile in sin, lost in his own personal darkness and haunted by evil monsters glooming overhead. Guevara's sketch was linked to a *Tumblr* page on the internet, but sadly the link no longer exists. This drawing would have been lost. This is a rare drawing of Dzhokhar and it should be saved. It depicts Dzhokhar as a lost person.

AN AWKWARD AND UNEXPECTED DAY

On April 30, 2015, there was a big media turnout. Although Jahar's relatives arrived in Boston a week ago, the government planned to fly them back the next day. They hoped they would be able to testify today. The five Russian women were escorted through the courthouse toward courtroom 9 wearing ankle monitors. They seemed nervous as they gazed at the Boston skyline. The city was overwhelming compared to the green mountainous landscape of their homeland. They wore long skirts and were accompanied by a Russian translator.

Jahar had not yet arrived in the courtroom, but Miriam arrived wearing a deep bright red suit with a pile of papers in her hand. *"At the prosecution table, an attorney is looking at old photos on laptop of Tsarnaev family, including his parents holding Tamerlan."* – Bailey. Alexa Guevara who cried in court was *"Back on the stand ...We are waiting for judge, jury and defendant. Tsarnaev will have to walk right past Alexa Guevara. Right now, Miriam Conrad at the stand chatting w/ her, smiling,"* – Bailey. Courtroom suddenly hushed. *"Jahar strutted in with hands held together in front of him. He looked down as he passed by her. Alexa pouts,"* – Sweet. Alexa tried to make eye contact with Jahar, but he never regarded her. Jahar looked awful; he had very dark bags under his eyes and his hair was a mess like he hadn't slept in months.

View the Court sketch of Jahar and Alexa by Art Lien. (http://courtartist.com/2015/05/during-the-break-sketches.html)

Jahar sat between his two lawyers and talked with them. He glanced back towards the gallery searching for his relatives. Wen tweeted, *"Awkward scene: Tsarnaev & former buddy, Alexa, sit 10 ft away from each other waiting for court to begin. Alexa looks at him, but he looks down."* Jahar seemed to ignore her or he felt ashamed looking at his friend. They were once very tight, reported Cullen. *"Alexa offers a slight smile to Tsarnaev who appeared to glance her way. He's still talking to Judy Clarke,"* – Bailey.

Judy was smiling and talking to Jahar. Miriam seemed to enjoy talking with him too. Jahar was extremely quiet. *"Tsarnaev is looking down, slouched back in his chair,"* – Bailey. Alexa, who was waiting to be cross-examined by prosecutors, rocked in her chair. Alexa kept glancing sadly at Jahar. She yearned to see through him. Suddenly, Miriam walked up and whispered something to her.

The Judge's door opened. Clerk Lyness came in and called attorneys back to the judge's chambers. Jahar was removed and returned back into custody. Alexa was escorted off the stand. Jahar did not look at Alexa, who also looked away from him.

"As you know, I had some strong reactions to yesterday's testimony. But if I put myself in Guevara's shoes, this must be dizzying apparently, was this pivotal figure in her life, imbuing her with a desperately needed sense of self–worth. And now – He's a convicted terrorist who won't even look at her." – From Adam Reilly, wgbhnews reporter

Court was delayed for one hour and it was unclear why there was this delay. There was much whispering and anxious looks exchanged among the attorneys, U.S. Marshals and the FBI. Judge O'Toole arrived without the jurors following. Clerk Lyness told the U.S. Marshals to retrieve Jahar. When the door opened, Jahar was fixing his shirt collar. He glanced at the reporters as he entered the room.

Judge O'Toole made a public announcement: "A juror is sick. So, we're stopping the trial until Monday." Of course, the government was not happy with this delay. Unfortunately, the government would have to keep Jahar's Russian family over the weekend. Sixteen FBI agents would have to guard the family at the government's expense.[185]

Tears Finally Fall

"When Dzhokhar was 4 or 5 years old, he watched "The Lion King"
and when Simba's father, Mufasa died, he was crying. He was very
sad. Our family was struck by his ability to feel compassion."
– Raisat Suleimanova, cousin

Day 4 – May 4, 2015

THREE SEDANS PULLED UP at the federal courthouse
carrying the Russian family members of Dzhokhar Tsarnaev.
Today, Jahar was happy and buoyant. He smiled at his attorney
Miriam Conrad, shared a chuckle with Judy Clarke and chatted
with David Bruck. He wore an impressive black European
fashionable suit. The testimony of classmate, Alexa Guevara, was
suspended in order to hear from his Russian relatives. Judge
O'Toole and the jurors entered the courtroom. When Jahar stood up
he had a big smile on his face as his attorney called their first
witness to the stand.

Raisat lingered at the stand staring at Jahar, trying to
recognize the young cousin she once knew. She smiled at Jahar,
who was now all grown up. The 25th WITNESS WAS RAISAT
SULEIMANOVA. Raisat was born in Russia in Dagestan. *"She lives*
near Moscow now, but was born in a village near Caspian Sea; jurors see a
map. Witness is an ICU nurse in Russia," – Armstrong. She had a
daughter. Raisat said Zubeidat was the youngest sister of her
mother, Shakhurzat. She bore some resemblance to Tsarnaev's
mom, Zubeidat. She was the maternal cousin of Dzhokhar. Raisat
was a tall, dark-haired woman with long hair who spoke softly
with the aid of an interpreter. She gripped tightly, clasping her
hands nervously as she testified. This was the first time she had
ever left her home country. *"'I came for the sake of my brother, whom I*
love very much,' she said thru a translator," – Cullen *"I have no right not*
to come here. I categorically reject what he did, it's a great tragedy."

"Why do you refer to Dzhokhar as your brother?" asked Defense attorney William Fick.

Raisat explained that she did not have brothers, so she clarified, "I usually refer to my cousins as brothers," reported Cullen. The jurors saw a photo of her in Dagestan with the Tsarnaev family during one of their visits one summer. The Tsarnaevs visited her family every summer. "My sisters and my cousins," she emphasized, pointing to the photo. Dzhokhar was a baby in the photo. Before Dzhokhar was born, Raisat said she did not have much contact with her sister's cousins that much. It was until 1991, her family went to visit the Tsarnaev family in Kyrgyzstan.

"*She last saw Dzhokhar in person when the Tsarnaev clan left for the US in 2002. Asked to describe him, says, 'I can only say good things,'*" – Reilly, and it wasn't because he was her cousin. When Dzhokhar was born in 1993, as a young child, he had a warm, lovable personality. Bailey tweeted, "*He was a sunny child. If you looked at him, you would want to smile even if you didn't feel good...*" While she testified, Jahar did not make direct eye-contact with his cousin. His eyes focused straight ahead, and he listened. Raisat continued, "I don't think there is anyone in our family who didn't love him. Everyone in the family loved him," reported Wen.

Defense raised more questions. They wanted Raisat to share several childhood stories about Dzhokhar for the jurors to hear. Raisat smiled and gazed at Jahar whom the family doted on. "When Dzhokhar was four or five years old, he watched "The Lion King" and when Simba's father, Mufasa died, he was crying. He was very sad. Our family was struck by his ability to feel compassion...
Dzhokhar used to cry when he watched "The Lion King" and the king died. He understood tragedy, she says," – Armstrong.

Raisat told another story about their aunt, "*...because Jahar had such a wonderful smile as a little boy, he'd make other people smile, even if they were strict,*" – Stevens. This aunt was very strict, and Dzhokhar's gentle way had an impact on this aunt. "We couldn't go out of bounds with her. But when Dzhokhar was staying with us she would allow him to do whatever he wanted. When we watched *"The Lion King,"*and when Simba's father died, Dzhokhar was crying. She said, *"I can't understand how a small child could sympathize. She even said to herself, 'This child has changed me.' Raisat's aunt changed after that and started loving everybody including the children,"* – Cullen.

"Describe Tsarnaev's mom?" asked William Fick.

"She is a very strong person. Bright personality. She wanted everything to be "ideal," – Wen. Zubeidat loved to wear bright colored clothing. Her children always dressed the best. Jurors saw a couple of photos of Zubeidat: one of her wearing a light green top and skirt, and a necklace. A second photo showed Tsarnaev's mom at an airport, with a pink dress on, wearing heels and sunglasses. – Wen.

"None of us have seen any of these pictures before. Don't want to slow things down necessarily, but we want to see them," stated prosecutor William Weinreb.

"All of these have been provided to the government," said William Fick.

Judge O'Toole cut in, "We'll proceed as we have been admitting them, if an issue we'll deal with it." – Cullen.

Fick continued to ask Raisat. "What about Zubeidat's personality? Was she shy or outgoing?"

"She wasn't shy at all. She had a bright personality, outgoing, very social. She was loud," – Cullen. Zubeidat wanted everything in her life to be excellent and beautiful. She was strict with her children. She wanted all the best for her and her family, reported Valencia. Defense asked Raisat about Uncle Anzor. She replied that he was the total opposite of Zubeidat. He was quiet and worked hard with two to three jobs in order to provide for the family. He always wanted to help other people and did what he could to support Zubeidat and his children. – Cullen. Anzor was also in love with Zubeidat and he wouldn't let her go anywhere without him.

The Tsarnaev family moved around a lot. Raisat said, *"They always lived out of suitcases. We said, 'you are like gypsies.' They lived in Siberia, Kyrgyzstan, Chechnya, and Dagestan,"* – Cullen. The jurors saw a map of the different countries and the locations where the Tsarnaev family lived. Raisat would visit them often during the summer months, for three months or six months at their home near the Caspian Sea. – Valencia. Anzor was an auto mechanic and wherever the family moved he always searched for and found work. The family's frequent relocation was difficult on the children, so they did not adapt well.

The jurors also saw another childhood picture of young Dzhokhar in Russia. *"Now seeing photo of a New Year celebration, witness, cousins, along with Tsarnaev's sisters Bella and Ailina holding him as a baby."* – Valencia. *"We are looking at a class photo of Dzhokhar Tsarnaev in the first grade. He's tiny. Wearing a red shirt. Hands on lap. Looks scared,"* – Bailey. Raisat showed the picture of tiny Dzhokhar with tousled hair. Dzhokhar looked scared to be surrounded by unfamiliar faces as the Tsarnaev children switched schools a lot. Next photo was of Dzhokhar and his sisters, Bella and Ailina, celebrating New Years. *"It is New Year's, 2000, fyi. There's a Christmas tree in the shot,"* – Reilly. The siblings all looked very happy standing next to a small Christmas tree at a house party.

Fick asked, *"What role did religion play in your life, growing up?"* Suleimanova answered, *"because I'm a Muslim, we celebrate all our Muslim holidays,"* – Reilly. However, religion played a less significant role in Zubeidat and Anzor's lives. They did not pray the customary five times a day. They would only celebrate major holidays. – Cullen. When the family moved to the States, Dzhokhar's mother became more religious. Raisat spoke of the shock she experienced seeing for the first time the radical appearance of her aunt wearing a hijab, *"She used to be such a fashionable person. It was a shock not just for me but for my mother and everybody else,"* – Cullen. Bailey tweeted, *"It was a shock for me knowing the kind of person Zubeidat used to be. It was very strange."*

At the defense table, Jahar seemed to avoid making eye contact with his cousin whom he had not seen since he was eight-years-old. The jury now saw a startling picture of Zubeidat, *"Here's a photo of Zubeidat, wearing a hijab, standing in a depressingly ramshackle kitchen. Very different than the woman we saw earlier,"* – Reilly. Jahar stared at the picture of his mother. Fick asked Raisat, "What impact of crimes of Tsarnaev brothers had on you and your family?" – Cullen.

Prosecutor Weinreb objected. Attorneys from both teams went to sidebar to discuss matters with Judge O'Toole privately. Meanwhile, Raisat dabbed tears from her eyes. Suddenly, Jahar peered up at his cousin. Finally, Raisat caught Jahar's large dark eyes staring back at her. She smiled. Raisat refused water; instead she grabbed a tissue to wipe her tears away. Jahar turned away from her and talked to Judy. After the sidebar, prosecutor William Weinreb began his cross-examination. "Weinreb asked, "The defendant himself has never set foot in Chechnya, has he?

Raisat answered, "I cannot give you the exact dates, I was a child myself." – Armstrong.

Writer's Note: At this section, I am writing verbatim Kevin Cullen's tweets without interruption in the paragraphs, to demonstrate the level of tension that occurred during the cross-examination and the conversation flow between the government and Raisat.

Weinreb: "And because you were a child, you weren't keeping track of dates. But he moved here at eight, and lived in same place for five years?"

Raisat: "As far as I know, they lived in Kyrgyzstan, then Grozny."

Weinreb: "But Jahar was never in Grozny, was he?"

Raisat: "They didn't stay there for a long time."

Weinreb: "So, as a child, you don't know dates?"

Raisat: "I was fourteen-years-old when the war broke out in Chechnya."

Weinreb: "So he spent four or five years in Kyrgyzstan?"

Raisat: "I can't tell you for a fact."

Weinreb: "And they were able to spend summer on Caspian Sea?"

Raisat: "Yes."

Weinreb: "And spend time with family?"

Raisat: "Yes."

Weinreb: "You haven't seen him since he was eight-years-old?"

Raisat: "Yes."

Weinreb: "Growing up, he was much loved?"

Raisat: "Yes."

Weinreb: "He grew up surrounded by loving family members?"

Raisat: "Yes. He was such a sweet child, very loved. One couldn't help but love him."

Weinreb: "Family doted on him?"

Raisat: "Of course. He was the little one."

Weinreb: "Had his needs been met? What does a child need? Food? Well fed? Clothing?"

Raisat: "Zubeidat really took care of the clothes; the children were well dressed."

Weinreb: Was he comforted when sad?"

Raisat: "Yes, especially since he had sisters."

Weinreb: "He was a very lucky boy in that way?"

Raisat: "He has a lot of cousins."

Weinreb: "They helped him become a confident young boy?"

Raisat: "Yes."

Weinreb: "So when you saw him, they raised him to be a confident young boy?"

Raisat: "Yes, of course."

Weinreb: "So he wasn't intimidated by his strict aunt?"

Raisat: "She was strict toward us, but to a child of four or five years old, it's hard to be strict."

Weinreb: "But you said Dzhokhar made her less strict."

Raisat: "Yes. She changed because of him."

Weinreb: "But when faced by someone older who was strict, he managed to change them? "

Raisat: "He had such a smile."

Weinreb: "Because of that he could do whatever he wanted?"

Raisat: "I don't mean literally. In the bounds of the reasonable."

Weinreb: "But he had mind of his own, even at age eight?"

Raisat: "I don't understand the question."

Weinreb: "You talked about Dzhokhar's kindness, but you would agree that the bombing of innocent people was not an act of kindness?"

"At this, Miriam Conrad looks back at Fick and mouths, "OBJECTION!" He objects. It's overruled," – Reilly.

Weinreb: "Dzhokhar cried when Simba's father died?"

Raisat: "Yes."

Weinreb: "But he's indifferent to the pain and suffering of hundreds of — "

Defense: "OBJECTION!" **Judge:** "Sustained."

Weinreb: "You agree that someone who cries at the death of a cartoon character but remains indifferent to the death of innocent– –"

Defense: "OBJECTION, your honor!" **Judge:** "Sustained."

Weinreb expressed his mockery towards the defendant, scorning Dzhokhar for crying at the death of Simba's father, a cartoon character in "The Lion King," but all the while being "indifferent" and "unemotional" to the bombing victims.[186] Defense attorney Fick was clearly angry with the government's point and argument and insisted on a sidebar with the Judge.

The Prosecutors wanted the jury to keep their fuel of anger focused on Tsarnaev yet remain compassionate toward the victims. They did not want any jurors to become softened by the cute baby pictures of Jahar, nor to show him any mercy because he was once this loveable boy with a happy, attractive smile. The prosecutors wanted nothing more from Dzhokhar, but for jurors to remember his offense, his unrepentant heart, to punish him and seek justice for the victims.

After sidebar, Defense asked Raisat one last question about accommodations when the Tsarnaev family came to visit them. She told them, in a two-room apartment, more than twelve to fourteen people were cramped into the rooms. After questioning, she was excused from the stand.

26th WITNESS WAS NAIDA SULEIMANOVA, who was Raisat's older sister, and also Dzhokhar's cousin. *"Tsarnaev is turned toward witness stand, his hand resting on the left side of his face. Naida has short blond hair and looked as if she is about to cry looking at her cousin,"* – Bailey. Naida was emotionally sad when she finally set eyes on Jahar. She was dressed in jeans and a cardigan. Naida breathed heavily. She appeared to be nervous as she took the stand after her arrive in the States for the first time. She was from Moscow. In a very soft-spoken voice, she told the jury that she was born in 1976 in Dagestan, a rural village near the Caspian. Naida glared at Jahar as she spoke, but he did not glance over at her. She took several deep breaths trying to compose herself. She said she worked as a cashier at a gas station. She also babysat Dzhokhar twenty years ago. Suddenly, she shook, visibly nervous, *"Nadia appears on the verge of bursting into tears, speaking very softly. Very emotional for her."*– Cullen. She said, "Dzhokhar is my brother... my beloved brother."

"You seem to be emotional or teary up there. Can you tell us why?" William Fick asked. Long silence," – Bailey.

"Because I am seeing my brother for the first time in so many years and it is not easy," she shared in a barely audible voice, – Bailey. Jahar did not seem to look at her. Defense began showing the jurors an old family photo, *"The Tsarnaev family as kids in 1994. She was pregnant. She's holding baby Dzhokhar back in Southern Russia."*

"Who are you holding in that picture?" – Bailey.

"Jahar," she whispered in an anguished voice. She identified him in the picture to jury and smiled at Jahar. She last saw him in 2002 in Moscow," – Bailey. This picture brought back sad memories for her. The Tsarnaev family had come for a short visit and would return to Kyrgyzstan or Chechnya. "It was very painful because they were leaving," she recalled their last visit. "Nobody knew when we would see each other again," for they were moving so far away, – Bailey. In 2002, Anzor, Zubeidat and Dzhokhar immigrated to the United States.

"How do you describe Dzhokhar you knew as a child?"

"He was very cute, very nice, very kind. There was always a smile on his face," – Bailey. Defense displayed another family photo showing little Dzhokhar in a black suit similar to the one he was wearing in court. Naida glanced up to see if Jahar was looking in her direction. Defense repeatedly showed more and more photos of Jahar. The jurors stared at the pictures of the defendant. Naida said, "This is cute Dzhokhar, the little one."

"How was Tsarnaev as a child?"

"There was never an occasion that he did not have a smile on his face," said Naida. – Bailey. The court saw a photo. *View: cute little Dzhokhar sitting on a chair smiling.* *(http://bostondefender.org/wpcontent/uploads/2015/03/3507-021.pdf)* He was leaning against a stuffed pillow.

(Young Jahar picture is from *Tumblr*.)

"Next photo, little Dzhokhar on a chair, looking at the camera. Naida smiles sadly when she sees it," – Armstrong. Next, defense showed another photo of Dzhokhar sitting on the shoulder of big brother Tamerlan.

View:

(http://bostondefender.org/wp-content/uploads/2015/03/3501-10.pdf)

Nadia stated sadly, "Dzhokhar loved his older brother very much…. he would always listen to his oldest sibling," – Boeri. Nadia choked up and became teary eyed when she saw the picture of the two brothers. "This is the custom…you always listen to your older sibling. Your older brother, and follow his example," – Cullen.

Nadia also spoke about the changes in Zubeidat's dress. Like her sister Raisat, she *"called Zubeidat's change 'dramatic' and said, 'I'm a little scared of people who are completely covered,'"* – Palumbo.

William Fick played a recording found on Tamerlan's computer. Nadia identified the voice as belonging to Tamerlan. The voice said, *"'I have this rage of hatred inside me.' We hear a booming voice – it's Tamerlan,"* – Grossi. Naida wiped away tears as she listened to his voice; it stirred up painful memories. She gave a prolonged stare at her young cousin, but Jahar remained aloof. Fick played a second recording.

Tamerlan said in deep voice: *"I don't see life past 3-4 years. Somehow deep down in my heart I don't believe that the Caliphate will be established in my life time."* Naida was disturbed. She spoke about her feelings for Tamerlan. "What Tamerlan is saying here isn't what our parents taught us. They taught us to pray. I'm very far away from all this. I last saw Tamerlan in 2012 when he came to Russia at my uncle's house. I was very happy to see my brother." Tears welled up in her eyes. "But, I had two conflicting feelings. To see my brother and hug him." Naida began weeping on the stand explaining the conflict she had for Tamerlan.

The other conflict...Naida became afraid of him when she learned he embraced jihad. "I miss him.... I'm sorry this time I didn't have my heart completely open to my brother," – Cullen. Naida wept on the stand. She was clearly in pain from the loss, reported Wen. That year, she prevented her son from interacting with Tamerlan. She asked her son, *'Are you praying?'* and that praying was enough for her. Naida was done testifying. Jahar turned away as his cousin stepped down.

27th WITNESS WAS PATIMAT SULEIMANOVA. *"This is the aunt that Tamerlan stayed with,"* –Wen. Jahar smiled when he saw his aunt, Patimat. She was an elderly woman with gray hair pulled back into a pony tail bun. She walked to the witness stand with the help of another woman. As soon as she sat down, she began weeping. Jahar gazed at her quite seriously for he knew this aunt was close to his parents. She said in a soft voice that she was sixty-five and was born in 1950 in Dagestan. She showed the jurors a photo of the mountainous town village where she was born.
View: (http://bostondefender.org/wp-content/uploads/2015/03/3507-083.pdf)

Patimat spoke sadly. In the back of her mind, she was both very sad and upset. Her nephews had committed the most horrific terror attack, a crime so massive and unbelievable. She refused to think that they were involved. She was very upset with Dzhokhar and stared at him in agony. He was supposed to come home to Dagestan in May 2013 to visit his parents...and she would have been there also to welcome him.[187] However, that would never happen now because of his involvement in the bombings. Patimat could not keep her emotions in check, apparently, she was so distressed on the stand. She started hyperventilating and crying before she could say another word. Patimat grabbed some tissues on the stand and she sobbed, large heaving sobs with cascading down her cheeks. She could not stop crying. She placed her hand over her heart and wiped her eyes, breathing heavily.

Suddenly, her sobs shook Jahar. *"His aunt's anguish is the first thing that's gotten to him, in all of this,"* – Cullen. Tears welled up in Jahar's eyes and he started crying. He pulled a tissue from the tissue box.

View: "Tsarnaev has wiped his eyes and nose with a tissue several times. Miriam Conrad whispers to him," – Bailey. *(http://courtartist.com/wp-content/uploads/Tsarnaev150504_crying-copy.jpg)*

Jahar, for the first time broke down and cried in court, reported Wen. *"Tsarnaev seen with tissue in his hand and putting it to his eyes. And now he is using his hand to wipe his eyes. Patimat testimony affected him. Her cries sounded like woman w/broken heart,"* – Wen.[188]

Jahar had remained impassive in the past couple months, especially through the victims' testimonies and videos. But this day, he finally showed emotion. *"'Perhaps Mr. Fick we should take a break,' judge says. As she leaves the witness stand, Tsarnaev appears to wipe his eyes. He's crying,"* –Bailey. Patimat's loud sobs were still heard as she was led out of the courtroom. Jahar, showing remorse, realized now how his involved actions had impacted his own family, and that he had deeply disappointed the people who loved him. Yet, he cried only for his own kin and not for the victims. Liz Norden, the mother of two handicapped sons who both had lost their legs, left the courtroom distraught. She found Tsarnaev shedding tears for his family "troublesome."

"Dzhokhar dabs at his eyes and nose as Patimat leaves... he appears to be shaken up," because he had seen how his crimes ruined his own family. – Reilly. As Jahar wiped his tears away, the Defense brought up their next witness.

May 4th, Day 4 of the Tsarnaev's trial was a very emotional day for Jahar and his relatives. He couldn't hug them because of SAMs confinement and also because this was a capital case trial. He was not allowed to have human contact. Jahar broke down in tears for the first time as his Aunt Patimat cried on the stand. It was the first visible show of emotion from him, revealing his sadness, and his remorse at the deep pain he caused to his family.

28th WITNESS WAS SHAKHRUZAT SULEIMANOVA. Shakhruzat stared sadly at an old black and white photo from her childhood with Zubeidat. Shakhruzat was also Dzhokhar's aunt. She was born in 1955. *"Has 4 children, including Naida and Raisat, the last two witnesses,"* –Boeri. Like all the other witnesses she also cried observed reporter Cullen. Shakhruzat wept softly as she talked about her sister, Zubeidat. She peeked over at her sister's youngest son, Jahar, sitting a few feet away. She worked in a hospital as a nurse's assistant.

Shakhruzat took care of her sisters, Zubeidat and Patimat when their mother was ill with cancer. Zubeidat was the youngest of the three sisters. Shakhruzat shed tears as she viewed a childhood photo and identified herself with her mom, and her sisters (including Tsarnaev's mother) in the photo. Shakhruzat cried at the memory, "It was very hard for us," she told attorney William Fick who asked her about her role in the family. When their mother became ill and couldn't do much, Shakhruzat took care of the family. She cooked, did the laundry and supported her younger siblings. They asked, *'When would mother be back?'* She would provide comfort to the younger children.

When the eldest sister Patimat got married she moved to another home. She would travel back home two hours to help the family. When Shakhruzat got married at eighteen, it was very difficult and upsetting for Zubeidat because Shakhruzat had always taken care of her. *"At this time, Zubeidat was only 7 years old. Didn't want her older sister marrying and going to live with "strangers,"* – Wen. It was very painful time for them both.

On Shakhruzat's wedding day, Zubeidat cried at her wedding. *"She approached me under the table,"* hitting her legs. *"Crying, 'Shari, let's go home.'"* – Cullen. Three years after their mother died, Zubeidat went to live with her oldest brother, Muhammad Haji. When Zubeidat went to 9th grade she moved in with another brother.

Shakhruzat had gray hair and she had her long hair tied back in a bun. She continued to describe how Zubeidat was passed among family members after their mother's death. Shakhruzat did not look at Jahar as she testified. She seemed so sad, kept looking down…her eyes were somber. She spoke in a soft voice observed reporter Valencia.

Later, she described how her family didn't approve well of Zubeidat (an ethnic Avar) marrying Anzor (a Chechen). She showed a photo of Anzor and Zubeidat, as a couple from their time in Siberia dressed in thick coats and boots. "It's very cold," she said. *"Now, a series of photos of the young Zubeidat & Anzor first courting, now holding baby Tamerlan. Lots of Tsarnaev family backstory today,"* – Armstrong. "It's very painful when relatives live far away," said Shakhruzat. "We don't allow our daughters to marry a person from different ethnicity. Everyone wants their own people." She said the Tsarnaev children had a hard time switching schools with all the frequent moves.

The jurors saw several photos of the Tsarnaevs family taken in the early 90's displayed on the screen: *"A large family photo with everyone in Kyrgyzstan. Before Tsarnaev was born,"* –Valencia. *"Jurors getting pix of Tsarnaev's mom side of family: Girls marry young, patriarchal, poor, relatives lean on each other, cousins = brothers,"* –Wen. *"Shakhruzat, aka Shari, is holding Ailina, Dzhokhar's sister, who's using a pacifier. Tamerlan's maybe four. His head's shaved,"* – Reilly.

At this moment, Shakhruzat glanced up from the computer screen from the witness stand to peek at her little nephew. She felt so sad to see him sitting there alone, knowing he would never see his parents or relatives ever again. Jahar seized the opportunity to soak in the memory of his family from the photos that showed his family during their early years in Kyrgyzstan observed reporter Wen. He leaned in closer to the monitor. Shakhruzat stared down again, trying not to cry.

William Fick noticed the sorrow in her eyes. He asked, "When did you last see Jahar?"

"He was eight-years-old and in 2nd grade. I haven't seen him since. He was a very good boy – quiet, shy. He wouldn't hurt a fly," she said.

"What was he like?"

Little Dzhokhar (left) and young Tamerlan (right). Pictures are from *Tumblr*.

"When I told him something, he was so shy he'd turn his face away. The family was fun loving, very good family. Very hospitable," – Cullen. Aunt Shakhruzat said the Tsarnaev children had a hard time adjusting to different schools when they moved to different locations. She often sent her oldest daughter Nabisat to help the family. Nabisat would babysit the children. Shakhruzat was very sad to see the family move to the U.S. "We didn't want our little sister to be so far. She was like a daughter to me. I raised her. Then when Zubeidat came back to Russia to visit, she'd changed. We were scared. We were in pain." – Valencia.

"Were you worried when they left for U.S.?"

"Shakhruzat says they all cried a lot when Tsarnaev family moved to US. 'We didn't want them to go,'" – Boeri. The United States was so far away. They couldn't believe or understand the change in Zubeidat that happened in the U.S. – wearing black, the headscarf. It was even hard for them to comprehend Tamerlan when he returned home to Russia in 2012. He was a different person who started to talk about religion. They only prayed and fasted but did not talk extreme radical religion. Shakhruzat talked about Zubeidat, "My older sister asked, *'Do they dress like that in America? Why do you look like that?'* It was scary to look like her. We never had people dressed like that in our family. She used to be fun loving." – Cullen.

Aunt Shakhruzat sobbed when she was done testifying. *"Shakhruzat looks longingly at Tsarnaev as she steps down; he does not make eye contact. She sits in front row, sobbing,"* – Armstrong. In the gallery, a woman sat down next to Shakhruzat and consoled her as she cried. Shakhruzat sat at the back of Jahar contemplating while shedding tears of grief. Jahar could had heard her weeping.

While Nabisat Suleimanova was preparing to testify, Judy placed her arm around Jahar, leaned in and whispered to him. She could have been explaining something to him. He nodded as he stroked his chin.

29th WITNESS WAS NABISAT SULEIMANOVA who was born in 1974 in Dagestan. *"Nabisat is already struggling not to cry. She's Tsarnaev's cousin,"* tweeted Bailey. She was on the verge of tears at seeing Jahar. The court could still hear Shakhruzat crying softly in the front row observed reporter Wen. *"Defense hopes jurors would see closeness, caring and strong emotion in this Russian family,"* – Wen. Nabisat was seven years younger than Zubeidat and she babysat the Tsarnaev children when she was a teenager.

"Defense pulls up a photo of a house in Dagestan."

(http://bostondefender.org/wp-content/uploads/2015/03/3507-086.pdf)

"House of my in–laws," said Nabisat. Anzor Tsarnaev was in the photo. – Boeri. Zubeidat, an Avar married Anzor, a Chechen. It was an unusual marriage.

"What is the difference between Avars and Chechens?" asked Fick.

"A lot of traditions, but I don't know much about it."

"What about weddings?" – Cullen.

"In their tradition, the bride spends the whole day by herself. In our tradition, the bride sits at the table," tweeted Catherine Parrotta of *Fox 25*. Nabisat showed a photo of her wedding, she was at the head table with Aunt Patimat.

"Is there a difference in way children handled after divorce?" *"Defense now asks about the customs for divorce. Chechnya: children go with dad. Avar: They go with mother,"* – Boeir. *"But there's a similarity: "The older brother, older male, is in charge,"* in both cultures – Reilly. If the family had no brothers, then it would be the father's oldest brother who would be in charge.

Fick asked if the Tsarnaev family moved around a lot. Nabisat said they did. "Where was Dzhokhar born?" Dzhokhar was born in Tokmok, Kyrgyzstan. After living twelve years in northern Kyrgyzstan, the family left the country. Nabisat was asked where,

"Dagestan," she answered.

"How do you know he was born in Kyrgyzstan?"

"Aunt Zubeidat came to visit us," – Cullen. Jurors looked at Dzhokhar's birth certificate showing he had been born in Kyrgyzstan. *"Nabisat tells the jury that Dzhokhar was a premature birth,"* – Armstrong. Defense attorney pointed out that Dzhokhar's name was misspelled on the certificate. *"Nabisat said: I don't think so. Thinks there's an extra 'v' in the middle of Dzhokhar's name,"* – Parrotta.

"Have you lived with the Tsarnaev family?"

"Yes, in Kyrgyzstan," she responded. *"Nabisat was a frequent babysitter for the Tsarnaev children during 1987/8 (pre–Dzhokhar),"* – Armstrong. "I lived with Zubeidat. I stayed and watched the children, Tamerlan and Bella. I was fourteen." Nabisat's father opened a brick factory in Kyrgyzstan, so she moved there. The jurors saw a photo of a sun-dried brick block–like structure, a remnant of the house in Chechnya where she had once lived briefly with the Tsarnaevs. The house was quite rundown and abandoned. *"After being shaky and tearful early on, Nabisat is now totally without emotion. Sometimes looks to be glaring as she testifies,"* – Bailey.

"What is the in–law relationship between families of Anzor and Zubeidat?" asked Fick. Defense was exploring conflicts between Zubeidat and Anzor's family.

"Everybody wants a daughter–in–law from same ethnic background. There were some negative feelings. My mother–in–law didn't want my husband to marry me. Anzor and Zubeidat left for Dagestan because Anzor's mother was skeptical of Zubeidat because she was Avar."

"Was something happening in Chechnya when they left?" Fick asked.

"The war was unraveling there."

"Where did they move?"

"Dagestan."

"Did you see them often?"

"Not as often as I wanted to. I was married, had my own house. I had a child."

The courtroom saw another photo. Finally, a photo of the defendant, as a young boy was shown. Dzhokhar was in 1st grade and was smiling and doing his homework, reported Valencia.

View Dzhokhar doing homework:
(http://bostondefender.org/wpcontent/uploads/2015/03/3507-027.pdf)

The picture made his cousin cry. *"Nabisat's expression softens looking at the old photo of Dzhokhar Tsarnaev. Her voice starts to shake,"* – Bailey. Jahar stared at the photo of his younger self.

"What are your favorite memories of Dzhokhar?" asked Fick.

Jahar was a wunderkind and an unusual child.
(Photo from Tumblr)

Naibsat choked up, "There are so many, he was so warm and caring, you wouldn't want to let him go," – Armstrong. "He was an unusual child. A wunderkind." Suddenly, she smiled with a grin on her face as she remembered an incident Dzhokhar did as a child. "He was the first one who helped the wife of (uncle) Muhammad Haji discover her maternal feelings. She was a very strong woman who worked in security forces, and very pedantic...followed the rules all the time." – Cullen. Nabisat began getting emotional as she described Dzhokhar helping an aunt 'discover her maternal instincts.' "This stern aunt allowed Dzhokhar to urinate in her kitchen sink and it was very strange for us." – Wen.

Some jurors silently shook with laughter and chuckled after hearing her story about how Dzhokhar had charmed his aunt over so much that she would let him urinate in the sink. It was one of the funniest and embarrassing stories centering on the defendant that Cullen tweeted, *"Very weird that Jahar getting his aunt to let him pee in sink somehow shows a laudable characteristic. But, hey, who knows."* After the jurors laughed, *"Nabisat Suleimanova waved at Jahar as she left the stand crying."* – Grossi. *"Jahar has his head down, shaking it slightly* (possibly from this embarrassing childhood story) *as his aunt leaves the courtroom. He looked at her briefly before that,"* – Cullen.

When the U.S. Marshals led Jahar out for lunch recess, he glanced back at his sobbing Aunt Shakhruzat. Jahar grinned at his family as he left the courtroom. At that moment, he blew a kiss to his sobbing Shakhruzat, and to his cousins and aunts. The jury did not see this moment. It was one of the first rare moments the court had seen any form of animated emotion from the Boston Marathon bomber. The crying relatives got a kiss from Jahar and they waved goodbye to him.

Friends, A Coach, & A Teacher Remember Jahar

"We thought it was a joke, the idea that it could be him. But, that's not the person my friends and I thought he could be."
— Elizabeth Zamparelli, friend

JAHAR'S COLLEGE FRIEND, ALEXA Guevara, from Cambridge Rindge and Latin HS and UMass–Dartmouth, who sobbed on the stand returned to finish her testimony. *"Alexa took a long look at Jahar when she took the stand. She smiled at him,"* –Wen. Jahar's head tilted toward her, and this time he responded warmly. Previously, he had ignored her. He smiled in return, thinking how funny it was to see her back on the stand again. Alexa was relieved to see him smile. Miriam asked her if she knew where Jahar's parents were.

Alexa smiled and said she knew Jahar was from Chechnya because he did a Chechen dance in front of her and her friends twice. "We begged him to do this 'really cool' ethnic dance for us." Miriam finished questioning with Alexa.

Next, Attorney Nadine Pellegrini stepped up to cross-examine Alexa, *"Did you know what role the older brother took?"*

Defense: "Objection!" Judge: "Sustained," – Bailey.

Pellegrini asked, "Did he demonstrate Chechen dance for you and your friends?"

"Yes. Our friend Dias said Jahar could do a real cool Chechen dance. They begged him to do it. He did it. But, Dias said he didn't do it right. He did it again with a lot of quick movements," – Cullen.

"Did Jahar pay for pizzas?"

"Yes."

"You said he'd pay for pizza. He had extra money?"

"I wouldn't say so," – Cullen.

"But, he had all this extra money, he could buy pizza..."

Defense: "Objection!" A Sidebar," – Armstrong.

Pellegrini wanted to point out that Jahar made extra money selling pot. Pellegrini pressed further, "You also used your phone to communicate with him about using drugs?"

"No, that's not correct," said Alexa. Defense rose to object. Now, the government asked Alexa about Jahar's whereabouts over spring break and Christmas. She said he believed he went back home to Cambridge.

Pellegrini asked if she saw Jahar between April 11 to April 16 at UMass Dartmouth campus around the time of the bombings. Alexa replied that she did not see him. Pellegrini inquired about the fireworks the friends set off at Charles River. She asked if Tsarnaev retrieved those fireworks from a backpack in the trunk of his car. Alexa said "Yes." There were a series of questions the government asked that she answered "no" to until Defense raised an objection. "Did Tsarnaev warn you not to go to the Boston Marathon?"

"No," she said. – Bailey.

"Did you know about Tsarnaev's second twitter?"

"No."

"Did he talk about going to gun range?"

"No.

"Talk about owning a gun?"

"Objection!" –Boeri.

As cross–examination continued, Alexa admitted again that she smoked marijuana with Jahar. She also bought marijuana with him. Then Defense Miriam Conrad briefly asked, "Who was looking for marijuana to smoke on break?" – Cullen. Alexa's answer brought laughter, "It was a joint effort." *"Tsarnaev didn't provide the marijuana in spring break 2013, didn't smoke it either, though Guevara calls it a 'joint effort' with others,"* –Valencia. Jahar turned and looked at Alexa. He smiled and laughed at her joint effort pun.

The 30th WITNESS WAS ROSA BOOTH, a college art student, age twenty-one. She was Jahar's high school friend. Miriam Conrad asked this young witness on the stand how they knew each other. Rosa said, "We would sit together most days and talk and play this sketch game." Rosa Booth was another female friend of Jahar's who carried fond memories of hanging out with him. She said, "We would smoke together, too. We hung out at Emma's house or at Charles River and parties. At Rindge, while I had dance practice, I'd see him wrestling." *"There was fluidity in his friend groups. He did not stick to 1 group,"* –Wen.

"Good friends?" asked Miriam.

"He seemed like a sweet boy," – Valencia. "Yeah. He had sweetness about him. Maybe very shy. I was very shy," – Wen. Rosa was asked if she considered Tsarnaev a leader within their group. *"Rosa furrows her brow, shakes her head. 'No,' she says,"* – Reilly. Jahar would tag along with friends and go along with others.

Miriam asked her, "He was funny and goofy?"

"Yea goofy...just goofy," said Rosa, tweeted Valencia. Rosa moreover testified that she did not remember when he ever expressed political or religious views to her. The last time she saw Jahar was at a barbecue party in August 2012. The jury saw a photo of a group of Cambridge kids from the party. In the photo a shaggy poodle dog named Dempsey was staring at Jahar. Rosa was the one sitting next to Jahar in the purple dress. (This is a page spread from Rolling Stone's "JAHAR'S WORLD," July 2013.)

Jahar fed the dog treats. Photo is from *Tumblr* and *Rolling Stone*.

Miriam perked up when she saw the picture. "What was Jahar's relationship with Dempsey the dog?" It was Emma's dog.

"Dempsey. He really liked Jahar," said Rosa. Some jurors smiled and giggled. Rosa talked about how well he interacted and played with the dog at the party. She told the jury Jahar had a special relationship with Dempsey. He loved the dog. Everyone watched him played with the dog. Jahar also loved cats; however, he was allergic to cats.

Miriam chuckled delightedly when she heard these amusing stories about Jahar. "Did Jahar feed the dog treats?" She turned to look at the jurors to see if there was a reaction, but they sat there stone-faced. They no longer saw the humour in Rosa's account.

Rosa answered, "Yes." Rosa had posted this photo of her sitting next to Jahar at the barbecue on her Facebook, April 20, 2013, the day after his arrest. Miriam asked Rosa, "What do you remember about that day?"

Rosa answered, "Good food," – Boeri. Rosa reflected upon the barbecue party photo of Jahar again. She was surprised how muscular Jahar's arms were. "I recall Jahar bulkier in his arms like he'd been working out," she said, – Wen. Miriam asked her, "How were you feeling when you posted this picture?" Rosa felt her friendship had been betrayed. Miriam was done. Prosecutor Aloke Chakravarty started his cross-examination of Rosa.

"You didn't know Jahar very well?"

"I thought I knew him fairly well. I believed that I did," she said. Alexa who sat in the front row seat in the gallery started to cry again. "I knew him mainly from math class."

"One class together?"

"Yes."

"So, that's the scope of your relationship. You didn't have contact with him after barbecue in 2012?" – Cullen.

"I think on Facebook we did." Although the friends knew each other, Rosa was a very shy person. Chakravarty wanted to know if there was more to this friendship. He asked, "In school, you sat next to him?" Rosa replied "yes" and then she admitted, "I had a crush on him then." She next talked about the prom. Jahar had asked Rosa to go to the prom with him, but she didn't go with him in the end. Rosa also said she was friends with Stephen Silva (or both the Silva twins) in high school, but later learned they were drug dealers in 2013 after the Boston attack. - Wen. Prosecutors were done.

Miriam stood to re-question Rosa, "Why didn't you go with Jahar to the prom even if you had a crush on him?"

"I was a little shy," she replied.

Rosa was the last witness for the day. Judy patted Jahar on the shoulder as he stood. The Judge exited, and the jury left. Laurel Sweet tweeted, *"So to sum up what we learned: Jahar had better luck with a giant poodle than landing a date to the prom with a girl who liked him."*

Day 5 – May 5, 2015

Writer's Note: The witnesses are out of order, but the intent of this section is to keep together all the friends and teachers who knew Jahar. The defense called its 32nd witness for Dzhokhar Tsarnaev.)

32nd WITNESS WAS ELIZABETH ZAMPARELLI. Twenty-two-years-old Elizabeth was a student at UMass Boston. She was called, "Bett Zamparelli, aka Elizabeth." *"She went to high school at Cambridge Rindge & Latin. She looks briefly at Tsarnaev from the stand,"* – Armstrong. She was Jahar's friend and was in his graduating class of 2011. "How did you and Jahar meet?" Miriam asked.

"We met in driver's ed," she replied. Elizabeth said she and Jahar had a few classes together like Spanish II. They were also in "Best Buddies," where high school kids would interact with special needs kids. They attended their holiday parties and made gingerbread houses together with the kids. Elizabeth told the jurors that Jahar was a lifeguard at the Harvard pool. – Cullen. Their relationship was relatively close, but she never went to his house. *"Zamparelli said she didn't have easy time in high school & talked with Jahar. He made her feel better. 'He'd make me laugh…He made me feel good,' she said"* – Wen. Elizabeth said Jahar was a little sarcastic, but not mean sarcastic.

"Did you ever see him argue or fight with anyone?" asked Miriam.

"No.

"How did he treat girls?"

"Really nicely. He didn't demoralize them or demean them," – Valencia.

Next, the government Aloke Chakravarty stood to cross-examine Elizabeth, "What was Dzhokhar Tsarnaev like?

Elizabeth, took a long thoughtful pause, and smiled. "He was very caring," she replied. She also said that she and Jahar never engaged in any political or religion talks according to reporter Cullen. Asked if he ever talked of future plans, she answered that he thought of becoming an engineer. Elizabeth said she had never met Jahar's parents, but only knew of his sisters and had met Tamerlan once.

She did not know Tamerlan very well. She knew him through a friend and met him during her junior year of high school. She remembered the meeting that took place outside the apartment of Brendan Mess. She revealed, "I was intimated by Tamerlan because I was a lot younger than they were…it wasn't my crew of people."

Brendan Mess was Tamerlan's best friend who was killed in a triple homicide in Waltham in 2011. Aloke Chakravarty asked her if she knew what happened to Brendan. "He was murdered," she said. He asked if she knew if Tamerlan went to his funeral. Defense objected.

Miriam asked Elizabeth what she thought of Jahar after the bombings. Government objected. Finally, Miriam held up a photo of the bombers, "Do you recognize the picture?" referring to Dzhokhar's picture post on the news. Elizabeth said, "We thought it was a joke, the idea that it could be him. But, that's not the person my friends and I thought he could be," –Valencia.

Aloke Chakravarty wanted to ask if she knew about Jahar and the Silva twins buying and selling weed, but he was stopped by an objection from defense. Elizabeth said she smoked with them once or twice. She testified that Jahar was socially well-adjusted and said he was a proud Muslim. Chakravarty asked if she had less contact with Jahar once he went off to college. She said, "Yes."

36th WITNESS WAS HENRY ALVAREZ. Henry was a bank teller and was on the Cambridge Rindge and Latin HS wrestling team with Jahar. He graduated in 2012 (a year after Tsarnaev). Henry attended UMass Boston. "When did you meet Jahar?" asked Attorney Timothy Watkins.

"I met Jahar through the Cambridge Rindge and Latin HS wrestling team in my freshman year and he was a sophomore. We were both new to the team."

"How was wrestling?"

"When I first started wrestling, I hated it. It sucked," – Armstrong. He found the training hard and tiring. There was laughter in court when he said it sucked. "But, he liked it when he won though." Henry said they both bonded while talking over how much wrestling practice sucked. "Jahar would always try to encourage me when I got tired at daily practices, such as running stairs."

Henry described how intense wrestling practice was. Practice was held all week long with Sundays being optional. He also explained why he liked wrestling, "In football team there's 45 players; in a wrestling team it is small, so there's opportunity to bond with teammates." He also discussed how the wrestling coach emphasized having a good diet.

The court saw a photo featuring Henry in his freshman year and Jahar in his sophomore year. "Describe Jahar?" asked Timothy Watkins.

"He was a kind person. He had a very relaxed personality. I'd say mellow." – Valencia. "He never caused harm to anybody. Or disrespect anybody. Just a funny person," said Henry. – Wen. "He liked to dance before a tournament to relax his anxious teammates. He would dance to song *"Like a G6,"* to make his teammates laugh and lighten the mood before meets."

Henry also described the camaraderie between them. They would walk home together. They ate pizza together, even though he doesn't like pepperoni.

Watkins asked, "How did Jahar become a captain?"

"His coach believed he could lead by example."

"You ever talk about religion with him?"

"No, though I did learn he was Muslim," responded Henry.

Watkins asked if he knew Jahar's brother, Tamerlan. Henry replied that he knew Tamerlan was a boxer. "What was his demeanor in talking about Tamerlan?"

"I could sense some pride in talking about his brother, his boxing skills," – Bailey.

Now the jury viewed a photo of Jahar's arms around Henry and Coach Payack before Henry's wrestling match on Senior Night.

View photo of Jahar, Henry and Coach Payack at:
(http://bostondefender.org/wp-content/uploads/2015/03/3281.pdf)

Jahar leaned forward to view the old photo of him as a high school sophomore. He put a hand on his chin. Henry explained that Jahar would come back to high school 8 to 9 times to help with team practices even though he was now a college freshman. "What is Senior Night for wrestling team?" asked Timothy Watkins.

"It's the last match for seniors. You get a rose, and then someone takes a picture." The jury saw a photo of Jahar in the stands watching Henry wrestle. Next, the jury saw another photo of Henry on his Senior Night in 2012. Jahar was there as Henry's guest. It was a few months before the attacks in Boston. When Henry was asked about Jahar and the marathon bombing, "You learned Jahar was the bomber? That consistent with Jahar?"

"Never. I honestly never could imagine he'd do something like this," – Cullen. Henry did not once glance at Jahar as he left the witness box.

37th WITNESS WAS CAMBRIDGE RINDGE & LATIN WRESTLING COACH, ROY HOWARD.

Jahar gave Coach Roy Howard a slight nod when he got on the witness stand. Howard had coached Jahar in wrestling. "What was his weight class?" asked Watkins.

"He started at 112 and wrestled at the 135 weight when he was at his most advanced level. He wrestled for three years, from sophomore to his senior year." – Valencia.

"Describe Jahar?"

"He was a quiet and hard worker." The jury saw a yearbook, *"a montage of wrestlers, featuring Tsarnaev in his senior year,"* – Bailey.

View photo of HS yearbook, Jahar wrestling.
(http://bostondefender.org/wp-content/uploads/2015/03/3280.pdf)

The jury seemed very interested in the pictures. Jahar looked at his old HS wrestling coach. *"He became co-captain his junior year. He showed leadership, hard work and dedication to his peers."* – Cullen. Coach Howard talked about nutrition and conditioning and how he contacted parents and gave meetings at the beginning of the year, informing parents about it so they understood how they could help nurture their athletic child.

"What about Senior Night?" Watkins asked. Senior Night was the last match. Jahar was captain and it was his day. "On Senior Night, all seniors get flowers to honor end of season," – Wen.

"In three years," Howard said, "I've never met Jahar's parents or saw them support him at a single match. His parents did not come to his Senior Night. Jahar was co-captain of wrestling team his senior year, as well." Jahar's parents never came to any of the coach's nutritional meetings either. Sadly, they never attended or supported Jahar at his high school graduation or even took him to his first day of college. This was probably at a time when his parents divorced.

Coach Howard told the jury how Jahar came back after graduation to help direct practices. He came back in 2013 before he bombed the marathon. Coach Howard was also in disbelief to learn that Jahar was the responsible assailant. "Was his role in the bombing consistent with the same boy you coached?"

"No sir," – Cullen.

HOLDING ONTO DEAR MEMORIES

Before lunch break, Dzhokhar was seen flipping through old photos of himself and studying them at the defense table. He could not break his focus away until the guards took him away. Right after lunch, he went back and lingered near the photos to reflect upon his memories. He could not part his attention away from the old photos because he knew he would never see them again.

40th WITNESS WAS JENNIFER CALLISON. Callison worked at Cambridge Rindge and Latin as a transitional coordinator and student advisor to the "Best Buddies" program in 2010. "Best Buddies" club helped create friendships between students and special needs children including those with disabilities.

Jennifer Callison showed the jury photos from a "Best Buddies" end-of-the-year banquet party at Ryle's jazz club in Cambridge. *"Callison shows jury a photo from a Best Buddies end-of-the-year party; Tsarnaev is there. She says he attended many events,"* – Armstrong. *"We see photos of a Best Buddies event at a restaurant. Dzhokhar pictured at the table,"* – Whitehouse. Jahar was wearing a red and white hat. Callison said Jahar went to the "Best Buddies" prom where kids with disabilities could dance, have fun and eat pizza. – Cullen.

Callison remembered Jahar, "He was kind, respectful, like all our volunteers. He was nice to every student he encountered. He was a good member of the club." – Wen.

"How was he to disabled kids?"

"He was very nice to them."

"Can you imagine that person committing the bombing?"

"I don't believe the student in my club is the person I remember from years ago. I can't imagine him being responsible for bombing." – Cullen. She seemed upset as she answered this, gave Jahar a quick glance as she left the stand and walked away.

41st WITNESS WAS ERIC TRAUB, a former Cambridge Rindge and Latin HS teacher. He is now employed as software engineer. *"Traub once taught at Cambridge Rindge & Latin School; Tsarnaev was his math student in 2007 & 2010,"* – Armstrong. He taught Jahar Algebra I and Advanced Math. Traub said, "He was a kind student...I really liked having him in a classroom...he brought a fun energy," – Armstrong. Jurors saw another picture of Jahar, with one the Silva twins and Eric Traub.

See photo of Eric making a silly face and Jahar doing his homework at:
(http://bostondefender.org/wp-content/uploads/2015/03/3246.pdf)

In the photo, Traub was making a silly face and he was "photobombing" them. Jahar was smiling and doing his homework. *"Traub says he had a good relationship with Tsarnaev. Knew he spoke Russian and was Muslim, because he'd occasionally prayed in a nearby classroom,"* – Boeri.

When Traub was asked if he ever met Tsarnaev's parents, he replied, "They never came to one-on-one teacher meetings." Dzhokhar asked Traub to write a letter of recommendation for college.

View letter at:
(http://bostondefender.org/wp-content/uploads/2015/03/3247.pdf)

The December 2012 letter said, *"I write with enthusiasm...Dzhokhar is a smart, energetic and friendly student...Dzhokhar is a strong student with a positive attitude...good nature and positive spirit... always polite and respectful."*

Traub testified he was sincere about everything he wrote in the letter about Dzhokhar and he still meant it today. Yet, he was shocked when he saw his picture on TV and his name broadcast on the news as the bomber. *"As Traub steps down, he and Tsarnaev share a quick nod,"* – Armstrong.

A Deeply Disturbed, Dysfunctional Family

"I don't think there is anybody that has seen what has unfolded in the last year and a day who doesn't understand that if the government's indictment is true – this is about a family – and the search for an understanding of what happened is in large measure a story of this family and the relationships between people in it." [189]
– David Bruck's statement about this case.

Day 6 – May 6, 2015 – TROUBLES IN THE TSARNAEV FAMILY

31st WITNESS WAS AMANDA RANSOM

Amanda was college roommates with Katherine Russell – Tamerlan's widow.

Amanda witnessed Tamerlan being aggressive and knocked down a man on the street. She was shocked. Tamerlan punched a man in the chest and he fell to the ground after he said something to Katherine and Tamerlan that he didn't like.

Amanda also felt Katherine was "being emotionally abused" by Tamerlan.

Katherine became quieter and alienated from friends. She wore the hijab and fully covered her body.

In 2009, Amanda finally moved out of the second-floor apartment complex after hearing Katherine and Tamerlan fighting and throwing things around on the first-floor. She could hear Katherine asking for help. When Amanda went to Katherine's aid, she told her it was none of her business. Tamerlan shouted back and threatened Amanda and she was very scared of him. She ran back to her room. She and her roommate packed up their bags and left the apartment.

33rd WITNESS WAS MIRRE KUZNETSOV

Mirre owned a Russian video store until 2012.

She witnessed Tamerlan saying something "very powerful" to Dzhokhar. He was giving him an order to go back to the car. Dzhokhar followed his brother's order to drive the car.

Mirre was very "scared" after seeing Tamerlan's physical appearance change. She said she feared him because his religious looks reminded her of a terrorist and of the "war in Russia between Chechens and Russia." Tamerlan reminded her of all that.

34th WITNESS WAS DR. ALEXANDER NISS

Dr. Niss was the psychiatrist who once treated Anzor.[190]

He met Anzor Tsarnaev in Boston in 2003. Anzor was under his care until June 2005. Anzor was very sick and suffered from post-traumatic stress disorder. Anzor developed PTSD from the Russian-Chechen war. He was tortured and experienced a lot of flashbacks, panic attacks, hallucinations and nightmares. He was disabled, and he couldn't work. "I am scared," Anzor told his doctor in October 9, 2010. He was having neurological problems. He suddenly had weak vision, insomnia, vertigo and migraines originating from a skull fracture. In February 17, 2011, he wrote, *"If I am not getting better my wife would divorce me."* They separated and divorced in April 3, 2012, a year before the bombings.

Day 7 – May 7, 2015

38th WITNESS WAS ELMIRZA KHOZHUGOV

Elmirza was married to Ailina, Dzhokhar's sister in July 2006.

They were married for two years. At the witness stand he testified he was Tamerlan's friend. He spent a lot of time with the Tsarnaev family in Cambridge. He said Dzhokhar spent a lot of his time reading, writing and studying. He was not interested in computer. His mother would post his good grades on the fridge with a magnet. Dzhokhar was a quiet person and very responsible. Elmirza observed the relationship between Dzhokhar's parents. His views, *"It was not an exemplary one, I would say...had a lot of conflicts and arguments."* Zubeidat had more of an influence on Tamerlan. Tamerlan was very fond of his mother and she encouraged him to learn more about Islam. Misha, a friend of Tamerlan's taught him Islam, politics and religion and offered his own views. One evening, Anzor came home and Tamerlan and Misha were in a deep discussion about radical Islam. Zubeidat stopped him because she did not want their conversation interrupted. She told Anzor, "Misha is teaching your son good things."[191] The talks were about religion and it was intermixed with politics and conspiracy theories. Misha converted Tamerlan. Tamerlan quit boxing because it conflicted with Islam. Islam said he shouldn't hit people.

Tamerlan also adored Dzhokhar very much. He loved to spend time talking with his younger brother and Dzhokhar would listen to Tamerlan. He went along whenever Tamerlan said let's do this or that. Tamerlan was the leader.

Defense's Expert Witnesses

35th WITNESS WAS MICHAEL REYNOLDS

Reynolds was a Princeton University professor who specialized in Russian studies. Defense provided a historical study of the Chechens, so jurors could understand the Tsarnaev brothers' background, although neither of the brothers were born and raised in Chechnya. However, they were both identified as Chechens.[192] Here is what he spoke about:

"The Chechens are mountain people. They have lived in the Caucasus for thousands of years without any centralized rule. They are isolated but interdependent."

"It is the Chechen custom... The eldest brother is expected to look after the material wellbeing of the family. It is a position of honor and a position of great responsibility. It's expected that the younger brothers will listen to their older brothers."

"It's very common for a young Chechen to go online to learn about his country, or Chechen roots, and to see his country intertwined with the cause of international jihad. Tsarnaev brothers saw "motivational videos" from the Caucasus region which attracts and inspire young men to be part of the jihad."

39th WITNESS WAS DR. JAY GIEDD

Dr. Giedd was a medical doctor at the University of San Diego who was an expert on child development and teen brains. Dzhokhar was at age nineteen when he bombed the marathon and was vulnerable to the influence of his older brother, seven years his senior.[193]

"Adolescence starts with puberty and ends in society." The age when the brain is having the most dramatic changes and matures is between the ages 25 to 30, not 16 or 18. The brain still develops through a person's late 20's.

Teen brains have an explosion in their passions. They are at their physical peek, but they are at most, reckless with hormones surge…"

Defense Judy Clarke asked Dr. Giedd, "Where is the balance at age 19 or 20?"

Dr. Giedd answered, "From ages 12 to 25, on the scale the 19–year–old brain is about halfway to full maturity. Therefore, at age 19 the brain is still a work in progress, but not damaged."

Government's Nadine Pellegrini said, "At the end of day, age might just be a number when it comes to maturity."

Dr. Giedd said, "yes."

Pellegrini asked, "Can a 19–year–old fully plan and premeditate an action and understand its consequences?"

Dr. Giedd replied back, "yes."

ADX, "A Clean Version Of Hell"

43rd WITNESS WAS MARK BEZY

At the time of the trial, Bezy owned a correctional consulting company. He once worked in the federal prison system. Bezy described the prison conditions at ADX Supermax to the jurors.

Dzhokhar is currently imprisoned at the highest security-prison. The ADX Supermax facility in Florence, Colorado houses the nation's worst and most violent offenders and terrorists. More than 400 prisoners are locked and secured inside 7 x 12 cells. They live, contained within by steel doors and gray, concrete walls with faint natural sunlight coming from a slit window. A light in the facility is on all the time. No talking with guards. No human contact. ADX Florence was called "A clean version of hell." A warden who once worked there confirmed, "It's squeaky clean and quiet. Everyone there is locked down. It's a very abnormal environment." Inmates are let outdoor for recreation inside a caged yard surrounded by high concrete walls. Above them is a chained-metal roof that allows prisoners to see nothing but the sky. Inmates are isolated 23 hours in their cells and receive their meals through a small flap in the door.[194]

Tsarnaev has been housed under SAMs (Special Administrative Measures) since the summer of 2013. He is not allowed to have contact with the media or with other inmates. Tsarnaev lives in a single cell in ADX H Unit under special security. He is allowed a 15-minute phone call to his immediate family. His calls are recorded and monitored by FBI and prison officials. He is allowed two phone calls a month. He can receive books and magazines to read. He is not allowed to have physical contact with visitors. He can see one visitor at a time behind a security glass partition. The only visitor who can see him is his immediate family. No friends are allowed. Tsarnaev will stay in prison at the Supermax for the rest of his natural life.

JAHAR SAID "I'M SORRY" FOR OBSCENE MIDDLE FINGER

When Bezy was finished with his testimony, Jahar appeared somber after hearing how he would be tortured, chained and locked up at ADX Supermax prison. It was another dismal, lonely prison facility, similar to the one in Devens. Miriam turned to Jahar and attempted to cheer him up with a smile.

Next on the stand was 42nd WITNESS KEVIN ROCHE, a deputy U.S. Marshal. Shortly after Tsarnaev's arrest, on April 21, 2013, Roche first met Tsarnaev at Beth Israel Hospital where he was being treated for his injuries and gunshot wounds. He personally escorted Tsarnaev to doctor visits. Roche described about one of those visits, *"The first time, he was still pretty lethargic...he may have still been medicated,"* – Reilly. Defense asked if he observed injures to his face. He said yes, *"He had a wound that appeared to be sutured. And his head was deformed. His left side seemed swollen,"* – Cullen. Roche said he was aware Mr. Tsarnaev had been shot and he followed directed instructions.

Roche also interacted with Tsarnaev during his July 2013 arraignment. Defense asked, "Have you seen middle finger video?" Roche replied, "Yes." But *"he didn't actually see it at first. Someone told him, so he went to talk to Mr. Tsarnaev,"* – Bailey. In the holding cell where nineteen–year–old Tsarnaev was locked up, Roche went *"to speak to Tsarnaev with a supervisor after that gesture. He listened to us and 'didn't have much to offer.' He apologized,"* – Armstrong. Defense wanted to know what Roche said to Tsarnaev. Roche told Tsarnaev what they had observed, and the middle finger gesture was completely unacceptable. They told him such behavior would not be tolerated here.

Defense asked, "What was Tsarnaev's demeanor?"

Roche answered, "Tsarnaev acknowledged why we were there. We asked if he was going to be a problem all day."

Tsarnaev said, "No, I'm done. I'm sorry," – Armstrong.

A Surprise Up Lawyers' Sleeve

"What unrepentant, unchanged, untouched jihadi is going to meet with a Catholic nun, connect with her, talk with her and have her enjoy the conversation with him?"
– Defense Judy Clarke

Day 9 – May 11, 2015

TSARNAEV'S DEFENSE TEAM WAS behind closed doors today with Judge O'Toole. They had two witnesses left and would rest their case today. Their 44th and last witness was a Roman Catholic Nun, SISTER HELEN PREJEAN. The team hoped the famous anti–death penalty advocate would be their last witness; but the prosecutors hoped to block her testimony. Sister Prejean rose to fame with her book *Dead Man Walking* (1993) and it was later turned into a 1995 Oscar winning film starring Susan Sarandon and Sean Penn. Her autobiographical experience was portrayed by Sarandon. The Judge had not agreed to her testifying. Both trial teams were fighting. If the prosecutors blocked Sister Prejean's testimony, the defense would be forced to rest their case. Mr. Tsarnaev would not be taking the stand to testify to the jurors regarding how his brother Tamerlan had led and directed him to set off the bombs. It was his lawyer's call that he not testify. Since the trial began in March, the jury had heard testimony from more than 150 witnesses.

Jahar entered the room. Still, his eyes avoided eye contact with people in the back of the room. As he slowly walked in, he placed his right hand on his left rib. He was sullen-faced and appeared tired. He settled down in his seat. Jahar wore a dark blazer and a dark gray collared shirt. His hair and chin beard had grown quite long, curly and unruly.

View court photo:
(http://courtartist.com/wpcontent/uploads/Tsarnaev150511_enters-copy.jpg).

All the lawyers emerged from the Judge's chambers. Judy and Miriam were both smiling and appeared triumphant. However, the prosecutors were not smiling. Jahar sat down with them and began chatting, wondering what the consensus was. His lawyers whispered to him and Jahar chuckled. His chuckle was a little too loud that he shyly put his head down quickly. They seemed to have a surprise up their sleeves. Their next witness, Sister Helen Prejean would testify after all, but why? Jahar smiled and seemed relaxed as his legal team whispered to him. He poured himself a glass of water. His team appeared to be relaxed and very happy. Miriam stood at the podium, flipping through a thick file and holding a cup of water. Judge O'Toole and the jury entered the courtroom.

Sister Helen Prejean, a woman wearing a necklace with a cross smiled when she came into court, reported Wen. As she entered some jurors may have recognized her and knew of her reputation. Sister Prejean stood at the witness stand and raised her hand as she took her oath. Jahar glanced at Sister Prejean. Miriam started asking her a few questions. One was asked, "Are you a Catholic nun?"

View Sister Helen Prejean:
(https://peopledotcom.files.wordpress.com/2016/08/helen-prejean-1024.jpg)

"Yes, I am," she said. *"Prejean, based in New Orleans, is a member of the Sisters of St. Joseph. Became a nun in 1957,"* – Boeri. Sister Prejean used to teach middle and high–school English. She also taught adults in a Catholic church and then later established a prison ministry. Her ministry is focused on death row inmates as well as with keeping in touch with victims' families. Her ministry also started a group called "Survive" for murder victims' families.

Sister Prejean told the jury how she met Jahar. Miriam asked, "Have you met Dzhokhar Tsarnaev?"

"I have," replied Sister Prejean. She had been asked by defense to meet him in early March. – Bailey. Recently, she had met him five times (from guilt and penalty phases) and other inmates like him who had committed terrible crimes. This was the surprise...no one in the room except for the Defense team and perhaps the government knew that this nun was counseling Dzhokhar privately. How did Sister Prejean meet with Mr. Tsarnaev under SAMs? Dzhokhar had met with the nun and had spoken with her and may have even confessed his remorse privately to her.

Sister Prejean smiled at Jahar and pointed him out in court. "First visit was in early March, after testimony began."

Miriam asked, "Why?"

Sister Prejean answered, "Not to convert them but be by their side and know that they have a dignity," – Bailey.

Jahar peeked up at Sister Prejean. Miriam asked, "And before you met with Jahar, did you know that he was Muslim?"

"I knew Tsarnaev was Muslim before I met with him; I looked into the Qur'an and Islam, to see what we had in common." – Armstrong. Sister Prejean had prepared herself before her initial visit. She read and studied the Qur'an and Islam, so she could understand the deep spiritual core beliefs in both Islam and Catholicism.

Miriam asked Sister Prejean when she first met Dzhokhar, how did he react to seeing a nun. Sister Prejean replied, *"Very open and receptive. It was good,"* – Cullen, adding that she wasn't sure if he had ever met a nun before. She said she had a pleasant talk with him. Sister Prejean also recalled her first meeting with Dzhokhar Tsarnaev and her own reaction. Defense asked, "What do you remember about the first meeting?"

"I walked in the room and I looked at his face and I remember, *'Oh, my God, he's so young,'*" – Bailey. Sister Prejean said that Dzhokhar was very young, that young people are open and responsive. "I sensed he was very respectful…easy to establish a rapport," – Bailey.

"What types of topics did you discuss?"

"I told him I was dedicating myself to God. I talked about Louisiana and being a nun," – Perrotta. She talked with Dzhokhar about being a Catholic and about serving God. She shared with him that she was familiar with Islam and that Islam is similar to Catholicism. She said to him, "As a Catholic, like a Muslim, our goal is to do the will of God," – Armstrong. Sister Prejean turned to Jahar and smiled at him. Jahar made eye contact with her.

Miriam asked if they talked about the differences and similarities between Catholicism and Islam. Prejean said, "Yeah. They kind of naturally emerged. Like I talked about how in the Catholic Church we have become more and more opposed to the death penalty--" The government raised an objection, stopping Prejean from continuing to share her opinion on the death penalty.

During their meetings, Sister Prejean said they talked about scripture. They both talked about Islam and Catholicism, but Dzhokhar did not agree with everything she said. Those disagreements *"revolved around the God of love."* Miriam asked if they were respectful to each other. Sister Prejean said "yes" but then she said "no." She felt he was respectful and wanted to ask him about his faith because she did not know a lot about it, reported Wen.

Jahar's Tweet from Tumblr & Twitter account.

"At some point did he express to you his feelings about what happened to the victims in this case?" asked Miriam. - Wen. The attorney asked if they had ever discussed his crimes. Sister Prejean said in low voice, "yes." After they had established trust with each other, she talked with him about the victims of the bombings, reported Wen. "What did he say to you about the victims?"

"Conrad wants to know what Tsarnaev said about the victims."

Sister Prejean answered, "He said it emphatically. He said no one deserves to suffer like they did," - Reilly.

Miriam asked, "And when he said that, how did you perceive his sincerity?"

"As absolutely sincere," said Sister Prejean. - Cullen.

In the gallery, the victims shook their head. They couldn't believe Jahar was remorseful.

Miriam asked, "What did you observe about him?"

"That his response was so spontaneous, and it's not like he was hedging or it's not like he was trying to -- he just simply said, *'Nobody deserves to suffer like that.'* And I had every reason to believe that it was sincere," said the nun. Sister Prejean described his facial expression when he said, *'Nobody deserves to suffer like they did,'* reported Wen. She said, "Well, he -- his face registered it, and he kind of lowered his eyes. And it was the -- it was his voice when he -- because I had said to him, "Look at the--""

Defense received another objection from the government.

Miriam tried again to ask, "What, if any, observations did you make about his voice when he said that?"

"It was -- it had pain in it, actually, when he said what he did about nobody deserves that, and -- And I just had every reason to think that he was taking it in and that he was genuinely sorry for what he did." - Cullen.[195] When Sister Prejean finally revealed Jahar's feeling of "remorse" and "shame," he "bowed his head toward the table."[196]

Miriam asked, "Do you believe Tsarnaev is untouched--"

Government: Objection. *Judge:* "Sustained. Nothing further. Weinreb to cross," – Armstrong.

Miriam tried another way to ask it, "Do you feel that Jahar is unrepentant?"– Bailey.

"Objection, Your honor." The government kept objecting. They did not want jurors to hear the nun's answer. The prosecution wanted jurors to keep believing that Mr. Tsarnaev was this non–human entity, this unrepentant, untouched monster. There was no way they wanted Sister Prejean to speak on Jahar's behalf certifying that he was indeed sorry for his victims and giving an inkling that he still retained some of his humanity. So, they censored and blocked her words.

Miriam asked, "When you told us that you believed that Jahar was sincerely remorseful for what he had done and the suffering he had caused, --"

"Your Honor, she can't vouch for her own credibility. I would object," stated government's William Weinreb. Miriam then declared she was done.

Finally, at the end of Sister Prejean's testimony, Judy did a redirect, reported Wen. *"Would you tell this jury that he was sincerely remorseful if you didn't truly believe it?"* – Cullen.

Weinreb objected, "She can't vouch for her own credibility."

Judge O'Toole said, "Overruled. She may answer it."

Judy reworded her question differently again, "Would you tell the jury that he was sincerely remorseful if you did not believe that?"

"No, I would not," said Sister Prejean.

Judy and the Defense team finally concluded, "We rest."

Read a full transcript of Sister Helen Prejean's testimony. See Reference number 197.[197]

Sister Helen Prejean's testimony was the closest answer the victims and survivors would ever hear from Mr. Tsarnaev himself. It revealed his first feelings about the victims. It was the only confirmation of his remorse. He had said, *"Nobody deserves to suffer like they did,"* but what did he mean by that? It was his statement, yet did it truly express his remorse for the suffering he had inflicted on them? It did not address regret for what he had done. Was it enough to save him from the death penalty? Did the jury buy Tsarnaev's remorse after hearing it through a second person, a nun? Liz Norden did not believe in Sister Prejean's testimony. She said if he was genuinely sorry then he should have taken the stand to express his true and deep remorse to his victims. Another survivor Karen Brassard said it was a little too late for him to express he was sorry. Throughout the long, drawn out and anticipated trial, the jurors and surviving victims searched for any clue of emotion or remorse from Mr. Tsarnaev, but it just wasn't there for them to find.

Closing Arguments

"His actions destroyed so many families. And he and he alone, is responsible for his actions in causing so much sadness, death and fear." – Prosecutor Steve Mellin

Day 10 – May 13, 2015

THE COURTROOM FILLED UP with people quickly – survivors, law enforcement, media, and the public. Many of the victims' families: slain MIT police officer Sean Collier's family, Bill and Denise Richard arrived for the closing statements. There were other survivors and families in attendance including Eric Whalley, Liz Norden, Karen Brassard, and Carlos Arredondo, the man in the cowboy hat who helped save survivor Jeff Bauman. U.S. Attorney Ortiz and anti-terror unit Chief Jim Farmer sat in the first row. FBI Boston Special Agent in Charge Vincent Lisi and Watertown police Chief Ed Deveau also sat in the front row seat. Everyone was nervous. In the courtroom, everyone waited silently for the closing arguments to begin.

Shy Jahar Tsarnaev, with clasped knuckles strode into the courtroom once again. The twenty-one-year-old sat between Judy and Miriam. Jahar dressed well on his last day; he chose to wear a black suit and gray shirt open at the collar in the hope of impressing the jurors. He had a shy smile. At the counsel table, Jahar read Judy's closing statement. His left leg bounced under the table. After he read the closing, he helped himself to water, then, refilled Judy's glass. Jahar's mood seemed much lighter since the jury began deliberations. He shared a rare laugh with his lawyers and said "Hello" to David Bruck. Miriam and Judy leaned in to talk to him, he smiled and engaged in conversation. David looked beat; he rested his head on his two fists. Judge O'Toole and the jury entered the courtroom. Jahar stood up for them, with head bowed down and hands wringing in nervous anticipation.

A couple jurors took a quick glance at Jahar. Judge O'Toole instructed the jury that, "The choice is yours and yours alone to make between death and life without the possibility of parole." He reviewed the 18 counts. "Give careful and thorough consideration to all evidence, to weigh in "aggravating" and "mitigating" factors." He told them, if they could not unanimously agree to death, then Tsarnaev would automatically receive life. There would be no retrial. The jurors appeared to be attentive to the Judge's instructions.

The Judge also directed jurors to not take into account the defendant's behavior or demeanor as observed during the trial. He reminded them that the defendant had the constitutional right not to testify. "Do not draw any inference from his decision to exercise that right," said the Judge. Jahar looked down at the defense table as the Judge spoke. He told the jurors to weigh the 17 counts against him in isolation. After an hour of explaining the verdict sheet, prosecutor Steve Mellin stood to deliver the government's closing. THE FOLLOWING EXCERPTS WERE EXTRACTED AND SUMMARIZED FROM THE DOCUMENTS REFERENCED #198.

PROSECUTION'S ARGUMENT & EXCERPT SUMMARY

1. **He did not value lives.** Prosecutors argued the defendant placed no value on the lives of others and didn't care what impact his actions and his killings would have on others.

PROSECUTOR STEVE MELLIN: *(Excerpt found on Page 67, line 11 through Page 59, end line 1.)* The defendant, Dzhokhar, did not value lives. He killed people and maimed them forever. The just punishment for his crimes was that he should be given the death sentence because this "loss is overwhelming in scope and impact." He caused a lot of pain and suffering, and yet he did not even have a care in the world or even shed tears for what he did. After the bombings, Dzhokhar went and bought a half gallon of milk. He remained "remorse-free."

2. **He killed them using a weapon of mass destruction.** Prosecutors argued the defendant used bombs to create grave risks of deaths to additional people and to the victims who died. He also planned to make the bombs.

PROSECUTOR STEVE MELLIN: *(Excerpt found on Page 69, line 15 through Page 70, end line 9.)* The defendant used a weapon of mass destruction to kill people. Terrorists used this tool. It is a tool to kill "indiscriminately" and to "destroy." *"It's clear the defendant killed more than one person by using a weapon of mass destruction in this case."*

3. **He engaged in substantial planning and premeditation.** Prosecutors argued the defendant took time to deliberate, plan and carry out the attacks.

PROSECUTOR STEVE MELLIN: *(Excerpt found on Page 70, line 10 though Page 71, end line 18.)* The defendant took time to carry out the attacks. He downloaded and read the *Inspire* article, "Make a bomb in the kitchen of your mom." It was a recipe book on how to make a bomb. The defendant acquired the 9–millimeter semiautomatic weapon. The brothers went to the firing range to learn to shoot the gun. On April 7, the defendant tweeted, "If you have the knowledge and the inspiration, all that's left is to take action." Within eight days they bombed the marathon. On April 14, the day before, he purchased a SIM card to call his brother to give him the go–ahead to detonate the bomb.

4. **He made a political statement.** Prosecutors argued the defendant not only went out to kill but was ordered to make a political statement to punish America, and he took credit for what he did.

PROSECUTOR STEVE MELLIN: *(Excerpt found on Page 75, line 19 through 25.)* The defendant wasn't out just to kill. He also wanted to make a political statement. *"He knew these bombs would make people suffer because murders are more terrifying and they make a better political statement this way..."*

(Excerpt found on Page 85, line 2 through 20.) In the boat, he wrote a manifesto to explain their actions and took credit for what they had done. He clearly wrote, "I can't stand to see such evil go unpunished." He didn't write "we." He did not write, "My brother made me do it."

(Excerpt found on Page 88, line 4 through 10.) Dzhokhar found terrorist writings. He read books and listened to their lectures. He acted on the beliefs and the writings and he acted on it to carry out a terrorist attack. He was an adult and was old enough to make decisions.

5. **He had no remorse.** Prosecutors argued the defendant demonstrated a disturbing lack of remorse.

PROSECUTOR STEVE MELLIN: *(Excerpt found on Page 80, line 21 through Page 81, end line 5.)* Dzhokhar's lack of remorse when he was charged with detonating the bomb is disturbing. About 20 minutes after exploding the bomb, while his victims lay dead and dying or bleeding, he goes shopping for milk at a Whole Foods like it was an ordinary day.

DEFENSE'S ARGUMENT & EXCERPT SUMMARY

1. **Tamerlan was becoming very radical.** Defense argued that Tamerlan who had unrealistic expectations had changed dramatically by becoming more radical.

DEFENSE JUDY CLARKE: *(Excerpt found on Page 100, line 6 through 15.)* Dzhokhar arrived with his parents to the United States when he was 8-years-old. They left behind 15-year-old Tamerlan and his two sisters in Kazakhstan with relatives. A year later, the whole family reunited in Cambridge with hopes and dreams. They had hopes for Tamerlan who would become an Olympic boxer and would be the "savior of the family." But, he lost his motivation in boxing and began to change.

(Excerpt found on Page 104, line 9 through line 17.) Later in life, Tamerlan left for Russia to become a jihad warrior. He wanted to take up the fight. However, he was rejected by the group.

(Excerpt found on Page 108, line 24 through Page 109, end line 8.) *"When Tamerlan returned from his unsuccessful join-up with the jihadi movement, he was frustrated and determined to find a new war to express his rage."* This was how he became more radical and anti–American and began plotting the attack.

He also received instruction from Misha, *(Excerpt found on Page 103, line 15 through 21* and *Excerpt found on Page 110, line 25 through Page 111, end line 3.)* Misha, an Armenian man who *"brought his own special version of Islam into the home and began to teach Tamerlan."* After this, Tamerlan began to develop ideas and *"obsessions about conspiracy theories and about religious extremism."*

2. **Dzhokhar was the invisible kid.** Defense argued Dzhokhar was a shy, quiet, respectful, and hard–working kid who kept his head down and did his homework.

DEFENSE JUDY CLARKE: *(Excerpt found on Page 100, line 16 through Page 101, end line 11.)* Unlike his brother Tamerlan, Dzhokhar was a good student and "quickly absorbs new ideas." He was friendly with peers and adults. He was polite and respectful. Teachers loved him and "he enters class with a warm greeting." *(Excerpt found on Page 102, line 16 through Page 103, end line 14.)* Dzhokhar got involved with the Model U.N. club and "Best Buddies" and he was good with disabled kids. His wrestling coach, Roy Howard, remembered Dzhokhar who volunteered, and helped as a wrestling coach. Howard never got to meet Dzhokhar's parents. His parents did not support Dzhokhar or even showed up for Senior Night, the big day for wrestlers when they receive their roses.

(Page 102 line 3 through 6. And Excerpt on Page 107, line 4 through 7.) Clarke stated to the jurors, *"One thing that was consistent in all of the family chaos and craziness was Dzhokhar remained the invisible child. His parents weren't there for his wrestling match. His parents never met his teachers in high school."*

3. **Dzhokhar's parents and their troubles.** Defense argued Dzhokhar's father was becoming more disabled, and his mother had changed wearing darker clothes.

DEFENSE JUDY CLARKE: *(Excerpt found on Page 99, line 19 through Page 100, end line 1.) (Excerpt found on Page 103, line 22 through Page 104, end line 8.)* Dzhokhar's father, Anzor, was described as "quiet and a hardworking dad." His mother, Zubeidat, was "fashionable, flashy and loud." However, overtime their lives changed while they lived in the States. Zubeidat began covering herself and wearing dark clothes which shocked her family. Anzor's health began declining. *(Excerpt found on Page 104, line 18 through Page 105, end line 23.)* He was becoming disabled and suffered a "series of mental health problems."

4. **Tamerlan influenced Dzhokhar.** Defense argued that Tamerlan was a major influence in Dzhokhar's life when their parents divorced.

DEFENSE JUDY CLARKE: *(Excerpt found on Page 107, line 24 through Page 108, end line 17.)* When Dzhokhar's parents divorced, he had little parental support when they left for Russia. His mother *"wasn't available, even with her limited parenting skills, to help this kid, to be there to provide any guidance or support that a parent does."*

(Excerpt found on Page 108, line 18 through 110, end line 8.) By fall of 2012, Dzhokhar's only source of family guidance, his older brother stepped in to provide him support. *"Tamerlan had charisma. Tamerlan was bigger than him. Tamerlan was older than him."* In the Chechen or Avar culture, a younger brother would revere and adore an older brother. When Tamerlan left for Russia, *(Excerpt found on Page 113, line 18 through 22,)* he began sending "jihadi kinds of materials, radical extremism materials," to Dzhokhar to influence him. Tamerlan transferred files of *Inspire* magazine, radical materials from his computer to Dzhokhar's.

(Excerpt found on Page 117, line 2 through line 13.) While Tamerlan was in Russia to wage war, Dzhokhar sent Tamerlan emails about cars. Dzhokhar was a kid who talked about cars, but his brother encouraged him to look at the jihad radical extreme materials he sent. Dzhokhar was in his sophomore year in college and to say, *"that Dzhokhar was a jihadi in his -- the beginning of his sophomore year in college is just wrong,"* pointed out Clarke. Meanwhile, Tamerlan was rejected as a warrior when he tried to hook up with radicals. It's because *"he couldn't fit into any movement. So he created his own."* *(Excerpt found on Page 119, line 9 through line 19.)* When Dzhokhar hid in the boat, he already had absorbed jihadi teachings, *"he wrote words that had been introduced to him by his brother; words that he had listened to, that were sent to him by his brother; words that he had read that were sent to him by his brother until at least -- he could at least recite them."*

5. **Tamerlan was the mastermind planner and the real jihadist of the bombings.** Defense argued that Tamerlan planned the terrorist attack, made the bombs and had a gun to kill people. He also was determined to die, but Dzhokhar wanted to live.

DEFENSE JUDY CLARKE: *(Excerpt found on Page 117, line 14 through Page 118, end line 2.)* Tamerlan consumed with rage planned the attack by finding extremist articles online and he also watched violent YouTube sites. He searched for a gun, the P95 Ruger and for all the bomb-making parts. He ordered all the materials that he used to build the bombs with. Tamerlan's prints were all over the tools used to make the bombs, and not Dzhokhar's. *(Excerpt found on Page 119, line 4 through 8.)* Tamerlan also shot Collier and murdered him. Tamerlan's prints were on the magazine inside that gun. *(Excerpt found on Page 128, line 18).* Although Dzhokhar was found legally responsible for the death of Officer Collier, he did not pull the trigger. *(Excerpt found on Page 119, line 9 through 12.)* Tamerlan wanted to die a martyr in a "blaze of gunfire" but Dzhokhar "panicked and got into the car and escaped.

6. **Dzhokhar followed his brother Tamerlan.** Defense argued Dzhokhar followed his brother and did whatever he was told to do and what to believe.

DEFENSE JUDY CLARKE: *(Excerpt found on Page 101, line 20.)* When Dzhokhar was young, he followed his big brother around the boxing gym like a puppy. *(Excerpt found on Page 118, line 3 through line 11.)* The "tragic truth" was Dzhokhar followed his brother down Boylston. He carried a backpack with the bomb in it, and "he put it down in a crowd of people, believing that it would be detonated, and people would be hurt and killed." He believed in what his brother believed in and became a participant. *"Dzhokhar would never have done this but for Tamerlan. The tragedy would never have occurred but for Tamerlan. None of it."*

7. **Dzhokhar was not the worst criminal.** Defense argued that the death penalty was reserved for the worst criminals. Prosecution's theory painted him as a 'bad seed' and that Dzhokhar had everyone fooled and he should be executed for the heinous crimes, but defense argued for his life to be spared and to receive punishment of life in prison without parole.

DEFENSE JUDY CLARKE: *(Excerpt found on Page 122, line 18 through line 23.)* Clarke turned to the jurors and asked them, *"Is his a life worth saving? Is there hope for him? Is there hope for redemption?"* *(Excerpt found on Page 124, line 15 through 22.)* Clarke said, "Dzhokhar is not the worst criminal." There was "nothing to suggest he was difficult to supervise, manage or house in prison." Since his imprisonment under SAMs he has *"never tried to influence anybody about his beliefs. He's never tried to break the rules or disobey the law."* The government portrayed Dzhokhar as a remorseless, unrepentant person who had flashed his middle finger at the camera. The government only showed a stilled clip out-of-context.

(Page 125, line 6 through 12.) Dzhokhar was only acting stupid and he apologized for the middle finger gesture. He said, "I'm sorry." *(Excerpt found on Page 136, line 15 through 20.)* With this in mind, Defense proposed that Dzhokhar be sentenced to life in prison without the possibility of release. Clarke said, it "allows for hope," the possibility that Dzhokhar could be redeemed. It also "allows healing for everyone." Defense pled for mercy for Dzhokhar. *"It's a sentence that reflects justice and mercy. Mercy's never earned; it's bestowed. And the law allows you to choose justice and mercy."*

8. **Dzhokhar was remorseful.** Defense argued that although Dzhokhar was very young and had made a bad choice when he committed the crime, he has "potential for redemption" and to change. He already had repented and was growing more mature.

DEFENSE JUDY CLARKE: *(Excerpt found on Page 125, line 13 through Page 128, end line 11.)* Finally, a glimpse of remorse from Dzhokhar was seen through the eyes of Sister Helen Prejean who testified that as she sat and consoled him, it *"gave you the opportunity to see is that this kid is on that path of growth and remorse."*

Clarke described how Dzhokhar had changed in the past two years and how he now regretted his actions and the crime he had committed. *"The young man that Sister Helen sat with is not the angry, vengeful, uncaring, unrepentant, unchanged, untouched young man that the prosecution has described to you. What unrepentant, unchanged, untouched jihadi is going to meet with a Catholic nun, connect with her, talk with her and have her enjoy the conversation with him? The critical thing is that Dzhokhar is remorseful today. He's grown in the last two years. He is sorry, and he is remorseful."*

Read the full transcript complete arguments from Tsarnaev's trial found in Reference number 198 from Tsarnaev's trial.[198]

The trial teams moved to sidebar. Music was played so people could not overhear what they were saying. Suddenly, the Defense became angry that the government was able to make claims, especially about *"defense witnesses that they could not rebuttal,"* – Cullen. Miriam argued loudly over the music about Weinreb's closing, reported Cullen. Meanwhile, many jurors looked directly at Jahar. They began contemplating and wondering if his life was worth saving as he chatted with his attorney Timothy Watkins. Could they sentence him to death? Back from sidebar, Judge O'Toole reviewed legal instructions with the jury and then sent them off to deliberate. That day the jury deliberated for less than an hour before the Judge sent them home. Jahar was brought back into the courtroom. He sent a warm smile to his attorneys as he was escorted away. Twelve jurors were chosen to decide Tsarnaev's fate, and they sat in the jury box. The other six alternates sat on the side. When they returned to the courtroom, *"they chuckled as they noticed a change in seating in the jury box. Jahar turned to them and cracked a small smile."* – Quinn.

LIFE OR DEATH?

Below are actual public comments from a poll asking if Dzhokhar deserves life in prison or the death sentence. We uplift Dzhokhar to God in our prayers.

*Just lock him in a prison cell with some pressure cookers full of nails that can explode at any point in time in the future.
* Life in a cement cage. He should live another... 60 years. Let him live knowing his feet will never know the sweet feeling of wet grass in the morning, a hot bath, a loving touch from your spouse.... yeah, let him live in a box.
* Or allow a spitting gallery, once a-day-visitors get to walk past his cell from overhead and spit on him. Two hours a day should do it.
*Wipe him from the earth...he's evil and we don't need him here.
* He should have died in the boat.
*Kill the low life. * Lock him up & throw away the keys!
* Torture the prick! * Do not show his ugly face.
* How about we amputate his legs and give him life.
*Make him live in a pig pen with 10 hogs until death.
* Let the piece of crap rot in prison and hope he gets gang raped every day for the rest of his miserable life. * He should die!!!
* He is worthless. *Let him fry! * Die, he is a monster!!!
*Kill the little bastard, that's what he wanted to do, was kill people.
* I want to stop seeing his ugly face. * Shoot this little prick.
* Why should we spare his life? * Feed him pork then execute him.
*Life in prison in a 6x8 dimly lit cell 23 out 24 hours a day.
No contact with the outside world. No internet, newspapers, etc.
* Blow him up at The Boston Marathon finish line.
*Kill the shitbag! * Die Creep Die!

"Father, may Jahar meet You in prison and fall in love with Your grace. Show him who You are. May Your love for him be real. May he find new life in You. Thank You Lord for protecting Jahar in the boat that night and shielding his body from all those bullets."

Now We Will Kill You

"A death sentence is not giving him what he wants. It is giving him what he deserves. ....The only sentence that will do justice in this case is a sentence of death."
— Prosecutor Steve Mellin

Day 11 – May 14, 2015

"*JAHAR ENTERED THE COURTROOM gripping the lapels of his brown jacket. He smiled, looking strangely at peace wondering if he would live or die.*" – Sweet. The trial was nearing the end and he began his usual day, chatting with Judy and Miriam. Jahar was laughing about something with Judy. "*That's the first time I have heard Tsarnaev laugh; he kind of caught himself and brought his hand to his mouth. Jahar chatting it up with his legal team...it even brings an audible chuckle from the convicted terrorist,*" tweeted Armstrong. Perhaps his lawyers were putting him at ease. Today, the jurors would have a full day of deliberations, weighing the fate of Dzhokhar. The jurors came in the morning very alert and responsive. Twelve jurors headed back to a room to deliberate. As the jury left, Jahar scratched his head, apprehensively, wondering what they would decide for him. He lingered for a bit as Clerk Lyness talked to his lawyers. Judy touched his shoulder and he immediately exited the courtroom swinging his arms.

The jurors had a question after three hours of deliberation. It was about how they should apply the gateway factors to specific counts. 4 gateway factors were: 1 –Tsarnaev intentionally killed, 2 – he intentionally inflicted serious bodily injury that led to death. 3 – Tsarnaev intentionally participated in an act knowing lethal force would be used and people would die as a result. 4 - Tsarnaev participated in act of violence that created a grave risk of death and reckless regard for human life.

The question they asked: Did Dzhokhar "intentionally kill" if he had no such intent, but helped (aided) Tamerlan who had evil intent? If the jury focused on the word "intent," it could bring in mitigating factors, such as Tamerlan's influence. If the jury could not agree to any of the gateway factors, Dzhokhar would automatically receive a life sentence. If the jury found that Dzhokhar killed a victim, they would also have to find he intended for that person to die.

As all nine lawyers huddled together to discuss the question, Jahar was brought in and sat undisturbed and alone at the defense table observed Wen. A defendant should never be alone, but he was so obedient and well–mannered, drawing on a paper cup with a highlighter. His U.S. Marshals stood a few feet away watching him. Judge O'Toole said the determination must be based on Mr. Tsarnaev's personal actions and intent and not anyone else's or on Tamerlan's.

Day 12 – May 15, 2015 – THE PENALTY VERDICT IS IN

Reporter Laurel Sweet on Twitter announced in 14.5 hours that the verdict was in for Jahar Tsarnaev. She compared the jury deliberation time to another high-profile terrorist case. It had taken jurors only 11 hours of deliberations to convict and condemn Timothy McVeigh to death in the Oklahoma City bombings. Several of Tsarnaev's lawyers rushed into the courtroom and drew closer together...flipping papers. There was this nervous energy inside everyone. Defense attorneys William Fick and Timothy Watkins got to their chairs first. They flipped through the 22 pages of the long verdict slip. Miriam, Judy and David finally arrived. Soon after, the government team arrived: Steve Mellin, Aloke Chakravarty, Nadine Pellegrini and William Weinreb.

On May 15, 2015, the mood in the courthouse changed from being loose and relaxed to serious and somber. Victims, families of victims and survivors also now arrived. Bill and Denise Richard were present to hear the verdict. The Collier family, Liz Norden, Karen Brassard, and Carmen Ortiz all took their seats. The courtroom became packed again with public law enforcement officials, and survivors and their families. They all waited to hear the fate of Dzhokhar Tsarnaev who had taken the lives and injured so many innocent people.

Jahar appeared sallow and walked in quicker than usual. That day he chose to wear a dark suit and a slate gray dress shirt, yet like any other day he showed no emotion. He sat at the wooden table between his maternal cloak, Judy and Miriam, reported Cullen. He talked a bit, but they did not smile at him. They gently patted him on the back. The courtroom was deathly quiet as people shuffled in and took their seats. Jahar could sense a stream of people coming in behind him, though he heard no noise or talking. He became quiet. Miriam broke the silence, whispered something in Jahar's ear. He suddenly became fidgety and nervous. He cracked his knuckles. Attorneys on both teams, appeared somber and nervous as they waited for the Judge and jury. The courtroom was packed to capacity with people. They waited in eerie silence as all eyes focused on the condemned, Jahar. His legal team called him the "invisible kid" because that was what he was in his family. Jahar felt the stares of the people sitting behind him. He rubbed his itchy head worriedly and kept talking lightly to Miriam and Judy. Soon at about 3:00 in the afternoon, Judge O'Toole and the jury entered the courtroom. None of the twelve jurors who decided his fate could look at Jahar. The Forewoman handed over the envelope containing the verdict. Judge O'Toole opened it and read the verdict form. He handed it to Clerk Paul Lyness. The Judge asked the Defense team and the jury to stand. *"Jahar stood with his face down and arms crossed in front of him,"* -Wen. They stood waiting nervously for Clerk Lyness to read the verdict form out loud.

(All verdict tweets were from Jim Armstrong at Boston WBZ.)

"Was Tsarnaev at least 18 years old at time of offense? Yes, all counts"

"Did Tsarnaev intentionally kill the victim(s) in each count? YES, to some counts."

Jahar whispered to his lawyer as Gateway counts were read. He wiped his eye.

"Did Tsarnaev contemplate that the life of a person would be taken? YES, to ALL counts."

There was a long, awkward moment of silence. Jahar rocked back and forth. His eyes stared at the table in front of him. Judy glanced at the jury as the next counts were read.

"Did Tsarnaev intentionally inflict serious bodily injury resulting in death(s)? YES, to some counts. (1,4,5,6,9,10,14,15)"

"Did Tsarnaev's participation constitute "a reckless disregard for human life"? YES, to ALL counts."

"Death(s)/injuries occurred during commission of, or flight from, another offense? YES, to ALL counts."

"Did Tsarnaev knowingly create "a grave risk of death" to 1 or more persons? YES, to SOME counts. (1,4,5,6,9,10,14,15,16,17,18)"

"Did Tsarnaev commit offense "in an especially heinous, cruel & depraved manner"? YES, to SOME counts (1,4,5,6,9,10,11,14,15)"

"Did Tsarnaev substantially plan and premeditate an act of terrorism? YES, to ALL."

"Did Tsarnaev intentionally kill and attempt to kill more than 1 person in 1 criminal episode? YES, to ALL"

"Tsarnaev targeted Martin Richard due to his youth. YES."

In the gallery, Denise was resting her hand on her chin when she heard the jury characterize Martin as a targeted vulnerable victim. Up front in court, Jahar was wringing his hands and his attorneys looked grim as Clerk Lyness continued to read the verdict form.

"Did Tsarnaev make statements suggesting others would be justified doing more violence/terror against the USA? NO."

"Did Tsarnaev cause "injury, harm, and loss" to Campbell/Richard/Lu/Collier families & friends?

YES, to ALL."

"Did Tsarnaev target the final stretch of the iconic Boston Marathon? YES, to ALL."

"Did Tsarnaev demonstrate "a lack of remorse"? YES, to ALL."

Jahar rocked back and forth at the jury's finding that he lacked remorse.

"Did Tsarnaev murder Officer Sean Collier, who was engaged in his official duties at the time of his death? YES, to ALL."

"Did Tsarnaev participate in "additional uncharged crimes of violence" on 4/15/13 and 4/19/13? YES, to ALL."

As the verdict was being read, all the survivors and families of survivors stared at Jahar who was engaged in reading the verdict sheet. Jahar was both fidgety and nervous. He cracked his knuckles twice. He consciously touched his face, but he stopped and folded his hands in front of him.

"Now to MITIGATORS: Tsarnaev was 19 years old at the time of the offenses. Jurors who agree: 12"

"Tsarnaev had no prior history of violent behavior. Jurors who agree: 11"

"Tsarnaev acted under the influence of his older brother. Jurors who agree: 3"

"Tamerlan Tsarnaev's age/size/aggressiveness made Dzhokhar "particularly susceptible" to his influence. Jurors who agree: 3"

"Tsarnaev's brother Tamerlan planned, led, and directed the Marathon bombing. Jurors who agree: 3"

"Tsarnaev's brother Tamerlan shot and killed MIT Officer Sean Collier. Jurors who agree: 2"

"Tsarnaev would not have committed the crimes but for his older brother Tamerlan. Jurors who agree: 3"

"Tsarnaev's teachers knew him to be "hardworking, respectful, kind, and considerate." Jurors who agree: 12"

"Tsarnaev's friends knew him to be "thoughtful, caring, and respectful." Jurors who agree: 11"

"Tsarnaev's teachers and friends still care for him. Jurors who agree: 3"

"Tsarnaev's aunts and cousins love and care for him. Jurors who agree: 12"

"Mental illness & brain damage disabled Tsarnaev's father. Jurors who agree: 12"

"Tsarnaev was deprived of stability and guidance because of his father's mental illness. Jurors who agree: 2"

"Tsarnaev's father's mental illness made Tamerlan the dominant male in his life. Jurors who agree: 2"

"Tsarnaev was deprived of stability and guidance b/c of his mother's emotional volatility and religious extremism. Jurors who agree: 1"

"Tsarnaev's mother facilitated his brother Tamerlan's radicalization. Jurors who agree: 10"

"Tamerlan Tsarnaev became radicalized first, and then encouraged his younger brother to follow. Jurors who agree: 5"

"Tsarnaev's parents returned to Russia in 2012, made Tamerlan the adult male in Tsarnaev's life. Jurors who agree: 2"

"Tsarnaev is highly unlikely to commit/incite acts of violence if sentenced to life in federal prison. Jurors who agree: 1"

"The government has the power to restrict Tsarnaev's communications from prison with outside world. Jurors who agree: 2"

"Tsarnaev has expressed sorrow and remorse for what he did and for the sufferings he had caused. Jurors who agree: 2"

"Here comes the sentence."
"BREAKING: Tsarnaev SENTENCED to DEATH on SOME counts DEATH for Tsarnaev on counts 4, 5, 9, 10, 14, 15." (These counts are using WMD resulting in deaths.)

To view the counts, click the Jury Completed Verdict Slip, view Reference number 199.[199]

Judge O'Toole told the Defense team to retake their seats. Miriam, shocked at the death sentence verdict, sat with her hand over her mouth. Jahar swallowed hard, observed reporter Armstrong. Jahar did not flinch, but, nervously swept his hand through his long, curly hair that bothered him at the neck. At the moment the death sentence was announced, there was no sound or emotion. The air was heavy. Even the Prosecutors looked very somber. Jahar was zoned out, despite just being sentenced to death. *"The Richards, who opposed death, are bent over, dry eyed, looking at judge. Liz Norden, who wanted death sentence, wipes tears,"* – Cullen.[200]

Attorney Bruck wanted the jurors polled one–by–one. As the jurors stood they each said in clear, affirmative voices, "YES" to the verdict that corresponded to theirs, and that it was their true final verdict, reported Valencia.

Jahar stared down and showed no sign of emotion as each juror was polled. He then glanced at Miriam. His head tilted toward the jury, shifting slightly in his chair. When the juror polling was over, Jahar sat up straighter, and briefly rested his head on his hand. He could not face the Judge as he spoke.

The Richard family sat calmly, leaning forward and listening intently to the last remarks from the Judge. Judge O'Toole thanked the jury and the alternates saying, "And thanks on behalf of the citizens of Massachusetts. We ask of you the important and difficult task of reviewing this evidence. Your work here should stand as model for future juries. You should be justly proud of your service in this case," reported Cullen.

Jahar leaned back in his chair uncomfortably as he listened. It was awkward for the Judge to thank the jurors for their service that ultimately resulted in a sentence of death for him. The judge's words made him squeamish. Judge also thanked both teams of lawyers, "They have conducted themselves with the highest level of professionalism." Lastly, he peered down at Jahar, and he praised the Boston Bomber, Dzhokhar Tsarnaev, for he had kind words for him respectively, reported Bailey. "Mr. Tsarnaev has comported himself with propriety," the entire time he acted appropriately and well-mannered throughout the trial, reported Wen.

Jahar stared ahead, unfazed, tapping his foot and rubbing his face. One juror fixed his eyes on Jahar as the Judge addressed them for the last time. Judge turned his attention back to talk to the jurors. He empathized with them and said, "You've sat through a long time that at times had terrible images and intense testimony. You are now free to talk to your family and friends about the case and media if you wish. No obligations to talk. On behalf of a community seriously aggrieved...you show you can put emotions aside and make rational judgments. The inconvenience of this case to all of you has been considerable...yet you served with grace."

Relieved from their duty, final emotions began hitting the jurors. They could now go back to their regular lives. IT JUST HIT THEM that the whole trial was finally over! *"Three jurors are wiping away tears,"* – Valencia. *"One juror, a middle-aged man, takes his glasses off to wipe tears away. The jurors seemed wrecked. Several dabbing their eyes,"* – Cullen. Several of the jurors sighed heavily; even the forewoman, who played her role in court, wiped her eye with a tissue. They were glad it was over! These jurors did not listen to a word the Defense said to keep their minds open to hear, to learn or to understand Jahar. Some jurors even look zoned out during the Defense's presentation; however, they always paid close attention and agreed with arguments from the prosecution's attorneys. They rejected the Defense's argument that Jahar had been swayed by his older brother and ignored the evidence that Tamerlan had solely planned the bombings. The jurors continually stared at Jahar wondering if he was human or if he had a conscious mind. How can they walk around his head and know what he was feeling? They had quickly made up their minds that his life was not worth saving. The Judge had told them not to judge him by his demeanor, but they did judge his behavior. The evidence presented in this trial by the Prosecution team was so much stronger than that of the Defense team. The Defense did their best with what they had been given.

Meanwhile, some people sitting in the defense gallery, who had worked for Mr. Tsarnaev, the paralegals were crying for Jahar. They sobbed. It was such a shock for them. They had all come to like Jahar and it was sad and very hard to believe he would die by lethal injection. *"Defense attorneys looked somber as death penalty handed down to Tsarnaev. This may be one of 1st time Judy Clarke could not spare her client Jahar,"* – Wen.

Jahar shifted in his chair again, but otherwise appeared expressionless. Jahar wondered what the jurors thought of him. They only saw him as a terrorist who carried no remorse. It was so difficult for him to show his true emotions: he kept his emotions concealed inside of him.

The government won because they wanted to send a strong message. They would not tolerate such acts of terror. All that mattered to the government was for Mr. Tsarnaev to be responsible for the crime he had committed. And to suffer the worst punishment possible to force him to think what he had done to his victims by leaving them dead on the sidewalk. His doomed fate had been sealed by his heinous acts of terrorism.

After seeing the jurors cry, the Judge added, "It may not be too much to say you have formed some friendships." One juror nodded her head in agreement. – Valencia. The Judge said he would honor their anonymity until further notice. "You are now discharged. We rise in respect to you." – Wen.

Everyone in the courtroom rose. As a sign of respect, the Judge discharged the jury first. Afterward, the jurors were bused to "The Black Rose" bar in the Seaport District to avoid the media. At the Irish pub, they relaxed and drank a few beverages for a couple of hours. They talked among themselves and felt they had made the right decision to put Mr. Tsarnaev to death.

Jahar stood and watched each juror walked out of the room. He placed his hands in his pockets, but then he felt Judy briefly put her hand on his arm. It was a touch he was so familiar with. He turned to see her disheartened face. Judy reassured him and squeezed his arm observed by reporter Bailey.

Judge O'Toole ordered Mr. Tsarnaev to be taken back into custody and *"Jahar made a motion with his hands, his arms pointing downward asking to be handcuffed,"* – Bailey. Jahar surrendered his life to the authorities, but they motioned him to come to them. With one final grip on the arm from Judy, Jahar walked solemnly out of the room. Both Judy and Miriam frowned. They looked defeated as they sadly watched their client being restrained in handcuffs. When Jahar left with the U.S. Marshals, he turned quickly to glance back at his lawyers to say goodbye.

However, soon after the lawyers gathered all their belongings in the courtroom, they followed Jahar back to his holding cell to provide consolation for him. Laurel Sweet's final tweet from the trial was, *"Only 21-year-old, Dzhokhar Tsarnaev will be the first youngest person to be on Federal death row."* Outside the courthouse, someone who was close to Mr. Tsarnaev was seen avoiding the media. She fled and escaped the media crowd, crying. However, when DEATH was announced, there were also those who stood outside and quietly said, "Yes" and "Thank you."

SURVIVORS AND FAMILIES REACTED TO THE DEATH SENTENCE VERDICT

"Today the jury has spoken and Dzhokhar Tsarnaev will pay with his life for his crimes. Make no mistake the defendant claim to be acting on behalf of all Muslims. This was not a religious crime and certainly does not reflect true Muslim beliefs. It was a political crime, designed to intimidate and to coerce the United States."
– *Statement from US Attorney Carmen Ortiz* [201]

"He turned into a monster. Why that ever happened. We'll never know." – *Laurie Scher*

"There is no winner here today, but I feel the jury gave him the appropriate sentence… I have to watch my two sons put legs on every day, so there's no closure, but it feels like a weight's been lifted." – *Liz Norden*

"There is nothing happy about taking someone's life. I'm satisfied and grateful." – *Karen Brassard*

"This is nothing to celebrate. This is a matter of justice. He is going to hell quicker than he thought." – *Michael Ward*

"For me, it's not going to change my life [in] any way much, -- glad that it was over."– *Roseann Sdoia*

"We are glad it's over and we can continue with our healing,"
– *Celeste Corcoran*

"My mother and I think that NOW he will go away and we will be able to move on. Justice. In his own words, 'an eye for an eye.'"
– *Sydney Corcoran*

"My heart is with our entire survivor community. I am thrilled with the verdict!"– *Adrianne Haslet–Davis*

"Completely numb...and waiting anxiously for the day this is really over. My heart and prayers are with my Boylston Street family."
– *Rebekah DiMartino*

"Today, my thoughts are with the other bombing survivors and the jury who made what was likely among the most difficult decisions of their lives. The verdict, regardless of which one it turned out to be, doesn't bring me peace. It brings sadness and cause to reflect, again, on just how senseless ALL of the deaths and injuries resulting from this situation are." – *Heather Abbott*

"I think they did what they thought was right...It was tough for them to make that decision. He wasted his life by hurting other people. I feel bad for him personally...21–year–old kid that just got sentenced to death. Part of me has to feel bad for him, but he chose to put that bag behind a group of kids...It doesn't matter what he thinks. He's gone. He had a perfectly great life. He may not have been the richest person, but he had friends and that is all you need. He had a decent life..." – *Jeff Bauman*

TSARNAEV'S PARENTS

Dzhokhar's father, Anzor Tsarnaev groaned when he heard that his son had been sentenced to death. "What a parent can feel at such moment? It is hard," he said from Dagestan, Russia. "Hope exists always. We had hope and still do. We will fight until the end."[202]

Dzhokhar's mother, Zubeidat Tsarnaeva, said she hopes the United States burns in an "eternal and terrifying fire." "They think that they are killing us and they celebrate this, but we are the ones who will rejoice when Allah grants us the chance to behold them in the flames of an eternal and terrifying fire, an otherworldly flame."[203]

REACTION FROM THE NATION

All comments are from "New York Times"

"Many people are stating that Tsarnaev is unrepentant. He was silent during the trial, likely on the advice of his attorneys. This is the only thing we really know. There have been reports that he cried for three days in the hospital after capture. A very young person. We do not know why he was crying, and the nurses did not to try to talk to him about it, apparently. Legal instructions, no doubt. This verdict will close off our ability to understand one of the saddest, most tragic episodes I know of. It was an act of terror; yes. By someone who was in a fraught struggle for growing into manhood, a struggle most definitely secondary to the family situation which included asylum and then exit of parents from the U.S. Vulnerability writ large, with horrible consequences all around. He is too young for this sentence, and we are too unwise for it as well. Killing him will not make people whole. There is much more to be gained from a path of understanding, time, and forgiveness. Closure that is hoped for by victims will be partial and based in retaliation. Peoples of the world, who are experiencing terrorist actions, will continue to experience them. This brings no closure whatsoever. It just brings another round of vengeance." – *mjb, Tucson*

"I'm so torn over the death sentence received in this case. On the one hand, my feeling is that if there ever was a case that deserved the death penalty this is it. The callousness of this act and the amount of pain and suffering it caused was horrible. On the other hand, though, Dzhokhar is so young, and my feeling is truly that his brother was the mastermind behind the case. If his brother had not died I would have no reservations about him receiving the death penalty. Dzhokhar, though, is someone I feel was taken down the wrong path and too young to know what he was doing or to understand exactly how much pain he caused. A tragedy all around." – *NMY, New Jersey*

CHRISTIANS RESPONDED TO THE VERDICT FROM "CHRISTIANS FOR JAHAR"

Many Christians responded to the verdict praying and hoping that Dzhokhar Tsarnaev would come to know how much Christ loves him since he had been given the death sentence. Below are Tweets from **Christians For Jahar** after the death penalty was announced:

"Father, we trust You completely. For two years we have prayed for the sentence to be exactly what he needed to come to you, so we choose to believe that this is what he needs. Bring him home now Abba." – *Christians 4 Jahar*

"Sin gives us all eternal death sentence. Jesus paid our penalty. I want all people to know Him & accept His pardon—even Dzhokhar Tsarnaev." – *Franklin Graham*

"Praying for Dzhokhar Tsarnaev to know how much Jesus loves him before it's too late." – *Bethany Katherine*

"Saddened to hear the verdict of Dzhokhar Tsarnaev. So much life left. I pray the time he has left will be spent well and he will meet Jesus." – *JD Reynolds*

"Lord, please have mercy on Dzhokhar Tsarnaev and draw him to your Son Jesus Christ. Open his eyes and heart. In all things Your will be done." – *Jeremy*

"God loves Dzhokhar Tsarnaev. Praying for a world that doesn't believe killing the guilty brings healing or wholeness." – *Nathan Bledsoe*

"Tsarnaev found guilty in the eyes of man. I pray that before he dies he will repent and hold the hand of the ultimate intercessor, Jesus." – *Felipe Soares*

"Lord, please reveal Yourself to Tsarnaev. May he have an opportunity to know You before he's gone." – *Martha*

"Our Father desires Dzhokhar. LOVE him and PRAY for him, he may be redeemed. What a testimony that would be. God's broken heart. Lost sheep." – *I'mouthere*

"Here is where the Gospel can be considered scandalous. Even Dzhokhar A. Tsarnaev (suspect #2) can be saved."– *Richard Marroquin*

"I really hope he turns to Jesus in this time of his life. It makes me sad seeing people want him to die. The death penalty is wrong. They should let him sit in prison for his life instead. Hopefully during this time he finds Christ!" – *Jacob @cubs_15WSchamps*

"Thank you, God, for being gracious and limiting the bloodshed tonight. Lord, save Dzhokhar Tsarnaev's soul. May he be like Paul." – *Jordan Simon*

"Without forgiveness, there is no compassion. Revenge is never the answer." – *Ryan Traylor*

"Someday we must end the cycle of violence. Death cannot solve death. We are all in desperate need of grace." – *Nathan Stripp*

"To take a life when a life has been lost is revenge, not justice." – *Chris Stedman*

"My opposition to the death penalty is rooted in my faith. Tsarnaev is made in the image and likeness of God, as much as were his victims." – *Ireland /Ben*

"May we continue to pray for Dzhokhar." – *Brandan J. Robertson*

"As a Christian, I can't possibly scream, "Burn in hell Tsarnaev!" I long for him to receive the same grace that saved a wretch like me." – *Craig*

"Today I'm reminded Christ died for Dzhokhar Tsarnaev." – *2 Cor 5*

"We should not rejoice over the death of Tsarnaev. Instead, we should sorrow over the fact that he has not looked to the death of Jesus." – *Dayton Hartman*

"Everyone you see is important to Jesus. Remember that before you go around celebrating a death sentence." – *Gabby Gadapee*

"Jesus is weeping today - Tsarnaev." – *Stephen Carter*

"It was to a criminal like Dzhokhar Tsarnaev that Christ spoke to upon an adjacent cross saying, "Today you will be with me in paradise." – *Brandon McGinnis*

"Why does a rose represent love, when a rose always dies? Jesus loves Dzhokhar Tsarnaev too."– *Terezija Bjornsson*

"Pray for the soul of Dzhokhar Tsarnaev, and that he may encounter the love of God while awaiting his death." – *Danny*

"Pray 4 Tsarnaev's conversion & that he makes a final confession b4 his death. I hope he sees the light & maybe some good will come of this." – *LuvNThanks*

"I pray that someone can lead him to the Lord." – *Liberty Belle*

"My heart is broken for the boy I knew, and for our justice system." – *Becki Norris*

Victims And Survivors Confront Dzhokhar

"He's a human being. When I made eye contact with him, I wasn't looking into the face of a criminal, I was looking at the face of a boy."
– Henry Bogard, Survivor

"HE CAN'T POSSIBLY HAVE had a soul to do such a horrible thing. Those brothers took away an angel." Jahar was listening to KAREN MCWATTERS when he returned to court on June 24, 2015 for his sentencing. Karen (Rand) McWatters, who lost her leg in the bombings, confronted Jahar and relayed her feelings to him during his sentencing. Karen talked about her close friend, Krystle Campbell, who was killed in the bombing. She stared at Jahar and said, *"You took away a kind and loving person who never has hurt anyone. She was not the enemy. They didn't even know her,"* – Armstrong. As Karen spoke, Jahar faced her, but lowered his gaze. Miriam and Judy sat between Jahar once again and listened to the victims and survivors as they spoke about their loved ones and how their lives were forever changed as a result of the bombings. The sentencing took place about a month after Dzhokhar Tsarnaev had received his death sentence. Judge O'Toole, the jury and the survivors and their families reunited once again to impose the death sentence on Jahar. Jahar rubbed his left puffy cheek that had been injured. Armstrong tweeted, *"Tsarnaev sits in profile to me; his left eye is damaged, making it hard to tell when he's looking at speakers. But he largely looks away."* Jahar had put on a little more weight since the trial. His shaggy head of hair had grown longer, and his chin beard was fuller. At the start of his sentencing, Jahar shyly glanced out at the victims before he took his seat. He turned around and he saw two familiar faces, his best friends. *"Two young men seated in the defense section begin wiping away tears as they see Tsarnaev in court,"* – Palumbo.

At the jury box, jurors returned to the courtroom for a reunion and to listen in on Tsarnaev's sentencing. They were happy to see one another and were even hugging one another before the sentencing began. Now, they were in tears again as they listened to each survivor share how much their lives had been affected by the bombings. They kept peering back to see if Jahar would make eye contact with the victims when they addressed him. Karen continued, *"My grief over her loss has been the hardest part of my recovery. Islamic terrorist came to the most special event of our city and took something away from us."* Karen was frustrated as to why Jahar hadn't shown any remorse, *"Why didn't any of us who sat here this whole time see any remorse? You ruined many lives that day, but you also ruined your own. Today is the day you can share your remorse and regret if you really have an ounce of either,"* – Armstrong.

Jahar started to hear twenty victims and survivors shower him with words of hate for what he had done to them. He wanted to testify in court, and he signaled this inclination when he occasionally touched the witness box as he left court; however, he was advised by his lawyers not to testify on his behalf. Jahar and his lawyers turned their chairs around and faced the victims behind them in the courtroom listening as each of them spoke. Even though he was facing them it was still uncomfortable to be face-to-face with them. It wasn't easy for him to hear his victims directly express words of disgust or mockery towards him. The energy in and out of that room was very intense, as were the emotions emanating from the victims, the jury and the government towards Jahar.

Sean Collier's sister, JENNIFER LEMMERMAN who spoke next about her brother shared, *"There is an emptiness that I cannot manage to fill. The defendant has taken me away from me. I don't think I will ever be the same again,"* – Armstrong. Jennifer was very emotional as she talked about the empty void that now existed in her life and how she missed the joy her beloved brother, Sean had brought to her life.

Jennifer turned and directed her anger towards Jahar. *"He will never feel truly sorry for what he's done, only sorry for himself. He is a coward and a liar. He showed no remorse while their victims and their families stood in front of him. He hid behind a dead man who could not defend himself. He ran his own brother with a car. No wonder he had no problem shooting mine in the head. He is a leech abusing the privilege of American freedom, and he spit in the face of the American dream,"* – Armstrong.

Jahar stared at the ground when the bereaved parents of Martin Richard spoke next. They had no words to express their deep loss. BILL RICHARD said in a "flat" voice tweeted Bailey, *"He could have stopped his brother. He could have changed his mind. He chose to do nothing. This is all on him. We choose love, we choose kindness, we choose peace. That is what makes us different from him. On the day he meets his maker, may he understand what he has done and may Justice and peace be found,"* – Armstrong. The Richards also said they preferred a life sentence for Jahar, *"so that he had his life to deal with what he did. But now, he has "less" time,"* – Bailey.

During the whole sentencing phase, Jahar rubbed his face, leaned his face on his hand and slouched in his seat. He did not look remorseful whatsoever. He sometimes glanced up at some of the victims while they made their statements but did not stare at them.

"MY LIFE HAS CHANGED"

Many victims described how their lives were changed forever since the bombings. A couple families wept over how their children had been injured from the bombs. One of them was CAROL DOWNING, a mother who described her two daughters' injuries. She talked about her daughters: NICOLE GROSS and ERIKA BRANNOCK, *"I sob at the kitchen table, thinking of guilt I feel for my two daughters being at the finish line that day because I was running,"* – Armstrong. She felt like the invisible victim because she had to take care of her daughters by paying their medical bills and waiting with them at the doctor's office.

Carol Downing's daughter Erika Brannock described the loss of her left leg. *"I came very close to being a double amputee like other people. Mr. Tsarnaev did that, and changed the life I built for myself,"* – Armstrong. Erika said she had to quit her job working with children because she was no longer able to play with them. She was also not able to resume jogging again. She dropped out of the graduate school program that she had been enrolled in. *"What Mr. Tsarnaev did will not break my spirit,"* – Armstrong.

Another survivor was JENNIFER KAUFFMAN who described her current life to Jahar. *"My life has been completely altered because of the defendant and his brother.... I suffered massive internal injuries, neck and back injuries, heart arrhythmia, hearing loss. I suffer from PTSD; I used to be active and athletic – no more. My old "fun" life is gone,"* – Armstrong. Jennifer has been able to grant Jahar forgiveness. *I forgive you and your brother for the harm and terror that you caused me. I hope you're brave enough to drop your appeals,"* – Armstrong, so we all could move together in peace.

FINAL WORDS FOR DZHOKHAR

Although many survivors spoke about their emotional pains and sufferings, there were some survivors who talked directly to Jahar. There were some survivors who questioned Jahar, searching for any ounce of humanity in him. MICHAEL CHASE who watched the marathon and was near the second blast said he will never forget that horrible day. He helped stop the bleeding leg of victim, JANE RICHARD, by removing his own belt and using it as a tourniquet. He said to Jahar, "I do hope that he feels remorse for his actions."

Another bombing survivor, JOSEPH CRAVEN, who was near the site of the first bomb, said, *"I've tried my best to relate in any minor way to Dzhokhar throughout this trial, as hard as it was I whole heartedly believe in the benevolence of good people having power over evil. I ask you Dzhokhar to believe that as well,"* – Palumbo. He believed the defendant could rise out of this and ultimately do something good for humanity.

JOHANNA HANTEL who ran the marathon that day suffered from hearing loss, vision problems and a list of other physical complications. At the end of her statement to Jahar she shared that, *"I feel sorry for you, Mr. Tsarnaev."* She hoped Jahar would one day be able to do something positive in his life.

JEANNE-MARIE PARKER who was in the Forum Restaurant when the second bomb went off still had trouble hearing. She said, *"You have caused pain and suffering, a cancer you created that spreads so rapidly. I haven't seen or heard indication of remorse. I challenge you to write that,"* –Armstrong. She wanted Jahar to tell the court what *"he allegedly told Sister Prejean,"* – Palumbo. She also wanted Jahar to recall the time when he cried in court when his Aunt Patimat broke down in tears. *"You know what I mean, the way you caused your aunt emotional pain when she tried to testify here,"* – Armstrong. Jahar glanced up at Jeanne-Marie when she mentioned his aunt, but he quickly peered down at his knees. *"I saw you wipe your tears away because you were the cause of her pain,"* – Valencia. Jeanne-Marie continued, *"'You knew you caused your aunt pain – magnify that by all affected by the bombing.' Jahar shifts uncomfortably in his seat,"* – Palumbo. Jeanne-Marie wished Jahar would shed tears of remorse in front of everyone and she challenged him to speak out with a statement of regret.

HENRY BORGARD, the youngest surviving victim to give his victim impact statement said, *"No words could ever do justice to the atrocities that the Tsarnaev brothers committed,"* – Armstrong. Henry was twenty-one when he was walking home from work and happened to be on Boylston Street when the first bomb exploded. He remembered seeing Martin Richard before the second bomb detonated. *"I still wake up screaming sometimes from nightmares. I was genuinely afraid that I was going to die,"* – Armstrong.

Henry turned towards Jahar, searching for answers from him. *"I wanna know why and I was really angry and resentful...but I'm grateful for having my life today. I'm grateful for the fact that Boston has taught me to be resilient. I'm grateful for the fact that I've found a way to forgive the defendant for what he did to me,"* – Palumbo. Borgard also began crying, telling Jahar, *"I have forgiven the defendant. I want to spread good in this world."* – tweeted Rick Serrano of *LA Times.*

There were some survivors who were not so forgiving. They lashed out feelings of deep animosity at Jahar. A couple mocked him and described what they wished would happen to Mr. Tsarnaev. Such a feeling of offense towards Jahar was conveyed in the statement from survivor ELIZABETH BOURGAULT, who had watched the marathon from the finish line. She still suffered from both physical and emotional pain from the blast. She told Jahar, *"The defendant doesn't care about the negative impacts on my life; that's why he got out of bed that morning, to injure people,"* – Armstrong. As Elizabeth read from her statement, she shook her head at him. Jahar fidgeted with his beard and looked away from her. She continued to berate him, *"The defendant is a coward in the strongest sense of the word. The defendant will now die for what he did. The defendant's god will not welcome him, he will condemn him for the suffering he caused. I hope he never forgets and is always haunted by the fact that he failed to destroy the human spirit that day,"* – Armstrong. As Jahar listened, Judy turned and placed her hand on his arm to make sure he was still okay listening to all these hateful comments directed towards him. She saw that his head was bowed, and his face was still expressionless.

MEGAN ZIPIN also had suffered hearing loss. A marathon runner, she almost had her foot on the finish line when the bomb exploded. She spoke sadly how her two friends who were watching her race almost got blown up by the bombs. Her words for Jahar were, *"I watched the defendant, he sat there blank, never looking at any of us,"* – Palumbo. *"This defendant, to us he's already dead. He'll go back to a cell from now until forever. I'm the one who's alive."*

ED FUCARILE, Marc Fucarile's father stared at Jahar as he spoke, *"The first time I saw you in court, you were smirking. You don't seem to be smirking today. You took Marc's leg, but you haven't broken his spirit. Your sentence today should be as severe as possible. In the end, you have failed. We are stronger now,"* – Armstrong.

HEATHER ABBOTT, an amputee expressed her thanks to the jurors, *"I don't envy your choice to put someone to death. But the Tsarnaev brothers did the same thing. I didn't care much about Mr. Tsarnaev, whether he dies in prison or by lethal injection – as long as he can't hurt anyone else. By taking away my leg, he has taken away my independence,"* – Armstrong. Heather said she wondered if Jahar was happy with all that he had done. She added, *"Tsarnaev has also taken away his own freedoms. He robbed himself and his young life. I would like Dzhokhar Tsarnaev to know that he did not break me,"* – Armstrong.

The last survivor REBEKAH DIMARTINO, another amputee also thanked the jurors, *"I want to give you a hug after this is over, she tells them."* After that she focused most of her victim impact statement on Jahar. Rebekah stared intently at Jahar and said proudly, *"I'm no one's victim, not yours or your brother's,"* – Armstrong. When she spoke, the survivors cheered for her. Jahar peered down at his knees again. Rebekah was the only bombing victim who had written an *Open Letter to Dzhokhar.* In the letter, she poked fun at him, writing how he was her worst nightmare and how afraid she was of confronting him while giving her testimony in court during the trial phase.

However, when she gave her testimony during the trial, she found herself no longer afraid of Dzhokhar. It was a step she needed to take to gain back her self-confidence after facing her worst nightmare. She wrote, "*...you are a coward. A little boy who wouldn't even look me in the eyes to see that.*" Now, at Mr. Tsarnaev's sentencing, Rebekah displayed her fearless attitude while mocking him like he was a little bad boy she could fearlessly punch in defiance.

Victims were not allowed to mock the defendant, but she mocked him regardless, "*You fiddle with your pencil and crack jokes with your attorney as we tell our horrible stories. I remember how Miriam had to give you an aggressive nudge to stand for the jury on day two. On other circumstances, I would ask...is that how your mother raised you? Your brother is the one who blew me up, but since he's not here, I'll give you a dose of reality. Listen up,*" Jahar peered up for a sec. "*You did not achieve mass destruction. People all over the world have come to the aid of your victims. You may be proud of your bombs, but when people look back on 4/15, no one will remember your name or your brother's. All we will recall is the people, who were brave that day, have started foundations have become public speakers. You flipped off that camera, but that's what we are doing every day back to you – as we succeed. My 7-year-old son who was there that day said it best. You made us stronger. Think about that in your dark cell. Despite what you think you've done, you and your brother have lost. You've unified us. I'm sad you won't be here to see what happens next. We are Boston strong. We are American strong. Choosing to mess with us was a terrible idea. How's that for a victim impact statement!?*" – Armstrong.

As Rebekah ended her victim impact statement, Jahar sat still with his head down. William Weinreb stood up and spoke how Tsarnaev's actions had been politically motivated. *"He burned some, and blinded others. The harm to the victims cannot be undone,"* Weinreb says. *"They can never be made whole,"* – Boeri. Weinreb asked Mr. Tsarnaev to pay restitution to the victims of his crimes. He reminded him that he had received a public trial and it was before a fair and impartial jury. He ended saying, *"The trial of this case was the quintessential example of American justice. Sentence the defendant to death,"* – Cullen.

At this moment, Judy stood up quickly before the break and said the Defense team had legal issues to go through with the court. She finally announced, "Dzhokhar has an allocution to make." She asked for a lunch break. Everyone who heard this was very surprised. It was unexpected. No one knew that Dzhokhar Tsarnaev intended to address the court. This was the moment they all had been waiting for. What would he say? With that said, the court hurried off to eat lunch, but there were, *"no smiles from Jahar to his legal team as he exits,"* – Grossi.[204]

On The Path Toward Repentance

"Most of us hope that we have a chance to mature more from age 19 to age 21. And what Sister Helen gave you the opportunity to see is that this kid is on that path of growth and remorse." – Defense Judy Clarke

"I was shocked," said Juror 83. "I'm pretty sure my stomach kind of dropped. My heart dropped down to my stomach. It was very unexpected."– From Juror 83 when he heard Tsarnaev's apology.[205]

DZHOKHAR TSARNAEV'S FRIENDS APOLOGIZED TO BOSTON AND TO THE VICTIMS

Five friends of Dzhokhar were arrested in connection to the Boston bombings. A couple of his friends apologized during their sentencing.

"I want to apologize to lying to FBI. It was wrong. I do not support, and I am not a sympathizer of any terrorist organization. That's all I have to say." – Khairullozhon Matanov, apology tweeted by Milton Valencia of Boston Globe.

"Your honor.... I want to say how truly sorry I am to all the victims. I should have called the police. I regret it every day...Now I know that every decision has its consequences...not only for me, but for the victims. I really can't believe I acted so stupidly and irresponsible and if I could go back I would change it. I am ashamed sir. I am ashamed for my actions. I put shame on my family. I am ashamed I would be connected to this terrible event...I should have assisted and if I could go back I would have because of my stupidity and fear, I didn't...I know my decisions were wrong. In all this time, I've grown up. I'm a different person back then. I'm ashamed of the person I was. I wanted to ask for understanding." – Dias Kadyrbayev

"I am very nervous. I know I can't do anything to change what happened. I regret what I did because I know I could have made better decisions, never should have agreed to throw away the backpack. I apologize to the people of Boston for what I did...I disappointed a lot of people. I could have called police the moment I suspected it was Dzhokhar. At that moment I saw that one of my friends was alleged bomber, but I didn't know if it was true or not. I've seen how much it hurts my mom, worrying and stressing over her son, this pains me deeply. To my dad...I feel like I let him down...I could have been a better son, a better brother. I hope when I get out I can make him proud of me. I know my age is no excuse for what I did." Tazhayakov seemed to be fighting back tears as he said to his family, *"I love you guys. My parents taught me to do the right thing...to be a law-abiding citizen. I don't support a terrorist. I don't support any Muslim radicalism, it just makes me sick what Dzhokhar did on April 15th. I hope judge; you will find the time I served sufficient punishment. Thank you."* – Azamat Tazhayakov

Apologizes 🐦 *tweeted by NECN's Alysha Palumbo and WBZ News Radio's Carl Stevens*

IT WAS HIS REMORSELESS and unemotional response that gave him the death penalty, but, he did apologize to the victims and said the words that he so longed to say. Dzhokhar once tweeted on November 9, 2012, *"People that don't know how to apologize will be sorry one day."* How ironic it was that he was planning to do just that. Many people thought he would never apologize, never say he was sorry. However, after two years later, he was ready to apologize emotionally to the people he had hurt. A paper sat in front of him on the table when he returned from lunch. His guards uncuffed him and he sat at the table. He picked up the paper and began memorizing his speech. *"I am sorry..."* he read to himself.

Judy and Miriam read it over, made a couple of changes and told him to rehearse the confessed script. Pretty much what was written in the apology was close to his heart. He shared with his victims his thankfulness, his expression of fault and accepted responsibility, and his Islamic beliefs. It was the month of Ramadan and he was fasting. He was famished; however, this apology was far more important, and it could a leave an impression about him on others.

However, would his victims believe in his sincere words? No matter if Dzhokhar smiled, laughed in court or cried for his family, or had tears in his eyes, his victims would never be satisfied because it was difficult to see his true sincerity in all that. This trial was never about him, it was to achieve justice for the victims.

In Chapter 23, "Should We Kill Dzhokhar Tsarnaev?" it was mentioned up to that time Dzhokhar had shown no remorse. A terrorist or jihadist would never show remorse because his murderous acts were a righteous deed done in the name of Allah. If he showed remorse it would be taken as a sign of weakness. Sister Helen Prejean in Chapter 37 observed that she felt Dzhokhar was genuinely sorry for what he had done. To put it this way, terrorists or Jihadists do not apologize for their acts or their committed crimes. They are never sorry for killing infidels or innocents. They are always proud, defiant and unapologetic of what they've done. So, was Dzhokhar experiencing a change of heart? He would be going against everything a jihadist believed if he formally apologized for his actions and showed true repentance. On the boat, he wrote, "I don't like killing innocent people"; this seemed to show he experienced some remorse. He had even prayed for his victims.

Judy admitted that no jihadist would ever expressed such remorse to a nun. The court never heard most of the conversation that took place between Dzhokhar and Sister Prejean because the government blocked it, blocking the most crucial evidence demonstrating his remorse and repentance.

In his heart, he had never wanted to hurt anybody, and it pained him to see his victims suffer. Dzhokhar had been influenced by his older brother, Tamerlan. He had been brainwashed. He had obeyed Tamerlan. He had never been defiant to Tamerlan. Even his lawyers believed he never showed defiance, but utter compliance. He became a believer only because of his brother's influence. He went willingly along with his brother for the ride.

During his college years, he worried a lot about his own family, parents and relatives. He cared about people who no longer were there to support him. He struggled to pay his way through college, financed by his own scholarship. Dzhokhar wrote, *"This year I lost too many of my loved relatives. I was unable to cope with the stress and maintain school work. My relatives live in Chechnya, Russia."* Dzhokhar missed his parents and became disheartened in school. He struggled in life, to keep going to school and to maintain good grades. *"People come into your life to help you, hurt you, love you and leave you and that shapes your character and the person you were meant to be,"* he shared in a tweet a month before the bombings. The character of a lost boy had been shattered. He had now become a murderer. He had also been labelled the "invisible kid." No one knew he was really a lost, hurt, and depressed teenager. Wrong decisions and actions now haunted him, and he faced a dismal end – death. Juror 83, who wrote a book about his own experience about the trial shared about Tsarnaev, *"I kind of saw him as a disheveled, frail sort of person. He definitely looked like a kid who was existentially lost."*[206] Juror 83 admitted he would have changed his vote if he had known that the Richards were opposed to the death penalty.

When Dzhokhar first appeared to the public before his trial, Judy touched him gently on the shoulder in a sympathetic gesture. She asked prosecutor Weinreb, *"At what possibility of this trial that could end in a death sentence?"* Upon hearing the words *"death,"* Dzhokhar appeared to freak out. He seemed to be afraid that he would be executed for his crimes. He had always been referred to as the *"the lost puppy following his brother."*

The government wanted him to take full responsibility for his actions. But, what if he had wanted to die, a martyr? That is a whole different story and we don't know how he felt.

It was the images of dead Muslim children on his brother's computer that had fueled his anger. Tamerlan was obsessive over this fact and had seen photos of many children that were suffering, injured, naked or dying. They were his people. *"We Muslims are one body, you hurt one you hurt us all."* Dzhokhar recalled this when his attorney William Fick played a video for the jurors. It showed battle scenes, masked men in the forest, a jihad flag waving and a Muslim child being hit by a mortar bomb. This Muslim child was thrown into the air like the Boston bombing victims. This child was vulnerable to the bomb and so was little Martin. The prosecutors accused him of targeting children and he had allegedly targeted in them in retaliation, because of what U.S. had done to Muslim children during the war. From the teachings of al-Awlaki, he had been brainwashed to kill the enemies of jihad. After these images from his brother's computer finished playing, Dzhokhar had placed his right hand over his heart. Had he felt grief for the innocents who perished in these wars and did he now feel sadness and empathy for the bombing victims on Boylston Street? He must have realized they were not his enemies but were innocents too. He had heard how each of them suffered and died. He felt so sorry for the collateral damage that resulted from the bombings that he admitted to Sister Prejean, *'Nobody deserves to suffer like they did.'* His lawyers had given us a hint that Dzhokhar had changed. They stated in the Defense closing two years later after the bombings, that Dzhokhar was not the *"same angry man"* who had scrawled the message, *"I can't stand to see such evil go unpunished,"* ... *"I don't like killing people...but...it is allowed,"* on the boat. The note confirmed he had no regrets for his victims, but had he truly changed? Had he turned away from the radical Islam? Had he matured, and finally started the walk on the path towards repentance?

After lunch, the bombing victims, survivors and their families returned to the courtroom. Judge O'Toole and the jury arrived. Jahar sat calmly with his hands folded at the defense table listening to his attorney. Judy stood up to address the court. Palumbo tweeted, *"Clarke says much has been made of the perception that Tsarnaev lacks emotion. She says he will speak."* Although the government, the victims and the jurors all accused Dzhokhar for his lack of remorse, his lawyers defended him certifying that he did actually feel remorse and was sorry for his actions.

WHY DID DZHOKHAR NOT APOLOGIZE BEFORE THE TRIAL?

Why did Dzhokhar not apologize at his arraignment or after his arrest? Why did he not apologize sooner? Why now? Was it too late for an apology? Judy Clarke explained to the court how Tsarnaev in 2013 had prepared a statement of remorse/apology in return for a plea bargain with the government, but the government had rejected the offer. He had tried to apologize earlier. Palumbo tweeted, *"Clarke says it should be noted Tsarnaev was willing to 'resolve this' without going to trial."* However, the government declined all offers because they wanted to secure a death sentence for Tsarnaev. In these following tweets, Judy explained:

"Clarke says she wants to clarify for the court that Tsarnaev offered to settle without a trial and with a letter of apology in 2013," – Whitehouse.

"Clarke says Tsarnaev offered to plead guilty for a life sentence in October 2013, but government wouldn't take death off the table," – Bailey.

"Defense Attorney Judy Clarke tells court Tsarnaev offered to plead guilty and apologize in Jan. 2014. U.S. rejected," – Lawrence.

A series of rejections from the government could likely have made Mr. Tsarnaev indifferent to the trial proceedings. He had been willing to accept responsibility from the very beginning. He had also prepared an apology letter to the government; however, the government had power to rebuff his apology because these brothers had brutally murdered and maimed people and deserved no mercy.

The government sought absolute justice for their victims. Another reason why the government had refused the pleas deal might have been to set an example for other future terrorists inspired to carry out similar criminal acts.

Next, Judy discussed how Mr. Tsarnaev would pay victim restitution while in prison. If he was to make amends or work in prison, his lawyers asked that restitution be based on the limited wages he would earn at the prison. As Judy talked, Jahar began *"fidgeting with his shirt and pants a bit. A small piece of paper sits in front of him on the table,"* – Bailey. Jahar was nervous and was seen mentally preparing for his speech.

Lastly, Judy addressed Mr. Tsarnaev's execution and argued that his execution be closer to his victims (keep case localized) at a New Hampshire prison site. New Hampshire is the closest state to Massachusetts and she asked to move his execution there since the state has the death penalty. Judge O'Toole declined the proposition, and discussed that "Terre Haute, Indiana is where he will likely go," and is where federal death row inmates are housed and put to death – Whitehouse.

It was an unpleasant record for Judy Clarke's career. This was her first death penalty client. She *"didn't have a clean answer"* as to how Jahar who had never been arrested could have done it.[207] Judy was done talking and gave the microphone to Jahar.

Jahar stood up. This would be the first time anyone in the court would hear him speak. Jahar broke his two years of silence and it was his final opportunity to express his sympathy to the victims, survivors and their families. He was nervous, and he could not stare at them still. He could only glance up at them occasionally. Finally, with everyone leaning on the edge of their seats, ready to listen, the silent, lone bomber nervously spoke softly into the microphone…

"Thank you, your Honor, for giving me an opportunity to speak. I would like to begin in the name of Allah, the exalted and glorious, the most gracious, the most merciful, "Allah" among the most beautiful names."

Reporter Bailey described his voice: *"His voice is shaky and clears his throat. Tsarnaev sounded incredibly young. Soft voice with slight accent. He seemed nervous and emotional. Did not look back at victims as he apologized."* Islam does not believe in forgiveness without having regret. Jahar spoke without notes…he continued,

"Any act that does not begin in the name of God is separate from goodness. This is the blessed month of Ramadan, and it is the month of mercy from Allah to his creation, a month to ask forgiveness of Allah and of his creation, a month to express gratitude to Allah and to his creation. It's the month of reconciliation, a month of patience, a month during which hearts change."

Jahar talked quietly and as he confessed he began asking for Allah's mercy and forgiveness because he knew he would face judgment before Allah. This was the month to make a settlement, to be reconciled to God. He gave thanks to Allah. His victims sitting in the gallery strained to hear him. He had such a low gentle voice, with a slight "affected" Russian/Arabic accent. *"Tsarnaev is hard to hear, speaking in deeply religious terms,"*– Wen. Victims tilted their heads to listen to him. He continued again…

"Indeed, a month of many blessings. The Prophet Muhammad, peace and blessings be upon him, said if you have not thanked the people, you have not thanked God. So I would like to first thank my attorneys, those who sit

at this table, the table behind me, and many more behind the scenes. They have done much good for me, for my family. They made my life the last two years very easy. I cherish their company. They're lovely companions. I thank you. I would like to thank those who took time out of their daily lives to come and testify on my behalf despite the pressure. I'd like to thank the jury for their service, and the Court. The Prophet Muhammad, peace and blessings be upon him, said that if you do not -- if you are not merciful to Allah's creation, Allah will not be merciful to you, so I'd like to now apologize to the victims, to the survivors."

Jahar's voice became emotional. He paused. There was pain in his voice like the nun had claimed. *"Immediately after the bombing, which I am guilty of –"*

Overwhelmed by emotion, Jahar choked up. He had been condemned and punished. Humiliated and mocked. He fought back the urge to cry but lost the battle and began crying.[208] His voice was shaky when he spoke. *"If there's any lingering doubt about that, let there be no more. I did do it along with my brother –"*

Jahar added tearfully. He paused again and trembled. He wiped his eyes. He calmly admitted his guilt that he was partners with Tamerlan when they committed the bombings. He assured his victims that he had heard their pain when they testified about their sufferings. Jahar could not peer up to see their faces in the courtroom, but, his voice quavered with emotion,
"I learned of some of the victims. I learned their names, their faces, their age. And throughout this trial more of those victims were given names, more of those victims had faces, and they had burdened souls…"

Tweets: **Garrett Quinn@Garrett Quinn June 24**
"Immediately after the bombing, of which I am guilty of, there is little doubt about that. I learned their faces, their names." He's crying.
Retweets 99, Favorites 39

Holly Bailey account@hollybdc June 24
"I would like to now apologize to the victims to
the survivors." #Tsarnaev says. He chokes up.
Retweets 84, Favorites 38

Jahar paused a lot and tried very hard to remain poised throughout his speech. He was somber as he showed some remorse. *"I ask Allah to have mercy…"* He paused to clear his throat.

"Tsarnaev in apologizing was very nervous. He stood and spoke slightly in a thick accent. His arms shook. His body weaved back and forth…," – Serrano.

When Jahar finished the four-minute speech, the courtroom was *"silent and full of emotion,"* – Cullen. His apology surprised everyone. The Forewoman who presided over the jury and sentenced Tsarnaev to death wiped a tear from her eye. Denise Richard sitting in the gallery sighed and bowed her head. Jahar sat down and Judy and Miriam both rubbed his back or shoulders. Reporter Palumbo tweeted, *"The courtroom was completely silent as Jahar spoke quietly. Some survivors are now wiping away tears."*

Immediately after the sentencing, Dzhokhar's caring educator and teacher, Ms. Becki Norris tweeted this message, *"Dzhokhar apologized today, to his victims and to their survivors. He also said, crying, "Immediately after the bombing, of which I am guilty, there's little doubt about that…I learned their faces, their names."* Norris commented, *"I am so glad he has taken responsibility."*

Remembering Dzhokhar Tsarnaev

*"Whenever your name is mentioned, what will be remembered is the
evil that you have done. No one will remember that your teachers
were fond of you...that your friends found you funny...that you were
a talented athlete. What will be remembered is that you murdered and
maimed innocent people, and you did it willfully and intentionally."*
– Judge O'Toole

FOR A FEW SECONDS, the court was utterly quiet.
Everyone sat stunned. There was an eerie silence. No one expected
the killer to speak at all, and if he did speak, they feared he would
say political words that would magnify the pain his victims were
already feeling. Many people had mixed reviews regarding his
apology and doubted its sincerity. They said he threw in a lot of
"Allah" references and felt his words were empty, void of true
emotion and remorse.   The government stated that he did not
openly denounce terrorism or Islamic extremism in his apology. His
apology would also not affect his future appeals.

Survivors complained that Mr. Tsarnaev appeared to have
shown no remorse, no regret and no empathy at all.[209] They still felt
it wasn't there...and that it was already too late. (The survivors
needed to understand that Mr. Tsarnaev had been in solitary
confinement and it had blocked his senses and made him
unemotional.) Many survivors were not moved by Tsarnaev's
apology (thought his words rang "hollow" and it was like an
"Oscar" style speech.)[210] and after hearing him for the first time,
they were not ready to forgive him. Nevertheless, no apology could
ever satisfy or appease the survivors. But, some people accepted his
apology. One young surviving victim, Henry Borgard, said he had
quickly forgiven Mr. Tsarnaev. He shared, "For me to say he is
sorry that is enough for me" and commented that the defendant
was only a couple years younger than he was.

People who had wholeheartedly supported the surviving victims throughout their sufferings reacted to Tsarnaev's apology and called him *"a coward," "a creep,"* and a *"little bitch trying to escape his fate"* who should had kept his mouth shut. No one had expected a shred of sincerity from him and they believed he had been lying. Even though people did not hear the words they wanted him to say, Dzhokhar had gained nothing by saying he was sorry. In the end, he was still sentenced to death.

Mr. Tsarnaev had been caught by surprise by the death sentence and it might explain why he had been crying or in tears during his apology. Not many reporters had picked up on that detail; it was almost like the nurse who saw Dzhokhar crying in the hospital, but it was an unconfirmed incident. Perhaps he had almost cried and was on the *"brink of tears."*[211] A couple reporters had clearly seen him *"crying"* and *"choked up"* with tears in his eyes and reported that he had *"tearfully apologized."* Dzhokhar also appeared both emotional and nervous. He did carry feelings of remorse for his actions. He had choked up badly right when he was about to apologize to the victims. Even when he had cried a bit, it had not been enough for the victims to acknowledge him. They had been expecting a little bit more from him. However, it still must have been hard for him to speak in front of his victims. He should have been given credit for that at least.

Others believed his apology was sincere. They felt sorry for him and that he was now seen as a broken young man. His apology revealed that he understood the terrible things he had done to his victims. Furthermore, it showed he had matured and was making progress toward reaching morality. His speech was quite eloquent and intelligent. It was spiritual like a prayer.

Judge O'Toole turned his attention to the jurors and thanked them for their service. *"I invited the jurors to attend today and many accepted my invitation,"* – Armstrong.

The Judge spoke about the death sentence verdict Tsarnaev had received. Regarding the jury's decision, he said, *"Theirs was not the only possible verdict but it was certainly a rational one based on the evidence,"* – Palumbo. *"Their careful verdict satisfies me that they did their duty. The proof was in the pudding,"* – Cullen.

The Judge turned away from the jurors and laid eyes on Mr. Tsarnaev. Jahar stood still, his head hung. Jahar felt the Judge eyeing him but would not look up to meet his gaze. Judge O'Toole regarded all the victims and the survivors and their families in the gallery. For three months they sat in this courtroom listening to horrific testimonies and had viewed gut-wrenching images and videos of bloody, disfigured victims lying on pavement sidewalks that had turned hot after the explosion, and were littered with ball bearings, nails, shrapnel, blood, and debris. What could the Judge say to the defendant who had committed this evil and monstrous crime? The Judge only had harsh words for Jahar.

Judge O'Toole turned his attention back to Mr. Tsarnaev, the convicted bomber. He said to the court, *"I can't stop looking at Mr. Tsarnaev, who just openly admitted what he and his brother did, and apologized for it,"* – Armstrong. The Judge had been so moved by this case. He said, *"This was an extraordinary case. Those of us who sat through this, from beginning to end, heard things they will never forget, good and bad,"* – Valencia. *"We will never forget the victims of these crimes. Their courage throughout their extended ordeal was exemplary. We will all remember the heroes and there were many…after the explosions people in the crowd responded immediately to help where they could,"* – Palumbo.

The Judge continued, *"What I will never forget is how after the tragic events unfolded, victims…worried about somebody else,"* – Boeri. He recalled the help and rescue from police, first responders, EMT's and civilians who had all come selflessly to the aid of the injured.

There were many stories to recount. He thanked the victims and survivors for their courage to speak and share their incredible stories of survival during the trial. The Judge quoted Shakespeare: *"'the evil that men do lives after them.' The good is oft interred with their bones." So it will be for Dzhokhar Tsarnaev."*

Now, Judge O'Toole addressed Mr. Tsarnaev. Jahar stared forward, his head tilted down.

"Whenever your name is mentioned, what will be remembered is the evil you have done. No one will remember that your teachers were fond of you. No one will mention that your friends found you funny and fun to be with. No one will say you were a talented athlete or that you displayed compassion in being a Best Buddy or that you showed more respect to your women friends than your male peers did. What will be remembered is that you murdered and maimed innocent people and that you did it willfully and intentionally. You did it on purpose.

You tried to justify it to yourself by redefining what it is to be an innocent person so that you could convince yourself that Martin Richard was not innocent, that Lingzi Lu was not innocent, and the same for Krystle Campbell and Sean Collier and, therefore, they could be, should be killed. It was a monstrous self-deception. To accomplish it, you had to redefine yourself as well. You had to forget your own humanity, the common humanity that you shared with your brother Martin and your sister Lingzi.

It appears that you and your brother both did so under the influence of the preaching of Anwar al-Awlaki and others like him. It is tragic, for your victims and now for you, that you succumbed to that diabolical siren song. Such men are not leaders but misleaders. They induced you not to a path to glory but to a judgment of condemnation.

In Verdi's opera Otello, the evil Iago tries to justify his malice. "Credo in un Dio crudel," he sings. "I believe in a cruel god." Surely someone who believes that God smiles on and rewards the deliberate killing and maiming of innocents believes in a cruel god. That is not, it cannot be, the god of Islam. Anyone who has been led to believe otherwise has been maliciously and woefully deceived."[212]

Judge O'Toole paused in his address and concluded his remarks, *"Mr. Tsarnaev, if you would stand."* Jahar stood up with his lawyers. With his head bowed, he clenched his hands. *"It is my duty to impose the sentence that the jury has voted for… I sentence you to the penalty of death by execution. On other counts, I sentence you to life in prison,"* – Cullen. The Judge also told him he had the right to appeal both the conviction and the sentence. Wen tweeted, *"Tsarnaev shows no emotion as he stands, his hands crossed in front of him."* Dzhokhar had received six death sentences and twenty non–capital counts to life in prison without the possibility of release. Judy and Miriam talked with the Judge and asked him to identify the jurors who had attended the sentence, but the Judge rejected the request. When Jahar sat down, he *"drops tiredly into his chair,"* – (Sweet) and bowed his head in a gesture of acceptance and defeat.

At the end of his sentencing, U.S. Marshals arrived with the *"clink"*, *"clink"* sounds of the handcuffs. Jahar surrendered himself and they handcuffed him from behind in front of everyone in the courtroom. Judy and Miriam, his maternal cloak sadly gazed at their client one last time. Jahar never turned and glanced back at them, not even uttering a word of goodbye. He looked at no one and acknowledged no one as he slipped out the door, leaving the world behind. As he walked out the door, he felt vulnerable. Everything was being taken away from him. He would have nothing but his faith to sustain him and keep him alive. His fate had been sealed. He would face endless days of complete isolation in a cement tomb for the rest of his life. There would be nothing but his internal thoughts to keep him company…

Laurel J. Sweet@ Laurel_Sweet
#Tsarnaev, who turns 22 next month, will be the youngest condemned man on federal death row.

7:53 AM – 24 June 15

AILEEN'S CLOSING THOUGHTS AND REMARKS

Although his execution will be decades away, his life is over. Society says those with the death penalty are irredeemable and we are not to give them the least bit of sympathy or compassion. The condemned should pay for their crimes and live a life filled with regret and remorse.

Dzhokhar had difficulty expressing remorse, but he at least did have remorse. His whole life is currently being spent behind bars. He was young, but he knew what he was doing. He was old enough to make decisions, but still immature in my opinion. I don't know whether to say his apology was sincere. But, I think he was sorry for the pain he had caused on everyone, because when he cried through his Aunt Patimat's testimony, it reflected his own guilt and how his negative actions/decisions had affected others including the survivors. I would have liked to hear him say more about his regret and how he has changed since the bombings. He may still hold onto his radical beliefs because he did not say he was wrong. I think he expected the death penalty.

Terrorism has become more prevalent and widespread and for us to understand it, we could learn from Dzhokhar about his Jihadist mindset and gain insight into his consciousness. Personally, I think he needs help. From my research, I believe he was a lost person who was influenced by his brother and taken down the wrong path too young in his life. He believed in it, thought killing was okay and was cool about it…and hid it in his heart. He had no one to stop him. He did not have a good adult role model to discipline him. His parents were not physically there to support him when he was failing.

Dzhokhar had been brainwashed by Anwar al-Awlaki like many other young men, but, he can still be redeemed rather than being labeled only as a wasted non-human being who should no longer breathe... Rebekah DiMartino said, *"He's completely wasted what could have been a beautiful life,"* but, only if he knew what could change him. That's why we pray for him. I pray that he does something positive in his life...in prison. Someday, Dzhokhar will face death and the penalty (or punishment) imposed on him that he so deserved...but will this bring closure to the victims who died and to the victims and family members who survived the tragedy.

Dzhokhar prayed for his victims and he asked Allah to bestow mercy upon his victims. Dzhokhar knew his crime was not merciful to Allah's creation, thus Allah would not be merciful to him. He had murdered innocents. He had hurt them and saw them suffer. As the Judge pointed out, he said if Dzhokhar believes his god of Islam smiles upon killing innocents, such a god would be a cruel god, and that was not the god of Islam. Dzhokhar must have realized his heinous actions were rooted in Tamerlan's obsessive hatred of America and that he will now lose his life over it, consequently he felt the need to apologize.

Dzhokhar has grown up and is moving on the right path towards remorse. We hope that people will never forget his words, "I am sorry..." but sadly there are people who don't care about what has said. Why couldn't he have shown remorse earlier during all those victims' testimonies? I don't know why but his lawyers may have advised him to remain unemotional. His lawyers may have helped him write his apology statement, then later they could work on his appeals and ask for a new trial.

Following the trial, Judy Clarke, flew back home to San Diego where she received a warm standing ovation. She was honored with a lifetime award for her service to the courts and criminal justice. Judy was awarded with the "John Frank Award" at a "U.S. 9th Circuit Judicial Conference" in July 2015.

Judy Clarke, the death penalty lawyer said, *"For the last 20 years, I have come face to face with the machinery of death. And that experience has caused me to hope that in my lifetime, or certainly in the lifetime of the youngster I just finished defending at a trial in Boston, that the remaining 31 states in this country will wipe the death penalty off its books."* She went on to comment, *"Or that Congress or the United States Supreme Court can begin to see the death penalty as I have learned it up close and personal – arbitrary, barbaric and an international embarrassment – and remove it from our lives."*[213] Judy was devastated and sad to lose her client, Dzhokhar, whom she considers a "youngster," a child. She had never experienced a defeat in a death penalty case, so she *"suffered and had to pick herself up."*[214] When she met Dzhokhar for the first time, she told him she was going to defend him. Judy has no children of her own. She attends to her clients, especially Dzhokhar as her own children. She cares for him.

Dzhokhar will grow up in prison alone. He is an outcast in our society. It's hard to love those who we feel are undeserving of love. However, he is still a human being. He may feel he is so broken, but he still needs mercy, love and forgiveness. As Christians, we are instructed to love our enemy. Therefore, we must love Dzhokhar and desire the best for him. To love Dzhokhar is to pray for him and to have compassion for him. Someday, we hope he will be drawn to our God's narrative story and find our Lord in prison. Even though, it seems he has turned away from Him. Yet, our God loves him. We must continue to pray that he will see the light (Christ's love) and to have a purposeful life come out of this tragedy. We pray for him that he may listen or read about the gospel. We know he has been witnessed to and he probably knows the gospel.

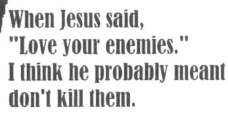

When Jesus said, "Love your enemies." I think he probably meant don't kill them.

Dzhokhar's lawyer, Judy was raised in a conservative family who attended church every Sunday. Judy's compassion for Dzhokhar went far beyond others that she invited Sister Helen Prejean to meet with him during the trial. We read that Sister Prejean and Dzhokhar had a meaningful conversation with each other talking about Islam and Catholicism. We pray that a chaplain or a jail minister could meet with him and share with him the love of Christ. Pray that he will have visions and dreams of seeing Jesus as some Muslims proclaimed to have seen. He watched the video *"Muslim has supernatural experience with Jesus,"* while he was reading all the jihad magazines. Pray that Dzhokhar will open his eyes to see the Truth and realize that there is a God in the universe who does not desire to make him his slave. There is a Father who loves him as his own child, who seeks a personal and loving relationship with him.

Dzhokhar already has reached a point where he is spiritually hungry to know more about Islam. He is a devout Muslim because he wants to be on the right path. He may have asked Allah for forgiveness. However, it would be a huge deal if he could come to know about God's grace and Christ's forgiveness of sins for him. Only he can take that step of faith in Christ, to have his sins be pardoned through Jesus' blood and righteousness.

When Judge O'Toole addressed Dzhokhar at the end of sentencing, he told him that whenever his name is mentioned, people will remember him for the bombings. He will always be remembered for the murders and for the maiming of innocent people. The Judge believes he will not be remembered for the good things he has done. The Judge forgot that our God will never forget or abandon Dzhokhar.

God miraculously spared him from getting killed from a hundred bullets on that night in the boat, therefore he could come to face-to-face with his surviving victims. It happened so he could see and hear their cries, their pains and loss. And consequently, he could receive justice, accept responsibility, and contend with the death sentence...and come to grips with eternal death.

Our God never forgets Dzhokhar and knows what is best for him...to come to Him. God loves him so much that many brothers and sisters in Christ have adopted him and pray for his salvation. If you feel led to pray for him, visit the online website devoted to Dzhokhar. You can read the past blogs.

Website: Christians For Jahar: https://christians4jahar.wordpress.com/

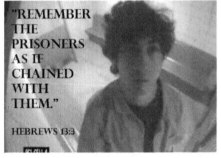

And at Adopt-A-Terrorist at https://atfp.org/adopt/terrorist/dzhokhar-tsarnaev/

"REMEMBER THE PRISONERS AS IF CHAINED WITH THEM."

HEBREWS 13:3

May it be your prayer to adopt Dzhokhar and pray for him daily, to see this precious, lost soul be saved by God's redeeming grace. Dzhokhar needs a lifetime of prayers and unending hope before his time comes. There are other people to pray for like his family and friends.

What will you remember about Dzhokhar Tsarnaev when his name is mentioned? We will remember him as Bomber #2 and for his horrific crimes, but there is an article online called, *"Dzhokhar Tsarnaev's Remorse Changes the Story, If We Let It,"* written by Amée La Tour. She hoped Tsarnaev would be able to do something positive in his life if he was given a chance.

She wrote, *"Tsarnaev's crimes can't be undone, but remorse that twist in events could change the course of his story.... I hope that he won't accept the judge's verdict on the sum of his life. I hope Dzhokhar Tsarnaev will make an effort to put the cautionary power of his remorse to use, aiming it at would-be fundamentalists.*

And I hope others will remember the full story: his corruption by fanaticism, the surety with which it drove him to inhumanity and the return of humanity once he was confronted with the names and faces of the fellow human beings he murdered and maimed."[215]

In that same article there appeared an interesting tweet. The source is unknown. It said, *"I'll remember Tsarnaev's pre-terror goodness and his post-terror remorse."* Yes, that should be our memory of him. The bombing was the bad, immoral part in his life, but Dzhokhar was once full of goodness and remorse. We hope he will live a full life in prison and during his suffering, he will find God's love in the darkest of places. I will be returning to Dzhokhar's story and his full apology statement. I really don't know what happened to Dzhokhar after his sentencing, but I know he was later transferred to ADX. I believe he was observing Ramadan and praying there. I'll end his story from the writer's imagination; it's fictionalized and conceived from his apology. Furthermore, there will be a few tweets from reporters that will show Dzhokhar was watching and listening; he was definitely paying attention.

I will bring you pictures depicting his youth and innocence, his achievements, his ordinary life as a college student and brother. These photos were discovered from *Tumblr* that showed Dzhokhar's pre-terror days, containing good memories of him. I don't know who posted these pictures, but it was such a delight to see photos of a young lively Dzhokhar. Yet, it was also sad to see a life full of potential end too soon because he chose to go down an evil and dangerous path. Lastly, I am not implying that Dzhokhar was innocent. People like him are unforgivable. However, will you consider praying for him? Many years from now, he will not be the same person who bombed the marathon.

DZHOKHAR'S APOLOGY AND REMORSE

Immediately after the sentencing, Dzhokhar Tsarnaev left the prison in Devens on June 25, 2015. He was flown from Worchester and westward across the country to ADX Florence in Colorado. After a couple weeks at the U.S. Penitentiary in the Florence federal prison, he was transferred to ADX Supermax, the high security prison facility also in Florence. He will call ADX home for now. It was a place where the worst criminals are housed. Eventually, Dzhokhar will be moved to Terre Haute, Indiana where he will be on death row.[216]

Dzhokhar walked down to the H-Unit area with the guards. There were cameras everywhere they turned…and dull gray walls. He moved slowly and tiredly. The iron shackles around his legs and wrists were unbearable like weights. *"Clink, clink, clink,"* clanged the chains on his legs as he walked.

The guards had wrapped a chain around his skinny waistline and he felt trapped inside. Thoughts went through his mind. *'I will live in solitary confinement for the rest of my life until I die. What is the meaning of my life now?'* Dzhokhar cried out to Allah and he felt a touch. He felt Allah had saved him for a greater purpose that will be revealed to him in heaven.

Allah bestowed upon him an undying energy to learn all he can about Islam. This became his new desire. A list of suggested books about Islam might be sent to him for his reading. (Some books are about the benevolence of Islam, books that renounce violence and promote humanity for others, and books about teaching Muslims how to pray. There are books about healing the broken heart and mind, and about cleansing the soul and body from sins.) Dzhokhar's eyes will now focus to worship Allah and to make amends for his actions. He will strive to live his life on the right path until death so that he will be reunited with his family in the Hereafter.

The guards took Dzhokhar to his tiny prison cell and released him. Alone in his cell he prepared to make himself at home. He set down a box of his personal belongings on a small immovable concrete desk in the corner. The box was filled with letters from his Mom and Dad from Dagestan. His sad dark brown eyes scanned the gray concrete walls and all the corners of the cell.

A small four-inch narrow window on one side of the wall overlooked out into the concrete courtyard where he will do his exercises. He sat on his hard-concrete bed and felt the soft thin mattress. He checked out the toilet–sink unit and fiddled with the sink knobs, pressing the button for water.

He washed his hands from the tip of his fingers to the wrists. He began washing his scruffy beard, face and feet. Above the sink he saw himself in a mirror on the wall. He hadn't had a haircut in five months. His hair had grown thicker, wavier and longer.

Dzhokhar rolled out his prayer rug and stood on it. He chanted. Dzhokhar performed the ritual afternoon prayer. Suddenly, his memory took him back to the courtroom. He saw himself standing in the room addressing the court. He had worn a dark sports jacket.

Deep inside himself he felt he had become a different person. He was not like the old Jahar who was shy of public speaking. Although he had been nervous, he had been prepared to talk. He cleared his throat and had said softly…

"Thank you, your Honor, for giving me an opportunity to speak. I would like to begin in the name of Allah, the exalted and glorious, the most gracious, the most merciful, "Allah" among the most beautiful names."

Dzhokhar remembered how hard it had been for him to see all the people in the room. He tried to remember every word he had written down…

"Any act that does not begin in the name of God is separate from goodness. This is the blessed month of Ramadan, and it is the month of mercy from Allah to his creation, a month to ask forgiveness of Allah and of his

creation, a month to express gratitude to Allah and to his creation. It's the month of reconciliation, a month of patience, a month during which hearts change. Indeed, a month of many blessings. The Prophet Muhammad, peace and blessings be upon him, said if you have not thanked the people, you have not thanked God."

In his cell, Dzhokhar bowed and prayed. Images and feelings tumbled again in his mind as he thought about his trial. The end of the long road stopped here, but this was only the beginning. There was no plan in his life, only a sustained torment that continued to echo. Dzhokhar searched for hope in this empty place. He longed for memories...an array of good memories. He remembered the fond moments he had with his attorneys: There was Miriam's sunny smile, her pep talks and her giggles. Judy's warm smile would make his day, her counseled advice, her laugh and her comforting hand rubbing his back. There was his other attorney, David Bruck, whom he enjoyed chatting with. He had spoken in court about them, thanking them. He had said,

"So I would like to first thank my attorneys, those who sit at this table, the table behind me, and many more behind the scenes. They have done much good for me, for my family. They made my life the last two years very easy. I cherish their company. They're lovely companions. I thank you."

Dzhokhar thought about the witnesses who came to testify for him. He will never forget his teachers, Ms. Charner–Lairds' and Ms. Norris' smiles as they talked about how good a student he was. He will never forget his Auntie Patimat's heartbroken sobs, his aunts' and cousins' tears, his friends and Alexa's smiles and cries. He thought about the jurors too. He remembered them from where they had sat: the man with glasses, the young juror who stared at him angrily, the Forewoman, the fashionable juror, the sleepy juror and the Led Zeppelin t–shirt juror. They had made their final choice to sentence him to death. Dzhokhar had thanked them all.

"I would like to thank those who took time out of their daily lives to come and testify on my behalf despite the pressure. I'd like to thank the jury for

their service, and the Court. *The Prophet Muhammad, peace and blessings be upon him, said that if you do not -- if you are not merciful to Allah's creation, Allah will not be merciful to you, so I'd like to now apologize to the victims, to the survivors."*

Dzhokhar spoke sadly with a shaky voice about the victims and his involvement. At that moment, he choked up - and had become reserved, trying to hold back tears. He suddenly felt so sorry for himself. He had not wanted to show such vulnerability. There was no point to it. Yet, he couldn't maintain control. He had been on the brink of tears. He felt no one would care if he was sorry or they perceived him as a wretch. He felt he did not deserve anyone's love or mercy. His life was over. He had brought this upon himself. As he spoke, he began to cry. [217]

Dzhokhar tried to remain calm, giving his apology statement to a room full of survivors who were crying. He had a flashback of Marathon Monday. He was walking behind Tamerlan. Both brothers were carrying heavy pressure cooker bombs inside their backpacks. Then Dzhokhar remembered standing with Tamerlan on Boylston. His brother was giving him orders on what he needed to do as he observed the race. He obeyed his brother and believed in his plan...to drop the bombs in the crowd with a clear intent of killing and injuring spectators.

"Immediately after the bombing, which I am guilty of" he had paused and choked up, *"-- if there's any lingering doubt about that, let there be no more. I did do it along with my brother--"*

Dzhokhar had said sadly, *"I learned of some of the victims. I learned their names, their faces, their age."*

Dzhokhar remembered his victims immediately after the bombings when he was in the hospital. When he admitted his guilt, he learned their names and saw their faces, of those who died and those he injured. He came to realize they all had *"good souls."*

Judge O'Toole said they were his "brothers and sisters in humanity," that his non–Muslim brothers and sisters were human beings and that he took their lives. He will never forget the testimonies of each and what he saw and heard in court.

During one moment in the trial, in the courtroom he glanced up quickly and saw little Martin Richard's tattered bloody clothes including a jersey that had a large hole on the left side. He saw Dr. Nields, the medical examiner opened a packet of six charred nails. *"Tsarnaev watches as Nields opens packet of 6 nails he extracted from boy's wrist,"*– Sweet. He listened intently to the testimony of Martin's parents that day. How could he not watch that chilling video of little Martin dying on the sidewalk, an image he was too ashamed to see. He thought right then there was no way his team will win him a life sentence.

Through Lingzi Lu's testimony, Dzhokhar watched her father's eulogy of her on a video that Boston University had made. *"Tsarnaev appears to be looking in the direction of the video screen in front of him playing this emotional speech,"* – Armstrong. Her father from China spoke in Chinese and a translator interpreted his speech in English. Dzhokhar viewed the monitor screen and listened. Lingzi's father said, *"She yearned for life... Your hometown lit you an everlasting candle, lighting up your path to heaven. There will be no more bombs or terrorist attacks...May you remain as jolly as a little elf in the Heavenly garden."*

At last, there was Krystle Campbell. Dzhokhar listened to Dr. Hammers' autopsy report, describing her injuries in excruciating detail, and he nearly caught an image of her autopsy. *"Jurors are shown photos of Krystle's autopsy, not being shown to Tsarnaev but he looks back at a monitor behind him briefly,"* – Palumbo. He wondered what his lawyers were doing, but he felt Judy's hand on his shoulder and he quickly turned around. He remembered Krystle's mom scolding him at his sentencing, *"You went down the wrong path. I know life is hard,"* she said to him, *"but the choices you made are despicable. What you did to my daughter is disgusting."*

Dzhokhar felt so awful. He prostrated and placed his forehead to the rug on the ground and prayed. There were so many more victims to pray for, including Sean, whom he could not forget. Dzhokhar recalled standing in the courtroom, telling the court his experience of learning all the names of the victims and remembering the handicapped victims who had testified in court. He related to their sufferings because he had been put through so much suffering from his own injuries. He acknowledged the devastation he had caused and said he was sorry. He said to them...

"And throughout this trial more of those victims were given names, more of those victims had faces, and they had burdened souls. Now, all those who got up on that witness stand and that podium related to us –– to me –– I was listening – the suffering that was and the hardship that still is, with strength and with patience and with dignity. Now, Allah says in the Qur'an that no soul is burdened with more than it can bear, and you told us just how unbearable it was, how horrendous it was, this thing I put you through. And I know that you kept that much. I know that there isn't enough time in the day for you to have related to us everything. I also wish that far more people had a chance to get up there, but I took them from you.

Now, I am sorry for the lives that I've taken, for the suffering that I've caused you, for the damage that I've done. Irreparable damage."

Dzhokhar had struggled to remain calm before a room full of victims and survivors. His hands had moved a lot when he spoke. Not glancing at anyone, he had told them he prayed for the souls that he had killed, and he prayed for healing for the survivors.[218] His voice had been soft–spoken and deep. It was not loud like his brother's or his mother's. It was his voice that most of the whole world had not even heard yet, and you know we will never likely hear from him again. Dzhokhar mumbled and prayed to his God, asking Allah to have mercy for his victims. He said to them these last words...

"Now, I am a Muslim. My religion is Islam. The God I worship, besides whom there is no other God, is Allah.

And I prayed for Allah to bestow his mercy upon the deceased, those affected in the bombing and their families. Allah says in the Qur'an that with every hardship there is relief.

I pray for your relief, for your healing, for your well-being, for your strength.

I ask Allah to have mercy upon me and my brother and my family.

I ask Allah to bestow his mercy upon those present here today. And Allah knows best those deserving of his mercy.

And I ask Allah to have mercy upon the ummah of Prophet Muhammad, peace and blessings be upon him. Amin. Praise be to Allah, the Lord of the Worlds. Thank you." [219]

"I am guilty. I did do it..."
"Now, I am sorry for the lives that I've taken, for the suffering that I've caused you, for the damage that I've done. Irreparable damage."

-Dzhokhar Tsarnaev

Photos credit: Associated Press

AFTERWORD

Tsarnaev's lawyers continued to meet with Mr. Tsarnaev, but they want his prison life at the Supermax to remain "private" from the government as they work on his appeals.[220] His lawyers asked for a new trial because they felt Boston was prejudice against Tsarnaev; however, the Judge denied their request. This won't be the last we will hear of him. The case continues...He needs our prayers.

PRAY FOR JAHAR

"Father, You love him. We know You do. Reveal Yourself to Dzhokhar. He said, "I am guilty." May he be made spotless in Your eyes. Bring him hope in the darkest places. Send him the light of Your love."

"Dear Faithful Lord, loving and compassionate Savior – pursue Dzhokhar relentlessly, Your beloved, lost son. People hate him and want him to die. His sin is unforgiveable. We pray for Dzho's heart to seek You. Lord, oh merciful Savior, bring this boy to the Cross. We ask You to soften the hearts of the world toward Jahar. We pray for the world to forgive Jahar for his sins. He needs people with good hearts, who will help him live – but not a life of a worthless criminal. You saw Jahar shed tears. He cries for himself. He is a human being who has seen how he ruined lives. Please Lord, draw near him as he continues to cry out to You and seek You with all of his heart and being. Wrap Your everlasting and loving arms around this broken child. Comfort and bless him with Your joy and peace in that hell hole. Let every person who comes to counsel him be messengers of Your amazing love and truth and may this love open Jahar's eyes to see Your presence everywhere. Now, we ask You to work within his appeals process. Spare Jahar's life, oh Lord. Have mercy upon Your son. Do not give him over to death. Let him live so that his life will be a testimony that will touch the hearts of many others who need a Savior.

In Jesus' name, Amen."

Pictures of Dzhokhar A. Tsarnaev aka "Jahar"

(from Tumblr) (From Toddler to age 19.)

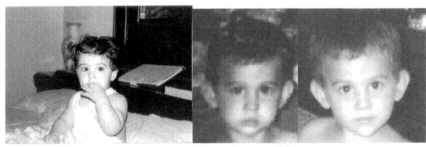

"YouTube" VIDEO TRIBUTES FOR DZHOKHAR

Here are inspiring and emotional videos about Dzhokhar Tsarnaev from supporters around the world.

"MY TRIBUTE TO TAMERLAN AND DZHOKHAR TSARNAEV"

By 19Blackvielbridesfan

https://www.youtube.com/watch?v=nWhjcMlP33s

"THINGS YOU DON'T KNOW ABOUT DZHOKHAR TSARNAEV"

By Justice Jahar

https://www.youtube.com/watch?v=hofyeSIWiCk

"ALL FOR ONE, JAHAR SUPPORTERS"–#FreeJahar Supporters"

By Turkish Malvina

https://www.youtube.com/watch?v=lbgYmyAOa18

"JAHAR'S 20th BIRTHDAY"

By Britt Faahs

https://www.youtube.com/watch?v=ux_R7uxdM8I

"JUSTICE WILL PREVAIL"

By FreeDat1993

https://www.youtube.com/watch?v=4dfx-RuiUCg

"DZHOKHAR TSARNAEV"

By Michelle Perez

https://www.youtube.com/watch?v=NplAK4xv6HQ

"WHAT HAPPENED TO MY CARING BEST FRIEND JAHAR?"

By rasjtna ev

https://www.youtube.com/watch?v=iMNYe7KrPPs

"HAPPY 20th BIRTHDAY JAHAR"

By withadrianna

https://www.youtube.com/watch?v=FMesVUGK5T0

"DJOHAR TSARNAEV"

By Грант Паремузян

https://www.youtube.com/watch?v=6uE1PpbM9ag

"JAHAR AND TAMERLAN TSARNAEV"

By Paula Sofia

https://www.youtube.com/watch?v=1iF5B9SPo6Y

"DZHOKHAR TSARNAEV"

By 19Blackvielbridesfan

https://www.youtube.com/watch?v=dAN8Sk_C3J4

"DON'T GIVE UP ON JAHAR"

By 19Blackvielbridesfan

https://www.youtube.com/watch?v=Rz1_cCYTOUw

"DZHOKHAR TSARNAEV"

By ishuthey

https://www.youtube.com/watch?v=JWm9pcqXAW0

"KEEP HOLDING ON JAHAR!"

By withadrianna

https://www.youtube.com/watch?v=eudLNsaLneU

"DZHOKHAR AND TAMERLAN TSARNAEV"

By MissNoxChiYuSo95

https://www.youtube.com/watch?v=uW1gefkJid8

"FREE JAHAR" (Dzhokhar Tsarnaev) – Supporters"

By freejahar

https://www.youtube.com/watch?v=mX7PH9nZzS4

ABOUT THE AUTHOR

AT THE AGE OF twelve, Aileen wanted to become an author. She has written many poems and was awarded "Editor's Choice" for her poem *"Fire on the Lake"* at the National Poetry Contest in 1995. In addition to writing articles for her church publication, she also has written several published short stories. She worked as a technical writer for a few technical companies from 1996 to 2000. In 1999, she published her first novel, which she considers "a masterpiece." It is a mystery/love story called, *"Under The Rose."* She also has written a couple screenplays. Her first screenplay is *"David and Jonathan Unveiled,"* a sweeping biblical epic story about King David's friendship with Prince Jonathan in 2010. In 2013, she wrote another screenplay about a devout mother and her unbelieving son in *"The Secret Joy Lover."* Her second book, a documentary about Tsarnaev's trial, *"Jahar The Lone Boston Bomber #2"* was a difficult book to write because it was about a person who had committed a crime. Yet, Jahar's story and his monstrous crime inspired her to write and share with others what she learned about him from her research. After BMB documentary, she is working on writing more books.

Visit the author's website.
http://abookaboutjt.wixsite.com/home

CREDITS

Here is a list of Twitter reporters in the courtroom reporting Tsarnaev's Trial. In Federal trials cameras are not allowed to record the proceedings so these reporters became our eyes and gave us information about Mr. Tsarnaev's story and about this case in Boston.

Jim Armstrong@JimArmstrongWBZ – *(Note: Armstrong no longer works at Boston WBZ.)*
Holley Bailey@hollybdc – Yahoo News
David Boeri wbur@wbur
Steve Cooper@scooperon7
Kevin Cullen@GlobeCullen – Boston Globe
Jesse Grossi@producerjesse – Fox 25
Mike Hayes@michaelhayes @BuzzNewsFeed
Lana Jones@Lanawbz
J.M. Lawrence@BostonJustice
Eric Levenson@ejleven
Alysha Palumbo@Alysha@NECN – NECN
Catherine Parrotta@CParrottaFox25
Jared Pliner@JaredPliner
Garrett Quinn@garrettQuinn – Boston Magazine - *(Note: Quinn no longer works at BM).*
Adam Reilly@adamreilly wgbhnews
Jenna Russell@jruss@globe
Hilary Sargent@lilsarg – Boston.com
Rick Serrano@RickSerranoLAT
Carl Stevens@carlwbz –WBZ News radio
Laurel J. Sweet@Laurel_Sweet – Boston Herald
Kelly Tuthill@wcvbkellyt
Bob Ward@bward3 – Fox 25
Gail Waterhouse@gailwaterhouse
Patricia Wen@globepatty – Boston Globe
Milton Valencia@MiltonValencia – Boston Globe

REFERENCES for JAHAR
The Lone Boston Bomber #2:

The Story about Dzhokhar Tsarnaev from his capture to his trial

*A Narrative Researched Documentary about Tsarnaev's Trial
and the Boston Marathon Bombing Case*

**This is the government website of all photos and exhibits from
the Tsarnaev's trial starting from Day 1.)
Website: https://www.justice.gov/usao-ma/tsarnaev-trial-exhibits**

1. *http://fox6now.com/2013/04/21/governor–we–have–a–million–questions–
for–bombing–suspect/*

2. *http://www.wmur.com/news/nh–news/dzhokhar–tsarnaev–sent–text–
messages–after–boston–marathon–bombings/20075866*

3. *https://twitter.com/J_tsar – Dzhokhar Tsarnaev's Twitter account*

4. *http://www.newsmax.com/TheWire/dzhokhar–tsarnaev–mechanic–suspect–
nervous/2013/04/19/id/500385/*

5. *http://www.dailymail.co.uk/news/article–2315718/Boston–Bomber–Twitter–
Dzhokhar–Tsarnaevs–chilling–tweet–sent–just–hours–deadly–attack.html*

6. and 6a. *https://www.youtube.com/watch?v=lgwZdlO4XtI Boston Marathon
Suspect Mother Zubeidat Tsarnaeva*

7.
*http://www.masslive.com/news/boston/index.ssf/2014/05/complete_transcript
_of_dzhokha.html*

8. *http://www.boston.com/metrodesk/2013/04/19/mit–police–officer–sean–
collier–killed–the–line–duty–during–confrontation–with–marathon–bombing
suspects/okOskoWUnFyGB1yQ6CxuBI/story.html*

9. *http://www.newyorker.com/news/daily–comment/the–tsarnaevs–and–the–
carjacking*

10. *http://www.buzzfeed.com/jtes/watertown–police–describe–their–12–
minute–shoot–out–with–the#.atEA8wpbQ*

11 and 12. *http://www.nbcnews.com/storyline/boston–bombing–
anniversary/108–hours–inside–hunt–boston–marathon–bombers–n76956*

13. http://www.washingtonpost.com/local/ruslan–tsarni–uncle–of–boston–marathon–bombing–suspects–denounces–them/2013/04/19/4644d43e–a91b–11e2–8302–3c7e0ea97057_story.html

14. http://www.nydailynews.com/news/national/watertown–man–finds–bomber–holed–boat–article–1.1322387

15. http://www.metro.us/news/anzor–tsarnaev–boston–bombing–suspects–father–says–son–is–angel/tmWmds–––d17vWYFYrmOns/

16. http://www.rollingstone.com/culture/news/jahars–world–20130717

17. http://m.salemnews.com/news/local_news/inside–the–swat–team–search–of–watertown/article_e9e9aba4–35df–5813–a29d–e3d99ab0ef7b.html?mode=jqm

18. – Boston Strong: A City's Triumph over Tragedy by Casey Sherman and Dave Wedge, February 3, 2015, page 197.

19. http://www.bloomberg.com/bw/articles/2013–04–26/how–boston–police–won–the–twitter–wars–during–bomber–hunt

20. http://fox2now.com/2013/04/29/source–dzhokhar–tsarnaev–arrived–at–hospital–covered–in–blood/

21. http://www.theblogmocracy.com/2013/05/20/dzhokhar–jahars–nurses–admit–they–feel–sorry–for–him/#sthash.yeqFMtB6.dpuf

22. http://www.rollingstone.com/culture/news/jahars–world–20130717?page=5

23. http://usnews.nbcnews.com/_news/2013/04/22/17860373–officials–hospitalized–bombing–suspect–says–he–and–brother–acted–alone–motivated–by–religion?lite

24a. http://www.scribd.com/doc/222749570/Doc–295–Motion–to–Suppress–Statements–050714

24b. http://www.dailymail.co.uk/news/article–2622796/Marathon–suspect–Statements–thrown–out.html

25. http://www.nydailynews.com/news/crime/accused–boston–bomber–died–grilled–atty–filings–article–1.1785155

26. http://www.rollingstone.com/culture/news/jahars–world–20130717?page=5

27. http://usnews.nbcnews.com/_news/2013/04/25/17918598–source–bombing–suspect–showed–no–fear–or–remorse–during–hospital–hearing?lite

28a. http://www.npr.org/2013/04/30/180083323/an–intimate–portrait–of–the–tsarnaev–family

28b. http://gardens–of–secrets.tumblr.com/post/65428773624/two–days–later–just–hours–before–the–shootout

29. http://www.rollingstone.com/culture/news/jahars–world–20130717

30. *http://www.dailymail.co.uk/news/article-2312049/Anzor-Tsarnaev-Weeping-father-Boston-bombers-overwhelmed-relief-told-19-year-old-son-captured-alive.html*

31. *Bombing Suspects Mom – America took my kids away – https://www.youtube.com/watch?v=2X_ZguVRoYs*

32. *http://www.cnn.com/2014/08/27/us/tsarnaev-sister-arrested-boston/*

33a. *http://www.cnn.com/2013/04/21/us/tamerlan-tsarnaev-timeline/*

33b. *http://www.vdare.com/posts/tsarnaev-family-and-asylum-fraud*

34. *http://www.rollingstone.com/culture/news/jahars-world-20130717*

35. *http://www.dailymail.co.uk/news/article-2312374/Andrew-Glasby-Friend-younger-Boston-bombing-suspect-Dzhokhar-Tsarnaev-speaks-out.html#ixzz3RMFJMtPv*

36. *http://finance.huanqiu.com/data/2013-04/3854697.html*

37. *http://www.bostonglobe.com/Page/Boston/2011-2020/WebGraphics/Metro/BostonGlobe.com/2013/12/15tsarnaev/tsarnaev.html – Fall of the House of Tsarnaevs –*

38. *http://www.rollingstone.com/culture/news/jahars-world-20130717*

39. *http://lynnfam.com/2013/04/20/trying-to-understand-what-is-not-understandable-dzhokar-tsarmaev/*

40. *http://finance.huanqiu.com/data/2013-04/3854697.html*

41. *http://www.wbur.org/2013/04/20/UMass-Dartmouth-suspect-profile*

42. *http://bluedreameruniverse.tumblr.com/post/51842816208/all-im-saying-is-this-case-is-a-special-variety friends say they cant believe Jahar*

43. *http://newsonia.com/report/friends-of-dzhokhar-tsarnaev-say-that-they-are-in-shock*

44. *https://twitter.com/J_tsar – Dzhokhar Tsarnaev's Twitter account*

45. *http://marathon.neu.edu/wburoralhistoryproject/peter_payack*

46. *http://justice4dzhokhar.tumblr.com/post/53868615755/thisisjohannabax-corresponds-with-the-wound-on*

47. *http://www.cnn.com/2013/05/10/us/virginia-boston-suspect-burial/*

48. and 48a. *http://fox6now.com/2013/06/04/parents-of-boston-bombing-suspect-share-phone-call-with-son/*

49. *http://www.dailymail.co.uk/news/article-2311653/Boston-bombings-Mother-Boston-bombing-suspects-arrested-year-stealing-1-600-worth-clothes-Lord--Taylor.html*

50. *http://www.insideedition.com/headlines/6225-friend-of-dzhokhar-tsarnaev-speaks-out*

51. *https://www.youtube.com/watch?v=BuD4-qu2_CA – Mother Doesn't Believe Sons Were Behind BMB*

52. http://san0670.com/2013/04/25/zubeidat–tsarnaeva–bombers–mom–a–wanted–felon/

53. http://www.reuters.com/article/2014/12/31/us–usa–explosions–boston–idUSKBN0K912Y20141231

54. https://www.naausa.org/2013/index.php/news/naausa-news/130-boston-bombing-prosecution-team

55. http://channel.nationalgeographic.com/inside–the–hunt–for–the–boston–bombers/articles/how–they–identified–the–bombers/

56. https://christians4jahar.wordpress.com/2013/08/11/update–on–jahar–8–10–13/

57. http://www.vanityfair.com/news/2015/03/judy–clarke–dzokhar–tsarnaev–lawyer

58. http://usnews.nbcnews.com/_news/2013/05/01/17986289–tsarnaevs–best–defense–judy–clarke–who–keeps–clients–off–death–row?lite

59. http://www.voanews.com/content/reu–attorneys–for–accused–boston–marathon–bomber–due–in–court/1755244.html

60. https://www.bostonglobe.com/metro/2013/06/27/dzhokhar–tsarnaev–indicted–four–deaths–including–marathon–bombing–victims–and–mit–officer–sean–collier/23vhQHQIk8q1Kl9ZijwtoJ/story.html

61. http://www.bostonglobe.com/Page/Boston/2011–2020/WebGraphics/Metro/BostonGlobe.com/2013/12/15tsarnaev/tsarnaev.html *"Fall of house of Tsarnaev"*

62. http://www.newyorker.com/news/amy–davidson/tsarnaevs–kiss

63. http://www.dailymail.co.uk/news/article–2359218/Fury–Boston–bombers–victims–smirking–suspect–Dzhokhar–Tsarnaev–pleads–NOT–GUILTY.html

64. http://www.scribd.com/doc/221660596/Doc–280–Motion–for–a–Hearing–Re–Leaks–and–Public–Comments–by–LE–050214

65. http://www.boston.com/2013/10/03/dzhokhar–tsarnaev–alleged–marathon–bomber–received–nearly–letters–while–custody–according–attorney–general–filing/jn30BN1IcscKq4gjtXT9TN/story.html

66. https://christians4jahar.wordpress.com/2013/08/04/islamic–literature/

67. http://www.scribd.com/doc/181559783/Doc–138–Reply–to–Govt–Opposition–to–Vacate–SAMS–11042013–pdf

68. http://www.lawfareblog.com/2013/10/tsarnaev–files–motion–to–vacate–special–administrative–measures/

69. http://www.cnn.com/2013/10/02/justice/dzhokhar–tsarnaev–prison–restrictions/

70. http://www.huffingtonpost.com/2014/07/14/azamat–tazhayakov–tsarnaev–friend–trial_n_5584825.html

71. http://www.nydailynews.com/news/national/dzhokhar–tsarnaev–rant–scrawled–boat–article–1.1759675

72. http://www.bostonglobe.com/metro/2013/11/05/tsarnaev–lawyers–say–made–declaration–anticipation–own–death/gIY6dekdhCzJhfD7rkDSlO/story.html

73. http://www.bostonglobe.com/metro/2013/05/23/stark–overtones–waltham–triple–homicide/hooxNuDSCGdQsRNZI30QHK/story.html

74. http://www.bostonglobe.com/metro/2014/03/25/todashev/rt3K7PSMY1ykZiUo DaaiuI/story.html

75. http://thebostonmarathonbombings.weebly.com/more–questions–surround–the–death–of–ibragim–todashev–as–crime–scene–photo–is–leaked.html

76. http://legaltimes.typepad.com/files/dmasstsarnaevdoc144.pdf

77. http://www.wcvb.com/news/local/metro/he–should–be–suffering–more–survivor–says–of–dzhokhar–tsarnaev/22264748–October%2013

78. http://www.ndtv.com/world–news/lawyers–for–accused–boston–bomber–want–more–time–for–venue–motion–544802

79. http://www.huffingtonpost.com/2013/12/01/boston–bombing–death–penalty_n_4367908.html

80. https://www.bostonglobe.com/metro/2015/03/17/with–friends–like–these/rzPjdooY2q8fMXRzyY2VjJ/story.html

81. http://www.thewire.com/national/2013/04/dzhokhar–tsarnaev–dealing drugs/64529/%20"Fall%20Of%20The%20House%20Of%20Tsarnaev"

81a. http://www.bostonglobe.com/Page/Boston/2011–2020/WebGraphics/Metro/BostonGlobe.com/2013/12/15tsarnaev/tsarnaev.html

81b. https://www.youtube.com/watch?v=lt78NlT_rYo – Dzhokhar Tsarnaev the risk–taker, from The Boston Globe

82. https://www.youtube.com/watch?v=qtvoUtRCmus– Boston Bombers Seen at Gym Days Before Attack

83. http://www.rollingstone.com/culture/news/jahars–world–20130717?page=4

84. http://www.dailymail.co.uk/news/article–2312374/Andrew–Glasby–Friend–younger–Boston–bombing–suspect–Dzhokhar–Tsarnaev–speaks–out.html#ixzz3RMFJMtPv

85. https://twitter.com/j_tsar/status/321113224802099201

86. http://www.washingtonpost.com/sf/feature/wp/2013/04/27/the–tsarnaev–family–a–faded–portrait–of–an–immigrants–american–dream/

87. https://www.washingtonpost.com/politics/details-emerge-on-suspected-boston-bombers/2013/04/19/ef2c2566-a8e4-11e2-a8e2-5b98cb59187f_story.html?utm_term=.6826425bc25c

87a. http://www.bbc.com/news/world-us-canada-22229176

88. http://www.rollingstone.com/culture/news/jahars-world-20130717?page=4

89. https://www.youtube.com/watch?v=heMemMPaKRc – Dzhokhar Tsarnaev teasing his niece

90. https://twitter.com/j_tsar/status/205730924695007235

91. http://nymag.com/daily/intelligencer/2013/05/tsarnaev-brothers-had-complicated-relationship.html#

92. http://www.washingtonpost.com/sf/feature/wp/2013/04/27/the-tsarnaev-family-a-faded-portrait-of-an-immigrants-american-dream/

93. https://twitter.com/j_tsar/status/313792911932280832

94. http://www.rollingstone.com/culture/news/jahars-world-20130717?page=4

95. "Stronger" by Jeff Bauman – http://www.dailymail.co.uk/news/article-2599823/Boston-bombing-survivor-Jeff-Bauman-shows-walking-skills-reveals-haunted-thoughts-stopped-tragedy.html

96. http://hereandnow.wbur.org/2014/04/14/jeff-bauman-stronger

97. http://www.pri.org/stories/2014-04-13/we-remember-boston-marathon-tragedy-should-we-try-forget-alleged-bombers

98. http://www.glamourmagazine.co.uk/news/features/2014/04/boston-marathon-2014

99. http://www.bostonmagazine.com/news/article/2014/11/25/inside-mind-killer-tamerlan-tsarnaev-matanov/

100. http://abcnews.go.com/International/boston-marathon-bombing-suspects-twisted-family-history/story?id=19012097

101. http://articles.latimes.com/2013/apr/21/world/la-fg-wn-tsarnaev-mother-20130421

102. http://www.dailymail.co.uk/news/article-2312767/Tamerlan-Tsarnaeva-Boston-bomber-phoned-MOTHER-final-shoot-told-Mama-I-love-you.html

103. http://www.washingtonpost.com/world/national-security/us-to-seek-death-penalty-in-boston-bombing-case/2014/01/30/c15465d8-8785-11e3-833c-33098f9e5267_story.html

104. http://fox17online.com/2014/01/30/feds-seek-death-penalty-for-boston-marathon-bombing-suspect-tsarnaev/

105. https://www.bostonglobe.com/metro/2014/02/12/judge-sets-november-trial-date-for-boston-marathon-bombing-suspect-dzhokhar-tsarnaev/JNcq6FzQewvCtgYAO2smSM/story.html

106. http://www.politico.com/blogs/under-the-radar/2013/12/feds-ease-dzhokhar-tsarnaev-jail-restrictions-178716.html

107. http://www.bostonglobe.com/metro/2014/02/28/feds-alleged-marathon-bomber-dzhokhar-tsarnaev-allegedly-made-ill-advised-statement-during-visit-with-sister/j6lcoJD2HJLHRModBJz29K/story.html

108. *https://www.bostonglobe.com/metro/2014/03/05/defense–says–dzokhar–tsarnaev–was–being–humorous–when–made–statement–sister–prison/nNrIiBIxTBqvdCoRFi7UGL/story.html*

109. *http://www.nytimes.com/2014/07/22/us/jury–reaches–a–verdict–in–first–boston–bombing–trial.html?_r=0*

110. *https://www.bostonglobe.com/metro/2013/05/02/marathon–bombing–suspects–initially–planned–july–attack–officials–say/XSpTNQmjYMK8TCNUKjsh3K/story.html*

111. *http://www.nbcnews.com/news/us–news/martyrs–go–straight–heaven–tsarnaev–told–friend–prosecutors–n149661*

112. *http://www.boston.com/news/local/massachusetts/2014/10/14/guide–dzhokhar–tsarnaev–friends–facing–charges–phillipos–silva–tazhayakov–and kadyrbayev/0FvjciYlJl3bHANfSFH4nL/story.html*

113. *http://thebostonmarathonbombings.weebly.com/khairullozhon–matanov–writes–disturbing–letter–from–jail–cell–alleging–prisoner–abuse.html*

114. *http://muslimobserver.com/1st–bmb–trial–commences–as–jahars–birthday–approaches/*

115. *http://justice4dzhokhar.tumblr.com/post/104061564855/anyone–know–how–jahars–familys–doing*

116. *http://news.yahoo.com/lawyers–accused–boston–bomber–due–court–thursday–110650539.html*

117. *http://karinafriedemann.blogspot.com/2014/09/tsarnaev–case–inches–forward.html*

118. *http://thefreedombulletin.com/2014/11/dzhokhar–tsarnaev–status–conference–summary/*

119. *https://www.facebook.com/ExtremeMakeoverForBostonBombingVictims/posts/639207976151098:0*

120. *http://www.myfoxboston.com/story/26569687/fucarile–wants–tsarnaev–to–face–victims*

121. *http://www.nydailynews.com/news/national/jury–selection–underway–boston–marathon–bombings–article–1.2066045 – January 5*

122. *http://www.usatoday.com/story/news/nation/2014/12/18/tsarnaev–court–appearance/20575029/*

123. *http://www.theguardian.com/us–news/2014/dec/18/outburst–interrupts–dzhokhar–tsarnaev–hearing – December 18*

124. *http://www.sportingnews.com/sport/story/2014–12–18/dzhokhar–tsarnaev–hearing–boston–marathon–bombing–suspect–trial–death–penalty–December 18*

125. *http://davidabelmarathon.blogspot.com/2014/01/survivors–gird–for–trial.html*

126. http://www.bostonmagazine.com/news/blog/2015/01/05/jury–selection–dzhokhar–tsarnaev–trial/

127. http://www.latimes.com/nation/la–na–boston–tsarnaev–penalty–phase–20150419–story.html

128. http://news.yahoo.com/opening–statements–in–boston–marathon–bomber–trial–set–for–today–021336229.html – March 2

129. http://www.boston.com/news/local/massachusetts/2014/03/17/dzhokhar–tsarnaev–should–not–able–review–photos–marathon–bombing–victims–prosecutors–say/xgAzTvEx6qd7JuTUQ3Sa7K/story.html – March 17

130. http://www.nytimes.com/2015/03/04/us/boston–marathon–bombing–trial.html?_r=0

131. http://www.masslive.com/news/boston/index.ssf/2015/03/dzhokar_tsarnaevs_defense_it_w.html

132. Prosecution's Opening:
https://jimmysllama.files.wordpress.com/2015/06/boston–trial–transcript–day–1–27.pdf

Defense's Opening:
https://s3.amazonaws.com/s3.documentcloud.org/documents/1681442/tsarnaev–dzkokhar–trial–transcript–3–4–2015–clarke.pdf

133. https://www.facebook.com/newday.newhope.rebekahgregory/posts/770673919715226

134. https://www.youtube.com/watch?v=xIJSw3Mhyd8 – FBI Surveillance video at the Forum

135. http://www.nytimes.com/2015/03/10/us/videos–at–trial–capture–carnage–and–perpetrators–of–boston–marathon–bombing.html?_r=0

136. https://www.youtube.com/watch?v=gSJpYhlPuHI– after bombings, Tsarnaev goes to buy milk

137. https://www.youtube.com/watch?v=QmUkvZGvW2w – Tsarnaev at gym after bombings

138. http://www.usnews.com/news/newsgram/articles/2013/04/16/boston–bombing–funerals–will–be–picketed–westboro–baptist–church–says – April 16

138a. http://www.foxnews.com/tech/2013/04/20/alleged–twitter–account–boston–bomber–suspect–tsarnaev–uncovered/

139. http://www.theguardian.com/us–news/2015/mar/10/fbi–testimony–boston–marathon–bomb–trial–dzhokhar–tsarnaev

140. https://www.youtube.com/watch?v=DPNwoxAiy1A – MIT Surveillance video of Officer Collier's murder

141. https://www.youtube.com/watch?v=yj8zwPWXqWg– Shell Food Mart surveillance video

142. *https://www.youtube.com/watch?v=bUENGGnGSXk – surveillance of carjacking victim begs for help*

143. *https://www.youtube.com/watch?v=mfwZw6EyTwk – Tsarnaev at ATM machine*

144. *http://www.usatoday.com/story/news/2015/03/16/boston–marathon–trial/24843547/*

145. *http://www.thedailybeast.com/articles/2015/03/18/the–downfall–of–the–boston–bombers–gun–runner.html – March 18*

146. *https://www.youtube.com/watch?v=HHEcj2B12PI– Tsarnaev brothers visiting gun range before BMB.*

147. *http://www.masslive.com/news/boston/index.ssf/2015/03/dzhokhar_tsarnaevs_defense_gri.html*

148. *http://news.yahoo.com/extremist–literature–focus–boston–marathon–bombing–trial–110155744.html – March 23*

149. *http://www.nbcnews.com/storyline/boston–bombing–trial/tsarnaev–home–was–chock–full–bomb–making–tools–agent–says–n329961– March 25*

150. *http://boston.cbslocal.com/2015/03/25/video–shows–tsarnaev–leaving–target–with–backpacks–before–bombing/*

151. *http://www.huffingtonpost.com/anne–stevenson/inside–tsarnaev–trial–wil_b_6936704.html –March 26*

152. *http://www.masslive.com/news/boston/index.ssf/2015/03/boston_marathon_bombing_details.html – March 26*

153. *https://www.bostonglobe.com/metro/2015/03/12/krystle–campbell–peace–garden–introduced–medford–ceremony–this–afternoon/ZgfK2rA3WwDdaKhjFUetCN/story.html*

154. *http://www.npr.org/sections/thetwo–way/2015/03/30/396381083/prosecution–rests–in–case–against–admitted–boston–marathon–bomber– March 30*

155. *http://www.nydailynews.com/news/crime/autopsy–photos–boy–8–shown–boston–marathon–trial–article–1.2167284– March 30*

156. *https://www.bostonglobe.com/metro/2015/03/31/that–all–you–got/Rhw3hu59FPhA0xcrarCzOJ/story.html –March 31*

157. *http://www.usatoday.com/story/news/2015/03/31/boston–marathon–bombing–trial/70716808/*

158. *Prosecution's Closing: https://s3.amazonaws.com/s3.documentcloud.org/documents/1719848/tsarnaev–defense–excerpt–closing–argument–4–6–15.pdf*

158a. *Defense's Closing: https://s3.amazonaws.com/s3.documentcloud.org/documents/1719837/tsarnaev–defense–closing–4–6–15.pdf*

159. http://www.nytimes.com/2015/04/09/us/dzhokhar-tsarnaev-verdict-boston-marathan-bombing-trial.html?_r=0

160. http://www.bustle.com/articles/75033-survivors-react-to-the-boston-bombers-sentence-with-relief-exhaustion – April 8

160a. http://www.cnn.com/videos/world/2015/04/08/ct-boston-bombing-verdict-karen-brassard-intv.cnn

161. http://www.christianexaminer.com/article/boston.bombing.victim.witness.thanks.jury.for.verdict.credits.her.faith.for.strength/48730.htm

162. http://time.com/3819585/pope-francis-dzhokhar-tsarnaev-death-penalty/-

163. http://www.washingtontimes.com/news/2015/apr/9/dzhokhar-tsarnaevs-mother-zubeidat-calls-americans/#ixzz3XQ6dXscM

164. http://www.bostonglobe.com/metro/2015/04/09/boston-region-debates-death-penalty-for-dzhokhar-tsarnaev/AocXgm92PABL8pqolsdOFI/story.html

165. https://www.bostonglobe.com/metro/2015/04/13/sister-slain-mit-police-officer-sean-collier-opposes-death-penalty-for-dzhokhar-tsarnaev/oeqrJ8ji4DHMPxOBxdRN3O/story.html

166. http://www.bostonglobe.com/metro/2015/04/16/attorney-responds-richard-family-statement-tsarnaevpunishment/YKBYhU1mYBdEbTOEbLSeNK/story.html?hootPostID=d2fcd320b231b635471317a094163c62

167. https://www.bostonglobe.com/metro/2015/04/08/guilty-verdict-boston-marathon-bombing-leads-officials-hope-closure-will-come-for-victims-region/FJf7XpRCQw1roYj8weqVAI/story.html

168. Government's Opening: https://s3.amazonaws.com/s3.documentcloud.org/documents/2004183/tsarnaev-dzhokhar-opening-statement-transcript.pdf

169. https://www.youtube.com/watch?v=XlEkjknGPcA – Dzhokhar Tsarnaev Jail Cell Surveillance

170. http://www.huffingtonpost.com/2015/04/22/dzhokhar-tsarnaev-middle-finger_n_7118730.html – April 22

171. http://www.cnn.com/2015/04/24/opinions/blecker-tsarnaev-penalty/ Dzhokhar Tsarnaev's punishment should fit horror of his crime

172. http://www.cnn.com/2015/04/24/us/tsarnaev-trial-middle-finger-13th-juror/

173. http://www.boston.com/news/local/massachusetts/2015/04/23/final-prosecution-video-martin-richard-appears-reach-for-mother-dies/dhD7AUxofOiPAUhAkjHmaJ/story.html – April 25

174. https://twitter.com/globecullen/status/599289230959841280 – May 15

175. http://nypost.com/2015/04/28/boston-marathon-bombers-lawyer-urges-jury-to-spare-his-life/

176. *Defense's Opening:*
https://jimmysllama.files.wordpress.com/2015/06/boston–trial–transcript–
defense–witnesses–50.pdf

177. *https://www.youtube.com/watch?v=-3h3DBLtYdE – Defense exhibit:*
Tsarnaev's at boxing gym

178. *http://www.cnn.com/2015/04/28/us/tsarnaev–boston–bombing–*
sentencing/

179. *http://www.newsweek.com/dzhokhar–tsarnaev–clung–life–while–his–*
brother–tried–die–court–hears–326793

180. *https://www.youtube.com/watch?v=4Z9nnDRK2L8 – Dzhokhar Tsarnaev's*
Schooling

181. *http://www.cbsnews.com/news/boston–marathon–bombing–trial–*
dzhokhar–tsarnaev–always–wanted–to–do–the–right–thing–teacher–says/–

182. *http://www.huffingtonpost.com/2015/05/03/becki–norris–tsarnaev–*
teacher_n_7197072.html

183. *http://cognoscenti.wbur.org/2015/05/04/tsarnaev–becki–norris – May 5*

184. *http://wgbhnews.org/post/kinder–gentler–tsarnaev–described–defense–*
witnesses–2nd–week–penalty–phase May 1

185.
http://www.bostonherald.com/news_opinion/local_coverage/2015/04/tsarnaev
_trial_on_hold_until_monday_due_to_sick_juror

186. *http://www.cnn.com/2015/05/04/us/boston–bombing–tsarnaev–*
sentencing/ –

187. *http://rt.com/news/tamerlan–tsarnaev–relative–boston–160/*

188. *http://abcnews.go.com/US/cracks–ice–boston–marathon–bomber–*
dzhokhar–tsarnaev–cries/story?id=30794563

189. *http://www.theguardian.com/world/2014/apr/16/dzhokhar–tsarnaev–*
defense–lawyers–strategy– April 16

190. *http://www.cbsnews.com/news/boston–marathon–bomber–dzhokhar–*
tsarnaevs–father–had–ptsd–doctor–testifies/–

191. *http://www.cnn.com/2013/04/24/us/boston–brainwash/*

192. *http://wgbhnews.org/post/tsarnaev–trial–its–cultural–identity–versus–*
personal–responsibility– May 4

193. *http://blog.expertpages.com/general/convicted–boston–marathon–*
bomber–turns–to–neuroscience–expert–witness–in–sentencing–trial.htm – May
13

194.
https://www.bostonglobe.com/metro/2015/04/25/thealcatrazrockies/aoBWrZjR
pmQatMsfmsFUOL/story.html

195. http://www.washingtonpost.com/news/morning-mix/wp/2015/05/11/boston-marathon-bomber-genuinely-sorry-sister-helen-prejean-tells-jurors/

196. https://theintercept.com/2015/05/11/dead-man-walking-nun-tsarnaev-feels-remorse/-

197. Sister Helen Prejean's Testimony transcript: https://s3.amazonaws.com/s3.documentcloud.org/documents/2077686/tsarnae v-trial-day-58-penalty-5-11-15-sister.pdf

198. Closing's Arguments: https://s3.amazonaws.com/s3.documentcloud.org/documents/2081648/tsarnae v-trial-day-59-penalty-phase-5-13-15.pdf

199. Jury Verdict Slip Form: http://ftpcontent3.worldnow.com/wfxt/pdf/Tsarnaev%20Completed%20Jury%2 0Form.pdf

200. http://abcnews.go.com/US/boston-bomber-dzhokhar-tsarnaev-sentenced-die-eerie-quiet/story?id=31080965

201. http://www.nbcnews.com/storyline/boston-bombing-trial/boston-marathon-bombing-survivors-call-verdict-justice-n359796 – May 15

202. http://www.news.com.au/world/north-america/boston-bomber-dzhokhar-tsarnaevs-father-anzor-says-we-will-fight-until-the-end-after-death-penalty/story-fnh81jut-1227357735743– May 13

203. http://www.masslive.com/news/boston/index.ssf/2015/05/dzhokhar_tsarnaevs_mother_says.html – May 15

204. http://www.dailymail.co.uk/news/article-3101302/At-20-Boston-Marathon-Bomb-victims-set-speak-Dzhokhar-Tsarnaev-s-death-sentence-hearing-scheduled-June-24.html

205. http://boston.cbslocal.com/2015/08/13/boston-marathon-bombing-trial-juror-interview-jim-armstrong-wbz/

206. http://kosu.org/post/he-was-just-year-older-boston-marathon-bomber-when-he-sentenced-him-death#stream/0 – September 4

207. http://www.masslive.com/news/boston/index.ssf/2015/05/defense_argues_that_dzhokhar_t.html– may 14

208. https://news.vice.com/article/dzhokhar-tsarnaev-breaks-silence-in-court-before-judge-sentences-him-to-death– June 24

209. http://www.upi.com/Top_News/US/2015/06/24/Boston-survivors-say-Tsarnaevs-apology-lacked-remorse-sincerity/7691435156321/

210. http://www.masslive.com/opinion/index.ssf/2015/06/when_an_apology_means_nothing.html– June 26

211. http://news.yahoo.com/boston-marathon-bomber-sentencing-123758333.html#-

212. http://www.bostonglobe.com/metro/2015/06/24/judge–excoriates–
tsarnaev–before–imposing–death
sentence/s4IVL9PTCeznIqEYcTuJMN/story.html?p1=Article_Related_Box_Articl
e_More

213. http://www.sandiegouniontribune.com/news/2015/jul/13/boston–bomber–
lawyer–judy–clarke–award/–2015

214. http://www.newyorker.com/magazine/2015/09/14/the–worst–of–the–
worst

215. http://cognoscenti.wbur.org/2015/06/24/dzhokhar–tsarnaev–remorse–
amee–latour

216. http://www.cnn.com/2015/07/17/us/boston–marathon–bomber–moved–
to–supermax/–

217. http://www.hngn.com/articles/103837/20150624/boston–bombing–trial–
tsarnaev–cries–apologizes–during–formal–death–penalty–sentencing.htm –
June 24, 2015

218. http://www.vice.com/read/dzhokhar–tsarnaev–spoke–to–the–public–for–
the–first–time–since–the–boston–bombing–today–624

219. Dzhokhar Tsarnaev's allocution:
https://s3.amazonaws.com/s3.documentcloud.org/documents/2110708/13cr1020
0–tsarnaev–tn–sent–x–tsarnaev–06–24–15.pdf

220. http://www.necn.com/news/new–england/Whats–Life–in–Prison–Like–
for–Boston–Marathon–Bomber–Dzhokhar–Tsarnaev––337448791.html –
October 27

94186939R00248

Made in the USA
Columbia, SC
27 April 2018